THE
LONGSTOCK
CHRONICLES

JOSEPH MARVICI

Olympus Story House

Contents

Technical input and editing by Leonard Lea Frazer. who helped me greatly to get this book published.

This work is dedicated to my Mom, Peggy Sullivan, without her influence in my life. I would not be the person that I am. May she always live in our hearts and minds and never be forgotten.

The Longstock Chronicle
Volume 1: The 70's

Chapter 1

Looking for Land

It was 1972, the hippie back-to-the-land movement was in full swing in the U.S. I arrived in Denver in January with Katy and a new baby boy about 2 1/2 months old.

Katy and I had spent two years in the high desert in New Mexico on a forty-acre piece of land that we had a 99-year lease on. It turned out that the fellow who gave us the lease possibly didn't own the land. There were apparently two deeds on the same property, which wasn't really too unusual in New Mexico at that time. Towards the end of 1971, Ed Labato, who was one of the people with a deed, began to become an irritation to the point that Katy and I decided to leave.

After about 2 months of traveling around, we ended up in Denver. We knew people in Denver, having lived there off and on since 1969. I got a job doing concrete forming for a company that several of my friends worked for. After about 6 months, I was making real good money and Katy was driving me crazy wanting to leave Denver and go to some place out of the city. I knew with the job I had, now making it to Foreman, and the money I was making, that if I stayed in the city another year, I would be able to buy a piece of land outright.

The only solution for my sanity was to give Katy some money and the van and send her on a land search. We had a few

1

thousand dollars in the bank, sufficient for a down payment. Katy, and Chico, our six month-old son, left Denver in search of land.

My sister Cathy was in Seattle in June of 1972, so Katy drove there first, picking up her and her daughter Jennifer, who was 3 years old. She also picked up my cousins Carolynn and Ron Carter and the six of them traveled north together.

Katy and I had a few maps of B.C. We had talked to some people who had land around Mahood lake in the 100-Mile House area. We decided that area would be our target. The four adults and two children crossed the border and headed north on the Trans-Canada Highway, then north again on Route 97, which runs through 100-Mile House.

After inquiring at the Real Estate agencies in 100-Mile and finding the prices very high around there, they decided to go further North, driving to Prince George. In 1972, Prince George was basically a logging town. The city was amalgamated a couple of years before, doubling its population overnight.

After getting to Prince George, Katy started hitting Real Estate offices. It wasn't long before someone referred her to David Parson. As real estate agents go, David Parson was different. As a matter of fact, he was as different as anyone goes, an eccentric man and a story-teller. He was one of those people who told the wildest stories that were very hard to believe, but swore up and down that they were true. He had a hissing kind of laugh and was sure to laugh at everything he said.

David did have some good points as a real Estate agent though. He had put a lot of time into finding and listing rural land which nobody valued much. Most of the land he was listing was in the Fraser River Valley east of Prince George and much of that land belonged to one owner, listed as Weinberg Land And Investment. Apparently, Mr. Weinberg went around to tax sales in B.C. in the 50's and 60's, buying up land. He accumulated thousands of parcels of land, or at least that's the story David told me. According to David, the Government put an end to tax sales as a result of Weinberg's buying so many parcels.

It had been about two weeks since Katy left Denver, when I got a call from her from Prince George. At that point, I wasn't sure where she was, as I hadn't heard from her for about a week.

"I met this guy in Prince George" Katy told me on the phone. "He's got listings for a lot of cheap land, mostly quarter sections. There's a couple of places for sale in a place called Longstock," she said. It was the first time I'd heard the name Longstock. "I think you should fly up here and we can go check these places out."

I bought a ticket from Denver to Prince George. We traveled in a modern jet from Denver to Calgary and then changed to this very large propeller plane. "Air Canada," I thought," I think this could be the oldest plane I've ever flown in". I remember looking out at the wings and I could see the flex in them. After a quite bumpy ride in the rain, we finally landed in Prince George. Katy, Chico, Cathy, Jennifer, Carolynn and Ron all met me at the airport.

We got in the van and went to David Parson's house. There were David, Shirley - David's wife, and four babies. The twin boys, John and David and Maryanne and Jennifer. The place was a madhouse, with kids crying, and Shirley yelling at the kids, kids yelling at each other and David telling us some

3

absurd story that was beyond belief. Every once in a while Shirley would pop up with something like, "Oh come on now, David" when his stories got a little too outrageous.

We stayed that night at the Parsons, all the time having to listen to David's stories.

The next morning we all went to his office. It was an agency called John Neff Real Estate, of which David was one of four agents in the office. He had one of these little cubicles with separators about 5 feet high so that you could look over into the next cubicle when you were standing up.

The walls of David's cubicle were covered with maps. There were highlighted areas all over the map of the Fraser valley and the eastern end of the valley, which was known as the Robson Valley. The highlighted areas marked the many properties that David listed for sale in the last couple of years.

We were particularly interested in two little places on the C.N. rail line east of Prince George. Penney and Longstock were about halfway between Prince George and McBride. Both of these little communities were on the North side of the Fraser River, with no road access. This was the kind of property that we were looking for: a place that was isolated from the civilized world. It was the hippie ideal that we brought with us that made us want to be in the most isolated place we could find, and both fit the bill.

Admittedly, Longstock was the more isolated, with a sixteen-mile ride down the Fraser River from the Penney landing to get there. Even then, it only got you to the river at Longstock. It was still another two-mile walk to get to the center of town. (The center of town was really the Post Office and a few houses, population 15 in a area of 8 square miles).

We checked out the maps in David's office, and decided to look at the place in Longstock first. We really liked the isolation aspect. We copied a couple of maps on the office copier and hit the road for Longstock.

In June 1972, the Fraser River was at the highest level it had been at since 1936. There was a trailer court down by the river on First Avenue in Prince George where the water was right up to the windows. The trains were not running because of high levels of water at some of their rail bridges, so the only way to get to Longstock was to drive out to the Penney landing, try to catch a ride across the river and walk in down the tracks.

We headed out of Prince George on the Yellowhead Highway going east, crossing the old C.N. Railbridge that had vehicle lanes on either side of the bridge and train tracks in the middle. There was an island in the middle of the river that was completely under water, with just the trees sticking up.

It was about a sixty-mile drive to the Penney Access Road. Then it was another five miles before you got to the banks of the Fraser River opposite the town. Because of the high water, the lower half of the road was under water. People in Penney who had boats were tying them in the creek bed about half way down the road.

We drove down the Penney Road and came upon a few boats tied by the creek. There were a few people loading groceries into one of the boats. I got out of the van and walked up to the boat.

"Can I get a ride across?" I asked. "Where are you going?" a man replied.

"We're going to Longstock to look at some land".

"Oh yeah, what place are you looking at? By the way, my name is Jack, Jack Boudreau, and you are?"

"Louie Carmen," I said. "I just came up North from Denver. We're looking to buy some property in this area."

I went to the van and got one of the maps we had, taking it over for Jack to look at. He studied it for a minute and said, "I think that's old Jack Hemming's place. Jack used to grow strawberries there. I guess they grow real good, 'cause he used to sell them all over. You know that it's about 10 miles on the tracks to walk into Longstock?"

"Yeah, I know" I replied.

"We're going over to Penney right now, if you want a ride".

"Great!" I said, and went back to the van to get the others. "Let's go. We've got a ride across, and then a ten-mile walk along the tracks." Everyone got it together rather quickly, which was quite amazing with that many people. We piled in the riverboat with Jack and his wife and brother Clarence.

It was a long narrow boat about 30 feet in length, with a 40hp outboard on the back. The paint looked new, as if it had been painted very recently. It was my first time in a riverboat. I was impressed at the stability, even with 10 people.

We pulled out of the creek and swung out onto the river. The river was wide and muddy gray - so wide, objects on the opposite riverbank looked really small. The surface of the river was covered with patches of foam. Sticks and logs floated down with the current. Trees lined the riverbank on each side. The sky was partly cloudy, filled with big cumulus clouds that get in and out of the way of the sun, causing hot and cool and hot and cool throughout the day.

We headed up river, and the old beehive burner at Penney came into view. The Penney Sawmill had been one of the last independent sawmills in the area. Small mills like this used to inhabit all the small communities along the C.N. rail on the one hundred forty-mile stretch between Prince George and McBride.

Just below the burner, a few boats were tied up. The riverbank on the Penney side was pretty high and with the high water, people had to tie their boats up the ramp and into the parking area.

We landed on the other side after about a two-mile boat ride across and up river. We got out of the boat and piled into a funky little Jeep with no muffler that belonged to Clarence. He gave us all a ride to Jack's house.

Jack was also the Postmaster for Penney. The Post Office was in his house, identified by the official-looking Canada Post signs around the house.

We sat around the kitchen drinking coffee and listening to Jack's stories about the area. Many years later Jack would write a book. I remember one story in particular he told about old Harry Olson:

Harry was fishing out at Toneka Lake near Longstock. He would go out to the lake for a few days at a time on a regular basis and stay in a small fishing cabin he had built with old John Flotten. He was on his way back one day with a packload of fish. Rather than walk the road, Harry took the shortcut through the bush that day. Part way down the trail from Toneka Lake to Longstock, Harry surprised a grizzly on the trail. He was packing a .22, but never even had time to get it off his back. He did, however, get the grizzly in the face with an axe he was

7

carrying. The bear killed Harry, and they found his body on the trail a couple of days later. About two years after that, a grizzly was killed up near Penney. It had a big scar on its face that looked like it had been made with an axe. Jack figured that it was most likely the same bear.

I thought it was almost like an initiation or something for the locals to tell you a grizzly story just before you headed out into the bush. Maybe they figured that we might need something to think about on the long walk to Longstock.

After a while, we realized that we had to get going, as we had a long way to walk. We went back towards Clarence's place, which was on the West end of Penney and set out down the tracks.

It was a slow-moving operation with the 7 of us, but we plugged along with kids on our shoulders and finally arrived at the Longstock train station at about 4 o'clock in the afternoon. The station was about eight feet by sixteen and had a wood stove inside. We lit the stove with the intention of cooking some rice. After going through our packs several times, we realized that in our hurry to get to the boat we had forgotten to pack any food, though we did have a pot to cook in, and some bowls.

Between the 5 of us adults, we had a total of 4 oranges; and so here we were, 7 people, way out in the middle of nowhere, with no food.

I remembered David Parson telling me about some people he had recently sold some land to. As a matter of fact, we discovered that he had marked it on the map.

"Maybe somebody will sell us something to eat," I said, "let's take a walk and see." My sister Cathy and I took off down the road trying to find some food while everyone else waited for us at the station.

After walking South from the train station for about a half mile, we came upon a homestead that looked lived in. The map said Chad Allen, so I took it that a fellow named Chad Allen lived there.

We entered the yard, where a log cabin was under construction. There was another little structure that looked kind of like a hog pen with a roof. It was built out of very small logs, with big gaps like a corral.

I yelled out "Hello!"

A few seconds later a skinny, thin-faced man ran frantically from the hog pen building with a gun in his hand. Nervously the little man yelled out "Who are you and what do you want?".

I thought, "What the hell? This is the kind of greeting I would expect from the neighbors pit bull." I wasn't quite ready for this.

We had met Chad Allen. Chad was basically an uptight, disagreeable man, suspicious of everyone. He was an American who came to Canada in 1971 from California. Rumor has it that he was shell-shocked in the Korean war, which seemed quite believable upon meeting him.

"Are you Chad Allen?" I said. "Who wants to know" he replied.

"My name is Louie Carmen, and this is my sister Cathy. We came here to look at some land. David Parson gave us your name."

"And what do you want with me?" he said suspiciously.

"We walked in from Penney on the tracks and in the rush

to get a ride across we forgot to bring food. We have a couple of kids with us. I would like to know if I could buy some food from you," I replied.

Chad just looked at me for what seemed like a long time and then said, "You know, I've backpacked all over the world and I never forgot to bring food. If you're so stupid as to forget the food, I think you should go hungry."

"Does this mean the answer is no?" I asked. "It sure is." Chad replied.

Cathy and I turned around and started walking back to the train station. "Man, I hope everyone in this town isn't like that guy" I said. "I'm not too sure about living in a place like this if they are."

As we were walking back, I remembered there was another name on the map, Bob and Paula Hooty. The turnoff to their place was on the way back, so we followed the map. We turned off the main road onto a driveway that was nothing more than a foot path with willows bending over, making a kind of tunnel effect. We soon came upon an old log house that was all weathered a dark brown color. The house was partly sunk into the ground from many years of freezing and thawing. There was a huge Weeping Willow tree growing next to the house, with a large branch of the tree laying right on the roof. You had to walk under the huge tree, alongside the house and a few steps down to get to the door.

Cathy and I went to the door, not knowing what to expect after our last encounter. As we approached the house, a dog started barking from inside. It sounded like one of those little yappy dogs. I knocked, and a man answered the door right away. As he opened the door, a small dog that was mostly hair came running out barking at us.

"Hi, you must be Bob Hooty. My name is Louie Carmen and this is my sister Cathy," I said, trying to talk over the dog that was barking and jumping all around us. "We came out to look at some land we're thinking of buying. David Parson gave us your name."

Bob had a thin build, with an enormous head of hair, and an extremely heavy beard. He looked a bit like John Lennon in his real hairy days with the Beatles. He had a big smile on his face as he greeted us. Either he was really glad to see us or really stoned. I guessed it was both.

"Rufus, shut the hell up!" he yelled at the dog, though it didn't seem to make any difference. "Yea, I'm Bob Hooty, come on in," as Rufus barked incessantly.

It was obvious we were in friendlier territory. We were greeted very warmly by both Bob and Paula as we came in. Paula was a thin woman with a big friendly smile. She had jet black hair cut in a Cleopatra cut. "Come on in," she said. "It's nice to get some company. We don't see many people out here in the bush. Would you like a coffee?"

"Well, we have a little problem and wonder if you can help us first," I said.

"What's your problem?" asked Bob.

"We walked in from Penney today and in our hurry to get a ride across the river at Penney, we forgot to bring food. We were wondering if you had some food we could buy? Oh, did I mention there's five more of us."

"There's 7 of you and you have no food?" said Paula.

"That's right," I replied.

"And where is everyone else?" Paula asked. "At the train station," I said.

"We won't sell you food," said Paula, "but if you bring everyone here, we will feed you all, that is if you don't mind moose meat and potatoes. It's just for a couple of days, eh?

"Yeah, just a couple of days," I replied. Cathy and I went back to the station and got everyone and came back to the Hooty's.

Bob and Paula were the real friendly sort. Bob was a draft evader who went to Canada in 1970. His family was quite well off and lived in Connecticut. Bob and Paula had been living in Longstock for a couple of years. Every few months a check would arrive from Dad. Paula knew how to make it last. Bob was kind of the lazy sort. He wasted away many days reading and hanging around doing nothing while Paula did most of the chores. It seemed to work for them, as they both seemed pretty happy.

I had crossed the border with a big chunk of hash and now seemed like a good time to break it out. After a good feed of moose meat and potatoes, we spent the evening smoking hash and drinking Bob's homemade wine - that Paula made.

At one point in the evening, I looked over at Bob and said "I met Chad Allen. He told me if I was so stupid to forget the food, I should go hungry."

"I'm not surprised," said Bob. "We don't get along with Chad very well. He's basically a real asshole."

We all crashed out at the Hootys and got up to a breakfast of pancakes and coffee before we headed down the trail to find the property that was for sale. We spent a couple of nights with

Bob and Paula, who became really good friends for many years.

The road heading West from the crossroads was the one we wanted. The road got narrower and narrower the further we went and finally became entirely grown in. It had a groove to it that caused all the water to set in the middle of the road. I found out later that one of the old timers had skidded logs down the road with a Cat, and had left the road in a big groove.

We found the drive, which was nothing more than a path with the willows growing in leading into the property. About 50 yards in, the road broke out into a clearing, getting to a point where we could see all the mountains. To the South were the Caribou Mountains, with the saddle of Sugarbowl Mountain looming in the foreground. To the Southeast was the mountain at Penney. To the North was Longstock Lookout Mountain, where the fire lookout station was. It was only manned during the fire season. Further to the East was Mount Baldy, a magnificent rock rising two thousand feet above the timberline.

The place was beautiful and Katy and I fell in love with it right away, although we still had reservations about the town after meeting Chad Allen.

Longstock's history was all about old timers who lived, worked, and settled the area. Some still lived here. Many books have been written about those times, though the history is relatively short, having been settled about 1911 when the railroad came through.

The hippy movement in North America was a direct contrast to the isolation in Longstock. Bob and Paula were the first hippies to come in 1971. The people who lived in Longstock had virtually no contact with hippies prior to this, but that was about to change forever. Within a year, Longstock would be mostly populated with hippies. They took over and set the tone of the community for many years. Old timers who had lived through many different eras in the history of Longstock would be smoking pot, hash, taking acid and peyote with the hippies. There were numerous parties where young and old partied together and there were no fights - uncharacteristic for parties in Longstock.

We spent the remainder of the afternoon just walking around, exploring the property and smoking hash. I couldn't help feeling that I was going to have a long relationship with this land and Longstock. Little did I know how long it would last and how my life would change as I prepared myself for a life in the Canadian bush.

Three days later, we set out walking back to Penney, and were picked up by a rail crew who had been working on the tracks nearby. We rode the speeder for about 8 of the 10 miles to Penney.

We looked at several other properties in the next few days, but nothing made an impression like the property in Longstock. We went back to David Parson's office in Prince George, and told David that we wanted to buy the Longstock property. We put in an offer for $6,000. It was higher than any of the most recent sales in the area.

We would go back to Denver a week later and wait until October before Weinberg got back to us. He rejected our offer of $6000. He said he would take $7500. So we sent the down payment and the first month's payment in October, and paid it off the following May.

Chapter 2

The Big Move

It was the beginning of May 1973, and I couldn't wait to leave Denver. I had been working steadily since the summer, and had put together enough money to pay off the land in Longstock. We made the last payment at the beginning of May and had saved up close to $4000 to move and live on for a while. It was a really satisfying feeling.

We had been preparing for the big move from Denver to Longstock for several months. Every week we would go to garage sales and flea markets, always looking for things that would be useful to us in Longstock. Gardening tools and building tools were on the top of the list and I always managed to find something.

I was boarding my horses on a ranch high in the Colorado mountains. I decided to sell three horses to Bill Cummings, who owned the ranch. I would be taking one horse with me, Dondi, a Paint mare I'd had for about 4 years. I sold off two mares and a young stud colt to Bill, and made arrangements with him to pick Dondi and the horse trailer up at the end of May on my way to Canada.

About two weeks before leaving for Longstock, I decided to leave the stress behind for a few days and take a vacation at the hot springs in Jemez Springs, New Mexico. It was like a calm before the storm, with the enormous task looming before me. A couple of friends, Bobby Mach and Jimmy Rodgers came along and we hung around soaking in the hot springs and basically doing nothing. I was resting up for the adventure I was about to embark upon.

While in New Mexico, I decided to look up Gypsy, an old friend who was at Placidas, about 40 miles away. I met Gypsy in New York City in 1967. We had a mutual friend, Amen, who was my roommate when I lived there. We would always take Gypsy with us when we went to Avenue D to buy pot. It was a dangerous part of the city. We would feel safer if he was with us, as he was a really scary looking character and was usually armed with knifes and chains.

I ran into him unexpectedly at the hot springs in Jemez a few years back. I was sitting in the hot springs when a bunch of people from the communes at Placitas showed up. There were about twenty people in the pool. I didn't realize it was

Gypsy until he started talking about Amen.

"Does Amen live on fifth street?" I asked. "What!" he says really surprised.

"Does Amen live on fifth street?" I asked again. "Yes he does", he said, "Who are you?"

"I'm Louie, I used to live with Amen in New York on the seventh

floor right across from the 5th precinct."

"I'm Gypsy," he says with a thoughtful look on his face as he tries to remember me.

I remember him right away as soon as he started talking about Amen. We became good friends after that and hung out together quite a bit. He and his girlfriend, Angella, lived with Katy and me on our lease in Northern New Mexico in 1971.

He was a wild looking character with long, jet black hair and black eyes that gleamed like daggers as if he were looking right through you. Our paths had crossed on opposite ends of the U.S. and would cross again in Longstock.

Gypsy wasn't at his teepee that day. There were people at the commune where he lived who greeted us in a friendly way. They told us he'd been drinking heavily and had gone to the city to get some wine. I left him a note at his teepee.

Dear Gypsy,

I'm moving to a little town in the Canadian bush. A place called Longstock, about 70 Miles east of Prince George. Drop me a line.

My address is: General Delivery, Longstock, B.C. Louie.

The week in New Mexico was just what I needed to really get charged up on moving. I gave notice at work that I would be leaving the job for good in the middle of May. I got the usual "You'll be back, you'll see." They would prove to be wrong.

We lived in an old carriage house in an alley in downtown Denver. There were three parking spaces, two were mine and the third belonged to a Narcotics Detective on the Denver Police. I would see him every morning on my way to work. All winter I was dealing pot out of the carriage house right under his nose. It might have been the safest place in the city. I never got bothered.

In one of my parking spots, I had a 1946 Dodge Power Wagon. It was 4-wheel drive, with about 40 leaf springs on each side. I had a canvas cover on the box. We loaded it with everything heavy. I bought it out of a wrecking yard and had been working on it for almost a year. I spent many mornings and afternoons discussing the Power Wagon with my neighbor, the detective. Because he'd seen it every day, he was able to track my progress.

We put an ad in the Buy and Sell newspaper for a "wood stove with a water reservoir", and found an old Home Comfort wood cook stove, and yes, it had a water reservoir. It weighed at least 500 lbs. and took 4 people to move it. That was in the Power Wagon with the Ashley wood heater, I got at an auction for $50. All the tools, stoves, windows were packed in tight, right to the roof, front to back.

Next to the Power Wagon, I had a 62 Dodge panel truck. I rebuilt the 318 motor during the winter. It had a trailer hitch, as we intended to tow the horse trailer and Dondi to Longstock with it. We also had a raised bed in the back. Under the bed was packed solid with clothes and things.

A friend, Louise Flenner, volunteered to drive one of the trucks to Longstock for us. Louise was 4 months pregnant at the time and being the adventuresome type, she thought it would be fun. Katy was also 6 months pregnant, and Chico was a year and a half now.

May 24, 1973, we left Denver with two trucks, two pregnant women, a baby, and everything we owned and headed west to the ranch to pick up the the horse and horse trailer, then we headed North to Canada.

We left Denver on I-70 about 9 in the morning. It was all uphill drive for the first 50 miles as we headed West into the Colorado Rockies. The old Power Wagon pulled the hills at a steady 25 miles

per hour in 2nd or 3rd gear. It was a slow crawl up to the ranch, arriving there in about two hours.

We arrived just after 11am and had a coffee with Bill before we hooked up the trailer and loaded Dondi. We also loaded a couple bales of hay from Bill's barn on the other side of the trailer. Our two saddles and tack that we had stored at the ranch, we loaded into the front compartment of the trailer. After saying our last goodbye to Bill, we hit the road again.

We drove Northwest across Colorado, crossing into Wyoming, travelling along the Wind River Range, through Grande Teton Park and Yellowstone Park. When we were entering Grande Teton Park, we were pulled over by the Park Rangers. They said the muffler on the Power Wagon was too loud and we couldn't enter the park. I looked at the map and it's was a hundred miles back-tracking to get around the parks. I appealed to the Rangers that I would try to patch the muffler and make the Power Wagon quieter. We left the Power Wagon outside the park and drove the panel up to the restaurant at Jackson Hole inside the park. I went in the kitchen and asked the cook if I could bum some steel wool and an old tin can. I went back to the Power Wagon and stuffed the hole in the muffler with steel wool, and wrapped it with the tin can and baling wire. It smelled of burning soap for a little while but did the trick and they let us through the parks.

It was a long trip, with the Power Wagon only being able to go 50 miles per hour top speed, that's going downhill. On the uphills, it was only 25 or 30 mph. We also had to stop at least once in the middle of the day to let Dondi out of the trailer and walk her around a bit. About 5 days later, we made the Canadian border in Montana and that's where our progress ground to a halt. We couldn't get across the border.

When I was in Canada the year before, I made it a point to check out the Immigration situation. In 1972, the law was that you could show up at the border with everything you own and fill out your immigration papers at the border and file them right there. You were allowed to go in, they would process your application and you would get your immigration papers in a few months. The Hooty's had immigrated that way in 1971.

In November 1972, the Canadian government changed the rules on immigration. You now had to apply for Canadian immigration outside of Canada. You could no longer immigrate at the border.

This threw a major wrench into our plans. Here we are, 1,500 miles from home, which really doesn't exist for us anymore, as we have moved out of Denver. We had everything we owned with us, and nowhere to go.

After being turned away from the border, we drove to a nearby campsite. Katy and Louise were setting up the camp. I had to think:

What are we gonna do? I decided to take a walk in the woods to give myself some space. We had a couple of ounces of hash stashed in the air cleaner of the Power Wagon in a plastic container. I got the hash out and went for a walk.

I thought of every possible scenario, trying to run the border somewhere. I knew there were lots of back roads across the border. All I had to do was find one. I also thought of turning around and going back to Denver. After all, I could get my old job back in a flash and could then apply for immigration.

Or I could claim that we are going to Alaska. We certainly had enough money in cash to make it believable. "That's it!" A light bulb went off in my head; "We're going to Alaska." I said.

We made a big sign out of cardboard and colored it with magic markers and put it on the Power Wagon, "Alaska or Bust".

The next morning we hit the road again, this time heading for the border in Idaho. The next day we were denied entry again, this time because we didn't have the right papers for Dondi. It was about a test for a sleeping sickness in horses called the Coggins Test, that all horses must have to cross the border into Canada. There were only two places in the U.S. that did the test. One was an agricultural school in Illinois. The other was at the University of Washington in Pullman, Washington. It required a blood test that had to incubate for 3 days to determine whether or not the horse was carrying the disease.

So it was off to Pullman Washington with the whole

caravan to get the Coggins Test for Dondi. They did the test at the University, where they kept Dondi for three days while the test was incubating. We set up camp in a local campground while we waited.

Three days later, we set out for the border again. Dondi had passed the test and we had the proper papers. We had to keep changing border crossings so the Canadians wouldn't catch on to us, so we headed West this time to Blaine, Washington.

We rolled up to the border with our caravan. The white Dodge panel with Dondi and the horse trailer behind. Following was Louise and the Power Wagon with "Alaska or Bust" blazed across the canopy on both sides. The hash was re-stashed in the air cleaner oil bath of the Power Wagon. Our fingers were crossed that this time we would be successful. We told the Canadians that we were going to Alaska on the Al-can highway, 1500 miles of goat trail they call a highway. A truck like the Power Wagon was just what a person needs to drive the Alaska Highway. The sign, "Alaska or Bust" just looked like it belonged.

So far, the trip was being heavily influenced by Murphy's law and once again, while getting the papers for Dondi, Katy blurted out "Longstock" when they asked destination. At that point it was too late to change, so the papers end up saying: Destination Longstock.

Now we had to come up with an explanation for it. I told the border guy, "Dad sold the farm, and this is my sister's horse and I'm delivering it to her in Longstock."

He asked, "Are you leaving the Horse trailer in Canada? Because if you are, you will have to pay duty on the trailer."

I confessed that I was leaving the trailer in Canada, and Canadian Customs charged me $100 duty and we were in; except, we had to wait for the Vet to come and look at the papers and the horse and tell us the horse was okay to come into Canada. And because it was Sunday, the Vet was not readily available, but had to be called in and paid $100 to look at the horse. We waited about 3 hours for the Vet to show up. It took about 5 minutes for him to check out the horse and a lot less time to take the $100. We were finally through the border.

We didn't drive very far after the border, pulling off the road onto a dirt road which opened into a little clearing about 1/2 mile off the highway, somewhere near **Chilliwack.** What a feeling! After a week and a half, we finally arrived in Canada!

It was a really nice spot we found that night. The coastal mountains were in view. There was a nice little clearing with lots of green, lush grass for Dondi to graze on. It was a warm evening, with a few mosquitoes around. We collected a pretty good pile of firewood and sat around the fire long into the night, smoking hash and celebrating our success on making it across the border.

The sun was shining on the mountains across the valley when I woke up the next morning. I threw some wood on last nights coals, the fire started up easily. After breakfast, I loaded Dondi into the horse trailer, broke down camp and hit the road. Heading North on highway 97, our slow-moving caravan crept along. We made it almost to Williams Lake that night, rolling into Prince George the following afternoon. After stopping at David Parsons house for a visit, we drove East from Prince George, finding a little meadow beside the highway. We camped there for the night.

The first thing we had to do was to find a place to leave Dondi for a couple of days while we floated the Power Wagon across the Fraser River and drove into Longstock. There was an old road from Penney to Longstock. It was an old bush road that was hardly used anymore, with several bridges washed out and miles of gun barrel gray clay that could be the most slippery substance known to man.

The road along the CN rail line to Sinclair Mills was as close to Longstock as you could get by driving and be on the same side of the river. That still left ten miles to go. We drove along the rail line until we got to the end of the road. We met a man named Bob Crane who lived there. He was a very tall, thin man about 6'6", and looked a lot like Ichabod Crane in the Legend of Sleepy Hollow. here was Bob, his wife Carol, and three boys. All the boys were tall and thin, just like their father. Their place was about 10 miles from Longstock. Years ago, the government tried to build a road through to Longstock, but was not successful. There was just too much soft ground. A horse however, could make the trip with no trouble.

Bob Crane was happy to board Dondi for a few days while we moved into Longstock. We went inside for about a half-hour and had tea with the Cranes. It was the first time we actually had a chance to tell our story of our trip from Denver.

Leaving the Cranes that morning, we drove to the river at Penney. By bringing the Power Wagon into Longstock, we would have a vehicle on that side of the river and we would use the Dodge panel on the outside.

Clarence Boudreau, who was one of the people we met

the year before, while crossing the river in Penney, had told me that he had crossed vehicles on riverboats for people quite often. He would put planks across two boats and drive the vehicle on. The boats would handle the weight just fine, and he would power the boats with just one motor.

We set out to Penney that morning to find Clarence. Last year, because of the high water, we were only able to drive part way down the road; but the river was at a normal level now, and we drove right to the Penney Landing. It opened up into a clearing with a couple of big hunks of rusted iron from some industrial use that was unidentifiable. The beehive burner was now right across the river. There were pilings in the river that were used to secure the winter ice bridge. The road on the other side took off from there.

We were there about a half hour when a VW van drove in. I was already out of the truck and approaching the van when a tall hippie- looking man got out smoking a joint.

"Hi, I'm Louie Carmen," I said, extending my hand. "Alfred" he replied, passing me the joint.

"Going across?" I took a toke and passed it back to him.

"Yeah! Need a ride?" he said toking on the joint between words, then passing it back to me. Katy and Louise and Chico came over and everyone introduced themselves.

Katy and I crossed the river with Alfred and walked to Clarence's place.

It was about a 1/2 mile walk. I knocked on the door. Clarence's wife Olivia answered.

"Hi, I'm Louie Carmen and this is my wife Katy, we're looking for Clarence. We bought some land in Longstock and just moved North from Colorado."

"Oh yes," Said Olivia. "You were here last summer, eh! I remember Clarence talking about you. He isn't here right now. He's up in the cedar forest, cutting some shakes. I'll tell you how to get there if you want to go looking for him."

She gave us directions and off we went walking on the trail that headed up Red Mountain. As we followed the trail, the mosquitoes got increasingly worse. We frantically smeared ourselves with bug dope to keep the hoards off us. About a mile up the trail we could hear someone working, we followed the sound. We came upon Clarence in the forest. He had a massive cedar on the ground and was splitting it into shake bolts. It was warm and muggy, just the right environment for mosquitoes and there were millions. It didn't take long before Katy and I were slapping on the bug dope again and even then they were still getting through. There was a cloud of mosquitoes around Clarence. Mosquitoes full of blood sticking out all over his head. He ran his hand across his face and head when he seen us, pretty well killing the ones that were already biting him, and leaving small streaks of blood across his head. It didn't take long until there was a new batch of 'em filling up with blood.

"Hi! How are you Clarence?" I asked." Remember us? We were here last year."

He put down his tools and walked over to us, hand outstretched. "Yes I remember. So you came back. Did you buy the place in Longstock?" he said.

"We did buy the place, and we're moving in." I answered. "Want some?" I offered Clarence some bug dope.

"Never use the stuff." He said. "You get used to the bugs

after a while."

"We have an old Power Wagon that we would like to get across the river. I remember **you** telling me you crossed vehicles on boats." I said.

"When do you want to cross it?" Clarence replied. "ASAP" I said.

"How about tomorrow?"

"Sounds good to me, "I said" We'll probably camp across the river, so when you're ready, you can just come over."

"Okay then, I'll be there at nine." says Clarence as he brushed another crop of bloody mosquitoes off his forehead.

We didn't waste any time running down the mountain, trying to outrun the mosquitoes. They seem to thin out from the unbearable to just really bad as we got closer to the river.

When Katy and I got back to the river, Alfred was still there. "Did you find Clarence?" he said.

"Yeah, sure did. He's going to meet us here at 9 tomorrow morning and we're gonna get that truck across the river," I said, pointing across the river at the Power Wagon.

"Why don't you stay at my place tonight?" said Alfred. "I live just down the road."

"Sounds Okay to me, but we got to be here by nine." I said.

"No problem," said Alfred, lighting up another joint, and passing it to me.

We crossed the river and picked up Louise and Chico, who had been waiting at the trucks, then crossed back again, walking about a mile from the river to Alfred's place.

Penney was a small town nestled in a narrow part of the valley. There had been a sawmill in Penney that was operating into the late 1960's. The old beehive burner was still there. A lot of the mill apparatus was still there, albeit in disrepair. The river is narrow at Penney, narrower than most places. The people string logs across, and flood the ice to build an ice bridge across every winter. For anywhere from 1 to 4 months, they have a road across the ice.

On the road from the river to Alfred's there was a spectacular view, with the beehive burner in the foreground and Red Mountain with a touch of snow and its red twin peaks in the background.

It was nice to be staying in a house that night. The mosquitoes were pretty brutal, especially in the evening, and I noticed a marked difference in the length of days this far North. It was light at least two hours longer than it had been in Denver. The long days, when the sun comes up at 4am and goes down at 10pm, but doesn't really get dark until 11, make it hard to sleep. I never really got used to the long days all that summer. I was just tired a lot.

Of course, this made it longer evenings for the mosquitoes too! It seems to be their favorite part of the day.

We hung out with Alfred that night, smoking joints pretty well constantly... and crashing.

"I'll come down to the river with you and give you a hand tomorrow" Alfred announced at one point out of the blue. Alfred was from Chicago and he was dodging the draft. He'd been in Penney for about a year. He was part of a whole group of draft dodgers when he first came. One by one they all moved on and now Alfred was the only one left.

We were all up at the crack of dawn. Clarence showed up

about 9 am across the river. We all got down there within a few minutes of each other. Clarence lashed the two boats together and we all went across.

We tied the boats to the old pilings. This kept the boats solid to the bank. We put eight rough cut 2x12s across the two boats. The planks were spaced apart for the tires to ride on. Both boats were 30 feet long, with a 6-foot beam, so the two together made a boat 30 feet long and about 14 foot wide. The extra width was gained from having to keep about two feet between boats so the swell didn't boil up between them and swamp them.

After laying planks from the boats to the river bank, we blocked them to the ground to support the weight of the Power Wagon while driving it on and also so that we didn't tear the side of the boat off. Everything looked right to load the Power Wagon.

Clarence yelled "Okay Louie, let's give er' a go, eh!"

I got in the Power Wagon and started it up. Katy, Chico and Louise watched as we started to load. I had my head stuck out the window, watching as the front tires rode up on the planks. Up it went, you could hear the wood take the strain. My knees were shaking. I kept thinking, what if something goes wrong, I'd end up in the river and all my stuff would, too. This was a much bigger river than they've got in Colorado. I kept hoping Clarence knew what he was doing.

The back wheels climbed up the planks and went over the top and on to the boats. Just when I think everything is okay, Alfred starts yelling at me "Back er' off, back er' off! She's sinking the boats!"

I took a deep breath and stuck my head out the window and slowly backed off the boats. It was a good thing that we had taken time to block the planks well before we started. I rolled down off the planks with a sense of relief, and got out.

"What the hell you got in that truck, anyway, eh?" said Clarence. "Oh! She's heavy. I knew that. There's a couple of wood stoves in

there." I said.

"Well we got to unload it!" he said, "She's too heavy."

We opened up the back and took everything out and piled it on the river bar. After the Power Wagon was empty, I drove it back onto the boats. I stayed in the drivers seat and held the brake the entire way across. It was nerve-wracking, but fun, because you're sitting high up in the boats and higher still in the drivers seat. In later years, this would be old hat, as we crossed many vehicles and buildings this way, but this first crossing was quite the rush. Though the boats seemed really stable, I still rode with the truck door open, just in case.

Clarence carefully maneuvered the boats on the other side. It took a bit to get the boats blocked up properly so we didn't tear the side out driving off. I carefully backed the Power Wagon off the boats. Everything went as planned. It turned out that Clarence did know what he was doing.

Then we crossed again, and picked up the load that was on the river bank. I think the load was almost as heavy as the Power Wagon, by the way the boats sat. On the other side I backed right into the river and up to the boats and loaded everything back into the Power Wagon.

We were across the river with all of our stuff and all we

had between us and Longstock was 10 miles of bush road.

It was already afternoon by the time we were done. We all went up to Clarence's place to have coffee and talk about our success in finally getting that crossing behind us. Clarence and Olivia lived in a neat, little house. It was freshly painted a bright yellow, with white trim. A neat, little picket fence surrounded the house. We went inside and Olivia offered us coffee and cookies. Turns out Clarence had lived here his whole life. They had met in Penney, got married in Penney and lived in Penney together for 30 years.

Clarence was a funny character, who loved to tell jokes. Sometimes his jokes weren't very funny, but at least he would always wait for Olivia to leave the room before he told dirty jokes.

I asked Clarence to tell me about the road we had to drive. He told us about the washed-out bridge where you had to drive through the creek and about the other bridge that there was no boards left on. The only thing left was the log stringers which you had to drive across. All this talk about the condition of the road was making me a bit nervous. I kept seeing the bridges in their state of disrepair and the slimy mud we had to get through.

We decided to stay in Penney another night so we were sure to get an early start in the morning. Clarence offered a little cabin to stay in and we took him up on it.

When I opened my eyes in the morning, it was already daylight. Through the window, I could see the sun lighting up the top of Red Mountain. I laid there in bed for a while just looking out the window and thinking about the whole adventure. Over the next year, I would ask myself more than once if I was really up to this. The whole day played itself out in my mind. What would happen today? Are we finally going to get to our land in Longstock? It just kept playing itself over and over again. I had to get up.

Everybody else was still asleep as I got up quietly so as not to wake anyone else. I threw on my clothes and went outside. I walked around the barnyard, cruising by Clarence's house to see if any one was awake. I could see smoke coming out of the chimney and some movement inside. I walked up to the house and knocked on the door. The door opened and there was Clarence.

"Good morning Louie, can I get you a coffee?" he said, inviting me in.

"That would be terrific." I said, sitting down at the table.

Clarence poured me a coffee and leaned over the table; in a low voice, he said," I got one for you, Louie... What's the height of conceit?"

I thought about it for a minute and replied, "Gee, Clarence I don't know."

"A mosquito floating down the river on his back, with a hard-on, yelling, open the drawbridge!" he laughed. We were both laughing just as Olivia walked into the room, so that was the end of the jokes, for now.

A few minutes later Katy, Chico, and Louise showed up at the door.

Olivia made breakfast for everybody.

"They didn't waste any time waking up." I said, as the mosquitoes were buzzing around the windows outside.

"Thank God for the mosquitoes and the winters or this

place would be overpopulated!" Olivia piped up while looking over her shoulder from the stove where she was cooking. She was right.

It was about nine a.m. by the time we finished breakfast and were ready to go. We started putting on mosquito dope, getting ready to tackle the drive to Longstock. Clarence and Olivia walked out to the truck with us, wishing us luck as we pulled away.

The Penney-to-Longstock road was an old bush road that was basically impassable most of the time without a four-wheel drive. In the winter, there was too much snow on the road. Penney was in a real heavy snowbelt. It was nothing for them to have 6 feet of snow. It always snowed more in Penney than in Longstock.

This was the summertime now and though there was no snow, we still had to contend with mud. A long stretch of the road was gun- barrel gray clay. Hard as a rock when it's dry, slipperier than snot when it's wet. The road to Longstock took off in the back of Clarence's place and up the hill by Victor Malice's house through a sandy part of the road then down a long hill. The road cut sharply to the left, right by a beaver pond and that is where the slimy clay began. I had chains on the front wheels of the Power Wagon, causing mud to fly everywhere as we plowed through the muddy road.

We went along really well for the first few miles, until we came upon the first bridge. All that was left of the bridge was two logs on each side. All the boards were rotted away, just as Clarence had told us. I got out of the truck and walked up to the bridge to take a look before we crossed it. It was a span of about 15 feet, and about 6 or 8 feet above the creek. The bank was too steep to drive around it. Everyone else got out of the truck and walked over the bridge just in case it didn't hold. I slowly drove the Power Wagon across the bridge. It was no problem, a cake walk. We drove on.

As we were getting about halfway to Longstock, we came upon a long hill overgrown with willows. The ground suddenly became a lot more slippery. We had not gone very far before we were spinning out, even with chains. I backed up about twenty feet and tried it again, going only about 10 feet further. It was a long time getting up that hill after backing up many times, probably taking more than an hour. By the time we got to the top, the truck was covered with mud. What a relief! I was having visions of getting stuck out there and having to walk to get help.

Everything went along smoothly until we got to the second bridge. The bridge was actually still there, but was knocked off its supports and listing heavily. There was a two-foot gap between the road and the bridge. There was a trail right beside the creek that Clarence had cleared with his Cat. It went off to the left of the bridge going down to the creek and up the other side and swung back to the road. I got out and checked it out. The creek looked pretty swift right there. It was hard to tell just how deep it was, but I was pretty sure that we could make it. However, Katy, Chico, and Louise walked across the bridge.

I pulled down off the road, chains clanging and barreled down into the creek. I could feel the current pushing the front end over. At one point, the water was right up to the top of the 16-inch tires. I was hoping that it wouldn't drown the motor.

As the current hit the back wheels, it seemed to straighten the truck out. I gave it the gas and crawled up the other side, water just pouring off everywhere. I pulled the truck back onto the road and got out. We were getting closer to Longstock now. I figured we had only about 4 miles left to go.

"Everybody in!" I called out to the others as they got back in, and off we went. That proved to be the worst part of the road. The closer we got to Longstock, the more solid the road got. We drove through one area of very large cedars where the road was pretty rocky, but it made for better going with the Power Wagon. It was a really beautiful drive through these big trees. Some were as big as 6 to 7 feet through, and maybe 150 feet high. This seemed like a good time to stop and smoke a little hash. So we stopped for about a half an hour, having a little something to eat as well.

With the worst part of the road behind us and a little hash to smoke, the stress level dropped considerably. We would surely make it to Longstock before noon. We were pretty sure that there would be some mail waiting for us at the Post Office. That would be our first stop.

We got back in the truck and drove on. About a mile on further down the road, we came upon the railroad tracks. There was no regular crossing there, so we just jumped the tracks and kept going. The road was starting to look familiar as we got closer. I recognized the crossroads and I hung a right to the Post Office. I could finally

get the Power Wagon out of 2nd gear! The old truck made lots of noise as the chains pounded against the body.

It was mail day in Longstock. The mail came 3 times a week

off the old Weigh Freight. The Weigh Freight was a train that serviced the local area. It ran from Prince George to McBride on Monday, Wednesday and Friday and from McBride to Prince George on Tuesday, Thursday and Saturday. It was made up of an engine and combination freight-and-passenger car. It was the mail train on the 140 miles between Prince George and McBride, hauling mail, picking up passengers, picking up and dropping off freight and freight cars where needed.

You could order your groceries on the telephone from Prince George and the store would box up your order and deliver it to the Weigh Freight and they would drop it off. It didn't matter if it was at a station or not, they would drop groceries right beside the tracks. Many of the old-timers had been getting their groceries that way for years. They'd be waiting by the side of the tracks when the train pulled up.

Mail days were busy days at the Longstock Post Office. Almost everyone came to get mail nearly every mail day. The Post Office was operated by Teresa McCoby. She had taken the position as a temporary job 30 years earlier. She lived right across the street with her husband Jonas and three grown sons, Dave, Bob and Wayne.

Teresa knew we were on our way, because some mail had come for us. Chad Allen was there that day, along with Bob Hooty, Ross Turner, Steve Worthy and old man Jack Hemming.

Chad could hear the Power Wagon coming for more than a mile away.

He went outside the Post office and listened intently. "What's that noise?" he said. The chains clanging against the body were pretty loud, and he was beginning to get flashbacks of Korea. He imagined a military vehicle with a machine gun on the top and started breathing heavily as we got closer. He was starting to sweat as the noise got louder and he started to freak out. All of a sudden he started yelling "Run!" at the top of his lungs. "Run, run for your life!" and he took off running into the bush.

Everyone else in the Post Office was pretty well oblivious to what was going on outside with Chad and really didn't hear us coming until we were really close. As we pulled up to the Post Office, everyone inside looked out at us.

"These must be the new people!" exclaims Teresa. I jumped out of the truck and let out a hoot. We had finally made it to Longstock. Everyone was excited, even Chico. We all got out of the truck and huddled around each other, talking excitedly. "I don't believe we're here!" said Katy.

"I didn't think we would make it, for a while there," I said. "I'm just glad we didn't have any babies on the way."

Bob Hooty and his cousin Steve came out to say hi. "Good to see you folks again, he said. "You here to stay?"

"Yep, we sure are. Just crossed the Power Wagon yesterday in Penney and it's got most of our stuff in it." I said. "We still have another truck and a horse and trailer to take care of yet. Did you get my letter?" I had written to the Hooty's from Denver asking them if we could stay with them for a couple days while I'm fixing up the one building that we have on the property.

"Yep, we got your letter and it's no problem. You can stay with us for whatever it takes," replied Bob. "By the way, this is my cousin Steve, he's living in the house we were in last summer. We built a cabin last summer, down the hill from the old place."

Just then Chad came out of the bush and started walking towards us. He walked right by us and into the Post Office like we weren't even there. It did, however, have the effect of changing the mood and I thought I should see if we had gotten any mail.

"Hi!" I said, as I walked inside. "Do I have any mail?"

"You're Louie Carmen?" Teresa says. "Yep." I replied.

"There is some mail for you." She turned and reached into a wooden box and passes me several letters. One letter was from my Mom and one from Gypsy, though I had to put them away for the time being because everyone was talking to me.

"Where you from?" "What place did you buy?" "Are you going to build a house?"

Chad was sitting there too, but was keeping pretty quiet. I don't know, but maybe he didn't expect to see us again after refusing to help us out with some food the year before.

Old Jack Hemming introduced himself: "Hello, I'm Jack Hemming, I got the homestead on that place back in 33. Jack was an old man now in his mid 70's. He had probably been about 5'8" at one time, but was hunched over pretty badly, and probably was only about 5'3". He had the ability to smoke a cigarette most of the way down and the ash wouldn't fall. Jack would be talking away, and he did talk a lot, and this ash would just hang on. As he's talking, the cigarette is bouncing up and down, but do you think the ash will fall? No way! And Jack was a chain smoker, lighting another cigarette off the short butt. You could almost never find Jack without a butt in his mouth, and an incredibly long ash hanging on.

Then there was Ross Turner: a man in his 50's, he wore an old, beat-up cowboy hat. He had a leathery face that made him look ten years older than he was. He would almost always have a big chew of tobacco in his cheek. Ross lived down by the Fraser River on the family homestead. He had lived there since he was 5 years old, when his dad homesteaded the place. The Turners had a working farm for many years. Ross was one of 9 children who worked the farm with his dad. One by one, each of the kids left for one reason or another, but Ross stayed. After his dad died, he was the only one left there. He lived a hermits existence during the 60's and early 70's.

Ross would have a wealth of knowledge about living on the land and subsisting on very little. He was full of old stories and tales about people in the area. He would become best of friends with many of the hippies that moved into Longstock and would do anything, smoke pot, take mushrooms, drink anything alcoholic. I once saw him, when a 4-gram piece of hash was passed to him to look at, swallow the whole thing. He passed out for about three days after that.

Steve Worthy was Bob Hooty's cousin from Washington State. Steve and his women, Jenese and daughter ELEFIG [pronounced-E- LEF-I-GEE] were a couple of hippies from Washington who were caught up in the Back To The Land Movement of the times. Cousin Bob was in Longstock, so they moved North. It was convenient that Bob and Paula had built a new house, leaving the old homestead cabin available for them.

Chad still remained quiet, but seemed intent on sticking around, for what reason I don't know. Maybe he just didn't want to miss anything. But I did overhear him telling Steve, "I thought I was back in Korea when I heard that truck coming. I was gonna go home and get my gun."

"I think it'll be all right, Chad," Steve reassured him.

After leaving the Post Office, we piled back in the truck and headed for our place. The first half-mile of the road was good, but after that it was back into the mud, though nowhere near as bad as the Penney Road.

We were all excited as we came to our driveway, if you could call it that. The willows were so thick that it was like driving through a tunnel. We broke out into the clearing on our land. What a feeling! A year later, and here we are! We drove right up to the front of the goat shed, or at least that's what Jack Hemming called it. It was the only building standing on the property. It was going to be our home for a while, until I could get a house built. The mosquitoes weren't really that bad yet, but it was the middle of the day.

We spent the rest of the day cleaning out the goat shed so that we could make it into a place we could live in for a while. We actually made pretty good headway on it that day. We cut it short for our first day there, and headed over to Bob Hooty's.

We had been on the road for the last 15 days and it was nice to be here. We left Denver on May 24th, and it was now June 7th.

Chapter 3

The Homestead

It was a couple of days later, and the whole situation hit me with a bang. Maybe it was just fear of the unknown, or maybe I was taking too much for granted. Sure, there was an ideal that brought me and a whole generation together to revolt against the rat race society that we knew only too well. We rejected the idea that progress was better and embraced simplicity, self-sufficiency, and going back to nature. But now the reality of it all was looking right at me. Feeling a bit apprehensive about the whole situation, I could tell my confidence level was beginning to slip.

I seemed to slip into a minor depression for a few days and could not shake the feeling that I had gone too far in order to live up to my ideals. Katy was a bit of a fanatic about the whole situation though; she seemed to have a positive attitude about things, and sloughed off my doubts saying, "What are you worried about anyway?"

But for me the brave spirit of adventure that got us here was running smack-dab into reality. I spent some time alone for those two days, just trying to sort things out and get another wave of motivation. I asked myself, "So now what? Here I am in the middle of the Canadian bush, no place to live, and a baby on the way. I hope I'm not crazy to be out here, so far from everything." It was scary.

I thought, "I gotta have a plan. I gotta get busy. That's the way to get on top of this." I started making a list of all the things we needed to do. Then I realized that what I needed was a house to live in. Nothing else mattered. If I just focused on building a house and forgot everything else, the tide would turn. It was like a revelation.

Within a couple of days, my energy levels were back again and I went at it, first fixing up the goat shed; after that, cutting logs for the house would take priority.

After another few days, we had the goat shed fixed up enough to live in. It was a log building about 15 feet long, and 12 feet wide that Jack had built 35 years before. By this time, the logs were all weathered and gray. The log walls had sunk into the ground so that the bottom logs were only half-exposed and the ceiling inside was pretty low. I had to duck to get in the door, the overhead beams just brushed the top of my head.

I could see daylight through the shaked roof, but incredibly it didn't leak. We nailed up an army tarp over the side with the most daylight showing through, just in case. The floor, which was a mess of rotten wood and dirt, was cleaned and replaced with a new floor of used lumber we found around the homestead.

Once we got the floor in, it was time to get the cook-stove inside. It was still in the back of the Power Wagon. Somehow I had to figure out how to get it inside by myself. With both women pregnant, I couldn't count on any help from them for something so heavy. I backed the Power Wagon right up to the door and took every bit of iron off the stove that I could get off, stripping it down to just the main body. I was studying the situation, trying to figure the best approach, when Katy handed me a pipe with a chunk of burning hash. Taking a few hits, I went over possibilities in my head. This was going to be no easy task.

My plan to get the stove inside all of a suddenly became clear. I would lay some planks from the truck to the ground, where I could wrestle one end of the stove up on the planks and slide it down to the door. I'd tie a rope around the stove and run it through a pulley, and have Katy and Louise hold the rope and lower it as I slid the stove down the planks.

With the stove stripped down I could manage to lift one end, although not very far. I took my time moving the stove a few inches at a time until I got it to pivot on the planks. Once the center of gravity was passed, the stove started to slide down the planks. I was pushingg as the girls let the rope out slowly, until the stove slid down the planks and settled at the bottom with one end poking inside the door of the shed. I got

Katy to slide another plank under the stove while I tipped it up. I pushed and pulled, jiggled and pried, until I got the stove inside and in position. I lifted one end at a time while Katy and Louise positioned the legs underneath. It was definitely my limit as to what I could lift, as I groaned under the weight. Within a few minutes, the legs were positioned and the stove was ready for its parts to get put back on, and the stove pipe to be connected. We hooked up the pipes and lit our first fire. It was starting to feel like home.

Katy and Louise began unpacking household things. It wasn't long before it was time to have another toke and savor our accomplishments. We had the shed quite livable by the end of the day and spent our first night on our land.

Before I could start work on the house, I still had to go to Bob Crane's and get Dondi. Now that the shed was together, I walked the ten miles to Sinclair Mills the next day. I rode Dondi back to Longstock along the railroad tracks. As we had no fences yet, she was staked out on a tether in our field. The field was grown up with a lot of small trees, so I couldn't give her much rope without her getting tangled and had to move her at least twice a day. It was summer, so there was a lot of green, lush grass around for her to graze on.

Aside from the goat shed, the old homestead cabin was still standing, though it was in pretty bad shape. The floor inside was heaved up with a big crown in the middle. Again, the log walls were sunk into the ground from years of freezing and thawing. One side of the roof, the South-facing side, was completely rotten, while the other side was basically intact. With a little work we could probably use it to store hay.

Right beside the old house were the remnants of a root cellar. It had been reduced to a big pile of dirt, with a lot of brush and raspberry bushes. A close inspection revealed how Jack had put it together. It looked as though there was a small room in the very middle made out of logs. A larger wall encircled the smaller one, with about a three-foot space between. That area was filled with dirt, and the whole thing was covered by another three feet of dirt. With a double-door entrance, it would store vegetables in the coldest weather.

You could almost see the outline of the old garden Jack had told us about. It seemed like a good place to put our garden. Though it was going to be up to Katy and Louise to plant and take care of the garden. I had to get a house underway. That was still my priority.

The next day at the Post Office I ran into Ross Turner.

"Hey Ross, do you have a roto-tiller?" I asked.

"Yeah," answered Ross, sounding a bit suspicious as he peered at me from under the greasy brim of his weather-beaten cowboy hat.

"Could I hire you to roto-till my garden?" I said.

"Yeah," said Ross.

"When would you be able to do it?"

"When do you want it done?" he said.

"How 'bout today?"

"How 'bout tomorrow?" "Okay."

"Want a fish?" asked Ross.

"A fish? Sure," I replied.

"Better follow me to my place and I'll give you a fish," Ross said as he got up, walked out, climbed on his old Ford

Jubilee Tractor and took off down the road.

I jumped in the Power Wagon and followed Ross down the road to his place. He drove the tractor like a maniac, wide open in high gear. The tractor was weaving all over the road. I followed at a good distance till he stopped to open his gate and I caught up to him. We both drove through and I jumped out to close the gate. Ross took off down the driveway. It was about 200 yards to his house, a small place built out of plywood, with a layer of faded blue and white paint and a tin roof.

He had already gone in by the time I got there. I walked up to the house. Finding the door open, I went in. Ross was stuffing kindling into the cookstove, then set a match to it. The fire immediately started crackling as he slid the stove lid back into place and asked without looking at me, "Drink of wine?"

"Sure," I said.

He took out two glasses and a gallon jug of wine, something called Berry Cup. He poured a couple of glasses and sat down.

"So what the hell you doing up here, anyway?" Ross asked.

"What do you mean? It's just where we are, man," I replied. "Everybody's gotta be somewhere and this is where we are. What are you doing here?"

"I was born here and lived here all my life," he answered.

"So what does that tell me?" I said.

"It tells you why I'm here" he said with a laugh, taking another drink. "I want to know why you came here."

I said, "We're back-to-the-landers. You know. It's the new hippie movement." I'm not sure if he understood me or not as the conversation was getting drunker and drunker.

I had some hash with me and after we had had a few drinks

I figured this was a good time to find out what the old guy thought about dope. So I hauled out my chunk of hash and a pipe, broke off a little piece and loaded the pipe.

"What you got there?" Ross asked, leaning over the table to check it out.

"Just a little hash," I said "Want to smoke some?"

"Sure, I'll try anything," he replied. I lit up the pipe and passed it to Ross. It looked to me like he had smoked it before.

We talked for quite a while and I filled him in on all the details of the trip North from Denver. He was quite entertained as I recounted the events, describing in detail the two-week adventure, complete with three attempts at the border and the "Alaska or Bust" sign across the box on the Power Wagon.

Bear stories were always good conversation, especially when drinking wine in the middle of the day. Ross had quite a few stories about bear incidents, having encountered many bears in the bush over the years. He told me one story about the bear that almost got him. He was tracking a moose through the bush when he was surprised by a big grizzly. A tree that had fallen from the wind was held up off the ground on one end by the roots. The tree was about four feet off the ground and the only thing between him and the bear. Ross had a little yappy dog with him that day. The dog got between him and the bear, barking and jumping furiously, and kept it at bay while Ross emptied his 30-30 on him. He finally dropped the bear on his last bullet.

By this time the house was heating up fast. The fire had taken off and the wood cookstove was throwing off a lot of heat. I swear, it had to be 100 degrees in there. We started talking about gardening.

"Better go out and look at my garden," Ross said as he gulped down the rest of his wine. I drank up the rest of my glass and was feeling quite a buzz as we went outside. His garden at the back of the house was about 25' by 50' with neat, little rows of seedlings. We walked along beside the garden as he filled me in as to what everything was.

Then it was down to the root cellar, where he still had potatoes from the year before.

Handing me a potato, he said "Feel that." The potato was as hard as a rock. It felt like it had been dug just recently, though it had been in the root cellar for more than eight months.

"What kind of potatoes do you plant?" I asked.

"Wee McGregor, or the Green Mountain, they're the ones that do the best around here," Ross said.

"Can I get a few for seed?" I asked.

"No problem," he said, grabbing a burlap sack off a pile in the cellar. Ross filled the bag up with seed potatoes. "Here you go," he said passing me the sack. I took them right out to the Power Wagon so I wouldn't forget them.

Pretty soon we were out at the wood shed, checking out his wood. In all the years I knew Ross, every time I went down to his place I had to look at his wood shed, especially if he had been getting wood. Wood in the woodshed or hay in the barn were bragging rights in Longstock.

Then it was off to the barn to check out Comet, Ross's Appaloosa stud. The barn was on the opposite side of the house from the woodshed, so it only made sense to stop at the house and have another glass of wine on the way. After checking out Comet, we stumbled down the hill to a large hayfield of about

50 acres. It was the largest cleared field in Longstock. Looking down from the top of the hill, I could see the river just beyond.

We walked down the hill and out into the field on our way to the river. The view was fantastic. You could see all the mountains in the area. To the Northeast, the Canadian Rockies loomed in the distance. To the South the Caribou Mountains with their scenic Sugarbowl Peaks. The winter snow pack was still hanging on to the mountain tops as the warmer weather and melting snow swelled all the creeks and rivers. This was the time of year when the rivers and creeks were the highest, as the high level snow pack began melting.

"Come on, lets get you a fish," Ross said as he headed down the hill toward the river. We walked across the field and down the riverbank. Ross started to pull on a chain connected to something in

the muddy water. As he pulled, I could see something coming close to the surface. It was a large wire cage with two big fins. As he dragged it out of the water and onto the river bank, I could see that it had a lot of fish in it.

"What the hell is that thing?" I asked.

"It's my fish trap," said Ross. The cage was about 4 feet long, 2 feet wide and 2 feet high, with two, 2-foot by 3-foot fins sticking out on one end. The entrance was a cone-shaped cylinder that intruded into the center of the trap. With the trap facing down river, fish swimming up stream swim into it and can't find their way out.

Ross reached for a gaff hook he had hanging in a tree nearby. He reached into the trap with it, gaffing a big Dolly Varden, he pulled it out of the trap.

49

"Here's your fish," he said, handing it over. Ross then picked up the fish trap, lifting it over his head, tossed it into the water, still loaded with fish. It slowly sank until it disappeared under water. I could just see the outline of one of the fins below the water. Ross explained that the fish traveled up river close to shore, so it was more effective if it was in the shallow water. The gray, murky water made it hard to see more than an inch or so into the water. The trap with its contents was virtually undetectable.

"It's not totally legal, eh," said Ross, referring to the fish trap.

We then headed back to the house across the field. The cheap wine was making my head spin by this time. I could feel a headache just beginning to surface.

I was getting the feeling that Berry Cup was mostly grape juice, sugar and some kind of hard liquor like vodka. I found out later about the incredible hangover that it produced. I could feel the throbbing getting more intense by the minute as I walked the fish back to the truck and threw it in on the seat.

"Well Ross, I think I better get going. I'm all set. I've got fish and potatoes. I'll see you tomorrow," I said as I jumped in the Power Wagon and started it up.

"See you later," said Ross, as I drove off.

I had just left Ross's place and turned on to the main road, when the fish started sliding off the seat. I tried to grab for it but it got away and fell on the floor of the truck. I reached down to grab it, but it was just out of reach. As I leaned over further to grab it, the truck drifted over to the left and went right off the edge of a culvert into the ditch. It turned out the culvert ended up right underneath the truck, hanging it up in the air.

I had no choice, I had to walk back to Ross's to ask for a tow.

He was in the house when I got there, so I walked right in after a quick knock on the door and said, "Hey Ross, I'm stuck and need a pull. The damn fish fell on the floor and I was trying to get it, and next thing I know, I'm in the ditch."

"That's the last time I'm giving you a fish," Ross said, chuckling under his breath. Of course, we had to have another glass of wine before we went out to pull the Power Wagon out.

Ross hooked a chain on behind the tractor and I jumped on the running board as we drove out to the road. I hooked the chain onto the Power Wagon and gave him the okay. He was backed up to the truck and threw it in gear, taking off and hitting the end of the chain really hard. The jerk popped the Power Wagon right off the culvert and onto the road.

"See you tomorrow," said Ross as he drove away.

On the drive home I was feeling pretty loaded from the wine and the hash, all I can remember is giving Katy the fish and passing out.

Ross showed up the next morning with his roto-tiller and started roto-tilling. We marked out the garden in the place Jack Hemming had told us to. Some of the ground was covered by really thick sod. It was like some kind of lawn grass. The sod was so thick that you could barely get a shovel into it. Ross had one of those front- mounted tillers that hopped all over the place whenever he got into the heavy sod area. We had high hopes for the garden, but in a real sense, it was just about too late for anything, except maybe potatoes. We went through the motions anyway planting all kinds of stuff. Ross hauled a couple of loads of old manure for the garden, which would probably help a little, but not that first year.

With the goat shed and the garden happening, my thoughts were occupied by the house I had to build. In about 4 months we would probably have snow on the ground and though there were a million things to do, I had to focus on building the house now.

I worked in the construction industry for several years and though I had never built a log house, I was pretty confident I could do it. I had several books on log building that I brought from Denver to help me formulate a plan of action.

While I was working on the house plans the next afternoon, Chad Allen showed up. This was one person I really did not like, but I was polite to him anyway.

"Hi Louie, how ya' doing?" Chad asked, as if we were friends or something.

"I'm doing okay, how about you?" I asked. "What can I do for you?"

"I wanted to offer you a job. I'm running this wilderness camp for kids and I could use a few extra hands. I was wondering if you were interested in working," he said.

I was thinking, "Is this guy a moron, or what? I mean, what kind of an asshole refuses food to people out here, especially people with kids? Do I really want this guy as my boss?"

"No thanks man, I've got a house to build before winter. There's really no way I could take a job," I said graciously. I couldn't get over how this guy acted like we were old buddies. I had to think of something to do quickly in order to get rid of this guy. I really didn't want to make small talk over coffee with him.

"Sorry to run off, but I've got to go look after my horse," I said as I got up and went out the door. I hung out in the field with Dondi for a while, hoping that Chad would leave soon. He made conversation with the girls for a few minutes and when I didn't return, decided to leave. I stayed out with the horse until I heard his tractor start up and take off down the driveway.

A couple of days later, we got another visitor from the wilderness camp. A young kid about fourteen years old knocked on the door while we were eating lunch. He was a short, stocky teenager whose parents had paid Chad for their son to go to the wilderness camp.

"Hi, my name is Burke," he announced as I opened the door. "I'm living at the child concentration camp down the road."

"I thought it was a wilderness camp," I said.

"He might call it a wilderness camp, but it's more like a forced labor camp instead," Burke said. He continued telling us about the work that Chad got out of all the kids at the camp. "He wakes us up at five in the morning and feeds us gruel. We're out working by seven o'clock, cutting and peeling logs for his house. He works us steadily until noon, and then gives us a half-hour for lunch, then back to work right through until supper time. It's grueling, working day after day on Chad's building projects, garden, firewood, and umpteen other jobs. We sleep in a tent and shit in a trench and my parents paid this guy for this. I hate it here. I'd like to escape."

"Man, I'm glad I turned him down! He was over a couple of days ago and offered me a job at the camp," I told Burke.

At one point in the conversation, Burke asked me if I had any pot. I was a little reluctant to give him a joint because of his age and the possibility that if Chad found out, he might make a lot of trouble for me. He pestered me for a joint, I figured, 'what the hell' and rolled a few joints, smoking the first one with him and giving him a couple to take with him.

Burke would show up at least once or twice a week after that, looking for some pot and telling us about the latest from the concentration camp. He had to sneak away from the work gang when nobody was looking and would not say a word about where he'd been. He always ended up with extra work when he returned.

Chad asked me on a couple of occasions if any of his camp kids were showing up at my place. I always denied that I had seen any of them.

It was a mystery to him where Burke would disappear to and where he was getting the pot. Chad could smell pot on the work crew sometimes, but was never able to catch Burke with any, even as the smell reeked through the tent after lights-out each night.

When I left Colorado, I had planned to build an octagon-shaped house. I'd read a book about circular-type houses such as these. One of the main benefits of round-shaped houses was air and heat circulation, which I felt would be a real benefit in the North. They were said to have a better energy flow as well.

However, the eight-sided house, if ten rounds of logs were used, would take 80 logs, or twice as many as a square or rectangle. It would also mean twice as many notches. This was going to take more time to build, time that I might not have. Yet I still wanted to go for the round shape and thought that if I reduced the number of sides to five, it would only increase the logs by ten, instead of forty.

"That's it!" I thought out loud. "A pentagon. I'll build a pentagon." The pentagon involved the least logs and notches I could do, while still maintaining a basically round shape. I went to work on the plan that would require twenty foot logs. The building would be five hundred square feet per floor and it would have two floors.

The next day, I went looking for trees that were about twelve to fourteen inches in diameter. I found a patch of trees about one hundred yards from where we decided to build. I figured I might as well get started cutting trees.

I'd bought a new chain saw before I left Denver. I knew next to nothing about chain saws when I went into Montgomery Ward, looking to buy one. I told the salesman where I was going and what I wanted the chain saw for. He assured me that this little Mac 10 would do the job. I'd cut a little firewood with it, and it seemed to work okay. I'd never felled trees before, but the next morning I had breakfast, got my tools together, and headed into the woods.

I guess I invented the cuts I used for falling the trees. It probably would have been good to look at a book on the subject, as, when I looked at the cuts years later, I was appalled. As a faller, I was basically a menace in the bush. My saw sputtered and smoked, sometimes overheating and refusing to run, but I managed to get half the trees on the ground on the first day. I limbed and peeled the logs right where they fell and soon had a whack of building logs ready.

Some of the logs were fifty yards further than I could get to with the Power Wagon. With a couple of come-a-longs and a lot of chain and cable, I could reach all the logs, and move them close enough to hook up directly to the Power Wagon and drag them to the building site. The trees were quite wet with sap at this time of the year and took several days to dry on the outside after I got them peeled. Up to that point, they were extremely slippery, and impossible to handle.

I needed about sixty-five logs for the walls and about twenty more for floor and roof beams. I limbed, peeled and skidded the first group of trees to the site and then cut the rest.

One day some friends arrived, surprising us by just showing up, with no warning. They were from Denver, and had come to check things out in Longstock. Mark and Donna Mohser and their friend Jerry, had driven out to Prince George, left their truck there and taken the Weigh Freight out that morning.

Mark and Donna wanted to go in with us on the land when we bought it the year before, but had backed out after they heard how isolated it was. It was just a little too far out there for them and they had decided to pass on it. They were very curious, though, and wanted to check it out. We were glad to see friends from Denver coming out to visit. It made the move seem a little easier and less drastic.

For a couple of days, Mark and Jerry helped me drag logs out of the woods and line them up along the edge of the bush where I could get them with the Power Wagon. It was nice to have some help, as it made things move a little faster.

One morning we were sitting around drinking coffee after breakfast and I mentioned that I still had my flat-bottom canoe up at the Penney landing. I wanted to bring it down the river to Longstock so I would have a boat to make the river trip with to Penney. The Dodge panel was still parked there. I took it to Prince George whenever I could get a boat ride to Penney. Ross Turner had a boat, but no vehicle and was glad to boat us to Penney and catch a ride to town with me. Katy usually took the train, rather than endure the hour- long boat ride.

Mark and Donna were only planning to stay a few days and suggested that we get out to the Penney landing and bring the boat down the river. They would see us off and drive around to catch the Weigh Freight back to Longstock the next afternoon.

We took the train to Prince George and drove out to Penney early the next morning. The canoe was stashed in the bush by the river and we had the three hp motor with us. We carried the boat down to the river, put the motor on the back, gassed up the tank and pushed off down river. Jerry was going with me; Mark and Donna would meet us in Longstock later that day.

About halfway to the highway there was a creek that flowed into the river. This was the creek we took off from the year before, when we were looking for the land. Mark and Donna stopped at the creek, waiting for us to go by. There were a couple of guys from Penney working on a boat at the landing that morning when we started off downriver.

It was a really nice summer day. The sun was shining and the temperature was warm, a perfect environment for mosquitoes. The river was wide and high from the high-level snow pack melt. There was a lot of debris in the water and a lot of foam on top, indicating that the water was still rising.

After we got out on the river, the mosquitoes seemed to be way thinner out away from the river bank. It was a pleasant start on our sixteen-mile river trip. The little three hp motor chugged right along down river, though it was probably going to be much slower going upriver.

We got only about a mile downriver and hadn't yet passed the point where Mark and Donna were waiting for us to go by, when the motor conked out. We were drifting along as I tried to start it up again. I hadn't realized that the vent on the tank was still closed, causing the motor to run out of gas, while I was messing around, trying to figure it out, Jerry yelled, "Louie! We're gonna hit a branch!"

It was a big branch from a tree sticking up out of the water, with the rest of the tree hung up on something below the water line. The branch reached out across the water about twenty feet, and was about three feet off the water. This was commonly known as a sweeper and was very dangerous if one should drift into it.

"Let's paddle around it to the left," I yelled to Jerry. I picked up my paddle and quickly started paddling on the right side of the boat. It only took a paddle or two before I noticed that Jerry was paddling on the left side. This had the effect of pushing us right into the sweeper very quickly. I switched to the other side, but it was too late. We drifted into the sweeper and Jerry grabbed onto it. In an attempt to keep it from hitting him in the head, he slid over to one side of the canoe, tipping it and water started pouring in.

In a split-second the current flipped it. We were both thrown into the water. We got a hold of the sweeper and held on. The canoe disappeared down the river, upside-down, as we pulled ourselves up onto the sweeper. With both of us sitting on it, the branch went down to just below the water line.

At first, Jerry was going to swim for it and took off his shirt and threw it in the river. Realizing that the water was so cold that he might not make it to shore a couple hundred feet away, he quickly changed his mind. We were both scared, but pulled ourselves together long enough to talk about our situation.

"Jerry, there were a couple guys at the landing. Do you think they would hear us if we started yelling?" I said, trying to stay calm.

"Let's hope so," said Jerry, and started yelling frantically.

We both started yelling at the top of our lungs for help. It was Mark and Donna who heard us first. They drove back to the landing where the guys were working.

"Hey, our friends are in trouble," they said excitedly.

The two guys immediately pushed their boat out, started the motor and came out for us.

"I hear a motor," I said to Jerry, "somebody's coming." Only a few minutes had gone by, but already we were starting to get very cold as the water was pouring across our legs. It was about up to our waist as we sat there.

"Here they come," I said, as I could see the boat now rounding the corner. "What a relief!"

The boat pulled up to us and we had to get in very carefully, one at a time, so as not to swamp the boat. One of the guys got to the other side of the boat to counter-balance as the other helped drag us into the boat. I realized that in a situation like this, a person should swim right away, because after just a few minutes in the water it would not be possible.

After they got us in the boat, we went upriver to the Penney side and one of the guys drove us up to Clarence's place. He and Clarence went downriver to find the canoe while Jerry and

I sat by the fire, wrapped in blankets, warming up. We must have been close to hypothermia because it took six hours of sitting by the stove before we stopped shivering.

Clarence and John, one of the guys who rescued us, retrieved the canoe and hauled it back to Penney in Clarence's river boat.

The whole incident gave me a lot of respect for the river from then on. I would never take a boat as light as that on the river again and was really concerned with river safety at all times after that. I was glad to be alive.

Every morning at nine am, and again at six pm, a local radio station in Prince George would announce messages to isolated areas. Anyone wanting to get a message to someone out in the bush would call the radio station with their message and the station would broadcast the message twice that day. We made it a point to tune in to the messages every morning and evening.

One morning in early July there was a message for us from Bobby Mach, my friend from Denver. It read, "To Louie and Katy in Longstock, I'll be on the Weigh Freight Tuesday - Bobby Mach."

Bobby drove up from Denver with his girlfriend Jamie. He had an old 52 Chev pickup, which he left in McBride where they caught the train. The Weigh Freight came in around half past eleven. Katy and I were there to meet the train. We were already at the station, and could hear it coming, a couple of miles away. A few minutes later we could see the headlight, as the train came around the corner about a mile down the track.

As it pulled up to the Longstock Station, you could hear the squealing brakes as the engine cruised right by the station. The passenger car was the fifth or sixth car back and approached us with the conductor hanging out the side of the car, giving hand signals to the brakeman in order that the train would stop right at the station.

The car pulled up to the station and stopped perfectly. The conductor jumped down from the train and put a step down on the ground for the passengers.

Bobby and Jamie got off the train and the conductor picked up the step and gave a hand signal to the brakeman. As the train inched forward, he stepped up onto the car and disappeared. The train picked up speed and pulled away.

"Hey Bobby," I said as I threw my arms around him in a big embrace, "How the hell are you?"

"It's good to see you," he answered.

I picked up one of their bags and crossed the track to the Power Wagon, throwing the bag in the back. Bobby and I got in the front seats and the girls rode in the back. I took it pretty easy, as Katy was starting to get pretty big. She was over seven months pregnant now. The last stretch of road was rutted up pretty badly. Katy and Jamie got out and walked the rest of the way.

I got all the news from Bobby on what was going on in Denver. Most of the old crew were still working for Barton Brothers, the company I worked for in Denver. It was really good to see Bobby. We were the best of friends and Bobby coming to Longstock to see me really meant a lot to me. I was in really good spirits when he was around and felt like I was bursting with energy and enthusiasm. We were in the foundation business in Denver and were both good at it. It just so happened I was ready to start the foundation. Bobby and I looked over the plan that night and figured out the layout on the pilings. The frost level was about four feet down, so it was

important that we go down below that.

He really liked the five-sided house plan. We stayed up late into the night talking about the house, old times, swapping stories back and forth. I still had a whack of hash left and Bobby had managed to get some pot across the border as well. We smoked joints and pipes of hash, until we eventually passed out.

Next morning, after having breakfast, Bobby and I headed over to Ross Turner's place. I really don't remember why we went. I think it might have been to borrow something or other. We no sooner got in the door than Ross had a glass of wine poured for each of us. Yep!

It was that rotgut Berry Cup. Berry cup had the amazing quality of starting the hangover while you were still drinking it and even though I'd been there before, I drank glass after glass, "'Cause that's the way Ross poured 'em," I explained the next day.

As we all got drunker, Bobby lit up a joint that he had with him and passed it around the table. After a while, Ross was insisting on giving us the tour through the garden, then the horse barn, and then down to the river to look at the fish trap, only this time, we were all really drunk. It was a sight to see. Three drunks trying to get that fish trap out of the water without falling in the river. I vaguely recall somebody falling in anyway. Hell, it could have been me for all I know. I'm not sure what went on directly after that, but we ended up back at Ross's place and sat around for a while, drinking some more.

Bobby and I decided that we were too drunk to drive the Power Wagon home.

"I'll give you guys a ride home," Ross piped up.

It seemed like a good idea at the time. I'm not sure why, because Ross was just as drunk as us but we piled on to Ross's tractor and headed to my place...might have been to get the girls in on the party.

Ross had this thing about vehicles of any kind: they were either wide open, pedal to the metal, or they were parked. We took off out the driveway with the pedal to the metal. There was only one seat on the tractor, that was the one Ross was sitting in. I was hanging on to the back of the tractor with my feet on the draw bar. Bobby straddled the hood of the tractor and Ross had it wide open. Between the bumps in the road, the potholes and Ross weaving from side to side, it was like riding a bucking horse. I was hanging on for dear life and Bobby had his hat in his hand, swinging it back and forth, yelling at the top of his lungs while bouncing up and down, trying to stay on.

"Whaaa—hooo! Ride 'em cowboy!" Bobby bounced around with one hand, holding on to the headlight fixture.

"Yaaaa—hoooo!" I yelled out from behind. Ross was laughing so hard, he could hardly keep the tractor on the road, running in and out of the ditch. We were making an awful racket. Katy and Louise could hear us coming quite a-ways away.

I don't remember much from that point on. I've had to rely on other people to recount it. From what I gathered, Bobby, Ross, and I stumbled in and all of us passed out within ten minutes or so. I could tell by the rough morning that we must have had a good time, although the girls were not impressed.

I awoke with a splitting headache the kind that throbs so intensely that it causes you to squint with pain. It took four aspirins and about forty more minutes in bed to get my headache dulled enough to get up.

Ross was crashed out on the floor next to the stove and was still there when Louise got up. She had a bed in the corner downstairs, while the rest of us slept in the loft. Louise lit the fire and turned on the radio to catch the messages to isolated areas. She had been waiting for her man, George, to come up from Denver to pick her up. It had been more than a month since we left Denver and that was the last time they had seen each other.

"Message to Louise at Longstock," came over the airwaves that morning. "I'll be arriving on the Weigh Freight from Prince George on Friday, from George."

"Oh good!" Louise exclaimed. Ross started to wake up. Louise had the fire going and hot water on for coffee when Katy and Jamie got up.

"So, George is coming," Katy said to Louise.

"Yes, he's coming tomorrow," Louise answered.

The girls sat around drinking coffee for a while before Ross finally got up off the floor. He immediately took a chew of snuff and shoved it inside his cheek. Louise handed Ross a coffee and asking "How do you feel, Ross?"

"I feel like I've been shot at and missed, and shit at and hit," Ross answered jokingly, punctuating it with a laugh.

A few minutes later, there was a knock on the door, and a

voice yelled, "Hello, anybody here?"

"I recognize that voice," said Louise, hurrying to the door. "Hi!" said George, as she opened the door.

"George!" Louise said." I thought you were coming on the train tomorrow."

"I was, but I would have had to wait around 'til tomorrow. I decided I'd drive as far as I could and walk the rest of the way. I left the VW in Sinclair Mills at Bob Crane's place, and walked down the tracks. Took about three-and-a-half hours. I followed the map," he said, and pulled a crumpled-up piece of paper out of his pocket. It was a map I'd given him in Denver a few weeks before we'd left.

George and Louise poured a couple of cups of coffee, going outside to drink them. About an hour later they came back in, just as Bobby and I were starting to come back to life. Ross had already gotten up, had a coffee, and taken off for home.

George and Louise were part of our circle of friends in Denver and so were Bobby and Jamie, so everyone knew each other. We all worked on the same concrete crew in Denver.

George stayed about five days in Longstock, spending most of his time with Louise, who was now five-and-a-half months pregnant. They were a couple who were very much in love. They had broken up for a year a few years earlier and each had different partners for a while. Then they both decided they belonged together and got back together about a year ago. Except for that year apart, they had been a couple for seven years and were now having their first child.

I was sad to see Louise and George go. Louise had been with us from the start on this adventure. She was one of those delightful people who was easy to be around, always in good spirits, positive and energetic. They would eventually leave Denver a few years later, after another child, both children were boys by the way and settle in the Ozarks Mountains in Southern Missouri.

Bobby and Jamie stuck around for a couple of weeks. We managed to get the pilings for the house foundation sunk during that time. We got the first two logs on the house up, as well.

Jamie was having a little trouble with the rustic lifestyle. She was not used to living without running water and electricity. It didn't seem to bother Bobby at all and they got into fights about it quite regularly. It finally came to the point that Bobby had to take her back to Denver. Katy and I saw them off on the Weigh Freight on a sunny morning in July.

It had been really nice to have friends around us up to this time, but now everyone had left and it was just Katy, Chico and I. The next week or so seemed pretty lonely as I worked on the house by myself and Katy looked after our goat shed home.

Chapter 4

The Hippie Invasion

"Hello, anybody home?" a voice called out from the front door of our goat shed home. Katy, Chico and I were eating lunch inside. I had just taken a break from working on the house and was busy making myself a coffee while Katy was making sandwiches, when a visitor arrived.

"Hi!" said Katy as she opened the door.

"Hello!" said the man in a rather happy tone. "My name is Theonius Toad." he says, extending his hand, and shaking hands with Katy.

"Glad to meet you." she said, happily. "Come on in."

"Don't mind if I do, eh!" he answered with a smile. "And hello to you, you must be Louie."

"That's me." I answered, as I poured myself a coffee. I filled a second cup as well taking it for granted that our visitor would have one too. "Want a sandwich?" I asked as I handed him a coffee.

"Don't mind if I do," he said reaching for the cup of coffee. "I just bought a place here in Longstock, and I thought I'd go 'round and meet some of the neighbors, eh! The name's Theonius Toad. Some people call me Theo, some call me Teddy and some just call me Mister Toad." He was a tall man, just over six feet and about one hundred seventy-five pounds, with a long handlebar moustache, and shoulder-length hair. He was a pleasant-looking, friendly sort of fellow, and very talkative. He seemed like the sort that would make a really good neighbor.

It wasn't really necessary to ask many questions, as Mr. Toad told all about himself in the next few minutes. It appears that he bought a piece of land up by the train tracks, about nineteen acres with a house on it.

"I just bought the place a couple days ago, eh! Don't figure to move out here 'til next year, though. I'm a forklift operator at the Giscome Sawmill, eh! Been working there about three years now, eh! I figure another year, and I'll be able to make the move here permanently, eh!" he rambled on. "Mind if I smoke?" he asked.

"No, go right ahead," I answered.

He just rambled on about things as he reached in his pocket, pulling out a bag of pot. He never did pause in the conversation, managing to roll a big, honking bomber of a joint. Passing the joint to me, he reached in his pocket and brought out a lighter. Reaching across the table, he gave me a light.

Showing up at someones house with a joint to smoke was pretty well the thing to do in the early seventies, especially in Longstock. It was unusual, as a matter of fact, that anyone would go for a visit to a friends house without taking a joint or something with you; or leaving one when you left, as Mr. Toad did that day. "One for later," as he put it when leaving.

It was about a week later that another family moved into Longstock. A French guy from Montreal, named Pierre Lablanque, and his wife Betty, and daughter Celine, moved in a place about a mile down the tracks. Celine was almost the same age as Chico and Betty was pregnant as well. Pierrïe had been a member of the FLQ in the late sixties in Montreal. He wasn't talking about what his involvement was, but in 1969 the FLQ had been responsible for kidnapping and killing a Member of Parliament in Canada, causing the Government to invoke the War Measures Act, which was basically Marshall Law in Quebec.

Pierre was a hard-looking, stiff kind of guy. He was always very serious and looked at the world that way. Any kind of humor seemed to be like an afterthought. Pierre would remark when faced with a joke of any kind, "I guess that was a joke, eh?" he would exclaim in a real serious tone. He'd loosen up a bit when he smoked dope, but would rarely laugh and joke with people.

The hippies were definitely starting to outnumber the old timers in Longstock by this time. It seemed as if every week more hippies would show up.

The next one to come to Longstock was a friend of Steve

Worthy. He was a rather strange character by the name of Skid Slimeheimer. Skid was a real homely-looking guy, with scars on his face and a glass eye. I'm telling you, that glass eye was weird. It seemed to follow you wherever you went. Sometimes, you couldn't get away from it, other times it seemed to be looking over your shoulder at something behind you. People couldn't help but to turn and look behind them to see what the hell this guy kept looking at.

I guess Skid was driving on the freeway outside of Chicago in 69, doing a couple hits of LSD and MDA, when he lost track of the road and ended up driving off the side of the freeway and landing upside down. He woke up in the hospital a couple days later, with serious injuries to his head and face and one eye missing. After that Skid seemed like he was a couple bricks short of a load in the brain department.

Steve Worthy knew Skid before the accident and felt that Skid had been affected quite a bit. Because they were good friends, Steve talked to Skid about coming to Longstock after he moved here. There was an old cabin about a hundred yards off the tracks that Skid fixed up and moved into.

Things were moving along nicely for Katy and I. The house-building was coming right along. I managed to get anywhere between one and three logs in place just about every day. The log walls were going up steadily.

Katy was getting bigger all the time, too, as she passed the eighth month of pregnancy. She fully intended to have the baby at home. We had been seeing a doctor in Prince George that was aware of the home birth. He was very helpful to us, taking us into his office and letting us look at medical books having to do with births, and explaining things in detail to me about how to know when things are not right and when it's time to call the helicopter. Katy was seeing him every two weeks until the last month, when she went every week. I usually went with her on the Weigh Freight every Tuesday and took the passenger train home the same night.

On one of these trips to town, we were riding the passenger train home and went to the bar car. We always rode in the bar car on the ride home. We usually met a lot of hippies from up the valley on the way. There was a general influx of hippies in all the little communities in the Upper Fraser and Robson Valleys. Because so many people used the train, it was easy to meet people.

We were sitting in the bar car that night and there were a few people from Ketchikan, Alaska that were getting pretty loud and loaded. We were drinking with some people from Dome Creek, a big guy named Ben and his friend Ken and his wife Sandy. The Ketchikan bunch was partying a couple tables over. We hadn't realized that they were getting off at Longstock until the train stopped there and they got up from their table, picked up their bags and got off. It looked to me like there were about five or six in their group.

We got off the train and walked across the tracks to the Power Wagon and started it up. "Where you going?" I asked, just in case they needed a ride.

"Just down the road, we're okay," somebody yelled through the darkness.

I gave them a wave and headed home.

The next day was a mail day and I decided to ride Dondi

71

to get the mail. There was a little gray house back off the road on the way to the post office where old Louie Lavangie lived. He was an old man that pretty well kept to himself; you would hardly ever see him. That day, when riding by his place, I noticed that there was a bunch of people around, outside his house. I recognized a person or two from the train the night before. A couple of people were close to the road and walked out to check out Dondi as I road by.

"Nice horse!" one of them remarked.

"Howdy." I said nodding my head. "Didn't I see you on the train last night?"

"Probably so, we did come in on the train." he said. "You're friends of Louie's?" I asked.

"Not really, we're gonna buy the place. We're doing the deal in a couple of days. Gonna go to town with Louie and pay him off on Friday. Moving in Saturday," he said.

"Wow!" I said, as a couple more people walked out to the road where we were talking. They looked like a really friendly group of hippies; everyone was from Ketchikan most recently, but hailed from all different parts of the U.S.

Bob Faddus and his girlfriend Kathy Haines were the couple I was talking to. They had a little girl about the same age as Chico. Her name was Colleen.

There was also Larry Gaylord, a short, red-headed guy with an equally red beard, who looked like he was on some kind of psychedelic drug all the time. He had a really spacey look and a perpetual smile. He liked to talk with big words even if he didn't really know what they meant, sometimes mispronouncing them as well.

Freddy Bartells was a schoolteacher in Alaska. He had long, reddish-brown hair and a scraggly beard and was a very slow talker. He was from Washington and gave it away easily when pronouncing words like wash, or Washington, with an invisible "r".

The last member of the group was Harry Half-dollar, though that was probably not his real name. Harry was a big, tall guy, about six- three and two hundred-fifty pounds, a comical type of person that always had something funny to say.

On that Friday, Louie would be packing his suitcase, and leaving Longstock after living there for over fifty years. It was a time of change for everyone, as the older generation left and the younger generation was moving in. Longstock would never be the same after that summer.

It had been almost eight years since Longstock had had this many people living there. Not since old man Jamison had closed the mill there, back in 65, had the population been this large. Prior to the Hootys moving there two years ago, there were only Bud Jamison and his wife and three kids; the McCobys, Teresa, Jonas, Wayne, Dave, and Bob, Ross Turner, Jack Hemming, Louie Lavangie, and old man Jon Floten: a total of sixteen people.

In the last two years, the Hootys and cousin Steve Worthy, Jenise and ELEFG, along with Chad Allen and his wife, moved in. In the last three months, fourteen more people had moved in, with two babies on the way as well. Though Chad could have been the farthest thing from a hippie, the new people definitely were in the majority.

It was the middle of August now and Katy was due to have

the baby within a couple of weeks. I had been working on the house pretty steadily and except for a few days of haying down at Ross's place, I stayed pretty close to home. We were having beautiful weather, though the days were getting shorter and the nights were starting to get a little cool by this time of year.

We were totally prepared for the birth at home. Katy was very confident about it. She had begun having Chico at home a few years earlier and relented, and went to the hospital. She felt afterwards that she should have just stayed home. The days of August were ticking off and still no baby. Katy was going crazy and wanted the baby to be born, she decided to try a spoonful of caster oil. On the last day of August, we went to bed that night and she woke me up around midnight, telling me that the caster oil was working and that her water had broken.

She went into labor a couple hours later. We had been sleeping upstairs in the loft, but had a bed downstairs by the stove ready for when we needed it. We smoked hash all the way through her labor, she said it made her relax. I had talked to the doctor quite a bit and knew that I had to track the baby's progress down the birth canal. He had given me several pairs of sterile rubber gloves, which I was to throw away after each use.

It was about seven in the morning when I was checking her dilation and felt the baby's head. Katy had been doing breathing exercises through the last months of her pregnancy and had been breathing all the way through her labor.

The goat shed was warm, with the stove going and things were well under control, when this dark-haired baby showed me the top of his head. I was braced to catch him, as I knew it happens pretty fast. A couple of contractions later, his head popped out and the rest followed right away.

I had the baby in my hands, still attached by the umbilical cord, but he wasn't breathing and the adrenaline was running through me. I got both feet in one hand and lifted him up by the feet, grabbing for the respirator I had by the stove. The fluid was starting to drain from his nose and month. I helped it along with the respirator. There was a gasp and a breath and then nothing. I put down the respirator and lifted the baby up, giving him a light slap in the butt. He immediately started crying and gagging with tiny body convulsions as he gasped for those first breaths. Within seconds he was crying loud, it sounded like he had a really healthy pair of lungs.

Katy was really played out, but motioned to me to lay the baby on her stomach. I laid the baby on her and had to sit down. The minute or so that went by from the time the baby was born until he was breathing and I knew he was okay, had to be the most intense moment I'd ever known. A life was in my hands and my hands alone. No hospital or doctor or nurses, nobody but me. Of course, Katy was there, too, but for that moment, it was only me and the baby.

"It's a boy, Katy said to me after I had sat down. I had completely forgotten to check. After a while I began to come back to life. The whole ordeal had left me quite drained. It was mostly the pressure of those all-important, few seconds where life begins. I've never experienced anything like it.

"Let's call him Zac," Katy says to me while she's lying there with him. And so it was that the baby, who was born in the goat shed, was named Zac.

Chico had just been waking up when Zac started to cry. He

75

lay in bed for a few minutes before coming down to investigate. Chico, Katy, and I all hung around together, googling over the Zac for a while, we smoked our last bit of hash that we had been saving for this day. It was a very happy day. Everything went all right. We had a new son.

After a couple hours, Katy and the baby were sleeping and Chico had gone down for a nap. I went for a walk down the road towards Longstock and back. I didn't really want to see anybody. I just wanted to thank God that it all turned out all right. It was about eight in the morning when I took off walking down the road. I felt like I was just coming down from the adrenaline rush and still high from the hash and the birth, as I walked down the road. Fall was already in the air as the leaves were already starting to turn colors and blow off the trees. A few leaves hit the ground as I passed by.

It was a time to reflect on things, as I had done several times since we arrived here. The house was partly built at this point. I was hoping I could get it done as quickly as possible, with two kids to take care of now. I visualized the steps I would be taking to complete the house. I could see in my minds eye the walls going up and then the roof going on.

My confidence level was growing again, as my thoughts of the birth of Zac seemed to fuel my enthusiasm once again and my determination to make this work grew stronger.

I turned around and started on the walk home with the fall wind blowing in my face. It was a beautiful, crisp morning, with the sun climbing over Mount Baldy as I walked. I turned the corner into our driveway and soon broke out into the clearing at the edge of our property. I could see the goat shed where

Katy, Chico, and little Zac were waiting. I found everyone asleep when I went in. I crawled into bed and closed my eyes and don't remember a thing, as I dropped off to sleep.

It was early afternoon when I awoke to the sound of a baby crying. I climbed down from the loft to find everyone awake and Katy and Chico googling over baby Zac. We were definitely a family of four now, with a son born in Canada. There was surely a reason to take the day off from the house building and just hang around and enjoy our family. Nobody came by that day. We had it all to ourselves and the neighbors didn't get the news about our new son until the day after, when Bob Hooty stopped by the following afternoon.

"Hello, hello!" Bob called out as he approached the door of the goat shed.

"Hello to you, come on in," I said as I opened the door. "Have a cigar" I said as I passed Bob a huge cigar-sized joint I'd been saving for this occasion. "It's a boy!"

"No shit! Katy had the baby?"

"Yesterday morning at seven o'clock." I replied.

"Everything went okay and everyone's healthy?" Bob asked in a serious tone.

"Come see for yourself," I said as I turned and motioned to Bob to follow me.

Katy and Zac were just waking up in the bed in the corner as Bob and I approached.

"Oh, hi, Bob," Katy opened her eyes, looking up at Bob and I. "Want to see the baby?

"Oh yes," said Bob, moving closer as Katy uncovered him and held him up for Bob to see. "Wow!" Bob remarked at the

77

full head of dark hair Zac was born with. After a few minutes of googling over Zac, we fired up the cigar joint and celebrated.

It was not long after Bob left that the news traveled like wildfire through Longstock. This was the first baby born in Longstock that anyone could remember. Even the old timers around Longstock could not remember a baby being born here.

Within a couple of days, the neighbors started showing up to visit and see the baby. Katy was still spending most of the day in bed and seemed to welcome the company, eager to show off the new baby. There was a steady stream of visitors for a couple of days running.

My work on the house ground to a halt for the time being. Between taking care of the house, Chico, Katy and little Zac, it was taking pretty well all of my time every day. It was about two weeks before things settled down into a normal pattern, where I had time to work on the house again.

Katy took the train into Prince George with little Zac to Doctor Jarvis for a check-up. The doctor gave Zac a clean bill of health. He wanted Katy to bring him in once a week for the first month or so.

The following week, Katy and I and the two kids got up early and got ready for the weekly trip to Prince George. It was a cool, crisp morning when we piled into the Power Wagon and drove to the train station. The Weigh Freight was supposed to come at 7:10 in the morning. We got to the station at about 7 o'clock that day. There was a work train we could see, working about a half a mile down the tracks that seemed to have the main line blocked.

We waited for quite some time and no Weigh Freight.

Trains being late was a pretty regular occurrence on this line, especially the Weigh Freight; it was delayed on a regular basis because it had to move and switch cars at different stops, as it worked along the rail line from McBride to Prince George.

We hung out there at the station for what seemed like a long time and still no sign of the Weigh Freight. After a couple of hours, we noticed that people were showing up to get their mail. It had to have been at least nine o'clock by then. I went up to the post office and asked if anyone knew anything about the train.

"There's a phone number you can call to find out," said Teresa McCoby. "Just go to the house and Wayne will show you how to work the phone."

I went to the house, which was right across the street from the Post Office and knocked on the door. "Come on in," a voice yelled from inside.

"Hi, can I use your phone? Katy and I have been waiting for the train since seven and it hasn't come yet. I want to call and find out what happened to it."

"No problem," said Wayne as led me to the phone. There was a separate room where the phone was kept. It was one of these older phones, where you had to turn a crank to ring the operator. After the operator came on, you had to give her the number and she would dial it for you. The lines ran along the train tracks and were owned by the railroad. Only people living close to the rail tracks could have a phone and this was the only one in Longstock.

"Hello is this C.N I'm talking to? I asked the person on the other end.

"Yes it is, how can I help you?

"I've been waiting for the Weigh Freight at Longstock and it hasn't come. Can you tell me where it is?" I said.

"There has been a derailment on that line and they do not expect to have the line opened until late this afternoon." she said.

"So there won't be any trains running today? "Not until they get the line cleared."

"Okay thanks for the information," I said, hanging up the phone. "Looks like there won't be any trains today." I said to Wayne as I walked out of the phone room. "Better go and tell Katy."

I left the McCoby's place and walked back to the tracks. Katy was waving at me as I got close. "Hurry up, we got a ride," she yelled.

"A ride? How can we have a ride, this is the train tracks and there are no trains," I thought.

As I got closer to the tracks, Katy was motioning me to follow her. She was walking towards an engine and caboose that were moving towards her on the tracks. I just caught up and the engine stopped and a man stepped out on the platform of the caboose and motioned to us to come over there.

We climbed the stairs of the caboose and went inside. The train started moving and soon was traveling down the tracks at a pretty good clip. There were several railroad workers in the caboose who seemed to be really concerned about the baby's health.

"Is he gonna be all right?" one fellow asked.

"Oh, God I hope so," said Katy, as the railroad workers looked on with a serious concern, as if something were terribly wrong.

They hurried us out to Sinclair Mills, where they had a work truck waiting. Stopping the train in Sinclair Mills, one worker said, "we'll drive you in the rest of the way." He motioned at us to follow him, as he disembarked the train and walked to the truck. I wasn't sure what Katy had told them, but I knew I had better go along with it for now.

He drove us into Prince George and dropped us off right in front of the doctors office.

"I hope everything is all right," he said, sounding very concerned just before driving off.

"Thanks for the ride," Katy said as he drove off.

"What the hell did you tell those guys," I said. "I called the C. N. and they told me that the line was closed, and that there would not be any trains until this afternoon."

"I was just hanging around the station waiting for you when the engine and caboose came down the track." Katy recounted the events. "As they passed me, I waved to the men on the train. I guess they saw me holding the baby with Chico beside me and they ground the train to a halt and backed up to where I was. One of the men came out on the platform of the caboose and asked me if there was a problem. I told him that we had to get the baby to the doctor today. Another man came out on the platform and they briefly talked between them, and then asked me to wait a minute, indicating they would be right back and then disappeared into the caboose. A couple of minutes later, they came back out on the platform and told me to get on the caboose, and they would get me into town. I think they thought it was an emergency. I just went along with it."

"I was wondering what was going on after I came out of

the McCoby's place and could see the engine and caboose stopped there," I said.

"I was looking at the road, hoping you would show up soon and asked them if they could wait a minute until you got back. It was perfect timing," said Katy.

Doctor Jarvis gave little Zac a clean bill of health: "I'm amazed that everything went so well and you have a very healthy baby here," he said as we were leaving. "See you again next week."

We had to wait in town until the next day to get the train back home. After doing some shopping, we took a cab over to Dave and Shirley Parsons house. They were used to having us stopping over whenever we had to wait for the train.

It was nice to have friends in Prince George to stay with. The Parsons had become very good friends by this time and liked having us stop by. They even put a room together in the basement for us to stay in. We spent the night visiting and listening to Dave's incredible stories, of which he had many.

The Weigh Freight was back on its regular schedule by the next morning, leaving Prince George at nine. It seemed everyone working on the train knew about how we had to rush the baby to the doctors the day before. We didn't have the heart to tell them that it wasn't really an emergency, so we just went along with it.

The Power Wagon was waiting by the station for us as we arrived in Longstock at about 11:30 that morning. On the drive home, I'd realized that I had not done any work on the house at all since Zac was born two weeks ago. It was time to get at it again and doubly important with two kids now.

The sun was peeking out from behind the clouds and then it slid back behind the big cumulus giants that populated the sky that afternoon as I stood in front of the half-built house, assessing the situation. There was one log that straddled the log walls that had not been notched in yet. Katy had helped me get up the day before the baby was born. It had sat up there, untouched, for the last two weeks. I figured that this was a good time to notch it in place and get things moving again.

Katy and I had a system for getting the logs up on the walls, that worked pretty well. We had a couple of poles with one end on the ground, and the other end sitting on top of the log walls. The poles were not that large, so we could move them around the walls to whatever side we needed them. We would drag the log to the side we wanted and line the log up with the poles. We tied a long rope to one of the floor joist logs and brought it over the walls and around the log we wanted to get up and back over the wall, and under the floor joist again. Katy would man the rope, taking up the slack each time I pushed, rolling the log up the poles. With this method we could get the logs right up to the top of the walls. When they reached the top, they would butt up to the butt end of the logs on the other sides. I would then stab the log with the peavey and lift it over the top, one side at a time. We had gotten all the logs up like this, up to that point. They were getting a little harder each time, as the walls got higher.

I climbed up on the log wall and started cutting the notch in the log that was not in place yet. It took about an hour to notch each log in and fit it tightly. I felt as if I should get someone else to help me get logs up. Katy was too busy with the kids and having just had a baby, I was worried about her hurting herself, especially with the log walls getting higher all the time.

I had been back working on the logs a couple of days when I got some unexpected company. An old-timer in Longstock, that I had met briefly before, Paul Miller, his wife Marge, daughter Eleanor, and her husband Bob all showed up one morning. Paul walked up to the building site where I was already working. He was a very tall man, over six feet tall. He had on big, leather logging boots with tassels in the front. His wool socks were pulled up over his wool pants, suspenders went over his shoulders and his red plaid wool shirt. He had a double-bitted axe over his shoulder. I swear he looked like Paul Bunyan.

"Can you use some help?" Paul yelled up to me as he walked up.

"Wow, a work crew," I muttered under my breath. Quite surprised at their arrival, it took me a second to realize that they came to help raise logs.

I climbed down from the log wall and greeted Paul with a handshake.

"We heard that you could use some help, so we came to help you out today," Paul said with a big smile on his face. Paul has lived in Longstock since the mid-1930's, when he homesteaded 160 acres. He built a log house in the first year on the homestead, out of timber from the great Longstock fire in 1936. It was said that lightning struck high up on Mount Baldy and started burning from there. There are still the remnants of a huge crater near the top of the mountain where the lightning strike happened. It was summertime, the temperature was in the high 90's and the bush was tinder dry. The fire spread like the wild fire it was and threatened the town. People were forced to evacuate the Longstock side of the river and set a makeshift camp on the South side as they watched the fire rage through the bush on the other. The river was rising a foot an hour for a few days straight as the fire burned. The ash that settled on the high-level snow in the mountains caused it to melt even faster coupled with the hot temperatures. The river was rising at an unusually fast rate and flooded some of the fields in the low-lying areas close to the river.

For three days the people in Longstock stayed across the river in their temporary camp until the worst of the fire burned itself out.

After it was over, there were hundreds of acres in Longstock covered with burnt and blackened trees. Most of the timber was charred on the outside, but still sound on the inside. It would only last a couple of years before the wood would start to deteriorate and be good for nothing. Paul harvested enough of the blackened timber to build a log house. It was a dirty affair, with the blackness of the wood getting on everything that came close. After a few years, the black seemed to wear off and turned the logs weather-beaten brown.

Paul had an old cable-blade Cat that he logged with. He worked for several years, skidding logs to the river in the winter and pushing them in the river in the spring for the mill down river at Sinclair Mills. He was an old, seasoned logger, well-liked by everybody.

The women went to the goat shed to take a peek at the baby and Paul and Bob started working, right away. Handling the logs with all the extra people was easy and fast. Paul swung his double-bitted axe with authority and accurately. The log walls grew.

I had been averaging three logs a day, notched in place, most days. We put up seven logs that day and got three more up on the walls for me to fit the next day. It was a colossal jump on the building progress and inspired me to keep it going. I have to say that the progress I made on that day was a definite turning point and made a real difference.

It was late in the afternoon as I saddled up Dondi and hoisted myself into the saddle. "I'll be back in a little bit," I yelled to Katy from Dondi's saddle, as I rode by the goat shed on my way to the neighbors, to line up some help for the next round of logs.

I was going to drop by at Bob Hooty's place, but as I rode by the crossroads at the center of Longstock, I heard a lot of noise coming from down the road, by the Alaskans place.

"Oh, what the hell!" I said to myself, and turned Dondi in that direction. As I came closer to their place, I noticed a bunch of people out in the yard in front of the house.

"Hey, Louie!" somebody yelled at me, "Come and have a drink!"

"Don't mind if I do! "I answered, as I reined my horse into the yard. I got off and tied Dondi to one of the two big weeping willow trees in front of the house.

"Have a beer, Louie," said Larry, as he handed one to me." We're having a little party tonight for my girlfriend. She's coming in tonight on the train from Alaska."

"I guess that's good for you, eh?" I answered as I took a swig of the beer.

"Good," said Larry," it's uncredible."

"Uncredible?" I thought to myself. I decided to leave it alone for now.

After a while, some of the other neighbors wandered by. It wasn't long before the tequila got broke out, and things started to get wild.

Bob Faddus had this old Harmony big-bodied guitar that he was playing. He had really big hands and he really liked to strum it hard. It was just one notch above beating on it. Bob could take a song like

"What'd I say?" and play it for hours, just pausing long enough to take a drink of tequila. Bob was about forty minutes into "Give me some of your love," when we could hear the train coming from several miles away.

"The Train!" somebody yelled out. The party poured out into the road and started for the train station, which was only a five minute walk. It was a really noisy procession, with Bob Hammering on his old Harmony, and at least half of us singing along with him, "just give me some of your love." The party was louder than the train. Every once in a while someone would yell "Quiet!" and everyone would just stop and be quiet so they could hear the train. When they were satisfied that the train was still coming, the noise would start up again.

I left Dondi tied up at the Alaskan homestead, joining the procession to the train to go meet Larry's girlfriend. When we got to the tracks, the train was already stopped by the station. We could see people getting off on the opposite side of the train. We hung out on the roadside of the tracks, waiting for the train to leave its passengers and pull away.

A couple of toots from the train whistle and the train began to pull away, leaving the station in the dark. We could see the silhouettes of at least two people across the tracks, when Larry yelled out, "Norma, is that you?"

"Yeah! That's me!" a voice answered out of the darkness.

"I'm over here," said Larry, as he tried to focus in the darkness.

They finally found each other in the dark, and embraced.

"Good to see you." I could hear Larry saying in the blackness, as the noisy party continued. Just then a flashlight went on and came towards me, blinding me.

"Hi Louie, how's it going, eh?" I recognized the voice as that of Theonious Toad, but could not see him as the light was right in my eyes.

"Kill the damn light, Toad," I said, "I can't see a thing."

Toad shut off his flashlight and joined the procession, as everyone moved on down the road, slowly and noisily, back towards the Alaskan homestead.

"You met these Alaska people yet? I asked Toad as we walked.

"Well kind of, but not really," said Toad.

"Hey everyone, meet Theonious Toad," I yelled out for everyone to hear.

A few people answered, "Hey, Toad!" and "Good to know you!" and

"Where the hell is this Toad?" one voice remarked.

The whole procession slowly moved back to the Alaskan homestead, noisy and partying all the way. Larry and Norma walked on ahead, arms around each other, and were the first to get back. Bob Faddus was still hammering on the old Harmony, singing "Tell me what I say," and the tequila bottle was still getting passed around, though it was almost empty by now.

We finally covered the eighth of a mile from the tracks to the Alaskans place and turned in to the house. It was a little, framed house, about twenty feet by about twelve, with a table and a couple of chairs, and a large bunk bed in the corner.

I stopped to check on Dondi, who was tied in the yard, waiting for me and I mumbled some drunken words about how much I liked her before heading for the house.

The little house was pretty crowded by the time I went in. There were a few joints going around, I squeezed in, and found a spot to sit on the wood box. Faddus had a chair pulled out in the middle of the floor, and was strumming that guitar like there was no tomorrow. I couldn't tell what song he was playing, and I don't think he actually knew either, but he just kept on playing until he could remember the words again.

'Hey, baby, don't you treat me wrong I wish I remembered the words to this song Hey, hey! Tell me what I say!' Faddus bellowed out, as he hammered his old Harmony guitar. Some people started singing along with Faddus, others talking and laughing. I was feeling pretty spaced out. I leaned back against the wall, just kind of looking over the situation. There were a few chairs and a couple stools pulled up to the kitchen table. A heated discussion was going on about Americans and Canadians. Toad was right in the middle of things, defending the Canadian perspective, and Harry Halfdollar was taking up the American side.

Larry and Norma were sharing a chair at the table and were engaged in a totally different conversation. Larry was asking

Norma for all the latest news from Ketchican, and every once in a while, he would throw a comment into the other conversation.

As I looked about the room, I noticed that Skid had joined the party. I hadn't seen him until this point, partly because it was dark and partly because there were quite a few people there. He seemed to be hanging out, being kind of quiet. Every once in a while, a joint would get passed to him, he'd take a hit and pass it on. He was holding a box of what looked to be dog biscuits. I was trying to see what the box label said, when I noticed Skid pop one in his mouth.

I leaned forward towards Skid and said, "Hey man, what the hell you eating there?"

"Milkbones you want one?" he said, holding the box up to me. "No thanks, I think I'll pass," I said.

"You sure?" he said, "they're really good!" He popped another into his mouth and got right down to chewing it up.

"I'll bet he's got good teeth," I thought to myself, as I turned my attention elsewhere. It was easy to do, with all the people in the room and several different conversations going on.

Just then Bob Hooty showed up with another bottle of tequila and started passing it around. There was a ritual that you had to go through when taking a drink of tequila: first you had to lick your hand and then sprinkle it with salt. With the bottle in one hand, you first lick the salt off your hand, then take as big a swig as you could and last, just before you gag on the stuff, you take a wedge of lemon and suck on it. Bob Hooty's bottle, and another that Faddus had, got passed around the room several times, until they were gone.

This created a situation where there were a lot of very drunk people getting drunk in a very short amount of time. More joints got passed around and even Skid's box of Milkbones came by me a couple of times. Some people even tried some, figuring, they can't be that bad, after all, Skid is eating them.

About ten minutes after the last bottle of tequila was finished off, I started to feel really drunk. I thought this might be a good time to get to my horse and got up to go outside. I had no idea I was so loaded, as the world started the familiar spinning head treatment that I usually try to avoid. My legs seemed to be on a holiday, or at least, thats how they felt.

The feeling brought back memories of about a year before, when Katy had found an unopened bottle of Mescal in the Goodwill box while dropping off some stuff. We thought it would be a good thing to drink at our weekly poker game with a few friends. There was a side pot for who got the worm, so we were all trying to get that worm. But every time you lifted the bottle up to take a swig, the damn worm would float up to the top. Needless to say, we were drinking a lot of Mescal as we tried to get that worm. I don't remember who got it, but the bottle ended up empty, so someone obviously did.

I woke up the next morning, and couldn't move my legs. I could feel like I was going to puke and though I tried to get up, I couldn't get my legs to do it and ended up puking all over the living room rug. I remember thinking at the time, "Well, at least it ain't my rug!" I was wrong. I found out later that my friends had packed me home after the card game and put me on my couch. I didn't remember a thing. It was around three in the afternoon the next day before my legs would even hold my own weight.

Just as I was trying to get to the door, I heard a voice, "Hey,

Louie, you need a hand?" It was Freddy Bartells, looking me straight in the face. He had a glazed look about him, but seemed quite willing to lend a hand.

"Fuck, no!" I answered. "Ive got a horse to ride home."

"Yeah! But your horse is out there," he said, pointing to the front yard, where the horse was tied. And you're in here!"

I bolted for the door, or maybe it was a stagger, though it felt like it could have been a bolt, and yelled to Freddy, "Now I'm out here, too!"

The cool air felt good on my face, and seemed to make me feel a little better. I looked around and could see Dondi a few feet away. I headed off in her direction, albeit a bit wobbly, but made it. I was feeling around, trying to find the bridle. I was pretty sure that I had taken it off and hung it on the saddle.

"Hey, where the hell you going with that horse?" Freddy yelled at me in the dark.

"Home, as soon as I find the bridle," I answered. I finally found it and got it on her. I got one leg in the stirrup and grabbed the saddle horn, moving up and down a few times, trying to get some momentum. Freddy gave me a push and up I went, damn near losing my balance and going right off the other side.

Freddy passed me a joint after I was on the horse. I sat there and smoked it with him.

"See you later," I said, as I nudged Dondi, she responded immediately. I don't remember the ride home. I think I passed out. I came too in front of the goat shed a while later. Don't know how long I was there before I woke up. I dropped the saddle on the ground right there and walked Dondi to a nearby tree and tied her up. I then went in the goat shed and crashed.

Chapter 5

The River

It was the end of September and fall had definitely set in. The mornings were frosty and the days were cool. Trees everywhere had lost most of their leaves and daytime temperatures were hovering below 50 degrees Fahrenheit. The air felt like fall, with a trace of winter on the way.

I had just got the log walls completed on the house and would soon be starting on the roof. Our goat-shed home was starting to be pretty cool in the mornings and we had to keep the fire burning even during the day to keep things at a comfortable level. Katy and I talked it over and decided to move into a house that was on the road to Longstock. It was about a mile away from our place. It was an old, framed house that was built sometime in the 1940's by Ross Turner's brother, Artie. It was a small, compact house that was more than twice the size of the goat-shed. The boards covering the outside were weather beaten brown and gold and the place was insulated with sawdust in the attic and in the walls.

The move changed my work schedule somewhat, as now I had to travel the mile-distance to work on the house. I put myself on a regular schedule each day, getting up early and packing a lunch and spending the whole day working on the house, returning home after dark.

Sometimes during the day, Katy would bring the kids down to have a look at the progress on the house. Otherwise, I would spend the whole day there and not see anyone. Though I was the only one in Longstock building a house, there were several other building projects going on which kept people quite busy getting ready for winter.

The Alaskans were working on the woodshed where Larry and Norma were living, trying to make it warm enough for winter. The house was small and pretty crowded, with Faddus, Kathy, and Colleen sleeping in the top bunk and Freddy in the bottom. Harry had a portable hammock that he hung up in the kitchen each night.

Just about everyone in town was cutting wood for the winter. Even when I was working on the house, I could hear the roar of several chainsaws working off in the distance.

The log work was progressing quite nicely, I knew I had to get some lumber soon. The money that we had brought with us was starting to get pretty low: we were down to our last $500, and needing quite a bit of lumber to finish the house. I was talking to Pierre about my situation one day when he and Toad stopped by the building site while they were out hunting moose. It was more like they were just walking around with guns. They ended up hanging around with me for several hours, smoking several joints and helping me lift a couple of roof poles up in place, then heading back home because it was too late to go further into the bush.

"I have a friend who has a small sawmill and he sells lumber pretty cheap," Pierre said to me. He wrote down his friend's phone number and drew me a map to his mill. Pierre had been bringing in lumber a little at a time for a barn that he wanted to build the next summer and talked to his friend quite recently. "I'll be talking to my friend in the next couple days," said Pierre, "I'll mention to him that you'll be by to see him."

It was still a 16-mile ride down the river to get things like lumber in to Longstock, unless you were able to bring a few boards at a time on the Weigh Freight, as Pierre had been doing each time he came back from Prince George.

I'd been on the river numerous times since Jerry and I had flipped the boat at Penney, back in June. I'd made several trips upriver with Ross Turner, as well as driving him into Prince George and back. He had a thirty-foot riverboat that belonged to Bud Jamison, that he could use whenever he wanted to. In exchange, he would have to drop Bud and his family off at the Penney Landing, and pick them up whenever they went came back. This was just about once a week, as Bud and his wife were both pretty serious alcoholics and they would only bring

95

enough booze out to last about a week before they ran out.

Ross had no vehicle on the highway side of the river, and it's a good thing the way he drove, so this partnership worked out well for both of us. I made plans with Ross and Bob Hooty's cousin, Steve, to go to Prince George a few days later. Ross wanted to get a 45-gallon barrel of gas, and I had to get gas too, as well as a supply of grain for our animals and groceries and, of course, lumber. I still had the horse trailer up at the Penney landing. We planned on getting so much stuff that we decided to take the horse trailer to fit it all.

It was a cool, cloudy day that morning, as we headed up the river for Penney. Hooking the trailer up to the truck, we drove the Penney road to the highway and we were in Prince George about an hour and twenty minutes later.

Bustling around town, we started to accumulate our load. We packed a ton of rolled oats into the truck, with groceries piled on top. Three barrels of gas were lined up on one side of the horse trailer, lumber on the other side, with the ends sticking up and out the back, to accommodate the long boards. We were loaded, to say the least. We stopped by the liquor store just before we left town, picking up a couple of gallon bottles of, you guessed it, Berry Cup.

It was about six o'clock in the evening when we pulled out of Prince George and crossed the old C.N. bridge and up the airport hill out of town. It was dusk, the sun had set behind us about a half an hour before. I turned on the lights in the truck and I noticed the amp meter was indicating a serious discharge, so I quickly turned them off again. We drove along for another ten or fifteen miles and it was getting too dark to see without the lights, I had to turn them on again. It was only a couple more miles and the truck started sputtering. I realized I had to shut the lights off if I was going to keep it running, so I shut them off. It was pitch dark when the lights went out. I struggled to get the truck stopped before we went off the road.

I got out with a flashlight and opened the hood. I banged on the voltage regulator while Ross watched the amp meter.

"It's charging," Ross said. "Now it's not, now it is. Now it's not, now it is."

"It's Got to be the regulator," I said. "I'll try to bypass it." I unhooked what I figured were the positive and negative wires and hooked them into the corresponding wires on the alternator. I had to do this with the truck running, because if I were to shut it off, it might not start again.

"It's charging," yelled Ross from inside the truck.

"Oh good, it's working," I said as I got back in the truck. I put the truck in gear and off we went. The lights were really bright, especially just before I shifted gears, when the motor was revving up. Just as I was shifting into fourth gear, the lights got really bright and went poof! Pitch dark again! Again I struggled to get the truck stopped, without driving off the road, horse trailer and all.

"What the hell do we do now?" Ross said.

"I don't know, got any ideas?" I said.

"We could flag someone down who's going past the Penney road and see if they'll let us follow them," Steve interjected.

"Sounds like a plan. Let's do it. We really don't have much choice, with all the stuff we're carrying," I said.

A couple of cars passed us by before we got one to stop.

It was a lady in a pickup truck, with a couple of kids in the truck with her.

"Sure you can follow me. I'm going to McBride, I go right past the Penney Road," she said.

"Holy shit, I wish that woman would slow down!" I said, as I stepped on the gas, trying to keep up with her. With the horse trailer on the back, I got pretty far behind on the hills. She didn't bother slowing down to wait for me to catch up, so I had to drive really fast to catch up on the flats. Sometimes she got so far ahead of me that I couldn't see the road at all in front of me. All I could see was what the road looked like five hundred feet ahead, where her lights were shining.

I finally lost her on a corner and was just about to pull over, when I could see lights around the corner shining up the road. She was pulled over waiting for me, which I thought was nice of her. I closed the distance and caught up, pulled up behind her, got out and walked to her window.

"There it is," she said. I looked ahead and I could see the 'Penney Access Road' sign.

"All right!" I said, surprised we were already there, "Thanks a lot."

She waved and pulled away, leaving us in the pitch dark, again.

Both Ross and Steve got out of the truck and shined their flashlights in front, so I could see enough to get pulled off the road onto the Penney Road. We pulled over there and got the Berry Cup out of the back. Good thing we had flashlights, as it was a black night with cloud cover that blocked out the stars and the moon.

We smoked a joint and had a couple of drinks of wine before we got going again, having to drive the five miles to the river where we left the boat, with Steve riding on the hood, shining a flashlight on the road. I could only see enough to go about two miles an hour. We eventually made it to the river.

We were feeling pretty good by this point. We weren't stranded on the road somewhere and it was only the boat ride between us and home. Time for another joint and another drink before we load the boat.

"What say we just take the ton of grain and groceries and come get the rest tomorrow," I said as we were finishing off our smoke.

"Sounds good to me," said Ross.

We loaded the grain, groceries, and a few, small hardware items into the boat, parking the horse trailer and truck. Shoving off into the blackness, we started downriver. Ross had been running this river for over forty years and had made the trip to Penney and back hundreds of times. The only things that really changed on the river were the river bars that seem to move around every year or two, and the logs floating down the river, or the deadheads or sweepers that are anchored to the bottom, that can split your boat in two, or knock a hole in the bottom that could sink you.

"As long as I can make out the tops of the trees on the river bank, I can get us down there," Said Ross. I couldn't see a thing and had to feel for the bottle of wine as it was being passed to me. Fortunately, I could see the joints because of their glow. We were in a big riverboat and I believed that Ross could get us there.

Everything seemed to be going really smoothly as the riverboat glided over the water, with Ross's little 25-horse Evinrude wound out at full throttle. It was sudden and smooth, I heard the sound of sand and gravel sliding across the bottom of the boat. I could feel the boat lift, and then come to a halt. The motor revved up as it came out of the water. We had slid up onto a gravel bar in the middle of the river. It was at least five to seven miles upriver to Penney and nine to eleven miles to Longstock.

"Oh shit!" said Ross, in a rather worried tone. "How deep is the water?"

I got out of the boat and stepped in the water with rubber boots. The water was about six inches deep, which was probably enough to float the boat empty, but we had a ton of grain in it.

"Better have a drink," Ross said, passing me the bottle of wine. I took a big swallow. We were all feeling no pain by this time, so we were probably not as bothered by the whole ordeal as we could have been. We smoked another joint by the lights of a flashlight and joked about our situation.

"Oatmeal, we got plenty of oatmeal! Oatmeal and wine, and how much pot we got?" said Ross.

"I've got a bag in my pack," I said.

"Hey, we can live out here for a month!" said Steve.

I could tell by the faint outline of the trees on the river bank that we were just about in the middle. We talked and joked about our situation for a while, finally deciding to try to get the boat off the bar. The three of us stepped out of the boat and tried lifting and pushing to get it to move, with no success. I grabbed a plank out of the boat and jammed it under the bow of under the boat. Pushing it under as hard as I could, I lifted, and pried the boat backwards. It moved! All three of us got on the plank and pried, moving the boat about an inch at a time. The entire boat was resting on the bar, with, maybe, four to six inches of water, so it had to move roughly thirty feet. The boat moved an inch at a time and after what seemed like forever, we could feel it trying to float.

"Whahoo!" I yelled as the boat broke free and floated again. It took most of an hour to free it.

Jumping in the boat and pushing it out into the river, away we went. We finally made it to Longstock at two am, and tied the boat where the Power Wagon was waiting, deciding to just take the groceries and cover the grain for the night.

We Spent the next day, getting the grain and then the gas and lumber up in Penney. Though uneventful, it was a nice day and a nice river ride. Especially when we could see where we were going.

It was about a week later that Ross, Pierre and I did the town trip again the same way. This time, we took Ross's twelve foot plywood skiff, as Bud was using his riverboat that day. Pierre was going to haul some more lumber with his two-ton truck. He agreed to haul a bunch for me, too. This would give me enough lumber to finish the house.

About half way to Penney that morning, I noticed a stream of water coming into the boat.

"Hey, Ross, look at this," I said, pointing to the stream of water. "What's that, we got a leak?" he replied.

"Yeah, we do, and it's leaking pretty good."

"Here stick this in it," he said handing me a screwdriver.

I took the screwdriver from him and looked at it. "What the hell," I said, and reached down and jammed the screwdriver into the hole. The leak stopped. I Never thought too much about it after that.

It was a normal trip to town... Got the lumber... Got the groceries... Got the Berry Cup... Always got the Berry Cup when you went with Ross. Heading out of town just after sundown, Ross broke it out.

It was a slower trip than usual, following Pierre in his big truck. I fired up a joint and Ross passed me a plastic glass, about half-full of wine. I passed him the joint. About halfway to Penney, it started to rain. The closer we got, the harder it came down. By the time we got to the river, it was coming down cats and dogs. We sat in the truck for a while to see if it was going to let up, but no such luck. After about forty five minutes, we decided to go for it.

Ross went down to the boat while Pierre and I wrapped the grocery boxes in plastic bags. We carried the boxes to the boat, we could hear Ross talking to himself.

"Man, there's a lot of water in this boat!" he said. I could hear the water splash each time he dumped his bailing can. I went back to the truck and parked it. When I killed the lights, it went totally black, I couldn't see my hand in front of my face. I picked my way through the blackness down to the river, having to yell, "where are you guys?" a couple of times. As I got to the boat, Ross flipped on his flashlight so I could see while getting in the boat. When he turned it off again: total blackness. We pushed off into the blackness and started on our way downriver. I strained my eyes, trying to see the tree line on the river bank, but I could not see a thing. It was still pouring rain as I thought about the screwdriver that we had jammed in the hole in the floor, thinking, 'gee, I hope it's still in there and not leaking.'

Pierre was sitting beside me on the seat and Ross was in the stern, running the motor.

"Can you see anything, Ross?" I said. "No!" he replied.

"Oh good," said Pierre, tapping me on the arm and passing me a bottle of whiskey he had just taken a slug from.

"Holy shit!" I remarked after taking a slug, thinking it was wine. A warm feeling went through me right away. It felt good, so I took another slug before passing it back to Pierre. It was too dark for Ross to see what we were doing. I thought, maybe that's not a bad idea, seeing as we're depending on him to get us to Longstock. We passed the bottle back and forth several times, when the motor started acting up. It sounded like it was only running on one cylinder and sometimes missing on that one.

"Water in the gas?" I yelled back to Ross.

"I don't know," he answered, "but either way, were going downriver."

'That's true,' I thought to myself.

When you're only running on one cylinder, you tend to use more gas and after a few miles of running like this, Ross picked up the gas tank and gave it a shake. "I don't think the gas is gonna make it," he said as he killed the motor. "We'll just drift a bit and save the gas for going through the rocks."

The rocks were these huge boulders, as big as houses that sat right in the middle of the river. The channels that we needed to get through were near the river bank on both sides and were only about twenty-five feet wide. We drifted for about an hour, before Ross started the motor heading down river again. It was still raining cats and dogs, still black as coal and we were still running on one cylinder, and almost out of gas. I never saw the rocks that night. As a matter of fact, I couldn't even see Pierre or Ross, or the river bank when we finally landed in Longstock. We did run out of gas before we landed and had to paddle and drift the last mile or so, but we did make it. I felt a little wobbly from the whiskey as I climbed the trail up the riverbank and started up to the Power Wagon. I gave Ross a ride to his house and since Pierre had his own truck, I drove home. Another ordeal with the river behind me...

"There's one," I said, pointing to a log on the river bank. We had already gathered three others to build a raft. The lumber was too much for the boat, so we were building a raft to get it to Longstock; that way, we could get all of it down river in one trip. There was too much lumber on Pierre's truck to take in the riverboat. It would be at least two or three trips downriver to Longstock, if we were to take it in the boat.

I jumped out of the boat and threw a rope around the log. Pierre jumped out, too, and the two of us, rolled the log into the water using peaveys. Ross stayed out in the boat and waited for us to throw him the rope. He towed the log across the river to the Penney landing, and then came back across to get Pierre and I. Faddus was with us, too, waiting on the landing for Ross to throw the rope to him. He pulled the log in to shore.

"That makes four," said Pierre as we pulled into the landing in the boat. We had Bud's riverboat for pulling the raft downriver.

We pulled the four logs into shore and tied them together

with ropes. It looked like a real skucum raft, and everyone agreed that it should carry all the lumber in one load. We had to push it out from the bank and anchor it there, so as not to get it grounded when it was loaded. We made a plank walkway from shore and began loading. There were about four thousand board feet to get on the raft. The first thousand, or so, went pretty well. By the time we got the second thousand on, we noticed the raft beginning to sink.

The more we loaded onto the raft the further it sank. When we finally got all the lumber on the raft, it was just about half underwater. The lumber that was on the bottom of the raft was totally submerged.

We had to keep pushing the raft out from shore as it sank, so we wouldn't ground it. So, it was well out in the water when we finally got it loaded, our tow line tied on, and pulled out into the current. It was a good two and a half hours, at the slow pace we were towing, before we got to Longstock. We partied all the way down, drinking Berry Cup and smoking pot on the way. When we finally got the raft to Longstock, we were all too screwed up from the wine and pot to think about unloading it, so we just tied it up, and came down to unload it the next day.

I met Pierre at the river the next morning. He had also driven his truck to the river. The lumber on the bottom was quite waterlogged, after sitting under water overnight. As we unloaded the raft, it came up in the water. When we were finished, the entire raft was back above water.

"It looks like a real good raft, sitting there with nothing on it," remarked Pierre, after we had everything loaded onto the trucks.

I drove my truck to my place with the load, unloaded and stacked the lumber beside the house and covered it with plastic. I had already gotten the downstairs floor put down, with the last load. This load would be mostly for the roof and the upstairs floor. A few weeks later, when I went to start using it on the roof, I found it frozen together into one solid, frozen, block of wood. There was no practical way to thaw it out. After hammering on the boards trying to break the ice to get them apart I was able to separate them, though the boards were still covered with ice. I began nailing them on the roof, ice and all.

It was a couple of days past Halloween and the first cold spell of the year was just moving in. It had been snowing for several days in a row. Ross and I had made plans to do a major town-run as soon as the river froze up. Otherwise the only way to town was the train, until spring. Katy usually went to Prince George on the train, but it had been a few months since I had taken it. Ross and I arranged our trips to town together regularly: him with no truck, and me with no boat, it worked out really well.

It was a cold morning. There was a ring of ice around the leg of the motor and a layer of ice along the river bank. The boat had about eight inches of snow in it, snow lined the river bank on each side. We pushed out onto the river and Ross opened the throttle. The air was biting. I had to get something in front of my face to block the wind. I crossed my arms across my face. It was always a different season when you traveled the river, but this was the coldest yet. The chill factor must have been minus-thirty. I hunched down in the big open boat and tried to stay out of the wind, which was next to impossible. Ross rode

106

in the stern, sitting on a board that was across the gunwales, up high and right in the wind. His eyes cringed, peering just under the brim of his old, beaten-up cowboy hat. A few tears streamed down his leathery cheeks from the cold wind. The parking lot at the Penney landing was covered with snow. It was nice to get in the truck with a heater, to warm up.

Again the drive to Prince George was uneventful; we just picked up groceries and some hardware items. We stopped at the liquor store and Ross passed on the Berry Cup, settling on a forty-pounder of rum. I took the lead from Ross and bought one, too.

We drove into the Penney landing late that afternoon. It was one of our earliest return trips we had all year. Though it was already getting dark. We could see that there were chunks of ice coming down the river. I walked out to the river bank and had a closer look. It looked like at least half the area of the river was covered with large chunks of ice. Some were as big as a house.

"What are we gonna do, Ross?" I said.

"We're gonna go home," he said. "We better get our asses going though, before this shit jams up and we can't get through."

We quickly loaded the groceries and parked the truck, and pushed out onto the river.

Ross gave the motor a pull, it started, and he put it in gear. As the first piece of ice scraped the side of the boat, I got really concerned. It was really loud. Just then, another piece scraped the boat, as Ross maneuvered through the chunks of ice. This may have been the slowest trip down the river yet. We couldn't go much faster than the ice flowed. As we got closer to the rocks, the ice seemed to move more slowly and get closer together. Up to this point, Ross had been moving between the ice chunks, but there was not enough room for that anymore. It was good that we were in a big boat, because Ross would gun the boat onto a big chunk of ice and break it in half. The ice crashed under the boat, the two halves would part from the weight of the boat and let us through. We pounded our way through the ice chunks until we reached the rocks. The last fifty feet, or so, was thick ice, but after that, it seem to thin out. After that, we made better time and the visibility was good, with the white snow on the shore and riding the tops of the ice chunks.

We made it all the way down that night, but two days later the ice jammed and froze the river solid. It would not thaw out until April, and that was November 5.

"Over here, Larry," I yelled, as I finished chopping the hole in the ice that we were going to use for ice fishing in the river. Larry was up on the bank cutting willows to tie the lines that we put though the ice. Steve was about fifty feet away from me, chopping another hole. Where I chopped the ice, it was about eight inches thick. It was thirty below zero already and was supposed to go down to forty below that night. It was dusk and you could almost feel the temperature falling by the minute.

Larry brought me four, long willows and threw them on the ice by me. I started getting them rigged with line and hook, while Larry went back to the bank to cut more willows for Steve's holes.

I got a couple of hooks rigged and baited two lines and stuck them through the ice. The lines were tied about three feet up off the bottom, not too far from shore. From the length of the poles, we knew it was about ten feet deep there. We were fishing for Dolly Varden, or Ling Cod, that stayed in the river during the winter, under the ice.

I was working on getting the third line together, when Larry walked toward me with four long willows for Steve. He walked the same route that he had walked before when he had brought me the last willows, only this time, the ice broke. Larry broke his fall by holding on to the willows that stuck out across the ice.

"Oh shit!" Larry yelled. I turned and looked in his direction. He was scrambling around, trying to get himself out of the water, but the ice was breaking on the edge of the hole.

"Grab on!" I yelled to Larry, as I pushed one of the willow sticks I had left, towards him. He grabbed hold of it and I pulled him out of the hole and slid him across the ice towards me. In only a few feet, the ice was solid enough to hold him up. He jumped up and started jumping around.

"Man, that's cold!" said Larry. "We are gonna have to hurry up with this."

"What, are you crazy?" I said. "You get the hell out of here and get up to Ross's place right now, before you freeze. It's thirty below! Go on, get going."

Larry took off walking as Steve and I got the rest of the lines set and baited, then headed off walking to Ross's, too. I'd left the Power Wagon at Ross's while we were getting lines together.

"It looks like you made it, all right," I said to Larry as we walked in to Ross's. He was hanging out next to the stove in his long underwear, trying to get some heat in his legs. They were actually Ross's long underwear that he was wearing. His wool pants and long underwear were hanging up next to the stove, drying out.

"I didn't think I was going to make it. My legs were getting real stiff by the time I got halfway here. My pants had froze so solid that they felt like they were made of wood and it was hard to walk. My legs were so stiff by the time I got here that I was only able to take small steps. It seemed like it was miles I had to go, when I finally seen the lights in Ross's place," Larry recounted the experience.

"Yeah, he looked stiff as a board when he came through the door. I told him to git them pants off. I got him some long johns to put on and a good stiff shot of rum," said Ross.

Ross poured a shot for each of us and added some hot water and cinnamon. "Have a hot toddie," he said, as he put the hot drink in front of me.

We hung around, drinking hot toddies and smoking joints for a couple of hours while Larry warmed up and got his clothes dried out. Ross burned the stove really hot, almost unbearably hot. Larry's pants dried remarkably fast.

"Man, that was strange!" said Larry as we talked, "I walked over that spot a few minutes before and the ice held me. Then it broke the next time. I wonder why it broke? What do you think, Ross?"

"I don't know, maybe a space between the ice chunks when it jammed, or turbulence under the water right there. It's a river with a current and even though it all looks the same on the top, it's not.

Good idea to chop holes and check the thickness when

110

you're going on the ice," Ross replied.

"I guess we'll be checking more carefully next time. That could be extremely bedangerous" said Larry, in his own language. We knew what he meant.

There lay a huge, smooth white plain that stretched far upriver and down river, that was lined by trees on the river bank. The river surface was completely flat from the wind-blown snow, which filled all the low spots in the ice jam. It was hard to believe there was a river under that plain of white. Trees lined the river bank on each side of this huge highway. I stood on there with Ross and Bud, looking out on this stretch of river.

"We'll head this way," said Bud and took off with his old one- lunger Ski-doo. I was riding on the back of Bud's Ski-doo and Ross was following behind on his Ski-doo, pulling a home-made toboggan with a load of willows tied on, as we headed across the ice. The sea of white had the appearance of being all-river, but in fact, it was at least half river-bar and half river-ice. We went what seemed like about halfway across before we got onto the ice. The snow was blown flat and about a foot deep on the ice. The snow everywhere else was a good three feet or more, but between the winds blowing the snow off and snow settling on the ice and soaking up with water from the bottom, it was much shallower there.

"We'll put one here," said Ross, as he started to untie the toboggan load of willows. Bud grabbed the axe, and started to chop a hole in the ice after kicking away the snow. There was a layer of slush under the top layer of snow and on top of the ice, which made it kinda messy to chop, with water splashing up with each chop of the axe. Bud swung the axe and it went through to the river.

"Looks like about six inches thick," Bud reported to us. He stuck a willow stick in the hole and packed a bunch of slush around it to hold it in place. We repeated this process about twenty times or more, until there was willows sticking up out of the ice in a line across the river.

"How come you mark it like this?" I asked Ross.

"That's so you can see the crossing in a snow storm or at night. You'd be surprised how hard it is to find this spot without these willows to mark it," Ross replied.

I looked back across from the South side at the crooked line of willows and the lone Ski-doo tracks marking the otherwise undisturbed whiteness of the snow.

Ross and Bud were going to check out a logging job that was across the river. Both had worked for years logging. Bud's Dad owned the last sawmill to operate in Longstock prior to the mid- sixties, when the last one closed down. He had been a faller for years, starting when he was fifteen and power saws were really heavy. These days, power saws were a lot lighter, but over the years, Bud developed really big arm muscles. He had a reputation for being a real tough, hard-drinking guy, that liked to fight, especially when he was drinking.

I was just along for the ride and thought I'd check the situation out, in case there was a possibility of a job for me.

After crossing the river, we unhooked the toboggan and ski-dooed along the river bank on the South side for about a mile and then drove the machines right though Hungary Creek, turning up the bank into a bush trail. The snow became much deeper when we got into the bush, sometimes bogging the ski-doo down. Whenever that happened, the trailing ski-doo would tear around the front of the other and break trail. Whoever was in front would go as far as possible, breaking trail until they bogged down and the trailing machine would take the lead for a while, until it bogged down. We came to a big hill on the trail and when we started going up, the leap-frogging of the ski-doos became more frequent, with the front machine only able to go ten or twenty feet ahead of the other, before bogging down. It was hard to get going on the hill, so we had to muscle the machines around so they could go downhill and get a run at the hill each time, getting a little further.

I got off and helped each guy get his machine turned around to go downhill. It was a slow process, but eventually we got both machines up the hill. It was not very cold that day and we were all dressed for the wind-chill of riding a machine. I was sweating from all the work of throwing around the machines by the time we got to the top. We stopped at the top and shut off the machines. Bud pulled a couple of beers out of his pack, offering one to me, which I refused, but Ross didn't. I lit up a joint instead.

After our little break, we got going again. The snow seemed to get deeper, the further we went. The powder snow was cascading right over the windshield, impairing our ability to see the trail.

We finally blasted through the snow bank and came out on a plowed road. We could hear the sounds of the cats and skidders working the bush close by, so we knew we were on the right block. We went from landing to landing and finally found the bossman. Bud knew Henry Ron, who was running the logging show.

"I heard you were looking for fallers," Bud asked.

"Yes I am, Bud. Are you looking for work?" he replied. "When do you want to start?"

"Tomorrow!" said Bud.

"Sounds good to me," said Henry Ron. "What about you?" he said, looking at Ross.

"Yeah, I can start tomorrow too," Ross replied. "You a faller, too?" He looked at me.

"Well, not really, but I'd like to learn," I said. "Any experience?"

"No not really, but I learn quickly," I said.

"I'm looking for fallers with experience. Sorry," he said, turning to Ross and Bud. "See you guys tomorrow."

I was a little disappointed about not getting hired as we headed back to the river. We picked up the toboggan and hooked it up and crossed the river on the way back. While we were gone, the ski-doo track that we made on the way over was completely filled up with water.

"Holy shit, there's water in the track," I said.

"So what," said Bud, as he gunned the machine across the ice. The ski-doo was working really hard, trying to beat its way across. I could feel the back end of the machine dropping as we went. It was quite nerve-wracking, but I figured these guys knew what they were doing. I felt relieved when we made it to the other side and hadn't fallen through the ice. When I looked back over the ice that we just crossed, the track was completely filled with water.

I had asked Bud to teach me how to fall trees and he agreed

to take me with him that first day and give me a lesson on falling. The next morning, we crossed the ice again, by morning the ski-doo track was frozen solid. It was my first time on any kind of a logging show and Buds experience as a faller for so many years made him a good person to learn from.

I spent the day cutting trees with Bud's saw. He felled the first two trees that day to show me how he wanted the trees felled and I pretty well felled everything else after that. Bud sat on a stump, drinking beer and snapped instructions to me the entire day, as I felled one tree after another. The job was directional falling to skid trails, tops ahead. The tops of the trees would have to fall on the skid trails for the skidder to grab. After about a dozen or so, trees were felled, I would have to climb over the fallen timber to the skid trail and cut the tops off to make it easier for the skidder to grab. Bud sat on a stump and yelled instructions to me as I climbed over trees to get to the skid trail and back again. He showed me how to aim the trees so they would fall with tops on the trail, as they were supposed to. He showed me how to make the trees swing, so that when they fell, they would swing around trees that were in the way by bypassing the trees and then pulling back around and landing tops in front of the standing tree. I learned to get the heavy, back- leaners to fall against the lean, using wedges to tip them over. I also learned to spot dangerous trees that could cause serious injuries or death.

"Always leave holding wood. Watch out for those loose branches, high up in the tree. Don't try to fall against the wind. Watch out for tops breaking off and coming back at you. Always have an escape route out of there. Don't pound your wedges too hard in frozen wood, because it could cause them to pop out of the cut and pinch the saw, or cause you to lose control of the tree." Bud snapped out instructions throughout the day.

I did lose one tree that fell the wrong way, causing Bud to have to jump off his perch on the stump and high-tail it to get out of the way.

It was like going to school for the day. I didn't get hired as a faller until several years later, but had lots of practice falling building and firewood trees over the next few years. When I finally did get a job as a faller years later, I was complimented by loggers that I worked for as being a good faller, whose trees were felled so that they were easy to skid. I have to give a lot of credit to Bud for teaching me how. He was one of the best fallers in the area, who had the reputation of being able to hit a dime with a hundred twenty-foot tree. No easy feat.

"Paul Miller is skidding the old cookhouse building from Jamison's old logging camp down to the river today," Ross said, as he stood outside the door talking to me. It was the end of January and the snow was pushing near five feet deep by this time. The ice on the river was over three feet thick on most of the ice bridge that was marked off by the willows which Ross, Bud and I had stuck in the ice earlier in the winter.

Ross had come to my place to get me. "I'm going down to see if he needs any help," Ross said. "I thought you'd want to come and check it out."

I gulped down the rest of the coffee and stepped into my boots. I got on the back of the ski-doo with Ross. The deep snow made the ski-dooing difficult. The trails were packed solid, but if one ski got off in the deep snow it would pull you off the trail and suck you into the deep snow. Once sucked in, it was quite a chore to free the ski-doo and get it back on the trail and moving again. Ross liked to drive at full throttle, so when he would get sucked over, he would have momentum and, most of the time, could get the machine back onto the trail without getting stuck. Sometimes the ski-doo would tip ferociously to one side, in which case, Ross, who was riding on his knees, would shift his weight to the high side, hang onto the handle bars and put all his weight on the running board, as if he were pulling the machine over the other way. As the passenger, I had to shift my weight along with Ross to make it work. Most of the time, this would straighten the machine out and get it back on the trail.

Sometimes, when the snow was too deep or powdery, it was a constant battle, with the ski-doo going off one side of the trail and then the other, back and forth, until it got off a little too far and bogged down in the deep snow.

It became a wrestling match, trying to get a heavy machine back on the trail now that it was packed with snow and weighed much more than usual. After wrestling with the machine, with Ross gunning it, the drive belt burning and smoking, and me pushing, we would finally get it back on the trail and going again until the next time we got stuck. The fresh snow on the trail made it hard to see, we were going off quite often. We had to go through this process every few minutes, all the way to the river.

When we got to the river, Ross shut off the ski-doo. I could hear the Cat working across the river.

"Is that Paul's Cat I hear?" I said.

"Should we go over and check it out?" said Ross. "Let's go!" I answered.

Ross pull-started the ski-doo and I jumped back on and away we went.

It was the same ordeal ski-dooing across the ice and up the road that followed the river where Paul was working. Stuck and go, stuck and go, until we finally could see the Cat.

Paul had already freed the building and had it on the move. The Cat was working, billowing a stream of black, diesel smoke out of the exhaust. The building looked huge trailing the D7 Cat, leaving a swath through the snow twenty feet wide behind it.

We pulled over out of the way, as the Cat passed us; giving a wave to Paul, we stopped, and watched. We followed behind the building, stopping every once in a while, to let the Cat and building get ahead of us.

Paul pulled the building right to the top of the river bank, right beside the ice bridge crossing. He unhooked the building and left it there, where it would stay for the rest of the winter. The following spring, using a thousand feet of steel cable, old man Jamison pulled the building across the ice with his TD20 Cat.

The sun shone brightly on a clear warm day in early April. The river was still covered with ice, although there was a channel cut out in the middle where the water slowly ate away the ice, making the channel a little wider each day. It had been raining for a couple of days and the river was beginning to rise. It was typical in the spring for the river to rise and lift the ice, breaking it free from the shore.

"I guessed it would go on the eighth and that's today, so we better go check on it," Ross said, slipping into his boots and grabbing his coat, and motioning for me to come with him.

"She won't last much longer, now," remarked Ross, as we stood on the river bank at his place looking down from the bank at the river. I stopped over at Ross's that morning for a visit and a game of cribbage. It was Ross's idea to go check the river, as it was like a contest, where people guessed when the ice would break loose and go down the river.

The river had risen considerably overnight, and the water was quite visible between the ice and the river bank. We were passing a joint back and forth and talking, when we started to hear a crashing noise that seemed to be coming from up river.

"What's that noise?" I asked Ross.

"It sounds like the ice is breaking up," he answered.

We listened intensely for a couple of minutes as the noise got louder. Just then, the whole river of ice started to move. The ice was breaking up, making loud crashing noises. We could see the wall of ice pushing its way down the river, piling and pushing the ice in front. It was noisy and swift, as the wall of ice swept the river clean of ice in less than an hour, except for a few pieces that spotted the river as they trailed the main body of ice.

We hung out on the river bank for quite some time, watching this yearly phenomenon of break-up on the Fraser River. It was a sure sign that winter had bowed out to make room for spring.

Chapter 6

Party time

It was the day after Halloween and Ross's birthday was a couple of days away. Marge Jamison was throwing a birthday party at her house for Ross and everyone in Longstock was invited. It had been raining for a couple days straight, not just raining, but pouring cats and dogs. Most people waited it out inside their houses, preferring inside work projects to anything outside. I went down to Ross's on Wednesday day and there was a steady stream of crib players dropping by. Everyone was talking about the party on the weekend. Ross started celebrating his birthday on Wednesday of that week. He had a couple bottles of rum, and a gallon of Berry Cup he'd been saving and was quick to offer a hot toddy or glass of wine to anyone who dropped by.

We played a round of crib and had a couple of drinks and a joint while we each won one game and were playing the rubber match, when Alaska Larry showed up with his girlfriend, Norma.

I was getting pretty loaded, and was having a hard time concentrating on the game. I made a couple of bad moves, and lost the rubber match to Ross.

"Your turn," Ross said to Larry, as I traded places with Larry and the game continued. That's the way it was for several days in a row, leading up to Ross's birthday. Someone else would always show up and the game went on.

We were hoping the rain would slow down before the weekend, but no such luck. It poured with no end in sight all day on Saturday and into Saturday night.

Marge Jamison asked me if I would drive up to the pole camp and pick up old Jon Flotten. Jon (pronounced Yon) was well into his eighties, an old family friend of the Jamison's. He got along pretty well for his age, still living in his own house and hauling his own wood and water. Sometimes, one of the neighbors would give him a hand, but it was mostly the Jamisons that looked in on Jon.

I drove the old corduroy road to Jon's in four-wheel drive. It was so rough, I had to go in bull low and it still rattled my teeth in my head. I pulled up to Jon's house and turned the truck around in front of the house. I caught a glimpse of Jon through the window. He was just puttering around the house like he didn't hear me drive up.

I went to the door and knocked. No one came to the door as I waited outside in the rain. I knocked again, still no answer. I knew he was in there, because I had seen him, so I opened the door slowly and started yelling, 'Jon, Jon, are you there? It's Louie!' I could see him in the other room and it looked like he was talking to somebody.

Whatever it was, it was in Swedish and he was pissed off at someone. I couldn't understand what he was saying, except that every once in a while I recognized the word, Jamison (Ya-maa-son). I figured out that he was pissed-off at Bud and didn't see or hear me. I didn't want the old guy to get surprised and have a stroke or something, so I walked in where he could see me.

"Oh Louie, I didn't hear yaa come in. I had my earing aid turned off" he said.

"No problem, Jon," I said. "I'm supposed to give you a ride down to Bud's place. Are you ready?

"Yaah, yaah, I'm ready," said Jon, as he got his rain gear on and grabbed his cane, as we headed out the door.

We bounced over the corduroy road and down the mountain and over the tracks to the Jamison's. It was early in the evening, only about six-thirty, yet people were already showing up at Jamison's for the party. Ross was over for dinner, so he was already there when I got back with Jon.

Marge yelled to us from the porch as we parked the Power Wagon, "Hi, Jon! Hi, Louie!"

I could tell she was feeling pretty good already and the

party was just getting started. "Appy birtday, Ross!" Jon said to Ross as we got in the house. There were a few people sitting around the table, talking and laughing. The table had a half gallon of Berry Cup on it and several bottles of hard liquor, some not opened yet. I brought a bottle of rum with me, which I opened and poured myself a drink, then put the bottle on the table with the rest.

The party was getting started, with people showing up one right after the other. I had a drink of rum, jumping back in the Power Wagon, and I went to pick up Katy and the boys. Katy had them ready to go when I pulled up to the house. We drove back to the Jamisons'. The crowd of people had increased in the short time I was gone. All the Alaskans had arrived, the Hooty's were there, Skid was sitting at the table with a glass of wine and his box of milk-bone dog biscuits. Toad was sitting at the table with Skid, firing sarcastic remarks that seem to go right over Skid's head. Bob and Wayne McCoby were sitting around the table next to Pierre.

The music was playing from an old eight-track stereo in the living room. Katy and the boys were hanging out in there with Betty and her two girls. The boys were close to the same age as Betty's girls.Katy and Betty traded the two babies back and forth, admiring and goo-gooing over them.

"Margie, where is Bud tonight?" Jon asked. You could tell he was already getting pretty tired and was not going to last much longer before it was time to go home.

"He'll be in on the train tonight, Jon," Marge answered. The passenger train was due in at 11 o'clock. "You're looking pretty tired, Jon. Are you ready to go home yet?"

"Yaah, I'm ready to go home," he said.

"Can you give Jon a ride back home?" Marge asked me. "No problem. Does he want to go right now?" I asked. "I think so," answered Marge.

Jon got himself ready, we walked to the Power Wagon, got in and headed to his place. We were bouncing over the corduroy road slowly, as not to shake Jon up too much. After dropping Jon off, I started back down the corduroy road, only this time, I was in more of a hurry.

I was feeling pretty good, which was probably the reason that I drove faster on the corduroy. The bouncing was pretty intense. It shook me up so badly that, I swear I could feel my organs jiggling inside of me. The Power Wagon felt like it was handling kind of funny when I got to the end of the corduroy, but it was still going all right, so I didn't think too much of it. When I got to the railroad tracks and started to cross, my forward movement stopped. The engine was running, but I didn't seem to be moving. I got out of the truck looking with a flashlight, trying to figure out what was the matter. After careful inspection, I noticed that the rear end was crooked. I looked closer and discovered that the rear end had slid backwards on the spring on one side. It had probably snapped the center bolt, causing the drive shaft to pull apart. It was still pouring rain, so I didn't feel like working on it right then, though I had to crawl under the truck and tie up the drive shaft, which was dragging on the ground. I figured out that if I put the Power Wagon in four- wheel drive, that the front wheels would pull me along and I could get back to the party and home afterwards. I could deal with fixing it the next day.

I threw it in four wheel drive...the front wheels dug a little hole in the gravel beside the tracks and the truck moved forward over the tracks. The back wheels were crooked over to one side. I had to compensate steering, as the truck was going forward down the road a bit crooked. I made it back to the party all right, parked the truck and went in and forgot about it for the time being.

Things were getting pretty wild by the time I got back. There were some psychedelic mushrooms going around and pot being smoked pretty well constantly. The music was blasting in the living room, and some people were dancing. In the other room, Faddus had broken out his old Harmony guitar and had started in on 'What'd I say?' There were a few people gathered around Faddus, and the bottle of tequila.

The kitchen table was full of glasses of various drinks and partially filled bottles of booze. The kitchen counter had an assortment of chips and snacks on it and a few people were hanging around the food.

Marge was getting pretty loaded by this time and seemed to be taking a shine to Larry, even though Norma was there. She seemed to be following him around and would laugh at everything he said, hanging onto and pawing at him. Norma could see what was going on and didn't seem to care. Bud would be showing up on the train in an hour, or so and Marge would probably turn her attention to him as soon as he got there.

The train was coming in soon, and a few of us walked to the station to meet it. The party was getting really wild by this time. The train came in and Bud got off with a pack sack full of beer, wine and rum. He was already half cut. As we walked back to the house, we could hear the power generator start to sputter.

"Sounds like it's out of gas," Bud remarked, as we detoured to the power shack. Some of the party went back to the house, except for Bud, Ross, myself, and Larry, who came with us just to get away from Marge chasing him around. We got to the power shack just as the generator was sputtering and died. Several of us were carrying flashlights, turning them on when the lights went out.

We stood around holding flashlights as Bud poured gas from a can that was in the shack.

Back in the house Marge was all distressed because the power went out, as well as because of her being extremely drunk by this time. She was also pissed-off because Larry had taken off to go meet the train. She noticed the lights out at the power shack and I don't know what she thought was going on out there. She came out and looked from the porch, went back inside, appearing a few minutes later with a twenty-two rifle.

"Hey, get the hell out of there," she yelled. Her voice sounded squeaky and strained. "What the hell are you doing?"

We were talking and laughing and didn't really hear her until she started shooting!

I heard a bang, as a twenty- two shell whistled by me, and went right through the plywood wall. That's when we realized what was going on. Bang! went the gun again, as another shell whistled passed.

"The crazy bitch is shooting at us," Bud yelled out. A couple more shots rang out as we all hit the ground. Bud scrambled back to the generator and hit the kill switch.

"Turn those flashlights off," he said as he hit the ground again.

We stayed on the ground for a minute or so, as Marge squeezed off a few more rounds into the darkness. She was not able to see us and started back into the house, yelling at us to 'get the hell away from the power plant.'

"What the hell are you doing, you crazy bitch?" Bud yelled back at her, as he walked towards the house in the darkness. She heard Buds voice as she was going through the door and turned and came back out onto the porch.

"Oh Bud, is that you?" she said. She had no idea that she had been shooting at him.

"Who the hell are you shooting at?" he said, as he approached her on the porch.

"Who? The guys thats screwing with the generator! They shut it down!" she said.

"You silly bitch! It ran out of gas," he said, "I was gassing it up."

"That was you? Oh, I didn't mean to shoot at you! Did I hit anybody?" she said.

"You might have, if you could shoot worth a damn, you crazy bitch!" he replied. "I'm going out to start it up again and you better not start shooting again or I'll break your damn fingers so you can't shoot! Crazy bitch!"

Bud went out and started the generator again and this time he got it going, without getting shot at.

The lights went back on and the party continued. Marge had turned her attention to Bud, now that he was home. Both Larry and Norma made comments about Marge finally leaving Larry alone.

The party was starting to wind down about three in the

morning, with a few people passing out on various pieces of furniture or floor. We gathered the kids up and limped the Power Wagon home. The rain was still coming down and continued to fall for several days afterwards, before turning to snow. The snow just kept coming down in the weeks that followed, as winter dug in. I think it snowed every day of November that fall and would prove to be the most snow that fell in Longstock for many, many years.

Old Jon Flotten swept off his porch every morning and recorded the snowfall in a journal. He would measure two hundred thirty-eight inches of snowfall that winter, setting records for snowfall in every month.

I could hear a ski-doo coming near. It had to be pretty close because, with it snowing like it was, sound did not travel very far. Katy and I and the boys, had just moved into the house a few weeks ago. There was three feet of snow on the ground the day we moved in and it snowed just about everyday since building up to five feet deep by that time. We were just finishing supper when we heard the ski-doo coming. Pretty soon, there was a knock on the door.

I opened the door to find Larry, and Bob McCoby standing there covered with snow from head to foot. Their faces were covered with beads of water from the melting snow on their faces. Larry had a jug of Berry Cup in his hands and a big grin on his face.

"How come you didn't knock the snow off the willows on your road before we came down?" Bob said. "They were all bent over from the weight of the snow and we're wearing most of it now."

He was right. The snow was stuck to both of them about three inches thick. They looked like Frosty the snowman and his trusty sidekick. They peeled off their outer layers, shook them off on the porch and hung them by the stove.

"We came to get you guys. There's a party at the Hooty's tonight.

It's Bob's birthday," said Larry.

"I think we're going to stay home tonight." Katy told them, looking over at me.

"We better have a drink and talk about it surspiciously," Larry said, in his own language. We knew what Larry was talking about, having gotten used to his original words, long ones at that, that he'd use quite often.

The boys had already gone to sleep, as we sat around the kitchen table, drinking wine and smoking a joint. Within a half-hour, or so, Katy and I were getting a pretty good buzz on and Bob and Larry had been well on the way to being loaded when they arrived.

"Aw, come on, you guys, let's go to the party," said Larry. Both he and Bob wouldn't let up on us and kept up the pressure to get us to go with them.

"Is there room on your ski-doo?" Katy asked Bob.

"We might have to tie a toboggan on behind," answered Bob.

We talked it over while we had another drink. Katy asked me if I wanted to go, I said, 'Sure, why not?' She got the kids up and started getting snowsuits on the boys. I went out with Bob and Larry and got the toboggan pulled up to the ski-doo, tying it on behind. We tied it on with a rope about twenty feet long, so we would ride far enough back to avoid the exhaust and the spray that the track threw off.

Katy yelled from the door that she had the boys ready to go and I went to help Chico make his way to the ski-doo. Katy got on the ski-doo behind Bob, holding Zac in front of her with Chico riding between her and Bob. Larry and I rode the toboggan, trailing twenty feet or so, behind.

It was still snowing pretty heavy. The trees and willows near the trail were weighed down and bent over from the weight of the snow. Some were still high enough to drive the ski-doo under and some were so weighted down that when the ski-doo went under, and it touched a branch, it would drop the snow, not on Katy, Bob and the boys, but on Larry and me, following behind on the toboggan. We hadn't gone very far, making it to the end of the driveway and out to the road, before we were covered with snow. I was feeling pretty good and a bit playful, as Bob got out on the road and opened up the ski-doo.

Larry was in front of me on the toboggan as we sailed down the road, snow flying in a whirlwind around us. As we got up to speed, I wrapped my arms around Larry's head and rolled both of us off the toboggan. We rolled off into the deep snow beside the ski-doo trail, crashing into the loose snow in a big spray of powder. Bob didn't notice that he had lost us right away and went up the road a ways before looking back seeing that we were not on the toboggan.

Larry and I picked ourselves out of the crotch-deep snow, scrambling up on the packed trail and ran to catch up. We reloaded ourselves back on the toboggan and off we went again. As soon as Bob got the ski-doo back up to speed, I grabbed Larry around the head again and rolled off the toboggan again, burying us in the deep snow again.

"What the hell are you doing to me?" Larry said, spitting snow out of his mouth and scraping the snow off his face. I could only laugh.

"What the hell's are you guys doing?" yelled Bob as we reloaded on the toboggan.

"Let's go!" I yelled to Bob, waving my arms back and forth.

Away he went. Within a minute or so, as we hit top speed, I had Larry by the head again and rolled off again, burying his head in the powder. It was definitely taking longer to get anywhere, but I was having fun dumping us in the snow. We finally made it to the Hootys party after many crashes in the snow. We were absolutely covered with snow. It was down our necks, front and back and stuck to our coats and touques in great big frozen balls.

We pulled up in front of Hooty's and could hear the party going on inside. Faddus had his guitar going and his singing and playing could be heard out in the yard. Larry and I peeled off our coats out on the porch and shook them off. Some people got a good laugh out of us, covered with frozen balls of snow.

We all went inside and the party was going full swing. The house was full of people, and there was a bag of psychedelic mushrooms and a tray full of joints on the kitchen table for anyone who wanted them.

There was one party going on in the living room, another in the kitchen, and another upstairs, where all the kids and mothers were. It's a good thing that we had been drinking before we came, or we would have been way behind everyone there.

I grabbed some mushrooms and started chewing on them,

as I migrated to the living room where Faddus was playing his guitar. It was obvious he was really high by the time we got there, the way he was playing and singing. He had a hard time remembering the words to 'What I say,' as he hammered out the chords, sometimes right and sometimes not.

Bob McCoby was sucking on a bottle of tequila and proceeded to get really drunk in a hurry. He was already blasted from the wine and joints we had had at my place before we got there, the tequila just finished him off. I think he thought that he was at a party of rednecks, instead of a party of hippies. He started picking on people, trying to pick a fight. It had been a tradition in Longstock to go to a party and pick a fight. A party wasn't really a party if there wasn't a fight. Unfortunately for Bob, he wasn't very tough, although you would think he was by the way he talked.

"When I see you on the road tomorrow, I'm gonna kick your ass!" he repeated first to one person and then another. Nobody paid any attention to him, which seemed to make him madder. His threats got louder and louder as the party wore on.

"What the fuck is his problem?" I heard someone say.

"Shut your mouth, asshole!" someone else yelled at him, but nothing seemed to get him to stop shooting off his mouth. I was reluctant to say too much to him, seeing as he had come and got us and given us a ride there. I tried to ignore him, but he made it impossible.

Faddus started singing, 'Stuff a sock in his mouth' as he played guitar. It finally affected the whole party, as he got louder and more belligerent.

"Mellow out or fuck off!" Harry Halfdollar said to Bob,

as he grabbed him and pulled him down and set him on his knee and administered a headlock and chokehold on him. Bob tried to get loose, but Harry was a big guy and held him tightly around the neck and head, making it impossible for Bob to escape. Bob started to gag and started to try and fight his way out of Harry's grasp, to no avail. Harry applied more pressure on him, looking him right in the eyes and said, "I'm going to let you go now, and if you start that shit again, I'm going to drag your sorry ass outside and and kick it. I can guarantee you that your night will be over." He then put one hand across Bob's face and grabbed onto it and pushed him away and onto the floor. Bob lay there for a minute, trying to get it together. He got up a bit wobbly, behaving himself for the rest of the party.

Meanwhile, in the living room, Faddus continued to beat on his guitar, bellowing out words to 'What I say.' It was a real mish-mash of lyrics, being unduly influenced by the mushrooms, tequila, pot, hash and whatever else was going around.

Bob Hooty had a second guitar that was leaning in the corner in the living room. I spotted the guitar and picked it up, joining Faddus in the never-ending 'What I say'.

Meanwhile Ross was sitting around the kitchen table with Bob and Paula Hooty, smoking a joint and drinking a glass of wine.

"What's this?" Ross said, picking up a large chunk of hash that was in a little bowl on the table.

"That's a chunk of hash," Paula responded, picking it up and breaking off a piece and loading a pipe with it. She sparked up a match and put it to the pipe, taking a long slow pull on the pipe. "Here, Ross, try some," she said as she passed the pipe over to him.

Ross puffed several times on the pipe, blowing the smoke out each time the smoke would surround his head in a cloud. Ross passed the pipe back to Paula and grabbed the chunk of hash, picked it up and was looking at it really closely. He had taken mushrooms a few hours earlier and seemed to be transfixed on the hash chunk, when, in a flash, he opened his mouth and popped the whole chunk in, and swallowed.

Neither Bob nor Paula actually saw him swallow it and continued to pass the pipe around. At one point, Paula turned to Bob and asked, what happened to the chunk of hash?'

"It was right there in the bowl," Bob answered. "Did you see it, Ross?" Paula asked.

"Yeah! I ate it," said Ross. "You what?"

"I ate it!"

"You ate it! Oh! Are you in trouble. Your going to get so stoned." Both Bob and Paula broke out into hysterical laughter.

Bob grabbed one of the joints out of the bowl and lit it. "Better smoke one of these, seeing as how the hash is gone."

Within about twenty minutes, Ross started to get this really spacey look in his eyes. His arms and legs seemed to be getting really heavy and he was finding it hard to move. That's the feeling he had just before his eyes rolled up in his head and he started to pass out. He had an uncontrollable urge to lie down and slid off the chair and onto the floor and passed out...and that's where he stayed for the next day and a half.

The kids were sleeping upstairs and sometime in the wee hours, Katy crawled in with them and crashed out. People were crashed out everywhere, except in one corner of the living room, where the party was still alive and well. I stayed with the party all night and saw the sun rise the next morning.

Paula was up and around early, making coffee and a batch of pancakes for anyone who wanted them. Skid showed up about nine that morning, ready to party and was quite disappointed that he'd missed the party. The hard-core Alaskans were still going strong in the living room. The last of the tequila was still going around. Skid passed on the pancakes as he joined the Alaskans in the living room, cracking open a new box of milk bones, slugging a shot of tequila to wash them down with.

Bob McCoby, who passed out shortly after his bout with Harry, dragged himself up and into the kitchen for coffee and a handful of aspirin. He looked like he had just returned from the grave.

We got the boys ready to go. Bob gave Katy and the kids a ride home on the ski-doo. I walked home later that morning, pulling the toboggan. Everyone was asleep when I got home. I crawled into bed too.

We had been living in our new house for over a month, and hadn't had a house-warming party, as yet. With New Year's Eve coming up in a few days, this seemed like a good time to celebrate both. We spread the word around Longstock that we would host the New Year's Eve party this year.

I took the train to Mcbride a couple of days before, to pick up booze and snacks for the party. When I got off the train in Longstock, the air felt especially cold. The Power Wagon was snowed in at home, so I was on foot from the train station to the house. I had all the party supplies packed into my Trapper Nelson backpack and I trudged down the road to the house.

It had been snowing for just about two months straight, but tonight was a crystal-clear sky. The air was crisp and clear and the Northern Lights streaked the Northern sky. The snow sparkled from the reflection of the sky, making it light enough to see the trail as I walked home.

When I got to the house, Katy and the kids were asleep and the wood heater had the place nice and toasty. I checked the outside thermometer, which read fifty below zero. That was the coldest temperature I'd ever seen, even colder than the thirty-six below zero that I'd experienced in New Mexico back in 1970.

The days were very short this time of the year, with the sun sinking behind the mountain at about 3:15 pm and total darkness by four o'clock. The nights were unusually bright if there was any light in the sky, because of the blanket of snow covering everything.

Larry and Norma showed up first, with Skid not far behind. We sat around the table and had a few drinks while Katy was getting the boys settled in bed.

We'd been sitting around for an hour or more when we heard the sound of ski-doos coming up the drive. Within a few minutes, there was a crowd of people at the door.

People piled into our warm house in a hurry. We had little furniture, but had brought in a dozen blocks of wood for people to sit on. The living room, empty of furniture except for the blocks of wood and the Ashley wood heater, was soon alive with people talking, laughing, drinking and smoking. The kitchen table was filled with bottles of rum, tequila, rye, wine and beer.

I had a tape deck rigged up to a twelve-volt battery. The

tunes were playing and people mingled. For most of the people, it was their first New Years in Longstock. There was a real festive feeling among everyone that night. The biting cold outside made the warm house even more inviting.

"What'd I say!" said Faddus, opening the door and holding up a bottle of tequila in each hand, with the old Harmony guitar strapped to his back. Kathy and Colleen came in right behind. The rest of the Alaskans showed up at the door a minute behind. They had walked the road in the cold night, passing a bottle of tequila around as they went. Freddy walked in, with Harry right behind, handing me a plastic lunch box that was full of cassette tapes.

"You can play some of these tonight so we won't have to listen to Faddus all night," Harry said, as he handed me the lunch box full of tapes. I opened it and checked out some of the tapes. The first one I looked at was 'The Cream.' Sounded good to me, so I stuck it in the tape machine and turned it up.

The party mood changed when the music got turned up. People started to dance on the spot and it wasn't very long before the rounds of wood were moved to create a dance floor out of the mostly empty living room floor. Bob and Paula started things off and were quickly joined by Larry and Norma. Katy grabbed Ross and dragged him to the dance floor, soon everyone in the house was dancing, all except for Skid, who was camping out at the kitchen table with a drink and his box of milk bone munchies.

The dancing went on for quite some time, everyone was having a ton of fun. This was the most lively of all the parties that year. The dancing making all the difference.

As people were dancing, Skid was getting pretty loaded, sitting there at the table. He had gotten up and gone outside without anyone noticing. I don't know how much time went by before Faddus went outside to take a leak and came back in saying that Skid was out there passed out in the snow.

"We better get him inside before he gets frostbite," Faddus said. A few of us went outside and found Skid curled up in the fetal position in the snow. The temperature had dropped down to forty-five below by this time. We had to get him in the house before he froze. We tried to wake him up and get him to come inside, but he was out and was not going to come around easily.

"Looks like we're going to have to carry him in," Toad popped up. Toad, Faddus, Harry, and I each grabbed an arm or a leg and carried him inside. He didn't come to, at all. It was like packing a dead guy. We laid him down in the living room corner and threw a blanket over him.

The tapes were still playing and people still dancing, a while later, when Skid started to come around.

"Ooooh! I'm cold," Skid moaned, as he started to wake up. I didn't know how long he had been lying outside, but it was long enough to get chilled to the bone. He staggered to his feet and headed right for the wood stove. He climbed on the stove and sat right on top of it. The stove was cast-iron, with a light, sheet metal cabinet around it. It was not really designed for people to sit on. I tried to get Skid to get off of the stove because he was bending the metal on top, but he would not move. I had the stove turned down low. With all the people in the house, it was quite warm anyway. I wasn't comfortable with Skid sitting on the stove and I felt like I had to get him off, somehow. I shoved a couple of big pieces of wood in the stove and turned it up. It took a few minutes to start getting hotter, but Skid managed to hang on for quite a while before it got hot enough to get him to get off. I guess he was pretty hot by that time. You could smell something smoking. I think it was the wool pants that he was wearing that were just about ready to catch fire. They were too hot to handle and the heat was getting through and burning his legs and his butt. Skid ran back outside and rolled in the snow to cool his pants off, rubbing his ass in the snow.

The party was really hopping, people dancing to the taped music filled the living room. The kitchen table was crowded with people and bottles of booze. Most of the old timers didn't show up to this party. With the exception of Ross and Wayne McCoby, it was all the hippies that had moved to Longstock in the last several years that came.

Just before the clock struck twelve, Toad came in from outside, saying that the Northern Lights were really happening. Everyone piled outside to check it out for a few minutes. They didn't stay outside very long, as the bitter cold chased people back inside.

"Ten, nine, eight, seven, six," Faddus started the countdown to the new year.

"Five, four, three, two, one, Happy New Year," everyone joined in, punctuating the ringing in of the new year with hoops and hollers and whistles. Everyone went to shaking hands and hugging each other, in a kind of frenzy.

Bob Hooty had a monstrous joint about two inches around and eight inches long, he was puffing on, trying to get lit. The smoke from the joint made a big cloud around his head as he puffed and then passed it around the room. We had shut the tape deck down during the countdown. I pushed play and turned it up again. The music permeated the house and the dancing started again. The house was rockin', and the party took on a new energy. It was now 1974.

The dawn was breaking on New Years Day and the party was still going on, although not everyone was still awake. There were several bodies scattered about the house, sleeping on the floor. On the kitchen floor, Pierre, Ross, and Skid were lined up, with Ross in the middle, using Pierre's butt for a pillow and Skid with his head on Ross's butt. They looked like three elephants hanging on to each others tails. By the time I noticed them stretched out across the kitchen floor, it was four or five in the morning. I threw a blanket over Ross, which completely covered him up. Pierre was partly covered, to the waist, at least, and Skid had his head covered up by the blanket. All three snored peacefully. We could hear the snoring going up and down, almost musically, as the trio snored an original composition.

Larry, Norma, Faddus, Toad and I were the only ones still awake. We watched the sun come up, though it was after nine in the morning before it got up high enough to clear the mountains and shine on the house. I made a strong pot of coffee and the smell permeated the house. The three guys in the kitchen started to stir and one by one, they got up.

The house was starting to liven up, as more bodies woke up and congregated around the kitchen table. I brewed up another pot of coffee and mixed up a batch of pancake batter. People were going to wake up hungry, so I started cooking a batch of pancakes. Once everyone got up there was quite a crowd of people. I fed them in shifts.

It was just another day, but somehow felt different. After all, it was a new year, a new day, in a new place. At first, it was just a few snowflakes in the air that morning. It gradually increased, and by noon was getting heavy about the time people started to head home.

The snow never let up for the next two months, reaching depths of up to seven feet deep by the end of February.

The ground finally started to show through the melting snow a few days before Mothers' Day. It had been an extremely long first winter in Longstock. Six solid months with snow on the ground and here we were in the second week of May and the ground was just showing out in the open. Snow lined the areas all around the edges of the open fields that were shaded from the direct sun. Even where the snow was melted, the grass underneath was quite brown, with not so much as a trace of any new green growth.

The baseball field at the crossroads was showing signs of the same brown grass poking up through the patches of snow. The word spread around that a Mothers Day picnic was being planned to greet the new spring that had been so long in coming. There was a buzz around Longstock for several days prior to Mothers Day. It had been quite a while since the last party and most people were quite ready for another.

The baseball field was the only real outside party place available to us, though it wasn't really very level. There were dips and doodles all over the place. A person could break a leg, running after a ball. It had a steady slant downhill to the trees, which made it one of the worst baseball fields I'd ever seen. The backstop behind the plate was in serious disrepair. But it was all we had, so the Mothers Day picnic was planned there.

Again, the old-timers around Longstock didn't come out for the picnic. Old Ross Turner was the only one that showed up. It was a warm, sunny morning, without a cloud in the sky. The temperature reached the low fifties early that afternoon and the snow was melting like crazy. Most people showed up with blankets and tarps, as the ground was still pretty damp. Faddus brought his guitar, as usual and I brought mine, too. The winter stash of pot was getting kind of low, but everyone brought some, as well as a bunch of really potent pot cookies that Larry and Norma had cooked up.

Blankets were spread out beside the diamond, as we chose up sides for the game. Larry was captain of one side, and Faddus the other. Most people ate a pot cookie, or in some cases two, before we got the game under way. By the time we had been playing for an hour or so, the game seemed to slow right down. Most people were heavily affected by the body stone that the pot cookies give you and there was lots of trouble negotiating the lumpy field. It got harder and harder as the game went on. There was increasingly more time between pitches and batters, with longer and longer delays between innings, as smoking joints seemed like a necessary thing to do before taking the field, or a turn at bat.

Everyone agreed that after so long a winter, it was a welcome event out in the sun.

The gardening season was coming on and there was

much talk about it. Larry had plants started at home and just couldn't wait to get them planted. He was an avid gardener in California and in Alaska, where he lived before coming to Longstock. Within a week or two, the snow was gone and the ground was warm enough to plant. In June had have spent an entire year in Longstock. It was a milestone, as we saw it. We had survived the first winter and the first year.

Chapter 7

The Inexperienced Hippie Moose Hunt Fiasco

The moose has got to be one of the ugliest animals known to man. Commonly referred to as 'Swamp Donkeys,' by many Northerners, these big-eared, big-lipped animals populate the North quite extensively. They are very large, sometimes getting as big as fifteen hundred pounds. They are really well-adapted to the deep snow, which made Longstock a perfect place for moose to hang out.

I'd seen several moose during the summer, but once winter hit, they seemed to be everywhere. It was nothing to see five or six moose, on the way to the mail. They blended right into the bush, especially when it was snowing. People survived in this area for long periods of time on not much more than moose meat and potatoes. That's what the Hooty's fed us that summer when we first came to Longstock.

Most people had a hunting license and hunted moose in the fall, when hunting season was on. The McCoby's would buy a license for every member of their family, even old lady McCoby and shoot a moose for each license, sometimes putting five moose in their freezer each year.

"If we got low, I'd just go bag another one or two," Bob McCoby told me one day. "Hell, there ain't no cops or game wardens here. Just be sure you shoot it while it's snowing, so it snows over all the blood and guts."

Bud Jamison was a really lazy hunter. He shot a moose by the train tracks one day. After going in, gutting and bleeding it, he cut off a hind quarter and the tenderloin strips and left the rest of the moose for the crows.

It so happens that Skid was down there the next day and saw the moose lying there with a hind-quarter cut off and wondered if someone was coming back for the rest. He finally decided that it was abandoned as the tracks had quite a bit of snow on them. He then hacked off the other hind-quarter and packed it out to the tracks, to a toboggan. As he was tobogganing it home down the tracks, the Weight Freight came by and he had to stand off the tracks a bit with his toboggan full of moose. The train crew could see the moose on the toboggan. They must have phoned the fish and wildlife branch, because Skid had the wildlife guys at his door the next day. He couldn't deny getting the moose, because when they walked up to his house, he was cutting the meat up and had pieces laying about.

"It got hit by the train," he told the wildlife officers. "It was lying off the tracks, in the bush, when I found it."

It was lucky for Skid they believed him, as there were many moose carcasses that had been hit by the train, littering the tracks between Prince George and McBride that winter. The deep snow forced many onto the tracks and roads that were plowed. Many were killed by trains and motor vehicles. It was especially bad on logging roads in the bush, where the moose would refuse to get off the road and sometimes even turn and charge the trucks, when they were too tired of running.

The train had taken over a hundred moose in the one hundred forty-mile stretch of track between Prince George and McBride up to that point in the winter.

'You have to get permission to take moose, even if the train kills it,' they told him but let him keep the moose.

They showed up at my place, wanting to look through my buildings, to see if I had any moose.

"Go right ahead," I said, knowing I had nothing...yet!

The fish and wildlife guys satisfied themselves that we were not hunting moose illegally and left.

Faddus, Skid, and I had been talking about getting a moose prior to the visit from the fish and wildlife people. They had come and gone and were not likely to come again this winter.

The three of us had agreed that we would all look for a moose and whoever got one would share it with the others.

It was early January and hunting season had been over for quite some time, when we decided that it was a good time to look for a moose. I loaded my old British 303 rifle and headed out into the bush alone one snowy day. I bought a pair of used snowshoes at a second-hand store, that were about six feet long. They were wood frame, with rawhide lacing. It took me a few minutes of walking on them to get the hang of them. I wasn't picking up my feet high enough at first and found myself stumbling along, barely able to stay upright. On several occasions, I stepped on a stick, or branch that stuck through the webbing and tripped me up. I was careful to keep the gun out of the snow when I fell over, holding it up over my head.

I had been seeing moose quite often just about everywhere I went in Longstock for several months and today was no different. There were tracks everywhere as I walked through an area that was thick with young spruce trees, anywhere from five, to about twenty, feet high.

There were fresh moose droppings and packed spots where the moose had bedded down for the night all over the place. With all the signs around, I was sure I would find a moose in this area. It was snowing lightly, which made the fresh tracks stand out from the older ones.

Sure enough, after a half an hour or so, I saw a moose through the trees. I lined up the moose in the sights of my rifle, trying to pick out the best spot to shoot at. I couldn't see the whole animal because of the trees blocking out part of it. I was contemplating where and when to shoot, when the moose moved out of sight. I followed it, trying to get another shot, but the moose kept moving around and I couldn't seem to get a clear shot. As I pursued the moose, I was making noise, scrambling through the bush, trying to catch up with it. Even though the noise wasn't very loud, being mostly snow falling off of branches that I brushed against, it was enough for the moose to hear and keep it moving away from me. I just couldn't seem to get close enough again to squeeze off a shot. I stalked the moose for a good hour or more, as he led me on a wild moose chase around and around through the trees. It was really tiring, walking on these long snowshoes, following the moose around. I crossed over my own snowshoe tracks several times as it led me around in circles. Once in a while, I got a glimpse of it, but never good enough to get a shot off.

Suddenly, there he was, standing in full view, between the trees. I brought my rifle up and had him in the sights for a split second. I clicked the safety off, but before I could squeeze off a shot, it took off again into the trees. I trailed that moose for a couple more hours and finally was so played out that I decided to give up for the day. I dragged myself through the deep snow back home probably walking way more distance than I had to. I got turned around in the bush several times before I finally found my way. I was totally exhausted when I finally arrived home.

I tried again every day for the next four of five days, to no avail. It was the same thing every day. I could get close, but not enough to get a shot off. Both Faddus and Skid were not having much luck either. There were lots of moose around, but getting a clear shot at one was another matter. A week had gone by since we had started hunting and not one of us had fired a shot, as yet.

It was another snowy day. I had been out in the bush, looking for a moose, since early in the morning. Again I saw moose, but they moved around between the trees, staying out of my sights, as if they had radar to avoid me.

I was getting pretty tired and was just about ready to pack it in and go home. Suddenly, I heard shots to the East. I heard quite a few shots, maybe nine or ten. They weren't very loud, as it was hard to tell how far away it was, because the snow seemed to muffle the sound. I had a feeling that it was either Faddus or Skid that had fired the shots.

I was tired and hungry as I headed for home. I went in the house and collapsed in the hammock, while Katy fixed some lunch.

"I heard a shot not long ago. Wonder if it was Faddus or Skid shooting at a moose?" I said.

"That would be nice," Katy replied, as we sat down to lunch.

I was relaxing after lunch, trying to revive my aching legs, when I heard footsteps on the porch. There was a knock on the door, Faddus walked right in. "Skid got a moose," he said, as he came in. "We gotta go help him deal with it."

I put my coat and boots on and took off walking with Faddus. "Where did he shoot it?" I asked.

"Over on the hill by Chad's place," Faddus answered." Right beside the road, on the hill."

We walked hurriedly down the skidoo trail on the road. The snow was a good four feet deep beside the trail. It was about a two-mile walk to where Skid shot the moose. When we got there, we found Skid talking to Chad, who had come down from his house after hearing the barrage of shots being fired.

"You know I had a pet moose around here," Chad is telling Skid. "I hope you haven't shot my pet moose. My old lady is

149

going to be real pissed off, if you did."

I guess the moose had been hanging around Chad's place for a few months and had gotten quite used to people. That's the reason Skid was able to get close enough to it to shoot it.

It was plain that Chad was really upset and had been ragging on Skid for quite a while about killing his pet moose, despite Skid's protests that 'it was a wild moose, he was quite sure.'

The whole situation was looking pretty tense and it was starting to look like Skid was going to find himself in a fight over it. Can't really blame Chad much, I suppose. Skid did shoot the moose on his land and pretty close to his house. I don't think I'd appreciate someone hunting that close to my home. Faddus and I tried talk to Chad, and tried to settle things down as things heated up.

Chad was pretty pissed off, but seemed to calm down right after he popped Skid with couple of punches, knocking him down and humiliating him. Hilarious! Skid just stayed there on the ground, not even making an effort to get up. I think he knew he would probably get hit again if he got up. Being somewhat the cowardly type of man, he stayed down.

"You funking idiot," Chad snarled at Skid, as he stood over him. "Get your funking moose off my property today, asshole, before I call the cops."

He turned and left at that point, with Skid still lying on the ground, he walked up the road back to his house.

"Man, that guy was sure pissed off," Faddus said to me as I offered Skid a hand to help him out of the snow.

"You okay, man?" I said to Skid, as I pulled him up.

"Yaa, I'm okay," he said, brushing himself off.

"Where's the moose? We better get it taken care of right away!

Chad's pretty pissed off, as you can tell," I said.

"It's on the hill," said Skid, pointing to a spot on the hill just off the road.

"Looks like your going to have a shiner," I said. Skid's eye was ringed with a red welt that was sure to turn into a black eye.

Skid started up the hill, following his own tracks through the deep snow. It was quite an effort, walking uphill through this much snow.

Skid broke trail, which made walking a little easier. The moose was lying about halfway to the top of the hill, in a little hole behind some birch trees. Skid had cut the moose's throat earlier, leaving a big patch of red snow around it. The moose still had to be gutted and cut up before we could move it. We stood around the carcass for a few minutes, talking about how we should do it. None of us had ever gutted an animal this big before.

It was a slow process making the cut across the belly. Skid slid his knife into the cut and drew a line across the belly and up to the moose's butt. The guts pushed their way through the cut, bulging out. Skid was trying to push them back in so he could see what he was doing. He continued the cut towards the animals butt as Faddus and I held the moose's back legs apart.

I had watched Ross Turner gut out a cow a few months earlier and he used a trick of cutting around the butt hole, pulling it out and tying it with a piece of twine to prevent any excretion from leaking out and getting on the meat. I was trying to talk to Skid about it, telling him what I thought we should do. He

151

didn't seem to want to pay attention to me and proceeded to hack away. As he split the belly a little further, the guts pushed their way out, rolling out into the snow. They were still attached inside the cavity by the butt hole and a layer of cartilage on the top of the ribcage. Skid hacked away, with his head inside the cavity, cutting away the spots that were still holding on. It was kind of messy, as he tried to dislodge the butt hole, spilling some of the contents of the guts out on the snow.

Faddus and I reached in and grabbed the guts, rolling them out of the gut cavity and onto the snow.

We then sifted through the pile of guts, trying to locate the liver, heart, and kidneys. Finding them among the massive pile was no easy job if you never had done this before. Each organ was surrounded by a thick layer of fat, which made it hard to identify. We finally found each one, and cut them out, then rolled the guts over, sending them down the hill a few feet.

After having completed the gutting, we started skinning the animal. Each of us started on a different part of the moose. Faddus and I started on the two hind legs. I took the right one and he started on the left, while Skid was working on the front legs. It was a slow operation, as the skin fell away from the meat and onto the snow. We started on one side and then had to roll the moose over to get the whole hide cut away, leaving it laying on the snow, with the carcass on top of it.

Hacking a moose into quarters so we could handle was another chore. There were bones holding things together that we were not too sure of and just when we thought it should be cut through, we would find a bone holding everything. Some places we cut through with a meat saw that Skid borrowed from Ross and others we chopped through with an axe. It was a grisly-looking job, but we finally got the moose hacked up into quarters that we could handle.

"How are we going to get this moose home?" I asked, as we stood over the pile of meat.

"Can your horse haul it for us?" Faddus asked.

"She probably could," I answered. "She could pull it on toboggans." "We should wait until after dark, so that nobody sees us," said Skid. Both Faddus and I agreed with Skid about waiting until after dark. We packed the liver, heart and kidneys into plastic bags Skid brought with him and decided to go to Faddus's place to divide them. We covered the quarters of moose with the hide, and buried them with snow. We also dug a hole in the snow and buried all the bloody snow. There was a light snow falling, which laid a blanket of white over everything. Satisfied that everything was taken care of for the time being, we took off for Faddus's place.

We piled into Faddus's, finding Larry and Norma sitting around the table smoking a joint and looking at some gardening magazines. Faddus laid the heart, liver and kidneys out on the counter to cut up. "Moose liver, all right!" Larry commented, he got up to inspect the meat. "Want me to cut it up?"

"Larry's really good at it, "Faddus commented, "he used to help his dad when he was a kid."

"Okay with me," I said. Skid nodded his approval as he took a hit off the joint.

Larry grabbed a favorite knife and steel that was hanging on the wall and started to sharpen the knife. He studied the meat lying on the counter as he worked the knife across the steel.

"How many pieces do I divide it into?" he asked.

"Thirds," Faddus said, looking at Skid and me for approval. We both nodded. Faddus held up three fingers to Larry. He turned around towards the meat and began cutting.

He cut each piece of meat into three equal pieces and made three piles on the counter. Then he sliced off five strips of liver and threw them in the frying pan on the cookstove. The liver sizzled as we talked about the experience. Recounting to Larry and Norma about Chad being so upset and punching Skid, giving him a black eye, which was starting to get some black and blue color to it. We all razzed Skid about the eye, laughing unmercifully at him. He took it pretty well, eventually started to giggle a little himself.

Larry passed each of us a piece of liver, stabbing it with a fork and handing it to us. "This liver is unscrupulous," Larry said, as he chewed on a piece with a satisfied look on his face. Faddus and I just looked at each other and grinned.

We split the piles of meat up, putting them in plastic bags and heading home. Our plan was to meet at Faddus's place after dinner. It was dark about four o'clock this time of year, so it was a good idea to get the toboggans together before dark.

I fed Dondi as soon as I got home and tied her so she would be ready when it was time to go. Katy had been really heavy on the vegetarian trip at that time, but had been really interested in eating some moose. I brought the meat in the house, she was very happy about it. We had not eaten much moose meat for a year and a half or so, since the Hooty's fed us moose meat when we first came to Longstock. She cut a couple of pieces of liver off the chunk and got it cooking pretty quickly. We feasted on our first moose, and it felt pretty good. There was something about the cold climate here that made a person crave meat. We devoured the liver and cooked a few more pieces. It was the best liver I had ever eaten. I was not wildly fond of liver all my life, even stuffing it down the kitchen table leg so I wouldn't have to eat it when I was a kid, but this liver was exceptionally good.

After eating, I lazed around in the hammock for a half hour or so, then got myself ready. I went to the barn and got Dondi ready to go. I had one toboggan, which I tied onto the saddle horn with a long rope. I rode her to Faddus's place. Skid was already there, waiting for me with a toboggan.

We rolled a couple of joints and headed out. It was pitch-dark by this time and we thought we'd be able to get the moose out of there without anyone seeing us. Skid was especially interested in moving it without running into Chad. His eye had gotten really black and blue by this time and puffed up so it was almost closed.

It was only the packed ski-doo trail that Dondi was able to walk on, as the snow was at least four foot deep beside it. We walked single- file, with Dondi trailing behind. The stars were out and the Northern Lights were appearing in the sky in streaks of light, coming and going as we walked. We had flashlights with us, but the trail was quite visible without them. We had three toboggans tied on behind Dondi, one behind another. She plodded along calmly, following us, with the toboggans following her.

We descended the big hill to the closest spot we could get to the moose. I turned Dondi around and tied her to a tree on the side of the road with a long rope. We lined up the toboggans on the ski-doo trail and tied them together. The three of us plowed our way up the hill to where the meat was and uncovered it. Each quarter weighed about two hundred pounds, and took two of us to drag it down to the road. Faddus and I dragged the first quarter about two hundred feet to the road and put it on the first toboggan. We went back up the hill to help Skid who had a second quarter dragged out and a little way down. Faddus and I grabbed that one and took it the rest of the way and loaded the next toboggan. We repeated this until we got the last piece down.

"We'll have to put it on Dondi," I said. That was easier said than done. Dondi flipped out, trying to run away from the hunk of dead meat. She didn't know what it was and she wasn't going to have anything to do with it. I tried but I could not get her to accept the quarter of moose. We finally gave up and rearranged the meat on the toboggans so that the smaller quarters rode on one.

We thought we were ready to go when Skid blurts out, "I forgot the hide up there. Just a minute," he said and plowed back up the hill to get the hide. We watched Skid climb the hill in the dim light and gather up the hide. He started down the hill, dragging the hide. As he got closer to the road, Dondi started freaking out. The hide seemed to scare her more than the meat did. We already had her hitched up to the toboggans and she wanted to take off. I was holding her with a rope, quickly grabbing her halter as she dragged me along for a few feet before I got her stopped. She wouldn't have anything to do with that hide, no matter what we did. Skid buried it in the snow beside the road.

I held on to Dondi while Skid and Faddus tied the load down on the toboggans.

"Let's go!" yelled Faddus.

I gave Dondi a click of the tongue and started to walk. She followed, leaning into the weight of the toboggans. Everything looked like it was going to work out great, as we neared the top of the big hill. The hill was our only obstacle and we just about had it behind us.

"What's that noise?" I said, stopping Dondi at the top of the hill. "Am I hearing ski-doo's?."

"I hear something, too!" said Faddus. "I don't hear shit!" remarks Skid.

"Quiet," I said. I could definitely hear something this time. It sounded like ski-doo's, lots of them. "Shit man, those are ski-doo's, and they're headed this way! What the hell are we going to do?"

There was no way we could get off of the road, except to duck into Chad's driveway. We didn't think that would be a very good idea, under the circumstances.

All of a sudden, panic set in. Who could this be? A whole bunch of ski-doo's! Maybe Chad had called the cops or game wardens.

"Let's get the hell out of here!" yelled Faddus.

I started running as I led Dondi, which put her into a trot. The toboggans really started to move, Faddus and Skid ran along behind. We could hear the ski-doo's getting closer and closer, but it was still about a half-mile to go before there would be a place to get off the road. My heart was pounding as I thought of what kind of shit we would be in if we got caught with this moose by the wrong people. I accelerated the pace out of pure adrenaline, trying to get to that spot on the road where we could ditch the ski-doo's. I looked back over my shoulder down the road and I could see the faint light of the ski-doo's, far down the road.

"We might make it!" I yelled to the others. I was sweating profusely and gasping for breath. It was incredibly hard to run on snow. This kind of frozen snow seemed to break loose when you step forward and push back a few inches. You lose about two or three inches with each step.

I looked back again and the lights were much brighter. I could see them flashing in the tree tops down the road.

"They're coming up the hill now. We're not going to make it. Let's get off the trail right now, instead of waiting until they get here," I said.

I stopped Dondi and slowly led her into the deep snow beside the road. Faddus and Skid helped the toboggans stay upright as they slid off the ski-doo trail. There we stood in the snow, as we waited for the ski-doo's to pass. I was hoping it wasn't the cops. It was now inevitable that we were going to be seen by somebody, as the lights got brighter and brighter. The sound was getting very close. I could see their headlights as the first one rounded the corner. Here they came, eight machines lined up in a single line, approaching fast.

The lights lit everything up like a baseball stadium, only brighter because of the white snow. I felt as if I were on television, as each machine roared by, with most ski-doo's carrying two passengers. It was old man Jamison and his wife (she had the reputation of being the biggest gossip in the entire valley). There were daughters and son-in-laws and friends and neighbors and who knows who else, passing us in full sight and well lighted, at that.

Our secret plan to move the moose unseen was completely shot to hell. It was quite possible that the incident would be recounted in every little community up and down the rail line to Prince George and beyond.

I couldn't believe my eyes as each of the eight ski-doo's passed us, careful to slow down and have a good look at our cargo. The last ski-doo passed and the lights headed down the road in front of us. You would expect that we would get the horse and toboggans back on the road and get going, but nobody moved. We just watched and watched, as the ski-doo lights got fainter, finally becoming a glow in the sky.

We stood there on the side of the road, in a kind of a daze. "I don't fucking believe it!" Faddus exclaimed. "I don't fucking believe it!"

We all broke out in hysterical laughter. My eyes were watering, as I was doubled over. Both Skid and Faddus were cracking up, too. Comments like, 'Boy, we sure pulled that on the sly!' sent us reeling into another bout of hysterics. We would have seen fewer people if we had hauled the moose on a mail day, in the daytime.

Finally Dondi had enough and jumped back up onto the road. We had to re-tie some of the load and then proceeded on to Faddus's place. It was hard to keep from bursting out laughing as we went.

Faddus's place was the first stop. We pulled Dondi up

in front of the house and tied her to a fence post. We then unloaded the toboggan with two quarters of moose meat on it. We all agreed that because there were more people living here, we would give Faddus the larger cut of the meat. Skid and I would take the rear quarters, which were a little bigger than the two front quarters. Faddus and I each grabbed onto one of the quarters and packed it into the house and put it on the counter. We went back out and packed the second one in too.

Larry and Norma were sitting at the table having a card game as we came in. Harry was at the table and Freddy was reclining in his bed. Kathy was lying in bed with Colleen, who had just fallen asleep. Kathy and Freddy got up as soon as we brought the meat in the house.

"All right! Moose meat!" said Larry, getting up from his card game to inspect the first quarter. Grabbing a knife and steel that were hanging against the wall, he stood over the hunk of moose, running the knife back and forth over the steel as if he couldn't wait to cut off a chunk of meat.

"Cut us off a round of steaks," Faddus said when we came in the door with the second quarter and saw Larry standing over the first quarter with the knife and steel.

Larry dove right in, first looking for the best place from which to cut some steaks. He cut a big chunk of meat off the backbone and threw it on the table and began slicing it into steaks. Freddy got the big frying pan on the stove to heat up and stoked the fire.

"Whoa, this looks good!" Freddy remarked, as he placed the steaks in the frying pan and they began to sizzle.

"How did it go?" Harry asked Faddus.

"Nothing short of a disaster!" he answered. "Why? What happened?" Harry asked.

"We got seen by a whole bunch of people on ski-doo's." said Skid. We proceeded to recount the events to everyone, with each of us butting in and telling a part of the story. We had a colossal laugh about the whole ordeal as we waited for the steaks to cook.

"Here you go," said Freddy, as he put a plate full of moose steaks and a pile of forks on the table. We all grabbed a fork and a piece of steak. It was a little chewy, probably because it was so fresh, but tasted very good.

After a while, Skid and I got ready to go. I still had to drag one of the toboggans to his place and then take the last one home. I left the toboggan that was going to my place in front of the Alaskan's, picking it up on the way back.

It was about nine o'clock when I finally got home with the last quarter of moose. I pulled the toboggan up in front of the house and threw a tarp over it for the night. I took Dondi over to the barn and gave her some hay and then went in the house.

Katy and the boys were already in bed when I walked in. She got up to hear how everything went. I told her the story. We had a good laugh about the whole ordeal.

The next day, it seemed like everyone in Longstock knew about the moose. Our efforts to keep the whole thing quiet was thwarted. I hung the quarter of meat in a tree in the bush the next morning, to give it a chance to cure. I would go out every week or so and cut off a piece of meat. It froze solid a couple of weeks later and was quite hard to get a piece off of at that point. It hung in a big, frozen block for several months before it thawed enough to be able to cut. I was still worried that the word of our moose hunt would reach the neighboring communities, and maybe the fish and game people, as well. I was careful not to go out in the bush very often, so as not to leave a trail to it.

About the middle of March, the meat thawed, and got a crust on it. Bits of mold appeared on the outside a few weeks later, when we brought it in to can.

It took a couple of days to cut the meat up and put it in jars. The fifty, or so, jars we put up lasted us most of the rest of the year. We finally used the last jar up the following August, during haying season.

Chapter 8

A Longstock Summer

S pring had definitely come, even though snow was still on the ground. The incredibly long Winter had dumped such an excess of snow that Spring was in the air long before the ground became visible. April brought day after day of warm, sunny weather, melting the snow quite quickly. The problem was that there was just so much snow that it seemed to take forever for it to go.

Like a lot of others, I was thinking about planting the garden. After shoveling the snow away, I built a small cold frame for starting plants out in the front yard. It was a space about two feet by six feet and about eighteen inches high, covered with plastic.

We had some tomatoes, peppers and pot plants started in the house that had to get moved outside where they could get better light. Soon after getting the cold frame built, we started flats of cabbage, broccoli, cauliflower, zucchini, kolirabi and more pot. The long days of sunshine and warm temperatures made the plants thrive in the cold frame.

The garden, however, was still covered with a couple feet of snow. Taking a bit of advice from Ross Turner, I spread a thin layer of wood ashes across the top of the snow on the garden. The bright sunshine on the snow seemed to reflect the heat, causing the snow to melt slowly, but when a layer of wood ashes were spread on top, it trapped the heat from the sun and it melted much faster. Within a week or so of covering the garden with ashes, the ground started to show through. Right beside the garden, where there were no ashes, the snow was still quite deep.

The ground took some time to dry out enough to work, but it was definitely way quicker than letting it melt slowly, without the ashes. Some of the neighbors used sand in the same way, which worked equally as well.

After a normal winter, the snow would be gone in April. Sometimes the ground was bare in early April and sometimes it would hang around until the end but it was rarely on the ground into May. This year was an exception, as the record snowfall stuck around into the second week of May. The open fields were pretty well bare by Mothers Day, but on the edges where there was some shade, there was still some snow right up until almost the end of May.

I managed to get the garden melted off in the first few days of May, but it would not dry up enough to work or plant until about the middle of the month. I piled up most of the winters manure from the goats and the horse, giving it a chance to compost for several weeks before it was applied to the garden. The pile heated up as it composted melting the snow underneath right down to the ground.

The first garden we had the year before, turned out rather pathetic. We were hoping that we could make this year's garden much better. We had always had good luck with our gardens since working on a five-acre co-op garden in Farmington, New Mexico back in 69. It was the first garden I'd been involved with and I really got the gardening bug from that. Our share of the vegetables from that garden was a colossal amount of every kind of vegetable you could imagine.

Since that time, I've made it a point to plant a garden every year, everywhere we lived. We planted a garden in the dry lands of New Mexico. We had to haul water every other day for it, until one day, when the rains came the water ran off the canyon walls and created little streams everywhere. We were able to dig some ditches and direct the water right into the garden, irrigating every row.

Later, while living in Denver, I dug up a part of the backyard and planted a small garden. I must say the neighbors in the city didn't appreciate my hauling and spreading manure from a local stable on my garden while they were having an outside barbecue. That was really the icing on the cake for these neighbors, who were not really impressed by the four or five houses nearest to theirs being populated by hippies. They moved out of the quaint, little carriage- house soon after the manure incident. Katy and I moved in.

We weren't the only ones in Longstock to have the gardening bug. Larry was a fanatic organic gardener. He had several cold frames filled with young starts of every kind of vegetable. He also had a cold frame full of just pot plants.

Freddy had a few cold frames full of plants, too. He had sticks with labels on each flat in the cold frames. Some were labeled tomatoes, carrots, beets, cabbage, but all the little plants looked the same. He explained it by telling people that they looked that way just because they were small, hoping to convince people that it was not all pot, as it appeared to be.

Skid was getting a garden space ready, too, though it didn't look like there were going to be any vegetables in it, only pot. He found an old manure pile from many years ago in a little clearing in the bush, down the tracks from his place. There must have been an old barn nearby that had collapsed and was swallowed up by the bush, leaving few signs of the old building close to the manure pile. After finding the pile, Skid worked a couple of days getting it ready by spreading it out over a larger space, and working it up.

Toad spent most of the winter working at the sawmill at Upper Fraser and would pop into Longstock on the weekends. He quit the mill about mid-April and moved into Longstock full-time. He was not really much of a gardener, though he was planning on giving it a try. With Toad, you could never be quite sure what he might be capable of. He had a way of reasoning things out in his mind, using ideas and principles that he thought up himself. It was usually quite illogical, but made sense to him, though not to anyone else. He got a garden turned up, but never really got it planted. There were stories about the little seedlings committing suicide and problems with the ground having way too much heavy sod in it so it couldn't be worked up very well. He recounted how the sun murdered the little plants when he put them out, describing the death of each individual plant, some turning white within hours of dressing them with way too much nitrogen fertilizer.

"Shouldn't they just grow faster, the more you give them, just like giving more gas to your vehicle?" he reasoned.

The Hooty's used the ashes-on-the-snow method, too. They had used the same garden space for several years. It was a very nice, sunny location and a sandy loam that was very well drained. Paula was one of the first ones in Longstock to get seeds in the ground that year. The location of the garden was excellent, at the bottom of a hill called the bench, which rose about two hundred fifty feet in elevation. The South exposure caused a hot spot, a perfect gardening area. They were able to grow corn almost every year there. Corn as a garden crop was hit-or-miss on the whole, but the Hooty's garden was one of the only places where corn would ripen every year. Paula was really proud of her strawberry patch, too. It was definitely the finest strawberry patch around, producing beautiful, large strawberries that melted in your mouth. It was the first crops to get ripe every year, producing a large crop of berries before the end of June. Paula canned dozens of jars of berries and jams every summer and still had enough left to give fresh berries to the neighbors. It was a real treat to get a bucket of strawberries early in the summer, before any other fruit or berries were ready.

Steve Worthy had grown a garden the year before that had turned out about as well as mine. He was determined to have a better garden this year. Steve had this compulsion to compete with everybody all the time. The gardening was no different. He would work on his garden very hard, in order to get the biggest and the best of everything, sometimes packing leaves or manure off the side of the road and babying the starts with plastic tunnels. He shoveled all the snow off the garden instead of using ashes or sand to melt it off, leaving large snowbanks on the side of the garden that were there until June.

Pierre and Betty had a garden turned up, as well, but Pierre insisted that it couldn't be planted until he finished the neat, little, wooden, picket fence around it. It had to be painted, as well, before any planting could begin. Pierre was very meticulous and had to have things just right before anything could begin. This included the garden fence, which looked like a picture out of Organic Gardenings most beautiful garden fences. It was kind of late in the season before the fence was done and Betty could begin planting. Pierre moved on to building 'The Barn', as Betty took over the garden tasks. Though it was a bit late in the season, she managed to get a modest garden in.

The old-timers in Longstock had their own set ways of planting. That was, turn the ground up and plant. When the plants were a few inches high, give them some chemical fertilizer and weed killer between the rows. A monthly dressing with chemical fertilizer and weed killer would keep the plants growing, and the garden, free of weeds. The concept of organic gardening seemed to be non-existent to most of the old-timers. I think that Ross Turner was the only old timer that didn't use chemicals to grow his garden. He had quite a bit of livestock and manure was abundant and money wasn't.

It was late February when I got the letter from my old friend Gypsy. He wrote to me from Gaspe', Quebec, where he had been living with a woman since November. He saved my letter when he left New Mexico, knowing he was going to Canada. He met Heather when she came to Placitas the summer before. She was a small, sexy woman, with blonde hair. Her well-rounded breasts and shapely figure got mens attention, wherever she went. Gypsy, like many of the guys at Placitas, got really interested right away. Heather took a shine to Gypsy, attracted by his long, jet-black hair and piercing, Gypsy eyes. She liked him so much, she offered to take him back to Quebec with her, assuring him she would take care of him and he wouldn't have to work at all. It all sounded pretty good to Gypsy, so off to Quebec he went.

He wrote me about plans to move out to B.C. in the summer. Heather was working as a school teacher in Gaspe', and would be finished at the end of the school year. They planned to leave right after her job was over. She liked the idea of re-locating out West. Heather had money and really didn't have to work. She had inherited a large sum of money several years earlier. I never knew the exact amount, but Gypsy said something about a half a million dollars.

I got another letter in April, saying that he was coming to B. C. at the beginning of July and wanted to know if he could come for a visit, for a week or so. I wrote back and extended an invitation to come visit and stay as long as they wanted to.

We got a pile of company that Spring, starting with Doug Miller and Shawn Green, a couple of guys I'd met in Denver a few years earlier. Doug was a journeymen carpenter and cabinet maker and insisted that we build a nice set of kitchen cabinets while he was visiting.

We took the Weigh Freight to Prince George one day, and bought enough lumber to build the cabinets, bringing it back on the train. There was still too much snow to drive the Power Wagon up to the station, so I walked the lumber home the next day, packing the boards on my shoulder. It took four trips from the train station to get it all to the house.

When I got the last of it to the house, they just about had the framing put together and were ready to cover it with the finished lumber. We gave it a cedar stain, which was a reddish color. It was the first piece of real furniture that we had and looked very handsome in the kitchen.

In the beginning of May, Moose Corrigan showed up. He was another co-worker from Denver. Moose had spent some time in B.C. a few years earlier, with a religious cult at One Hundred-Mile House. He was a short, stocky man, with a long, blond beard and long, blond hair and looked the epitome of the bush hippy, wearing sandals and denim coveralls.

He planned on staying for a while and came with a tee-pee. I had no problem with people setting up a homestead on the land. He found a spot he liked at the opposite end of the property and within a few days had the tee-pee set up. He got a little cookstove that he picked up in Prince George and set it in the tee-pee. Instead of using the traditional method of having an open fire with the smoke escaping through an opening in the top, he had a long stovepipe sticking up through the top of the tee-pee.

Kathy, who was Moose's girlfriend, was the next to show up. She came from Colorado also, a young, Jewish woman with dark hair and dark eyes, who talked a lot. I found Kathy to be a very nice person and got along with her very well. She was friendly and outgoing and made a lot of friends in Longstock quickly.

Kathy had a friend, who showed up a couple of weeks later. Trudy was a tall, long-legged woman with astounding good looks. She had an innocent air about her and a very sexy manner. Trudy liked wearing tight, muscle tee shirts, that clung tightly to her breasts. Fortunately for all the guys around Longstock, the tee shirts only covered about half of her large, firm breasts and fitting tightly over the rest. They bounced firmly whenever she walked. It was hard to keep my eyes off her when she was around. Trudy was very beautiful and she knew it, casually and innocently teasing the men that were clearly turned on by her looks. She moved into the tee pee with Moose and Kathy on the back forty.

Then there were Edith and Al, who moved into the cabin down the road. Edith was from California and Al was an older fellow who lived in the area for most of his life. Edith had acquired a twenty-acre piece of land out on the eastern end of town. They spent most of the summer cutting logs and putting the cabin up on her place. They finished the cabin late that summer but never moved into it before leaving in the fall.

By June of 1974, the population of Longstock was larger

than it had been for many years or since old man Jamison had had the mill operating at full tilt, ten or fifteen years earlier.

The homestead was a stir of activity that Spring, with Moose, Kathy, and Trudy around. After Moose got the tee-pee up, everyone jumped right into gardening. He spaded up a piece of ground nearby the tee-pee as soon as the ground was clear of snow. By the time Trudy arrived, Moose and Kathy had a fence built around the garden and some beds where Kathy wanted to plant flowers.

Trudy found herself the third person out at the tee-pee and soon started hanging out with Katy and me and the kids. She helped look after the two boys and enjoyed it immensely. Katy and Trudy became really good friends very quickly and I sure didn't mind having her around. She was a real turn-on. I had to keep remembering that I was married when I was around her. Trudy was a flirt by nature, as well. I think she liked the effect she had on men. I'm sure that there are very few men who would not be taken by her looks and sexy personality.

Ross came over with his roto-tiller one fine, sunny day and roto- tilled the garden for us. It was the first time he had met Trudy. She asked him if he could till up a little plot for her after he was done with mine.

"I'd love to roto-till your garden," Ross responded, when asked.

She was quite used to lewd remarks from men, as most of the men she met were interested in her. And of course, all men were on their best behavior and sure to put their best personality forward, in the presence of such a beautiful woman.

She snickered at Ross's obvious interest in her, as he did

a thorough roto-tilling job on her garden space.

"I think I'm in love!" Ross said to me when leaving.

I was crouched down in the garden one day, planting several rows of carrots, when Trudy came out to the garden.

"Hi Louie! What are you doing?" she said. "Planting some carrots," I answered.

"Need some help?"

"Sure," I said; even though I really didn't, I wasn't going to refuse her. I watched her as she walked to the end of the row and stopped and took off her tee shirt. Man, was I surprised! She was gorgeous, with her breasts glistening in the sun. Granted, it was a very warm day and I was working with no shirt on, too, but I didn't expect that. All she was wearing was a pair of tight jeans that were full of holes as she walked towards me down the garden row. I couldn't take my eyes off of her as she approached.

I watched her as she walked toward me. I had a string stretched out, marking several rows and was working on planting two rows at once.

"Should I plant these other two rows?" she asked me as she stopped in front of me.

"That's sounds like a good idea," I answered, reaching for the seed packets I had in my back pocket. I turned my head back to find her kneeling in front of me, her naked breasts just inches from my face. "Oh my!" I exclaimed as she took the seed packet from my hand.

I was trying to concentrate on the carrot planting and did, for short intervals, but my eyes kept coming back to Trudy. I got to the end of the row a little before her and stayed in a crouch as she planted her rows. She finally got to the end and stood up and gave a big stretch. She was beautiful and it looked to me like she was flirtin' with me.

I had just gotten an income tax return from the States and was looking to buy another horse. Dondi was getting older and we needed another riding horse, anyway. I was looking in the Prince George newspaper one day and saw an add for a three year old Pinto mare. They were asking three hundred dollars for her. One afternoon Moose and I drove to Prince George to check the horse out. She was a very gentle horse and was used to kids riding her.

She was actually kind of lazy, but I thought this might be a good horse for kids, too, even though I was looking for a horse for myself. The owners called her Chaperell, but I later changed her name to Daffodil.

I decided to buy her and returned a few days later with my horse trailer to pick her up. Moose bought a horse that day too and seeing as how the trailer could accommodate two horses, we picked up his horse, a little Arabian-Morgan cross, also three years old, named Rusty.

When we arrived in Sinclair Mills with the two horses Toad was waiting with Flicka which he wanted to ride into Longstock as well. He was going to have a friend of his ride his horse along with Moose and I. We left the truck and horse trailer at Bob Crane's place and rode the three horses from there. It was about a ten mile ride.

Daffodil was completely tired out by the end of the first mile and wanted to stop. I guess she was used to having her way with the kids that rode her previously, or she was accustomed to short rides, as it was hell to keep her going. She lagged behind the other horses constantly, lathered up with sweat, with me prodding and kicking her to keep up. After several miles of that, I was covered with sweat, too.

Moose, with Rusty and Toad's friend Rolly on Flicka, set the pace, with Daffodil always trying to catch up. We caught up to the others as they waited at Boulder Creek, where we had to ford the creek. They both had trouble getting the horses to go in the creek. I rode up to the creek on Daffodil. She stopped for a few seconds as I coaxed her into the creek. She went right in and slowly plodded across, stopping several times to drink water. The other horses, after seeing Daffodil go across, followed right along.

Daffodil was already out of the creek, behind her was Rolly on Flicka and when he came out of the water, Flicka jumped ahead, in back of Daffodil. Don't ask me why, but Daffodil suddenly kicked out with both feet, I presume at Flicka, with one foot hitting Flicka in the rib cage and the other nailing Rolly right on the kneecap.

"Yeow!" he exclaimed, grabbing his knee. Of course, Flicka wanted to take off running, and each time she came down in stride, giving

Rolly sharp pains running through his knee. Grimacing, he finally got the horse stopped and was doubled over in the saddle from the pain.

Moose and I both jumped down off our horses. "You okay?" I asked.

"Just give me a minute," he said, obviously in pain. "I can't get off this horse until we get there, now. I might not be able to get back on." We traveled at a bit of a slower pace from that point on. Rolly's knee was swollen up to the size of a football by the time we got him to Toad's place. He ended up staying for a week and-a-half, until his knee healed enough to walk.

I'd answered Gypsy's letter with detailed instructions on how to get to Longstock. I also told him about the 'messages to isolated areas' that the radio station put on every morning and evening. One morning, Katy, Trudy and I were listening when a message came on for Louie in Longstock, 'We will be on the Weigh Freight today - Gypsy and Heather.'

Heather and Gypsy were standing there, across the tracks, when the train pulled away. Trudy and I had come up to meet the train that morning and were just getting to the train station as the train was leaving. I pulled the truck up to the tracks and jumped out and ran right up to Gypsy throwing my arms around him, giving a big hug.

"Man, it's good to see you." I said. "What has it been, two and a half, or three, years since we last met in New Mexico?"

"Something like that," he answered. "This is my woman, Heather."

"Nice to meet you, Heather," I said, extending my hand for a handshake.

"Nice to meet you, too!" she answered. "I've heard a lot about you!" She grabbed my hand and pulled me into a hug, squeezing me very tightly.

Gypsy looked great, better than I'd ever seen him look. His face was bright and happy looking, clean shaven with a mustache on top of his six-foot frame. His long, black hair reached halfway down his back and was shiny and slick. He was dressed all in black: black tee shirt, black leather vest, black pants that were tucked into his black leather boots. His fingers were full of rings, with perhaps as many as fifteen different rings on his two hands. He had no fewer than four medallions around his neck and a black leather pouch dangled from his black leather belt. He had the appearance of a true Romany Gypsy.

Heather was a rather short woman, with short, blonde hair and a beautiful body. She had rather large breasts, but was otherwise quite slim. She had a round kind of face and seemed to be smiling most of the time. They seemed like somewhat of an odd couple, but who's to say.

"Hi! I'm Trudy," Trudy said, giving him a hug as she introduced herself to Gypsy. I'm sure that Trudy's hug was every bit as passionate as the one I got from Heather.

Both Heather and Gypsy had enormous backpacks. Gypsy swung his onto his back and I grabbed Heathers and we put them in the back of the Power Wagon. We all climbed into the front, having to squeeze together to get the door closed. Heather was squeezed up against me and Trudy was sardined between her and Gypsy as we started for home.

The drive to the house took a little longer than usual, as I drove kind of slow as we talked.

Chico came running out to greet us as we pulled up to the house.

Katy came out a few seconds later and gave Gypsy a big hug. "How have you been?" she said. "It's so good to see you."

They walked to the house with arms around each other. They had been good friends when we lived in New Mexico and it had been three years since they had seen each other.

We spent several hours visiting and recalling old times in New Mexico. It had been a really fun part of our life, convincing us that we wanted to live in a country environment.

They spent a couple of nights with us, walking around and checking out the land. Gypsy asked me on the second day there if he could build a cabin on the west side of the property. We walked out there and looked over the spot, I told him it was okay with me.

It was summertime and a person could get away with a makeshift shelter for a few months. They threw together a frame shelter out of plastic and mosquito netting in the bush by their building site.

He was really entrenched in the Gypsy culture, which was his true heritage, to the point of taking his mothers first name and maiden name as his own, while using his fathers first name as his middle name. Maria Savako Wood was the name he was using at this time, though some folks called him Vako. There had been other names he'd used over the years, but he was always known as Gypsy and was extremely proud of his Gypsy heritage.

For that reason, his plan was to build a house in the shape of a Gypsy wagon, just in case he wanted to jack it up and put wheels under it, hitch up a team of horses to it and travel the world. In the spirit of the Gypsies, that potential had to be there in any house that he built.

I have to say that Gypsy might have been a worse carpenter than Toad, if that was possible. One of the main differences was that Toad knew it and was reluctant to do much in that area, whereas Gypsy was not. Working with him was a danger in itself and it's a wonder he didn't break a leg or arm or something, the way the logs were slipping and sliding around. He would fell a tree, peel it, drag it over to the building and wrestle it into place right away. The logs hadn't had a chance to dry out at that point and were oozing with sap. They were slippery and extremely hard to handle. That certainly didn't deter Gypsy and Heather. Each day they recounted their experiences, with stories of how 'that log almost got me, or that one almost nailed Heather' as the logs slipped off the walls and on one occasion, one log broke in half when it hit the ground.

I guess he didn't feel the need to make the gaps between the logs very close, either, figuring he'd just fill them with chinking later on. Some of the gaps were four or five inches wide and made the place look more like a hog pen than a house. But, remarkably, the walls went up fairly quickly. It took them about a month to get the walls up on the long and narrow, sixteen by nine cabin.

Many nights, they came up to our house for supper after a hard days work all covered with pitch. Dishwashing liquid worked pretty well for getting pitch off. They took turns at the sink, trying to remove as much pitch as possible, although you can never get it all off on the first try.

It took about one more month to get the roof on before they moved in. It was a cozy, little cabin, at least during the summer months, but I suspected that winter was going to be cold in there.

Moose and I rode horses a lot that summer. I really needed to spend a lot of time with Daffodil to break her of a lot of bad habits that she came with. Most of her bad habits were born out of laziness. She always wanted to go back home. She had the unusual ability to untie knots by biting on them, pushing and pulling and would eventually get them loose and head for home, making me walk. More than once she would not let me get hold of her and would walk ten feet ahead of me all the way. The good part was that she always went home, no matter what.

We rode horses almost every day and spent at least one or two days a week riding all day. Moose and I were always looking for places to ride and rode to Penney about once every week or two. We'd drop in on Charlie and Olivia for coffee and some of Olivia's tasty treats. Then we'd ride over to Alfred's and see what's been going on. On the way back, we would let the horses run flat out at a place we called the Penney highlands. It was over a mile of good, flat road, perfect for a good run. It was there that I discovered how fast Daffodil was when she went into overdrive leaving Rusty behind like she was standing still. There wasn't a horse in the country that could keep up with Daffodil. It was amazing the way she left every horse in the dust while giving the impression that she was a lazy, old nag.

Some days, we would follow the old plank road network that was used for logging many years ago. By freezing up the plank roads with ice the loggers could carry monster loads of logs, pulled by horses and oxen. We investigated every trail we could find and because of it, got to know the area quite well.

Once in a while, Toad would come along on Flicka, but didn't seem to be into it the way Moose and I were. We were on the horses almost every day. Sometimes, Kathy and Trudy would come with us. Kathy would usually ride Dondi and Trudy would ride behind me. I looked forward to those days, having Trudy on the back of my horse, holding on tight, with her breasts poking me in the back. Once in a while, just Trudy and I would take off on the horses. She was a pretty good rider, having done some riding as a kid. We had lots of fun riding together, especially on those hot days when going for a dip in the river was the only way to cool off.

Before the summer was over, both Freddy Bartells and Steve Worthy had acquired a horse. Freddy bought an older sorrel gelding named Sinbad, and Steve bought a big, black gelding named Thunder. Sinbad, a spirited horse that liked to run, was very well trained and a good first horse for Freddy. Steve, on the other hand, had bought a completely unbroken horse. Thunder was a huge horse, probably around fifteen hundred pounds. He was trouble for Steve right from the day he got him. At four years old, Thunder had received very little handling up to that point and Steve had little experience with horses. Thunder started out as Bob Hooty's horse, but he was not able to control him. There were a couple of incidents where Thunder ran away with Bob and one where he reared up with Bob while he was pulling back on the reins and Thunder came right over backwards on top of him. Luckily, it was in deep snow, so it just drove Bob into the snow instead of breaking bones like it would have if it had been hard ground. After that incident, Bob sold Thunder to Steve.

Freddy was really taken by the speed of Sinbad, when he let him run. He had never been on a horse that was so willing to break into a run. As a matter of fact, he had only ridden stable horses that were lazy and gentle. After galloping on Sinbad, he was convinced that he was the fastest horse around. Freddy emphatically bragged about how fast he was and that he could outrun any horse in Longstock.

One day, Moose and I rode our horses over to Ross's place, and found Freddy and Ross playing a game of crib. Freddy rode Sinbad to Ross's and had him tied to the hitching post in front of the house. After visiting Ross for a while, we all left together on our horses. Daffodil had the reputation of being a lazy horse and Jerry was throwing around a few wisecracks about her, insinuating that his horse would outrun her while hardly trying. I knew Daffodil could run and felt confident that she was fast compared to horses I had ridden over the last five or six years.

"Can that nag run?" Freddy asked me in a condescending way, thinking that Sinbad would mop the floor with her.

I answered confidently, "One way to find out, man!"

Freddy turned to Moose, saying "Give us a three count, Moose." "Okay," said Moose, as he went into the count: "One, two, three!" and we were off.

"Yaa!" I yelled at Daffodil. She took a huge first leap and was in full stride in seconds. Freddy and Sinbad were immediately left behind on the first stride and we continued to put more distance between us. It wasn't even close. Daffodil outran Sinbad badly, opening up a lead of four or five boxcar lengths in the first quarter-mile. I reined in Daffodil, after it was clear who was the fastest horse. As we approached the bottom of the big hill, I slowed her to a walk as Freddy and Sinbad flew by me, and up the hill.

"Looks like we beat you," Freddy says to me from the saddle, when I approached the top of the hill where he was waiting.

"You got to be kidding!" I replied. "We kicked your ass man, it wasn't even close!"

Freddy didn't see it that way, insisting that his horse had won the race. As far as I was concerned, Daffodil could beat Sinbad every day of the week and if he wanted a re-match, I would be sure to have little mercy next time.

By the end of the summer, horses had become the main transportation around Longstock. I was riding just about every day and at least one day a week, Moose and I would ride out to Penney, or some other direction that kept us in the saddle most of the day.

I'd made arrangements with Ross to help him with his haying and get hay for my two horses in return. Ross had close to fifty acres of hay. It took him about a month to harvest and get it into the barn, that is, if it didn't rain too many days. A lot of rain could delay things, dragging the haying season out several weeks, sometimes right into September. It was quite hot and dry from about the middle of July right through until the end of August this year and the haying was going pretty well.

Ross had one of the old loose hay loaders that were common on the farms before there were hay balers. It picked up the hay after it was raked into winrows and lifted it up with rotating teeth and flipped it over the top and onto the wagon that trailed the hay loader. A person with a pitchfork worked the wagon on top, shifting the hay coming over the top around the wagon. There was a certain way of handling the hay as it spilled onto the wagon so as to keep it on the wagon, piling a large load without the load getting top-heavy and the hay falling off. Ross yelled instructions from his seat on the tractor to the person on the wagon, "Pile around the outside first and then the middle. The middle locks it in place."

There were several of us giving Ross a hand on the haying: Pierre, Skid, Moose, Freddy, Larry, and I were all there helping hay the field. We took turns on the hay loader. It was basically a one-man job on the wagon, as there was not really enough room for more than one person. It was a lot of work to keep up with the hay rolling over the top of the loader and onto the wagon in the hot sun.

It was my turn to work the wagon. I was sweating profusely in the first minute, as I pitched the hay to the left side and then the right, building the outside first and then filling in the middle. There wasn't time to think, as the hay kept rolling over onto the wagon. It was all I could do to stay ahead of it without getting buried.

Ross gave the tractor more gas, the loader was bringing up the hay faster and faster, until I couldn't keep up. The hay was coming too fast and was building up in the front of the wagon. I went into high gear, trying to spread the hay around, but I was losing ground quickly. Soon the hay overwhelmed me, just about burying me with hay.

"Stop the tractor," I yelled at Ross, as the hay piled up in front of me. I could barely work the pitchfork I was buried so deep in hay.

"Ha, ha, ha," Ross laughed, as he stopped the tractor giving me a chance to catch up. As each person took his turn on the hay rack, Ross sped up until the person yelled to stop because the hay was coming too fast. One by one, he went through the whole crew until everyone had had a chance on the wagon. When the wagon was loaded to the point where the hay coming over the top was as high as the load, Ross unhitched the wagon from the hay loader and hooked it to the tractor, pulling it over to the barn. One person worked the wagon, unloading the loose hay and pitching it into the opening in the barn. It was a chain gang of people, each taking his turn to shift the hay to the back of the barn, piling it right up to the roof. It took about an hour or so, to load a load and get it loaded into the barn. We worked from about ten o'clock in the morning, when the dew was off the hay, right up until it was almost dark each day. Each afternoon we would put a load on the Power Wagon to take with us each night when we headed home. It was usually dark by the time we got home. Moose and I would unload it into the barn before going to Ross's in the morning.

Day after day, the sun would shine hot and brightly as we plowed through the field, putting up more and more of it until, by the third week of August, it was done. Moose and I had the barn at my place filled with loose hay by this time. I figured that there were about ten tons of hay put up, enough for the three horses and a couple of goats, for the Winter.

There was a hell of a party at Ross's after the haying was finished. The Berry Cup was flowing freely, as well as a couple of bottles of tequila, as the whole crew got shit-faced. It was another hot, sunny day, which led to the party making its way to the river to check the fish trap. At least, I think that's why we ended up at the river.

We were all standing by the riverbank, watching Ross pull the trap, when Freddy took a run at Skid, bowling him over and right into the river. Skid got a hold of Freddy just as he was going in, and dragged him along with him. They both hit the cold river with a splash. Just then, I sprinted at Moose and knocked him into the water.

It was a free-for-all after that, as everybody was trying to knock everyone else into the river. I managed to escape getting pushed into the water for a few minutes, until Freddy and Moose, both soaking wet, attacked me and dragged me into the river. The water was cold, right around thirty-five degrees Fahrenheit. It took the wind out of you when you first hit the water.

It wasn't long before everyone was soaking wet, including Ross. It was a hot day, so the water felt nice, at first, that is, until you were in the water for a while, and your body temperature dropped. I started to shiver in the cold water, but only took a few minutes to get warm again, standing in the hot sun. We all had wet clothes, which were completely dry by the time we got back to Ross's place. After a couple more drinks, I started feeling like I'd been partying for days on end. Shortly after sundown the party broke up.

I stayed home for a few days after that, trying to catch up on some garden work that I'd been too busy to do. The garden had done very well that summer and was producing lots of vegetables. Katy had spent countless hours canning vegetables and making jams and jellies. Every time we made a trip to Prince George, we brought back a few dozen canning jars. By the time the summer was over, there were hundreds of jars of canned fruits and vegetables.

I built a small root cellar under the house, with a trap-door that opened under the stairs to the upstairs. One whole side of the cellar was shelves where the canning jars were lined up the full length of the cellar. The other side had two large bins for storing potatoes and an old washtub that I was going to fill with carrots and sand. I read in an old Foxfire book about storing carrots in sand. It was supposed to keep them nice and fresh and firm. It wouldn't be long before the potatoes and carrots would be ready to harvest and stored for the winter. Katy made a couple of crocks of sauerkraut that she canned in quart jars, as well. It looked like we would eat well this winter and would need to buy much less food than we did in the first year.

After the haying was done, it seemed that everyone was harvesting and canning. The warm summer this year had most gardens producing bumper crops of vegetables and it didn't matter whose house you went to, there were canned vegetables and fruits lined up on kitchen counters and water-bath and pressure cookers going constantly. The wild berries were prolific, especially the blue berries. We spent many hours picking them on the edges of the muskeg. Katy and I would pick a couple of gallons each in about an hour. Some years they were not very good, but that year they were thick.

The wild strawberries were slower picking, but extremely tasty. Mixed with rhubarb, they made delicious pies and jams, the combination being one of my favorites.

The pot crop had a really good year, too. Some plants had reached seven to eight feet high. Even old Ross Turner had a pot patch growing in an old pigpen. Judging by the size of the plants, I'd say that they really liked the pig manure.

I happened by Freddy's place one day and looked at his

garden. The little signs he had marked the ends of the rows, which said: carrots, beets, cabbage, and various other vegetables, but every row contained pot plants, about seven to eight feet high. The entire garden was pot, not a vegetable in sight.

The long, hot summer had created very dry conditions in the bush, with the fire danger rating at high. By the end of August, there were somewhere around three to four hundred fires burning at once in our area. Wayne McCoby was the acting fire warden and had been called out on several fires that summer. Wayne would work on fires as long as he could come home at night, but if he had to stay away, whether it was camping in the bush or staying in a motel, he refused to do it.

A fire started one night from a lightning strike and was burning out of control in the mountains, about twenty miles away from Longstock. The forest service was stretched to the limit, with all the fires burning at once. They were drafting guys from Prince George right off the street. It was a law in B.C. that if you were drafted by the forest service to fight a fire and refused, you could be thrown in jail. The word came to Longstock that the forest service was looking for volunteers to fight fire up in the McGregor Range, which was part of the Rocky Mountains. None of the McCoby's would go because it was going to be a fire that would require staying there for about a week. I got my name on the list, hoping to make enough money to buy a riverboat that I'd been looking at. It was a twenty four-foot plywood boat with a 33hp Johnson outboard on it.

They gave us an hour to get ready, picking us up near the train station. When I got there, I found Larry, Steve, and Skid waiting for the chopper, too. It was my first time in a helicopter.

I found it quite fun to fly in. The take-off was pretty well straight up. After clearing the trees, the pilot tipped the chopper a little forward and off we went.

We flew north over the mountain peaks that were visible from Longstock. It was neat to see the area from the air for the first time. The Torpy River twisted and turned below us, as we headed for the distant peaks near the Continental Divide. I could see the chopper approaching a mountain in front of us. The ground was several thousand feet below us as we approached. Slowly, the ground got closer and closer until I could see the tree tops clearly. The trees stopped and the alpine brush was below, getting closer and closer, until I could almost touch it. Suddenly, we passed the peak of the mountain and the ground was several thousand feet below again. The air currents caused the chopper to drop drastically after passing the peak. What a rush!

A few minutes later, we could see the camp where all the fire fighters were, along the side of a green/blue alpine lake. The chopper landed on a heliport made out of criss-crossed logs. We got out of the chopper and grabbed our gear from the rear compartment, walking away from the chopper with our heads down to avoid the spinning blades. The blades were probably high enough, but everybody was walking like that, so I felt like I should, too.

The previous day the crew was mopping up at the fire on the other side of the mountain, when a strong wind came up and fanned the fire into flames. It started burning everything in front of it as it moved uphill towards the fire crew. The guys dropped everything when they realized the situation and ran off into the bush. Tools that had been left behind were found later with the handles burned off. They were recovered the next day. Two of the fire-fighters were hours getting back to camp, each showing up alone about an hour apart.

By the time we flew in, everybody there wanted to get out pretty damn badly. Within an hour of arriving, we were the only ones left. They gave us instructions on what to do and how to find the fire and then everybody left. It was still daylight, so we walked over the hill and started working on mopping up the remaining hot spots before returning to camp that afternoon.

The crew that was there had left a huge amount of food. It was a beautiful spot, high up in the mountains. The walk over the hill to the fire was even better. You could see twisted, jagged peaks that made up the Continental Divide.

We awoke the next morning to heavy rain. It was a good reason to stay dry in the tents and let Mother Nature put out the fire. With the rain also came low clouds, in which a chopper couldn't fly. We were 'socked in,' as the forestry bosses told us on the radio. The rain was intermittent for the next seven days, but we were stuck up there. The chopper couldn't get in to get us out.

It was a lot of fun, hiking through the mountains during the time we were 'socked in.'

On one hiking trip, Larry and I saw a Grizzly track that I could put my foot in sideways and it was still bigger by a couple of inches. We saw mountain goats grazing on the side of cliffs. It was an awesome place to be stuck and getting paid for it.

Finally, after we had been up there for eight days, we got the word that they were coming in with a couple of choppers to get us and all the fire fighting gear. We worked pretty hard that afternoon getting hoses rolled up and tools and pumps gathered up to be ready to load when the choppers came the next day. It was virtually the only work we had done since that first afternoon we arrived.

They flew us out and we got our checks about a week later. I made just over six hundred dollars and the riverboat was going to cost me five hundred. I bought the boat the next day after getting my check. The next day I took the train to Penney and brought the boat back on the river. It gave me a real sense of independence to have my own boat.

I thought back, remembering the summer before, when I had a feeling of being overwhelmed. Things had sure changed. It was a year later and I was feeling very secure.

It was about the middle of September when the first frost hit. I went out to the garden that morning, to find about half the garden damaged by the frost. The potato plants were turned black, and were lying limp on the ground. Remarkably, all the cabbage family looked totally unharmed. The pot plants handled the frost quite well, too.

The sky was quite clear - not a cloud in the sky. The sunshine spread across the field and garden, burning the frost off. The days continued to be warm and sunny, with a cool, crisp feel in the air that identified fall on the way. It seemed to happen quickly from one day to the next, as only the day before, it still felt like summer. The air and the cooler sunshine made it clear that summer was over. It had been a really warm summer that year, much warmer than our first summer in Longstock.

The garden had done remarkably well, producing heavy

crops of almost everything. Even tomatoes and corn did exceptionally well, though they were hard to grow in this climate. It was a good year for growing pot as well. We harvested just over five pounds, more than we needed to get us through until the next summer.

Everyone who planted pot that year ended up with a bumper crop. Freddy and Skid seemed to get the largest crop, harvesting more than twenty pounds each. They, of course, didn't grow any vegetables, only pot. Even old Ross had a few plants growing in the old pig pen that did real well. It was the first time Ross had grown pot.

I think the McCoby's even grew a few plants that year, though they were paranoid about anyones knowing about it and tried to keep it secret. Apparently, Larry was wandering around the bush in back of McCoby's one day and came across a little patch tucked away in a little clearing. Wayne and Bob both denied that it was theirs, but where the pot was planted, it couldn't have been anyone else's. It probably wouldn't be any big deal, except that these grown men were worried that their sixty-year-old mother would find out about it and scold them or something. Or maybe they thought the cops would fly their spy plane over their place and see the pot and show up at their house and arrest them. It was pretty unrealistic, in any event and got a lot of laughs from the rest of the community. It was understood with the rest of the community that the McCoby's were bush people and not really in touch with the world as it was. They had lived their lives pretty well entirely in Longstock and had little knowledge of the world. Everything frightened them and they were overly careful about everything. They were extremely gutless about most things, with the exception of hunting bears. That was the only thing they did that didn't seem to frighten them, maybe because they felt safe with a gun in their hands.

Chapter 9

Sleigh Bells

It was a few days past Halloween. I was laying around the house, recovering from the Halloween party at the Alaskans place, when I heard something outside. I stepped out on the porch to have a listen and heard voices coming towards the house. There was about a foot of snow on the ground, which seemed to soak up the sounds so that you couldn't hear things until they were really close to you. I listened intently, trying to figure out what I was hearing, when I detected the sound of bells jingling and jangling as they approached the house.

I went back inside and threw on my boots and coat and went out to investigate further. As I stepped off the porch, I could see coming into view a team of horses pulling a sleigh with Ross and Larry riding on it. I recognized Ross's team of black workhorses pulling the sleigh. They looked very handsome in the harness as they trotted along. They were wearing sleigh bells that were hung below their necks from one horse to the other. It was snowing lightly, which caused a spray of snow to follow the sleigh in a swirling motion. Ross was holding the reins as they pulled up beside the house, he reined the horses to a stop.

"Want a ride?" Ross yelled at me from the seat.

"Why not!" I answered. "Be there in a minute!" I said as I ran back into the house to get some warmer clothes on. "It's Ross and Larry with Ross's sleigh, I'm going for a ride," I said to Katy as I headed out the door. I climbed up on the sleigh with Larry and Ross as Katy, Chico and Zac looked out the window and watched us pull away.

"Git-up," Ross commanded the horses, giving a slap on the reins. The sleigh was quiet as it slid over the snow, making but a faint noise as it slipped along. The horses trotted along together, sleigh bells jangling. Larry lit a joint and passed it to me. I'd had horses for several years but this was my first ride on a horse-drawn sleigh.

"Where did you get the sleigh, Ross?" I asked as we traveled along.

"I built it a few years ago," he answered, taking a toke off the joint and passing it back to Larry.

We went back to Ross's place, and turned the sleigh around and headed back to my place.

"Man, I'd like to have a sleigh like this," I said to Ross. "Could you show me how to build one?"

"First, you have to find a curved birch for the runners," he said. "After you find one big enough to make two runners out of, I'll help you build one."

Ross brought me back to my place and let me off. I took a good look at his sleigh before he left. I noticed that it had two sets of runners with a chain in between. The chain was connected to the back of the front set of runners and criss-crossed under the sleigh, connecting the front runners to the rear. It caused the rear set to turn when the front did. Each set of runners was about six feet long, with a couple feet between them, making the sleigh about fourteen feet long, not including the shafts that the horses were hooked to. There was a box on top of the bunks about the size of the box on a pick up truck with a seat big enough for three.

"This style of sleigh is called a bob-sleigh," Ross explained to me as I studied the design.

The summer before, I found an old set of runners from a logging bob sleigh out in the bush near the ruins of an old logging camp. I didn't know what it was at first, but figured that they would come in handy if I ever decided to build a sleigh. Moose and I wrestled them out of the bush and towed them back one at a time with the horses. They were more than nine and a half feet long. The sleigh that they were used on had to be more than twenty feet long and had been used for hauling logs across the iced-up plank roads. Ross had some old pictures of the logging out on the plank roads. One picture was of two teams of horses hooked to a large sleigh that was loaded with logs. I was impressed by the size of the load. It was a huge load, towering over the sleigh and horses pulling it.

The next day I went looking for a curved birch tree to use for the runners and found one on the river bank not too far from Ross's place. I cut the tree and trimmed off a chunk about seven feet long. The tree was almost a foot thick, and it looked like I could get both runners from the one log. I tied the log to a toboggan and pulled it about a half a mile to Ross's place.

"What you think of this one?" I asked Ross. "How wide are the runners?" he asked.

"Four inches."

"Looks like this one should work just fine."

We blocked it up to get it off the ground and nailed some braces on it to hold it steady in order to rip the log into runners four inches wide. The natural curve of the log gave it the sweep needed. The wood was rough on the outside from the chain-saw cuts and needed to be planed and shaped to fit the inside of the runners.

Ross showed up at my place the next day and we loaded the steel runners and hauled them down to his place.

Over the next week I went to Ross's every morning and planed on the runners for hours. It was a slow operation getting the wood to fit tight into the steel runners from the old bob sleigh. We set the runners up on blocks in Ross's kitchen where I worked on them. It took me pretty well the whole week to get the shape I wanted.

We set the steel runners up on blocks outside the door, and every once in a while we packed the birch runners outside and try them in the steel runners to check on the fit., It was a slow process, but each day I got a little closer to making them fit.

When they were fitting tightly onto the steel runners, I cut the excess off the steel with a hacksaw. The steel was a half-inch thick. It took over an hour of steady hacksawing to get them cut off.

The steel runners had large bolts in them that had to go through the wood runners, spacing blocks and bunks to hold it all together. Ross had quite an assortment of hand tools, including long drills and wood bits for drilling the holes. Amazingly, the bolts that had been sitting out in the weather for many years came right off with a little WD-40. After getting the bolts loose, I set the new birch runners on top and drew a circle on the wood from the bolt holes in the steel. After marking them, I brought them in the house again, setting them up on the blocks and drilled them. Once the holes were drilled, I put the new birch runners onto the steel and drove the bolts through the wood.

I cut a couple of fir blocks for each side and a piece of fir four inches wide and six feet long in order to give the runners a top piece to fasten the bunks to. Both the blocks and the top wood had to be hand-planed as well, to get things fitting as closely as possible.

After working every day for a week and a half, it was finally looking like the beginnings of a sleigh. Ross and I set everything up out in the yard and bolted it all together. It took almost another week to get the hardware and wood for the hitch and double-tree in place and the sleigh was ready, except for the box and seat.

I had been keeping my eyes open for some time for horse harnesses and found a pair for sale at a second-hand store on the outskirts of Prince George. Though I wasn't exactly sure how they fit on the horses properly. I threw the harnesses on Daffodil and Rusty. Moose and I rode them over to Ross's. The sleigh was just the runners and bunks when we hooked the horses up in the harnesses. Ross showed us how the harness's fit and hooked up to the sleigh. He then took them for a test ride up and down his driveway. Moose and I walked behind as Ross drove the horses along, stopping a couple of times to adjust the harness.

"She looks good," said Ross. "I think you can take her home." Ross had a way of referring to inanimate objects as 'Her,' as if it were a woman: She's' looking pretty solid, a damn good job! Just get a box on 'her' and some seats to ride on, and you got 'her' beat, eh?

Moose and I rode standing up on the bunks as we took 'her' out on the maiden voyage. It was a smooth ride home, with the sleigh quietly gliding over the snow.

"Wow! This is cool!" Moose said as we glided along.

As we pulled up to the house, we could see Chico, Zac and Katy looking out the window. The boys were really excited at seeing the two horses hooked up to the sleigh. They got their coats and boots on and came running outside. I laid a few boards across the bunks and gave everyone a ride across the field and back. Afterwards I parked the sleigh and unhooked the horses and turned them loose for the day. I rolled a couple of joints for Moose and I and started working on the box and seats. The sleigh was a pretty good size, so we were able to build a fairly large box on it. It ended up being about the size of a pick-up box, with seats that had boards that slipped into slots, rather than being nailed in. They could be easily removed for times when I was hauling firewood or anything else where the seats would be in the way.

We had the box built by the afternoon. It was a full moon that night and the winter full moon was so bright that it was like daylight.

"Come on up after supper and bring Kathy and Trudy with you. We'll all go for a ride!" I said to Moose as he was getting ready to go home.

That evening, right after supper, the whole gang showed up, including Gypsy and Heather for the first sleigh ride in the finished sleigh. The two benches were quite wide, with four people able to fit on each seat. We brought along a few wool blankets to lay across our laps and piled everybody in the sleigh.

"I hope it's not too heavy with all of us in here," Katy was saying seconds before the horses leaned into the harness and the sleigh started to move. They gave a jerk on the sleigh and away we went effortlessly. It was a beautiful, clear night, with the moon shining bright on the white blanket of snow.

I couldn't believe how easy it was for the horses. It was the first time Gypsy and Heather had ever ridden on a horse-drawn sleigh. Everyone was happily chattering and passing joints as we cruised along beneath the full moon.

"What say we take a burn to Ross's and show off our team and sleigh," I said, giving the reins a snap. The horses picked up into a trot as the sleigh slid smoothly and quietly along the road.

We pulled up in front of Ross's place and reined the horses to a halt. Ross and Larry were playing a game of crib inside. We made enough noise between all of us that they both came outside to see what was going on.

"Looks pretty good," Ross said to me as he studied the sleigh and horses. "Good thing I was helping you!" he said with a chuckle.

I tied Daffodil up to the hitching post in front of his place and we all went inside. Ross and Larry both had a hot toddy on the table.

"Who wants a drink?" Ross said, as he lined up a few cups on the counter preparing to make drinks for everyone. "Two, three, four, seven and Larry and I make nine," said Ross as he lined nine cups up and started making drinks.

It seemed like everyone was talking at once as Ross's kitchen bustled with conversation and Ross passed around the drinks.

He made a couple of hot chocolates for the kids and we all sat around the table, some of us on chairs and some on five-gallon buckets.

"Did you hear what happened the other night?" Larry confided in me. Everyone was talking at once, so Larry was just talking to me as several conversations were going on.

"No I don't think I did," I replied.

"Norma and I been talking about her going back to Ketchican for a couple of months to work. When she was getting on the train the other night, Bonnie, an old girlfriend of mine from California, got off the train here the same time Norma got on. They passed each other in the dark and I didn't even know who it was until the train left and Faddus asked her who she was coming to see. When she said, Larry Gaylord, Faddus gave a yell: 'someone looking for you, Larry!' I turned around, as he had already started down the road. He was really surprised to see Bonnie there. He'd written to her a couple of times last summer and she wrote back and said she would like to come for a visit. He really didn't expect her to show up here already. It would have probably been better if Norma were still here, but as she just left for Alaska, Bonnie had him all to herself. After sleeping with her the first night, he told her about Norma."

By this time, most of the people in the room had turned their attention to listening to Larry's story.

"Yeah, she wasn't too happy to hear that I'd been living with Norma, something I never wrote to her about," Larry continued. "She left on the next train. She said she was going back to California. I was totally surprised when Norma got off the next train as Bonnie was getting on. Neither one of them realized it, either."

By this time everyone in the room was listening intently and smiling in anticipation of where the story was going.

"I thought the situation was in hand when Bonnie returned on the very next train and walked in on Norma and me in bed in the woodshed. ÒOh, shit! was my first reaction. It was a real scene, with Bonnie crying and Norma wondering what was going on. We ended up staying up late, with a lot of heavy conversation going on. Norma and Bonnie were like a couple of long-lost friends even though they had just met. We ended up sleeping in the loft together, though neither one of them was impressed with me. To make a long story short, they left together on the next train and I don't think either one of them is coming back. Looks like I'm a bachelor again."

By the end of the story, we were all laughing and cracking

jokes about Larry the 'Casanova.' Though Norma did come back about a month later.

As soon as things died down a bit, we piled back into the sleigh and headed for home. Larry caught a ride with us to the crossroads, from where it was only a short walk home. The moon was still very bright and almost as light as daytime on the white snow as we pulled up to the house.

"That was an awesome sleigh ride," Gypsy remarked as we unloaded at the house. "It reminds me of the Gypsy life, with the horses pulling the sleigh."

"Did the Gypsies use horses and sleighs?" Trudy asked.

"They used horses to pull their Gypsy wagon homes around," he answered.

A couple of days later, I stopped over at Ross's place, hoping to get in a game of crib. As I approached the front door, I heard Ross yelling from the woodshed, "I'm over here!" I stepped into the woodshed and found Ross working on another sleigh.

"What do you think of my cutter?" he said. The runners, bunks, and hitch were all together and he had pieces of plywood cut out for the sleigh box.

"Cutter? How come you're calling it a cutter?" I asked.

"Don't you know what a cutter is?" he answered.

"No," I said.

"A cutter is a one-horse sleigh that is just for people to ride in. This one will carry two or three people."

I helped Ross pull the cutter out in front of the woodshed where he had a pair of pine poles cut and peeled to use for shafts. Paradoxically, a one-horse sleigh needed two shafts, one on either side of the horse, whereas a two-horse sleigh needed only one pole between the two horses.

I helped Ross drill holes to bolt the hardware to the sleigh and put the box together and then painted it. We painted it a bright red. I hung around for much of the day, helping Ross finish the cutter. When we were done we went into the house for some of Ross's moose stew, he referred to as Moose Mulligan, a favorite dish of his. It was late in the afternoon when we had the sleigh put all together. It looked pretty sharp.

"We better get a horse hitched up and give it a test ride, "Ross suggested. "You up for it?"

"I'm game!" I answered. "Let's do it!"

Ross fed the horses at the barn by the river most of the time, but every once in a while he'd feed them at the barn nearer to the house. The horses knew the drill when Ross started whistling and yelling from the top of the hill. At first, they all stopped and stared in our direction and then started towards the house. Before long, it became a stampede of horses and cows, with the cows following behind. Ross threw out a couple of bales of hay before they got there.

Ross had about ten horses and about a dozen cows. Lady, the big Perceron-Morgan cross, was one of the first to get to the hay. Ross got a rope out of the barn and a small bucket of grain; Let's get Lady!" he said as he walked by on the way toward the horses. Ross got a rope on Lady and led her into the yard where the sleigh was.

"You want to get a flake of hay for her?" Ross said to me, motioning towards the barn.

While I was getting the hay, Ross got out the harness and started putting it on Lady. I threw the hay down in front of her after Ross had backed her up to the sleigh. We gave her a few minutes to eat and went in the house to roll a couple of joints and mix up a thermos full of hot toddies.

"Here they are!" Ross said, coming out from the woodshed with a string of bells. He fastened them to the harness, underneath her neck. "There, we're ready to go now," he said, climbing aboard the sleigh. I got in and fired up a joint, Ross snapped the reins and Lady took off down the road. She was an older horse and quite used to the harness. It seemed as though she even liked it.

The sky was dark by now, with a slight remnant of dusk in the Western sky. It was a dark night, with no moon. The only light in the sky was a multitude of stars illuminating the sky. We silently slid over the snow, taking the occasional drink off the thermos and puffing on a joint, the sky suddenly burst into streaks of light. We seemed to have the best seats in the house for the Northern Lights show that night. It was one of the most beautiful displays of the Northern Lights I had seen yet.

We cruised all the roads in Longstock, just happy to be out for a ride in the sleigh and taking in the Northern Lights. We eventually ended up at the Alaskans; pulling the sleigh up in front of the house, we tied Lady to a hitching post in front of the house and knocked on the door.

"Hey, Ross, hey, Louie, what are you guys up to?" Freddy said while opening the door.

"Just out for a ride, trying out my new cutter!" said Ross. "Cutter?" said Freddy.

"Yeah, come have a look," Ross answered, waving his hand, motioning for Freddy to come out and check it out.

"Come on out and look at Ross's cutter," Freddy yelled to Faddus, Kathy, Colleen and Harry, who were inside.

Larry had heard something going on from the woodshed, and came out to the house. "What's going on?" he said, seeing everyone going out to where Lady was tied with the cutter.

"Wow, that's nice, Ross!" Freddy complimented. He really checked it out, walking around with a flashlight, looking at the sleigh intently. "You just build this?"

"Yeah, just finished it today, "Ross replied. "It's the maiden voyage!"

"How much?" Freddy asked.

"How much what?" Ross replied.

"How much do you want for it?"

"You mean to sell it?

"Yeah, that's right! How much will you sell it for?" said Freddy.

"Gee, I don't know, I hadn't thought about it."

"I'll give you a hundred bucks, what do you say?" Freddy said.

"Sold," said Ross and the deal was done.

"Come on in the house and I'll give you the money," he said, motioning to Ross to follow him. "You take it home tonight and I'll be down to your place with Sinbad tomorrow and pick it up."

Freddy gave Ross the money and then led him out to the woodshed to inspect the harness he picked up at one of the second- hand stores in Prince George a few weeks ago. I sat around in the house with Larry, Faddus and Kathy until Freddy and Ross came back in. Ross ran me home in the cutter and then took it back home. The next day, Freddy showed up at my place with Sinbad and his new cutter. "What do you think?" he asked, as we stood around admiring it. Freddy was really proud of his new transportation system and visited several of the neighbors that day, showing off his new sleigh.

Skid had acquired a workhorse named Sally early that fall. He had actually ridden Sally around a bit when he first got her, but found it too uncomfortable because she was so wide. After going with Moose and me on a ride to Penney, he had enough of trying to ride her. Skid had a hard time walking for a couple of days after that, telling us, "I think she spread out my hip bones and knocked them out of whack."

He decided that she was not the riding kind of horse, and only worked her in the harness after that. It was pretty funny watching Skid with Sally. He was on edge all the time when he worked with her; I think it was because he was scared of her. She behaved well when she felt like it. The rest of the time Skid would try to talk her in baby talk to try to get her to do what he wanted.

Skid bought an old sleigh from Chad that he hadn't used for a while. It was a heavily built sleigh that was just starting to get a bit rotten, but which still had a few years left in it. It took Skid a while to find a harness for old Sally and he ended up borrowing one from Ross at first. Watching Skid driving Sally in the sleigh, it wasn't hard to tell that he was awkward and unsure of what he was doing. Sometimes he had to get out of the sleigh and lead her for a bit to get her going, then jumped in the sleigh while it was moving.

Horse-and-sleigh power were on the increase and had outnumbered ski-doo's that winter as a form of transportation in Longstock.

Steve Worthy had come up with a sort of sleigh called the swing- dingle, or swing-a-ling. It had runners in the front with poles that pivoted on the front bunks and dragged along behind, kind of like the travois the Indians used behind horses when moving from place to place. His horse Thunder worked really well in the harness, although riding him was pretty scary.

That winter was like a throwback from the past, as horse- and- sleighs were bustling around Longstock every day. On a trip to the Post Office on mail days, one would encounter one or two sleighs on the way there and back. Sometimes I would harness up the horses to go for mail, especially if Katy and the kids wanted to go and pull up at the Post Office only to find several horses and sleighs lined up outside. On mornings like these, the Post Office was crowded with people hanging around, visiting and talking and generally getting a social fix. It was neat seeing so many horses and sleighs and it kind of made it feel like it was a hundred years ago.

The first winter in Longstock the roads were packed by ski-doos. Everyone traveled on the ski-doo trails, as the snow was so deep it made travel difficult if you weren't on the trails. This winter, the trails were predominantly packed by horse-and-sleighs. This brought a lot of complaints from the ski-dooers, as the horses made the trail pretty bumpy for the ski-doos. Luckily, the horses and sleighs outnumbered the ski-doos this year. Most of the complaints came from the McCoby's. They each had at least one or two ski-doos and rode them everywhere they went. Bob McCoby had a horse, but was not really into riding or sleighing much. I think he was afraid of horses, though he did try to ride his old horse at least once a year for ten minutes or so.

Katy and I decided to throw this years New Years Eve party at our place again. It was the second New Years Eve for us in Longstock and both years we had the party at our place. It was extremely cold for New Years, 1975, with temperatures hitting -50F.

I took the train into McBride the day prior to the party to pick up drinks and food. Catching the Weigh Freight in the morning and the Passenger train back to Longstock the same night. The Passenger train left Mcbride just after ten o'clock that evening. I hung out in the McBride Hotel Bar until the train left along with a few people from several of the communities in the valley taking the train that night. There was a party of Dome Creek people in the bar that I had been hanging out with. I left with them and got on the train heading right for the bar car with the rest of the party.

I met a woman who had just spent a week in Longstock at Skids place. Her name was Barbara and she was living in Dome Creek with my friend Ben. Apparently, Barbara had been thinking about moving in with Skid at Longstock, but after spending a week with Skid she decided not to. I guess Skid was just a little too weird for her. She was not much into dog biscuits either. Ben was on the train that night, too. I had been to his place on several occasions and we had become pretty good friends.

We drank and partied in the bar car for the hour and a half

before the train got in to Dome Creek. The bar car pretty well cleared out when the Dome Creek people got off.

It was about a half an hour later that the train pulled into Longstock and I got off with my Trapper Nelson backpack bulging at the seams with the load of party supplies. The air felt really cold on my face, though I was dressed quite warmly and not feeling too bad from the drinks. The walk home was comfortable, as carrying the backpack kept me warm. It was a nice night, the air was crisp and cold. The Northern Lights were lighting up the sky and made ice crystals in the air sparkle. I could see my breath, even in the half dark, as I walked the twenty minutes it took to get home. The trees were popping and cracking from the cold all the way.

A light shone from inside as I walked up to the house. I walked inside, feeling the heat from the stove. I worked the heavy Trapper Nelson off my back and set it on the floor. After shedding my coat, touque and mitts, I decided to check the temperature. We had a thermometer mounted outside the window that could be read from inside. I turned the flashlight on the thermometer and leaned closer to the window to read it. I thought I was reading it wrong and did a double take. It was reading 50 degrees below zero. I had never seen a thermometer that read -50 before. I had just walked a couple miles from the train and somehow it didn't feel that cold. It was pretty toasty in the house too, but it was definitely 50 below outside. I stoked up the heater stove with birch and went to bed.

The next day was New Years Eve and a fog was laying across the field in layers. Sunshine streaked through the patches of fog. The air was completely still and ice crystals were sparkling in the air reflecting the sunshine. It had a look of extreme cold. It was almost noon before I stuck my head outside. The temperature had warmed up to about 25 below by then, but the air was cold to breathe. It was important to be careful how you breathe in this weather, so as not to fill your lungs with air this cold. People had been known to freeze their lungs from breathing too heavily when temperatures were this cold.

I was thinking about the New Years Eve party that night and wondering if anyone would even brave the cold and show up at the party. Katy and I got things ready anyway, hoping we would have people showing up.

The sun sank behind the mountains to the south about 3:20 that afternoon. Wintertime brought a long, drawn-out dusk, as the sun traveled sideways in the sky just behind the mountains. You could feel the temperature drop quickly once the sun was hidden. It was evident that it was going to be another 50-below night.

Ross was the first sleigh to arrive that night. He had a few people with him, including Bob and Paula Hooty, Larry and Norma and a woman I hadn't met before, named Lana. They all had wool blankets across their laps to help keep warm. Lana had come from Kechikan, Alaska a few weeks before. She moved in with Skid at first, but couldn't hack it for long. "The guy is a weird one!" was the way Lana described her experience with Skid. She crashed out at the Alaskan's place for a while, not wanting to leave Longstock, but not willing to live at Skid's anymore. Ross had shown up with his sleigh at the Alaskan's that evening and after a few drinks, they piled in and headed to my place.

Ross pulled the sleigh up alongside the house and tied the horses. He had packed some hay in the sleigh and threw it down in front of the horses after removing the bits from their mouth.

A few minutes later, Freddy showed up with Sinbad and his new red cutter. He had a full sleigh, with Freddy, Faddus, Kathy and Colleen crammed into the seat and Harry riding in the back, on top of a bale of hay holding on to Faddus's guitar. They all disembarked the cutter and went inside, except Harry and Freddy. Freddy tied Sinbad next to Ross's sleigh and broke out a bottle of tequila. He and Harry had a few snorts before going inside.

I went outside and had a drink with Freddy and Harry, when I heard more sleigh bells coming. A few minutes later, two more sleighs came down the driveway. It was Skid, with his horse Sally in the lead and Steve Worthy with Thunder and the Swing-dingle. Skid had Pierre and Betty and their two kids with him and Steve had Jenise and ELEFG with him. They pulled their sleighs up alongside the others and tied their horses.

We were still outside, talking, a few minutes later when Moose, Kathy, Trudy, Gypsy, and Heather all walked up on us. The party was getting pretty lively by the time we went inside.

The kitchen table and counters were overflowing with food and drinks, people mingled in the living room and kids retreated to the upstairs to play with toys. Everyone was in a good mood and the party got off to a good start.

It wasn't long before Faddus had his guitar broke out and was strumming the favorite, 'What'd I Say?' The party got lively pretty quick as the music echoed through the house. After an hour or so of playing guitars we switched over to tapes. I had a car tape deck hooked up to a twelve-volt battery. It wasn't long before we had cleared the little furniture we had back out of the way and the room was filled with couples dancing.

The house was a mass of energy as everyone got into it, except Skid, who just sat at the table sucking on the tequila bottle. I felt sorry for Skid, he being the socially inept person that he was. He seemed like he was in a continual fog of depression, nobody seemed to pay much attention to him. He seemed to be into getting drunk that night, as he slugged down one drink after another. His glass eye seemed to look off into the distance, totally unaware of the good eye. It looked like they were focusing on two totally different things. The drunker he got, the more the glass eye looked out of place.

The party was really cooking, as the music of Jimi Hendrix, Cream, Traffic, Creedence Clearwater, The Eagles, The Band, and a few other bands filled the house. It was one of the liveliest parties yet in Longstock.

It was about an hour or so from midnight and everyone was up and dancing, when there was a loud knock on the door. It burst open and in came Toad! He had a woman with him, a short, petite woman, a cute little thing with freckles.

"Hi, everyone!" Toad yelled over the music. "Meet my new girlfriend, Annie," he said, mildly slurring his words as he talked.

The music kept playing loudly, a few people stopped dancing long enough to say hello to Annie. I was dancing with Trudy and having a great time as I yelled from the living room, "Howdy!" without stopping. Trudy was dancing in a very sexy way, moving back and forth. She had sexy eyes as she looked at me in the eyes, smiling.

Katy was getting drunk and had turned her attention towards Freddy, dancing with him and hanging on to him. I didn't really mind. I figured that if her eyes were on Freddy that she wouldn't notice Trudy and me getting friendly with each other.

The party went on for about another half hour, as Trudy and I had retreated to the upstairs. She was pretty drunk, and was coming on to me quite heavily. We were in the middle of a passionate kiss upstairs in the darkness of the bedroom, when I heard Toad yelling, "Hey Everybody, let's go for a sleigh ride! It's just over a half an hour 'til New Years. Come on outside!"

"Should we go?" I said to Trudy.

"Let's do it," she said. We got up and stumbled down the stairs. "Hey Louie!" Moose said, "Let's get the sleigh ready!"

"Okay," I answered, looking around for my coat, hat and boots among the masses of coats, hats, and boots that were piled into the corner.

Moose and I headed outside to the barn where the horses were. He caught Rusty and I got Daffodil. We led them over to the house where the sleigh was. As we hooked them up, people started pouring out of the house, hooking up horses and climbing into the sleighs. The temperature was 45 below, but it didn't seem to deter anyone.

Toad was already in his sleigh and turned around, waiting for everyone else. He had himself, Annie, Gypsy, and Heather with him. Ross was the next to turn around and pull up in behind Toad. Larry and Norma, Bob and Paula Hooty, and Lana rode with him. Lana seemed interested in Ross, sitting beside him in the front seat while the others crammed into the back.

Freddy's was the cutter. With him was Katy, Faddus, Kathy and Colleen all crammed into the one seat. Skid got Sally hooked up and pulled out in front of us. He was by himself at first, but when he went by us, Moose and Kathy decided to ride with him. We waved to Skid to stop while Moose and Kathy jumped out and changed sleighs.

We started to go just as Pierre and Betty came out of the house with their kids. I stopped and waited for them to get in with Trudy and me and the two boys. We followed along behind Skid in the procession. We had wool blankets on the seats over us and winter coats and boots. It was quite cozy as we slid along. Steve Worthy trailed the group with the swing-dingle and passengers Jenise and ELEFG.

Trudy brought along a few joints and lit one up. It was a fantastic night, crisp and cold and fresh. The crystals in the air sparkled, reflecting the light from the moon and stars. There was no artificial light anywhere, only the lights from the sky.

We went out of the driveway onto the road heading east toward Longstock. Toad was leading the procession. He led us south at the crossroads towards the river. Sleigh bells jangled and the hardware on the harnesses jingled, people talked and laughed, passing joints and bottles of booze back and forth between sleighs with someone jumping out of the sleigh they were riding in, passing whatever and getting whatever back, then sprinting back to the sleigh he got out of while it was still moving.

The horses traded off between walking and trotting, never getting too far off the pace. Horses, after all, don't generally want to lag behind other horses. We pulled up to the river and

Toad announced, 'It's two minutes to midnight.' We all climbed out and congregated on the river bank, drinks and joints on the ready. Toad counted down the final seconds: "Four, three, two, one, Happy New Year!"

Within a minute or so afterwards, the sky started to streak Northern Lights. We traveled home with the Northern Lights running wild the whole way. I have to say it was one of the most extraordinary New Years I'd ever had.

We went back to my place after the river and continued the party. It was nice to walk into a warm house after the sleigh ride. The next morning, the house was littered with people. I woke up in my bed with Trudy next to me and Katy and Freddy next to her. We all had our clothes on.

A hell of a party!

With the New Years Eve party behind us and the new year stretched out in front of us, cutting fire wood was the first thing on the list. The cold weather had almost emptied the wood supply so that cutting wood was high up on the priority list. The weather had warmed up quite a bit, with night time temperatures getting up to zero Fahrenheit.

Moose, Gypsy and I were going to work together getting fire wood for all of us. It was a couple of days after New Years by the time we got the wood operation started. The sleigh seats were built to come out easily, leaving a big box for hauling wood.

I took a walk through the bush north of the house the day before. The first time out in the woods, I walked through the trees marking the trail where I wanted to take the horses and sleigh. After returning, Moose and I hooked up the team and sleigh and went over the trail I had just walked in order to freeze it up. We went over it a couple of times with the empty sleigh and then headed out towards the tee-pee and Gypsy's cabin and made some trails there too.

I tried to cut some wood every day along the trail. I kept my chain- saw out in the bush and went out to cut some wood every day. I piled the wood in neat piles right beside the trail so that it would be easy to load when it came to hauling it. After cutting wood for about two weeks, I figured I had quite a bit to haul along the trail. Moose came over the next morning and we hooked up the team and set out hauling wood. It was incredible how much wood a team could haul in a day this way. We filled the sleigh right to the top, heaped up and stacked well above the sides. The horses needed a good jerk to get the load going but after that it seemed effortless pulling it to the house. We hauled something like thirteen or fourteen loads that day. The next day I took the sleigh to Moose's place and hauled another dozen loads between Moose and Gypsy. It sure made it easy and fun.

Everyone who used their horses and sleighs found the same thing: it was the easiest and fastest way to get wood.

Steve Worthy had the swing-dingle and was able to haul logs by taking the bunks and rear travois-type runners right off the front bunks. There were holes along the front bunks into which he stuck spikes. He could take birch logs that were short enough to handle and put one end up on the front bunks. The spikes would stick into the logs and hold them there. The more weight forward the better causing the spikes to stick into the logs and hold them while the ends of the logs dragged on the snow.

Unfortunately, Skid didn't wasn't having such an easy time. He was not really that good with horses or much of anything else for that matter. Sally took off on him several times, once spilling the load and and next wrecking the sleigh. You've got to give him credit though, as he always fixed it and tried again.

You might hear the odd ski-doo and once in a while one would pass you on the roads, but it was mostly horses and sleighs around Longstock that winter. It was like a throwback to old times. Life was care free and laid back here with the main thrust trying to live as close to the land and as self-sufficiently as possible, with a lot of time for spontaneous fun.

Horses fit right into the whole ideal, being as back to the land as you can get. They ate for nothing all summer, while still being used for transportation and work. In the winter they become the main method of transportation for people, wood, water and cargo of any kind. Horses also had very distinct personalities and became really good friends.

Longstock was the epitome of the early seventies back to the land movement and the horses played a vital role. People had done this type of thing in many different places during that era, but it was unusual to see a whole community go this way. Oh sure, there were a few people here who were not into it, but they were mostly people who had lived here for a long time and hadn't had enough of the modern rat-race cities that we all came here to get away from. Those people were really not a part of what was going on and seemed to be in a world unto themselves where satellite dishes and power plants and new ski-doos were the important.

The exception was Ross Turner, a man whose whole life was knowing how to do things the old way. In fact, he was like a walking encyclopedia when it came to knowledge about horses or doing things the old way. Ross was an old guy but young at heart and identified with the young hippies. He was indispensable to the success of the Back to the land movement in Longstock.

Chapter 10

Love That Summer

$\mathbf{I}$t was the end of March, and winter was winding to a close. The ice on the river had gotten really thick this past winter and was still frozen solid. Paul Millar's building had been sitting on the river bar across the river for over a year now. He made a deal to sell it to Chad after it was across to the Longstock side.

Ross came out to my place one morning on his old ski-doo. Katy and I were sitting around the kitchen, having coffee, when he showed up.

"Want a coffee?" Katy asked as he walked in the door.

"Sure do," Ross piped up as he sat down. "They're going to

pull that building across the ice today with Jamison T D 20. I'm going down to the river to watch and see if they need any help."

"Maybe I'll go with you," I said.

Ross had another coffee while I went out and hitched up the team and sleigh. Moose showed up at the house just before we were ready to pull out and jumped in with me. Ross took off ahead on his ski-doo while Bruce and I followed in the sleigh.

We pulled the horses out onto the river bar where Jamison's Cat was sitting, idling. He and Carl Jamison were trying to pull a cable across the ice to the building on the other side. The cable was 5/8 thick and was very heavy. They weren't having much success.

Moose and I left the horses reined into the sleigh and plowed through the snow to where the guys were working. It was plain to see that they were not going to pull such a massive hunk of cable by hand, across the ice. It was somewhere around a thousand feet of cable, coiled up in a roll that Jamison had dragged behind the Cat from his place that morning.

"Do you think you can pull it across with your team, Louie?" Ross asked me.

"How's the ice?" was my first question.

"Oh, it's three feet thick, we checked it!" Bud said.

"How did you check it?" I inquired.

"We sawed holes in it with a power saw. The thickest part, we couldn't get through with a 24-inch bar and the thinnest was just under twenty inches," old man Jamison tried to reassure me that it was safe.

"What's all this slush on top? How deep is that stuff?" I asked.

"It's anywhere from six inches to a foot deep, but there's lots of ice underneath. Don't worry, it'll hold your horses, no problem," Bud said, trying to convince me to go for it.

"What do you think, Ross?" I asked, turning towards him. Ross shrugged his shoulders, "looks okay," he said.

"What do you think, Moose?" I turned towards him.

"Let's try it," he answered.

"Okay, we'll give it a try," I said to Jamison as we turned and walked towards the sleigh. "You okay with this Moose, after all, one of these horses is yours." Moose nodded and said, "Let's go for it."

We got in the sleigh and ran it to the edge of the ice where they were standing by the cable. Everyone had their opinion of how we should hook up the one end of the cable and after listening to everyones opinion, we decided to run it right under the sleigh and hook it to the big hook on the front cross member. Old man Jamison, Carl and Ross stayed by the cable to make sure it uncoiled all right as we headed across the ice.

The horses were in slush about a foot deep almost all the way across. The slush got shallow as we got close to the other side. At first, the cable was a piece of cake for the horses to pull, but got increasingly harder as it uncoiled and we were pulling more and more of it. The cable ended up being about a hundred feet too short when we got to the other side; so we stopped the horses for a few minutes while they unhooked it from the Cat and let the end pull out onto the ice. We pulled the cable right up to the building, backing the horses up a couple of feet in order to unhook. We took the sleigh right around the building and headed back across the ice.

I drove the horses right up onto the road where there were trees to tie them to and they were safely out of the way. As I was tying them up Chad came whizzing by on an old ski-doo.

As I walked down to the river, I could see they were pulling the winch line out, hoping to connect to the long cable. They were short by about twenty feet. "I'll back up the Cat onto the ice!" Old man Jamison said. "We should be able to reach it then. Bud, you go over with Ross and get it hooked up to the building."

This was no small building they were dealing with. It was the old cookhouse from Jamison's logging camp, measuring fifty feet long and twenty-four feet wide. It was sitting on log skids and must have been fifteen feet high.

Bud and Ross buzzed across on Ross's ski-doo and got the building hooked up to the cable. Old man Jamison backed the Cat across the bar and onto the ice. I could hear ice cracking and some water squirted up around the Cat. He backed up just enough to get the cable hooked up.

We all stood on the bar, watching, as the Cat inched ahead tightening the cable. It creaked as it tighten just before the building started to move. Slowly, the building moved out onto the ice, piling up snow and slush in front of it. Jamison moved the cat ahead towards the road on top of the river bank. At that point, he ran out of room to pull. He backed down on the river bar again, doubling the cable up and clamping it. This gave him enough room to get the building across and onto the river bar on the Longstock side.

"We did it," yelled Chad, happily, as if he had anything to do with it. The ice was plowed off behind the building, leaving

223

a swath that filled up with water as wide as the building.

Bud unhooked the cable from the building and old Man Jamison pulled the full length of cable up onto the road to deal with later. He then backed the Cat down to the building and hooked it up to the winch. It was amazing how easily it followed the Cat. He pulled it up the road and up the big hill to Chad's place.

That was the last time I had the horses out with the sleigh that year. It was two weeks later that the ice let go. The weather turned sunny and warm and the snow was gone by the middle of April. It had been a very good winter. Katy was pregnant again and due in late August. We bought a few more goats in April and brought them in on the passenger train. I know it sounds funny and not totally legal but the baggage man on the passenger train was a nice guy and would take almost anything on the train as long as you asked him. He looked at me funny when I asked about the goats, but then motioned to load them on.

In the middle of April, after the ice let go, it was safe to put my boat in the river. In the fall I pulled it out and flipped it over, blocking the sides up to prevent damage from the snow load. There was still a little snow left on it when I flipped it back over after sitting all winter! Ross came down to the river with his tractor and helped me slide it into the water. I gave it a couple of pulls and the motor started right up. It was a sunny day so Ross and I took a little ride up river, just to test it out.

The highway department put in a road from highway 16 to the river for access to Longstock. Late in the winter the highways department spread gravel on a series of logging roads while they were still frozen. They also built a landing for us to park our vehicles in, as well as a ramp down to the water. The five mile trip down river was far better than the 16 mile trip up to Penney.

"Better take 'er for a burn," Ross.

"Ya reckon!" he answered. We pushed out into the river and headed downriver.

"Better head upriver!" Ross yelled to me over the sound of the motor.

"Why?" I said, thinking I wanted to go down to the landing.

"Just in case, "he said. "The motor hasn't been run all winter and this is a test run, isn't it? We can always get back if we go upriver."

"Okay!" I said, as I turned the boat around and headed east.

Satisfied that everything was working fine after a few miles, I turned around again and headed downriver to check out the new landing and road.

Moose took off to Northern Saskatchewan to work for several months. I helped out Kathy and Trudy, who were toughing it out in the winter in the tee pee. Kathy had a hard time with it. She took a vacation to Colorado during the winter, though Trudy seemed to be right in her element.

I would have gone for Trudy if my situation were different. Not only was she beautiful and sexy, but she was also a really nice person, happy, friendly and eager to please. Things went from hot to slightly lukewarm and back again with Trudy, though we remained close friends. I liked it that she enjoyed working with me in the garden. Katy even walked up on us more than once and didn't seem to mind a bit. She did not, however, see us getting physical, and never questioned us or brought the subject up. I was pretty young when Katy and I got married and she was pregnant at the time. I don't think we were ever in love, it was a sense of duty rather than anything else, her being pregnant with Chico at the time. It was because of that sense of duty that Trudy and I kept things under control.

Lana had moved in with Ross that winter, after being asked to leave the Alaskans for being hard to get along with and being drunk a lot. She really liked it in Longstock and wanted to stay around. Ross didn't mind the company at first, but with both of them being as stubborn as they were, they got into a lot of arguments.

Norma decided to go back to Ketchikan towards the end of March, after she caught Lana and Larry together in the woodshed. Lana was already living at Ross's by that time. Ross ended up sharing her with Larry. Larry ended up hanging around Ross's, building fences, chicken coops and such, disappearing down to the barn or the river with Lana a couple times a day. It was a strange situation.

Freddy and Skid were both going for it big time with the pot crops after having had such a successful crop the year before. Most of the people growing pot grew for their own use and maybe a bit to sell, like I did. With Freddy and Skid, they were going for the money, growing upwards of twenty pounds each.

Kathy and Moose were still together, but that was starting to look kind of shaky, too.

A few new people moved to Longstock during that spring and summer. One was a big, blonde girl from California. She was actually from Norway, but came to the U.S. when she was very young. Greta Bjorg showed up in Longstock all by herself. She looked at the map and said to herself, "I want to go there!" She was a big, hefty woman that looked like she could out-wrestle most men. She rented the little cabin that we lived in while building the house. It wasn't long before she had shot a couple of bears, skinning them, cutting them up and canning the meat by herself. I was really impressed by this woman that could work like a man. She ran a chainsaw, cutting wood and building things, as if it were second nature to her.

Ben and Daisy were two more newcomers to Longstock. They bought a place that nobody even knew was for sale. It was a hundred sixty-acre parcel that was right on the river. They had a young son, Frank, who was about four or five years old.

I met a couple on the road one day, who were visiting Greta, and were looking for land to buy in Longstock. Johnny and Maria Booth ended up buying eighty acres later that summer, also along the river.

Tony Bergoli bought a one hundred twenty-acre parcel down by Patty's Creek. He had his own boat and showed up one day without anyone knowing he was there. It was a week later, when he went to pick up his mail, before anyone knew he had moved in.

Gypsy and Heather came up one day to let us know that Heather was going to be leaving in the fall. They always planned everything in long-term plans and then carried them out. That's how they got here in the first place.

People came and went just like anywhere else, but the population continued to increase in the summer of seventy-five.

And what a summer it was that year! It was nice weather right from the beginning of spring, right through into the summer, which made it excellent for riding horses. Moose and I rode our horses almost every day that summer. With the extra goats we had now, there was a lot of cream for butter. We found that a ride of about three of four miles, with a couple of gallon jars of cream in the saddle bags, would make butter...a good reason to go for a ride.

The mosquito season was greatly shortened because of the lack of water in the muskegs where they breed. Surprisingly, the gardens flourished with the large amount of sunshine.

I traded some work building a foundation for a newspaper reporter in Prince George, for an 1949 Ford one-ton truck. I needed another truck as the van I drove from Colorado got vandalized at the Penney landing the year before. With the new landing down river, we only had to go five miles. It made going to town much easier. Larry, Steve and I left one morning for McBride to pick up a ton of grain for our animals. We took my riverboat down the river to the new landing where my truck was parked and headed off to McBride. The trip to McBride was slow. The old truck had a top speed of 50 mph and was slower on the hills. We got to McBride and went straight to the farm to get grain. That was the main purpose of the trip, to get a winters supply of animal feed. We put a ton and a half on the truck before it looked like it was loaded. The overload springs were just touching.

After stopping in McBride to pick up a couple of other things we headed for Longstock.

It was even slower now because of our load. The sun was shining and the air was warm as we picked our way through the mountains, up and down the hills. We got about fifty miles from McBride when the truck started handling funny. I decided to pull over, realizing that something was wrong and discovered that we were getting a flat tire on the back. I did have a spare and a jack that was underneath the grain bags.

Steve had been in a bad mood all day, though Larry and I just tried to ignore him. He was bitching about everything. He was a real pain in the ass that day. Changing the tire was just one more thing to complain about. It was going to make us get back late and he didn't like it.

I finally got the tire back on and the lug nuts on and let the truck down off the jack. Steve was standing there with the lug wrench, whining about how long it was taking. I grabbed the jack and went to the back of the truck to put the tire and jack away.

"You want to tighten the lug nuts, Steve?" I yelled. "Yeah, yeah!" he said, as if I were asking too much.

"What an asshole!" I thought, looking over at Larry, who was looking kind of pissed-off. We finally got back in the truck and got going. We had gone about five miles when all of a sudden there was a loud bang. The back of the truck dropped down and the tire shot by my window and was heading down the highway at fifty miles an hour. I managed to get the truck pulled over to the side of the road before it skidded to a stop. Steve apparently hadn't even bothered to tighten the lug nuts. I guess it was too much to ask, though he did manage to throw the lug wrench back in the truck.

We got out to see what the damage was. The brake drum was smashed to smithereens, parts lying all over the highway. We lost sight of the tire that went down the highway and off to the side of the road.

"Oh shit, now we'll never get there!" Steve said, just as a car pulled up to see if we needed any help.

The guy in the car offered to give us a ride to get help.

"You better go, Steve. You can let people know we're not going to make it," Larry blurted out. It didn't make a lot of sense to send him anywhere, but in the heat of the moment, he was in the car and out of there. What a relief!

"Better roll one up," I said as soon as the car pulled away with Steve. We smoked a joint and afterwards unloaded the whole load of grain and made a couch out of the bags on the side of the road. We had a case of beer that we picked up in McBride and rolled a couple more joints. We sat there drinking beer and smoking joints in the hot sun on the side of the road until we both passed out.

We must have slept for a couple of hours in the sun. It was still pretty warm when we woke up. It wasn't ten minutes later that a car stopped.

"What's the problem?" a fellow yelled from inside. "Tire fell off and busted the brakes up," I answered.

"That's easy, if that's all it is," he said. He pulled his car over to the side of the road and jumped out and popped his trunk.

"I'm going to look for the tire!" Larry yelled back at me and headed up the road in the direction it went.

We had already had the truck jacked up and the brake line pinched before Larry got back with the tire. Tightening up the last of the lug nuts, I threw the wrench back in the truck and we started loading the grain. The passer-by helped us get the truck loaded and we all had a beer and a joint when we were done.

"My name's Ken, by the way. Why don't you guys come stay at my place tonight?" he offered. "I'm just a few miles down the highway at Dome Creek."

By that time, it was getting late in the day. Larry and I looked at each other; "What the hell!" I said.

"Okay with me!" Larry answered. We jumped in the truck and followed Ken to Dome Creek. We parked the truck near the railroad bridge that crossed the Fraser River. Ken didn't actually live at Dome Creek, but across the river. We walked across the railroad bridge which was the only way across. That side of the river was called Bend because of a long bend in the river and in the tracks.

As we walked across the tracks, we could see a big house downriver from the bridge where Ken lived. We followed the trail that went along the river bank to the house. Ken walked in ahead of us, "I found some Longstockians on the road," he said. There were quite a few people in the house, as there seemed to be a party going on.

"Hi, Louie!" said a voice from the crowd of people there. I recognized several people from seeing them on the train over the last few years. It was big Ben who recognized me and pushing his way through the crowd. "Good to see you!" said Ben, extending his hand, shaking hands with me. "What are you doing here?"

"We had a breakdown on the highway on the way back from McBride this afternoon. Ken came by and gave us a hand and invited us to stay here for the night."

We stuck around for the party and slept in one of the spare rooms upstairs, though it was the wee hours of the morning before we crashed.

It was a beautiful morning the next day, the sun broke through without a cloud anywhere. I got up and went downstairs to the kitchen. Larry was already up and having a coffee with Ben.

"Coffee?" Ben asked, as he stood over a couple of cups with the coffee pot.

"Oh yeah!" I said, as he started pouring.

I sat down at the table and Ben sparked up a joint and passed it around the table. Within minutes, the whole house started waking up. It wasn't long before the kitchen was crowded with people talking, laughing, drinking coffee and smoking pot.

Both Dome Creek and Bend was populated mostly by hippies and just like Longstock there were a few draft evaders as well. There were some people that had migrated from the States, but many were from Prince George. Some of them went to school together in Prince George and had been friends for a long time. Ben was a kind of community leader and had gotten a grant for some community work that summer in Dome Creek. It created several jobs fixing up the school, playground, post office and the community hall.

He owned the property and the big house in Bend. Along with Ben, there were five or six other people living there while working on the community project. I originally met Ben on the train, like many others that lived up and down the valley. He was a big Dutch fellow, about six foot-two, and two hundred fifty pounds. His house-slippers were a large pair of wooden clogs. I slipped them on once to go out in the yard to take a leak. They were like wearing a couple of boats on my feet and clumsy to walk in.

While we sat around talking and drinking coffee, Ben asked if any of us in Longstock played softball.

Both Larry and I played a lot of baseball as kids, having grown up in the States, where it was popular.

"We want to challenge Longstock to a softball game," Ben said.

"You're on," said Larry quickly taking up the challenge. "When and where?"

"How about two weeks? Can you get a team together in two weeks?" Ben asked.

"You bet!" said Larry, looking over at me. I gave him the thumbs up and the challenge was on. We would bring a team to Dome Creek and play on their baseball diamond. The baseball field in Longstock was not very good, full of pot holes and on a slant from the infield to the outfield, it was pretty pathetic.

We took off for Longstock at about ten-thirty that morning, getting to the river just before noon. We loaded the whole load into the boat and took off against the current for the five miles upriver to get to Longstock. The boat was loaded pretty close to its capacity. It was a slow ride.

A couple weeks later, we crossed the river with the Longstock softball team heading for Dome Creek. There were mostly Americans on our team, though we did have Canadians: Wayne McCoby, Ross and Pierre with us. Including myself, Moose, Larry, Freddy, Harry, Faddus and the Norwegian woman, Greta, rounded out our team. Katy, the boys, Kathy, Trudy and Skid came along too. That way, if we needed any substitute players, we'd have them.

The baseball field in Dome Creek was in Ken Hookers hayfield. He mowed the hay a few days prior to the game. Ben had bases all in place which were made out of feed bags. A backstop was built for the big day.

There was so much beer being drank and pot being smoked that day, that it's a wonder we did as well as we did. Fortunately for us, the Dome Creek team was already loaded when we got there. We smoked them three games in a row, with scores of 10 to 0, 16 to 4 and 12 to 11. They were ahead of us 11 to 2 in the last game and were feeling pretty cocky, until we scored ten runs in the bottom of the seventh to take the game.

After the third defeat, they had enough and were happy to drink, smoke and party after that.

The game with Dome Creek started something and we got a challenge from Penney the following week to play them at home. Clarence Boudreau was the organizer of the Penney team, which we played four or five times that summer. He had a few friends who played mens softball in a Prince George league and were really good players. One fellow was a pitcher who could throw blazing fastballs. We were no match for the Penney team in the first game, as they trounced us 14 to 0.

It took me until the second game to be able to time my swings enough to hit off of this guy. Finally, in the second game, I was getting around on his pitches, reaching base all but my first time at bat. Harry seemed to get his rhythm and tagged a couple of pitches for extra base hits. We did better in the second game, still losing 10 to 8.

In the third game, they changed pitchers. This time, they had an older fellow who didn't throw that fast but had a lot of stuff on the ball. He would throw slower, lobbing-type pitches that curved and dropped and sometimes moved all over the place, as if he were throwing knuckle balls or something. The first half of the game, we were hopeless. The knuckle-ball pitch made us miss so badly that it looked like we'd never batted before.

We had a team huddle before batting in the fifth inning. "What do we have to do to hit this guy?" Larry said.

"I think it might help if everyone were to hold their stance when he releases the ball, instead of reacting immediately!" I interjected. "Wait until you pick up the ball as it's coming off its arch. Hold back, and then step into it!"

It sounded like a good plan, and the results were a bit better, but we still lost the game, this time 10 to 9.

We ended up going to Dome Creek once more that summer for softball games and to Penney two more times. One of the Penney games was a beer-ball game. The rules were that every time you reached first base, you had to drink a beer. Even if you had a hit that would go for extra bases, you had to stop and guzzle a beer before you could go to the next base. Fortunately, the team on the field was not in great shape, either, having just batted and drank a bunch of beer, too. There were a lot of errors in the field, causing the runners to be able to guzzle their beer and still be able to get to the next base before the fielders stopped throwing the ball away. The games lasted much longer than usual and by the end of a couple of games of beer-ball, everybody on both teams was shit-faced. We only played beer-ball that one time.

It was a long ride back to Longstock after the game of beer-ball. The best hitters seemed to end up being the drunkest.

Some crossed the river at Penney and drove their vehicles to the Longstock landing, boating in from there. I brought a crowd with me on the river and went back the same way.

It was a beautiful morning around the end of June when I got a visit from Bob and Wayne McCoby. I was the only one home at the time. Katy and the boys were visiting Betty and Pierre.

"Morning, Louie! How you doing this morning?" said Bob, as I answered the door. I was wondering what these guys wanted, having never had them drop by for a visit before.

I invited them in for a coffee. We sat around the table making small talk for a few minutes before I asked, "What brings you guys around this morning?"

"We want to talk to you about going through here to build a road to the lake," Bob said. Toneka Lake was about a mile west of our place.

"Why do you want to have a road through here?" I asked. "I thought there was already a road to the lake." There were old plank roads all over the place out that way, including one to the lake.

"We'd like to go this way 'cause then we don't have to go through the creek draw." Bob said.

"Yeah, but there's already a road. Why don't you just go that way?" I said." I'm not really into your having a road right by our place, especially seeing as how there's already a road."

Bob started to get a belligerent tone in his voice. I guess it was because I didn't just cave in to it like he wanted me to. "I've lived around here all of my life doing what I wanted until you fucking Americans come up here and tell me what to do!" he said.

236

"Now wait a minute, Bob! I bought and paid for this place and it belongs to me and not you. If you wanted to do anything you want here, you should have bought it. It was for sale a long time before I bought it!"

By this time, the conversation was getting heated up. "We want to put it on the strip of crown land next to you, anyway! Why should you give a shit?" he said.

"I give a shit because it runs right past my door, that's why," I answered.

"Well, it ain't your fucking land!" Wayne put in his two cents. "It ain't your fucking land, either!" I said.

"Oh yeah? I've lived around here all my life and that makes it more mine than yours!" Bob said.

"Go fuck yourself, Bob!" I said. "Fuck you, too!" he said.

"I think it's high time you two get the hell out of here!"

"I don't give a shit what you say! The forest service said we could build the road and we'll be showing up here with a cat on Friday morning and building the road! If you don't like it, it's too fucking bad!" Wayne said.

"Get the fuck out of here before you piss me off!" I said, even though I was already pissed.

They left, only pausing to yell a few threats back at me while walking away. I was fuming! They had a lot of nerve and who the hell did they think they were?

I took a walk out to Moose's tee-pee to talk to him about it. He was livid. "No way!" was his reaction. We walked over to Gypsy's place and told him what the McCoby's were threatening to do.

"I'll cut their fucking hearts out!" Gypsy snarled. "Just let them try it! Those little fucks try messing with us and it'll take a team of doctors to put their faces back together."

"I think we should go in and see the forest service and find out what they told those assholes," I said, thinking we might be able to squash the whole thing right there before we had to kick some ass.

Gypsy was very upset and had gone into a ferocious verbal assault on the McCoby's. We decided it might be better if Moose and I went. Katy and the boys were still gone when I got back to the house, so I left her a note telling her what we were doing. Moose and I headed for the river and Prince George.

It was a tense ride into Prince George, just thinking about the whole situation. We drove directly to the foresty office. Bob Richards was somebody I knew quite well, having worked on a few fires with him in the past.

"I'd like to talk to Bob Richards," I said to the receptionist at the front desk. He appeared at the front desk a couple of minutes later.

"Hi, Bob! How are you doing today?" I asked. "I'm doing fine. How can I help you? he said.

"We have a problem. It looks as though someone in your office gave Bob McCoby permission to push a road to Toneka Lake right by my house. I have a problem with that. Especially seeing as there is already an old road there," I said.

"Yeah, I did give Bob the okay on clearing the road, but there was no mention of any road by your place. Let's go into my office and look at it on a map," he said.

He had a large map of the area hanging on the wall in his office. I pointed out where the old road was and where they wanted to push the new road.

"I never told them that they could push any new road. It was my impression that they were going to open up the old one," he said.

"Well, they threatened to show up with a Cat at my gate tomorrow morning and start building the road right by my place, whether we liked it or not."

"They can't do that. I'll get in touch with them and let them know that they will have to shut it down for now until the situation gets straightened out. I'll phone them right now," he said. We sat in his office while he made the phone call. After hanging up the phone, Bob looked up at Moose and me and said, "Okay guys, rest assured, nobodys going to build a road by your house."

We left the forestry office in pretty good spirits and headed for home.

"I think I'll go up and talk to them before going home!" I told Moose after we crossed the river. I drove the power wagon up to McCobys and pulled up in front of the house. Jonas was working in the yard, splitting wood when we drove up.

"Hey, Jonas, is Bob around?" I asked in a friendly manner. "Yeah, he is," he answered, turning towards the house and yelling for him.

Moose and I stayed on the road in front of the house while we waited for Bob to come out.

Bob came out of the house and leaned across the fence between their yard and the road.

"We just came from the forestry office and it looks like you won't be building any roads by our place anytime soon,

239

that is, unless you want to take it to court," I said.

"Yeah," he said, "you guys will be going to court, too, for the scam you pulled with Moose working under your name. I'm turning you in, asshole!"

I looked over at Moose and then turned back to Bob. I was really pissed off at this point: "You want to come out here on the road and say that?"

"Why, so you and Moose can jump me?" he said.

"No, Moose won't lay a hand on you Bob, just me. I want to knock your fucking teeth down your throat, you chicken-shit, little asshole! Come on out here, that is unless you're too much of a chicken-shit!" I was pissed.

"Fuck you!" he said. I started walking towards him with my fists clenched.

"Come out here and say that to me if you think you're so fucking brave!" I said.

"Get the hell out of here!" he said.

"Come out here!" I invited him out again. To my surprise and delight, he opened the gate and walked out on the road towards me. He apparently thought he was going to talk me out of being pissed off and had no intention of getting into it with me. I saw things quite differently and figured the fight was on.

As he approached me, I took a swing at him. My fist went whizzing by his head, just missing him. It apparently scared the crap out of him when he realized he was about to get his clock cleaned right there in front of his house.

"Holy shit, you're serious!" he said as he ran back into his yard, hoping I wasn't going to follow him.

Then out comes old lady McCoby, yelling at me, "Why

are you coming up here making trouble, Louie?"

"It's your sons that are making the trouble," I said. "They came out to my place telling me their going to push a road right past my door to the lake and if I don't like it, it's too bad. Well, I don't like it and if anyone thinks they're going to do it, they're going to be paying the dentist a visit!"

She looked a bit confused, like she didn't know anything about it, turning to Bob and asked, "is that right, Bob?"

"Well, yeah," he said.

"And now you're not going to do it? she asked. "No, he's not!" I interrupted.

"Okay, Louie, you have the last word and then go home. It doesn't look like there's going to be a road," she said.

"Okay, here's my last word: There ain't going to be a road and if you ever threaten me again, I'm going to kick your ass all the way to the river and back again! I can guarantee you, you'll have a really bad day!"

Bob stood at the fence and said nothing. Old lady McCoby went back inside the house and Moose and I got in the power wagon and went home and smoked a joint.

This was the first time I'd had any problems like this with my neighbors in Longstock; it created a tension that lasted for several months.

Aside from the problems with the McCoby's about the road, Longstock was a nice place to be that summer. It was a really nice summer, very warm and lots of sunshine. Gardens grew and pot patches prospered. I had a couple of plants by the chicken coop, that were more than eight feet high by the beginning of August.

241

Both Freddy and Skid were looking at bumper pot crops.

Ross got a new hay baler just before the hay was ready to cut. It looked as if the old hay loader that he had used for so many years was getting retired. He had a lot of help that summer, with a lot of people looking for hay for their horses. Moose and I went to Ross's to help with the haying just about every day for almost a month. Larry was usually there too. He and Lana would sneak off to the barn any chance they got, usually when Ross was mowing or raking hay.

Between Moose and I, we needed about four hundred bales to feed all our animals through the winter. Every day, we hauled a load of hay when we went home, loading it into the barn in the morning just before going down to Ross's. Ross put up over three thousand bales from his forty acres of hay. It was hard to tell how this year compared to other years because it was the first year that he had the baler. But it's safe to say that it was a very good year and all the hay was in the barn, something that does not happen every year.

Pierre had an good old-fashioned barn-raising that summer. He and Betty invited everybody in Longstock. Pierre built the foundations and the floor and had all the lumber on site before calling the barn raising. I think everyone in Longstock showed up for it and a thirty by seventy-foot barn took a total of two days to put up. All the guys worked on building the barn, while the women cooked a colossal amount of food. Each night after it was too dark to work, everybody feasted and partied well into the night. At the end of the second day, the barn was looking good. The walls were framed and sheeted and the roof was on except for the tar paper. During the following week Pierre managed to get the tar paper on.

One day, Trudy stopped over at the house, looking for me. I had been working in the garden that morning when she walked up on me. I had been digging a few potatoes for breakfast when I looked up and saw her standing at the edge of the garden. She had a very worried look on her face, as if something were bothering her.

"Hi, Trudy, what you up to?" I asked.

"I want to talk to you, Louie, I got kind of a problem," she answered.

I stopped what I was doing and walked towards her. "What's going on?" I asked.

She was looking really upset and couldn't seem to find the words to tell me what was wrong. I could tell there was something bothering her. I looked into her eyes, then put my arms around her and gave her a hug. Trudy held onto me tight for some time, without saying a word.

"What's wrong?" I said.

Slowly she started to talk: "Well, ah. I'm gonna... I mean- Freddy asked me to marry him. I said that I would."

"Freddy asked you to marry him?" I repeated, not sure if I was hearing her right.

"Yeah! He never got legal status here in Canada and asked me to marry him so that he could get legal," she said.

"Is that the only reason? I mean, are you two involved with each other?" I asked.

"Well, not really. I mean, not any more than I'm involved with you. We slept together only once, but you know, he is a friend and I feel like I should help him out so he can stay in

243

the country," she answered.

"So what are you going to do?" I asked.

"That's the trouble, I don't know what I should do," she said. I could see her eyes getting teary. It was obvious that it was really bothering her.

"You already told him yes, eh?" I said.

"I did and I'm not feeling to sure about it now," she said.

"I don't know what to tell you, Trudy," I said, looking into her eyes.

"I know, I've got to figure it out myself," she started to cry.

"Let's go for a walk," I suggested.

"Okay," she said. We walked out the driveway and turned east on the old road. I had my arm around her as she leaned against me, not saying anything for a while. We walked out the old road to the lake that McCoby's had ended up opening up with a Cat. We walked along, hardly speaking as we went. There was an old trapper's cabin about a half a mile through the bush from where the road reached the lake. We walked along the lake shore until we came upon the cabin. It was just a one-room cabin with birch bark on the roof and only one window. People sometimes used it while fishing at the lake. It had a couple of beds with mattresses and sleeping bags and a stock of food that people left after staying there.

It was hot outside, but the cabin was cool. Trudy and I went inside and sat on the bed. I had a bag of pot and some papers with me. I rolled a joint. We sat there and smoked the joint, while not saying very much. It was obvious that the whole scene was weighing on Trudy very much.

We ended up staying there for most of the day. I think she

felt that it might be our last chance to be together and it was. About four in the afternoon, we headed back to the house.

The question of getting married to Freddy still did not sit right with Trudy, but she felt like she had to help him out and was going to go through with it right up until the day they were supposed to get hitched.

Trudy disappeared the next morning, catching the weigh freight with all of her things. It was six months later that I got a letter from her. She was in Ontario. She just couldn't go through with it and felt really guilty about going back on her word with Freddy. She felt like she couldn't face him and had to take off.

The time at the lake was the last time I ever saw Trudy.

One morning, about the second week of August, there was a message on the radio from some friends of ours from Denver. Barbara and Grizz were traveling to the west coast and decided to detour north to visit us. They lived in the house next door from us in Denver and Grizz worked on my construction crew.

Grizz was a big man, about six foot-three, and two hundred sixty pounds. I guess you could say that he was a fat guy. That's how he looked at himself and was proud of it. He once told me, when I remarked that working on our crew, he was likely to lose some weight, "Hell no, I'm gonna stay this fat if I have to go home after work and drink a pint of whipping cream every night."

He was quite the comic as well, and kept the crew in stitches often. He often bragged about things that only a fat guy would brag about.

"If you want to know how to do things the easy way, you should always watch the fat guy." According to Grizz, "If fat people did things the hard way, they wouldn't be so fat."

They were a comical looking couple, Grizz being the size he was, and Barbara who was very thin and as tall as Grizz. She reminded me of Popeye's Olive Oyl and kind of moved like her, too. They were two of our best friends from Denver, good-natured, funny people.

I hadn't heard from them at all since we moved to Longstock, until now. Katy and I picked them up from the train station that morning. Katy and Grizz were really good friends in Denver and she was anxious to see him. Moose and Kathy stayed with the boys while we drove up to meet the train.

"Wow, look at this place!" Grizz remarked as he stepped off the train. "Louie, Katy, how the hell are you? Holy mackerel," he said, patting her pregnant belly. "And when is the baby due?"

"Two weeks," she said. "How long are you staying?"

"About two weeks," he answered. "Maybe we'll be here for the birth! Will you have it at home?"

"Of course," Katy said confidently.

"Grizz, Barbara, it's good to see you," Katy said, while giving Grizz a big hug. "Now there's a bear hug," Katy said, after Grizz turned her loose. Grizz was a really talkative fellow, where as Barbara was a very quiet person. He talked about what they had been doing over the last few years, since we had last seen them, while Barbara hardly said a word.

"I quit form-setting shortly after you left Denver," he said. "It just wasn't the same, working for anyone else. I've been an apprentice to a shoemaker for the last couple of years in Durango, Colorado. Old Max the shoemaker has been ready to retire and was looking for someone to take over for him.

I met him in a bar in Durango and we hit it off real well. To make a long story shorter, I went to the shop the next day and we moved to Durango a week later. Been there for almost two years now." Grizz left his truck in Prince George not knowing about the road across the river. After he realized that he could park just across the river he decided that he would go back to Prince George and get his truck. He caught the weigh freight the next day and I picked him up with the boat in the afternoon.

Grizz seemed to be impressed by every thing saying "Wow, this is cool!" as we motored up the river"

"Is there any fish around here?" he asked. "Sure is. Do you want to go fishing?" I asked. "Oh yeah!" he answered enthusiastically.

"Let's go today!" I said. "There's nothing else doing today."

"Yeah, man, that's sounds great!" he answered. We drove the power wagon back to the house and gathered up a few worms and fishing poles then headed back down to the river. Driscol Creek was about four miles up the river. I had been there several times before and always caught fish. I thought it would be a good place to take Grizz.

"Let's catch some fish!" Grizz said, as we were pulling into the creek. I motored up the creek about thirty yards or so and ran the boat up on the mud flat. Grizz had his line baited and in the water right away. I was still getting the gear out of the boat when Grizz already had one on. He was fishing in the clear water of the creek. I walked past him and cast out into the murky river water, right where it meets the clear water from the creek. Fish like to hide in the murk, watching for food coming down the creek.

"I got one!" I yelled, as a fish hit my hook bringing in a nice rainbow trout.

"I'm moving over there!" Grizz said, as I was bringing the fish in. It wasn't long before he was yelling, "I got one!" and reeling in one of his own, too. It didn't take long before we had a string of fish, seven Dolly Varden and a couple of Rainbow Trout. They must have weighed at least twenty pounds altogether.

After a while, maybe a couple of hours, we decided we had caught enough fish and headed for home.

"Barbara, look at these fish!" Grizz yelled out as we got out of the truck at the house. "Barbara, look, fish!" he said, running to the house with the string of fish hanging from a willow branch.

"Holy!" Barbara said as she was coming out the door.

"It was awesome! I mean, it was wicked! Look!!" Grizz couldn't contain his excitement. "Come on! Oh! I know!! Let's cook them up! Man, this is far out! We got fish!"

"I like to cook them over a fire, Grizz," I said to him.

"Oh yeah, man! We got to cook them over a fire!" he said.

We built a fire outside in our fire pit getting it going really well and then let the fire die down. I had a couple of large grates that I cooked the fish on, laying the fish out on one grate, then wiring the other one on top. This way, you could prop the fish up next to the fire and turn them over and around with ease. After they had cooked for about an hour, I put some green Alder on the fire to make it smoke. I then laid the fish right on top of the Alder, right in the smoke for another half hour, or until the Alder caught fire and was getting too hot.

"Ah man, this is good!" Grizz said, as he gobbled a fish down. Barbara nodded her head in approval at Grizz from across the table.

It was great having Grizz and Barbara around for those two weeks. They were interested in everything and had a funny and happy demeanor about them regarding anything we did.

Both Grizz and Barbara were hoping they would be here when Katy had the baby. Neither one of them had ever been present for a birth before. They had timed their visit so that they would likely be here for this birth. Every day, Grizz would question Katy about how she was feeling and whether this was the day or not.

"Have you ever done the needle test to find out if it'll be a boy or girl?" Barbara asked one day. "A girlfriend of mine showed me it."

She got a needle and thread out of her pack and showed us how to work it: "First, you rub the needle across your wrist, right over the veins below your palm," she explained to us. "Then you hold the thread, and let the needle dangle over the vein. The needle will propel itself over the vein, either around in a circle, if it's a girl, or back and forth if it's a boy. It will reveal what sex your kids will be and how many you will have. When the needle doesn't move at all, it means that there won't be any more kids."

Katy and I both tried it and got the same results: the needle went back and forth the first two times and then around in a circle. On the fourth try, the needle stopped for her, but when I did it, it went back and forth one more time before stopping on the next try.

We both showed a girl for the third child, which convinced

us that this baby was going to be a girl. "I knew it!" Katy remarked after the needle test. "I felt like this baby was going to be a girl for a while, now and this confirms it." She had been picking up baby clothes for a few months and had collected a couple of baby dresses.

Now she was convinced that it would be a girl.

Like all parents, we started thinking of names for the baby, completely disregarding any boys names. Katy couldn't have been more convinced that this baby was going to be a girl.

Grizz and Barbara planned on leaving back to Colorado towards the end of August when, one day towards the end of their visit, Katy announced that she thought she was in labor. We were sitting around, having coffee in the morning, when Katy came downstairs and told us that her water had broken early that morning.

"Your water broke?" Grizz asked enthusiastically. "Does that?... You mean that you could, Oh shit! The baby's ready to!" Grizz tried to make sense, but he couldn't seem to get a whole thought out coherently, he was so excited.

"Yes, I'm having the baby soon," Katy said.

"What do we do?" Grizz said, looking very concerned. "Should we boil some water or something?"

"It's okay Grizz, we've been though this before and it's just a matter of waiting, now."

Katy started having light contractions right away. She moved upstairs to the bedroom as they started to get more intense. Grizz, Barbara, and I hung out upstairs with Katy while she went through one contraction after another.

Grizz was obviously concerned, asking Katy every five

minutes if it was time. He couldn't exactly sit still and went downstairs every few minutes to decompress, appearing back in the bedroom with more questions every so often.

Barbara sat on the bed with Katy holding her hand as each contraction waved through her. I sat on the other side of the bed holding her other hand and encouraging her to do her breathing.

It was about three in the afternoon, after she had been in labor for several hours, when the contractions started to get heavy. About a half an hour later it was apparent that the baby was coming any minute.

Grizz stood in the corner and was too taken by the whole ordeal to speak. He was a nervous wreck. The whole situation was pretty intense for him. "Holy shit!" was all he could say as he watched the baby being born. "Holy shit!" he repeated, as the baby slid out of the birth canal and into my waiting hands.

I lost track of everything for a minute or so, as I attended the baby. Within a minute or so, he was crying and breathing very well, as I laid him on Katy's belly.

"It's a boy!" I said. I couldn't help but start laughing. "It's a boy," I said over and over again.

"A boy!" Katy repeated. She was so totally shocked, having been so sure that it would be a girl. We all started laughing. Tears were streaming down Katy's face. I don't know if they were tears of joy or tears of disappointment, but we had a new son and he was healthy and had all his fingers and toes, even though he had no name.

Both Grizz and Barbara were in awe from the experience, as I cut the cord and clamped it, tying it off with dental floss.

A few minutes later, we could hear someone at the door

shouting "Hello!"

"Come on in!" I yelled. It was Moose and Kathy.

"What's going on? Did Katy have the baby? Moose yelled from the door.

"Yeah, it's a boy!" I answered. "Come on upstairs."

They both hurried upstairs to see the baby. The room was getting a bit crowded. Everyone pressed in to take their turn.

Grizz slipped out of the room and went downstairs. A few minutes later, I went downstairs to get Katy a drink of water and Grizz was lying spread eagle on the floor in the living room.

"You all right, Grizz?" I asked.

"Wow!" he said, "That was the most,- I mean I'd never, - What a, a baby, I couldn't, I can't even, - holy shit!" He couldn't seem to get out a complete thought about it, and mumbled half-sentences and words, trying to explain the way he felt without success. "Oh wow!" he said, looking up at me from the floor.

"I think I understand," I said, looking him in the eyes. Grizz had a glazed look in his eyes, looking mesmerized and totally blown away. He tried to talk, but nothing would come out. He sighed and looked up at me. I gave him the thumbs up and went back upstairs.

"Boy, that sure blew Grizz away. He's downstairs lying on the floor and totally out of it," I said as I walked into the bedroom.

"Is he all right?" Barbara asked.

"Oh yeah, he'll be okay, he's just in a state of shock," I answered.

Barbara went downstairs anyway to check on Grizz.

Katy should have been out of it, too, after the birth, but

was quite excited, talking to everyone and showing off the baby boy who had no name yet.

And so, the second baby was born in Longstock. This time, the birth was in our house instead of the goat-shed and there were lots of people around. It was a really happy day.

It was about five days later that we finally decided on a name. We named the baby, Chamuel.

Grizz and Barbara had stretched their time to the limit and now that the baby was born it was time for them to go. They left the day after the birth.

I took them across the river to their car that morning. Grizz confessed to me when we said goodbye that, "That was the most far-out experience of my life."

I was really sad to see them go and it choked up a little as they pulled away.

In early September, and the season was starting to change. The nights were a little cooler and the daytime sun seemed to lose some heat. It was a terrific summer for gardening and looked like it was going to be the best harvest so far. Even the tomatoes and peppers in the greenhouse produced a bumper crop. Katy was busy canning tomatoes, jams and jellys, putting up dozens of jars for the winter. We had been eating potatoes and carrots for a month and the fall crop looked like it would bear us quite an abundance to put in the root cellar.

A couple of days after Grizz and Barbara left Heather and Gypsy stopped over the house for a visit.

"Heather's going to leave tomorrow," Gypsy told us as they arrived. "We thought we would get a visit in with you guys before she goes."

"Where are you going?" Katy asked.

"I'm going to the Queen Charlotte Islands," she answered. "You know someone there?" Katy asked.

"Yeah, a girlfriend of mine lives there," she said.

They stayed for dinner and hung around until quite late. I played guitar and Gypsy sang songs, making up words as he went. Many of these songs were in Romany Gypsy, including a lot of wailing and mournful sounds. This went on for hours, only stopping long enough to take a toke off of a joint or a slug of wine.

We were all pretty blasted by the end of the night, when Gypsy and Heather decided to leave. After giving Gypsy a hand shake and a hug, I turned to Heather and gave her a hug and to my complete surprise, she laid a big kiss on me. It was not just a ordinary goodbye kiss by any means.

The next morning, Heather showed up at the house by herself carrying a backpack with all of her things. I was going to Prince George that day and Heather wanted to catch a ride with me. After coffee and saying goodbye to Katy and the boys, we left for the river in the power wagon. The sun was shining, burning off patches of fog that hung low on the water, as we boated down the river to the landing where my pickup was parked. I packed Heather's backpack up the riverbank to the truck and loaded it in the back. Ross, Steve and Larry had gotten to the landing just ahead of us and were just warming up Steve's truck when we got there.

We smoked a joint and talked for a few minutes. They pulled away ahead of us as my truck was warming up. I was just about to get in the truck, when Heather grabbed me and gave me another kiss. It was another juicy kiss, and this time, she kept kissing me. I was taken by surprise again, but remembering last night's goodbye kiss, I kissed her back.

It didn't stop there, as things became more intense: she started making noises like she was getting really excited. I had a canopy on the pickup and a foam mattress in the back. It wasn't long before we were in the back of the truck. She was very excited and sexy, grabbing me and being very aggressive. It was like an animal frenzy, as she grabbed and kissed me, first on the lips, and then moving down on me. "Man, what a little fireball!" I thought as she frantically kissed and grabbed me all over.

It's a good thing that nobody was there at the landing but us, as Heather made a lot of noise, moaning and shrieking, while we made love. She was completely shaved. I had never made love to a woman that was shaved like this before. It was extremely sexy. I thought It's too bad she's leaving.

The sun was shining into the canopy and heating it up, as we lay there in each other's arms.

"I guess we'd better get going," I said to her after lying there for a while.

"Not yet," she said, as she started kissing me again, and it started all over again. What a sexy woman, with a big appetite for sex! I had never met a woman like her. We made love again. She moaned and shrieked continuously the whole time.

After a while we got it together to head off to Prince George. Heather sat close to me on the ride into town. "You must have known that I was attracted to you for some time now Louie"

"No, I didn't know. Matter of fact I had no idea." "Why

255

don't you come with me to the Island?"

"How can I do that? Katy just had a baby. I can't leave."

"I'll take care of you. You won't have to work or anything. I have enough money to take care of both of us."

It was tempting but I couldn't walk away from Katy and the kids.

Heather cuddled up to me all the way into town. "So where are we going?" I asked.

"The Simon Fraser Inn. I'm supposed to meet my girlfriend there."

We pulled into the Simon Fraser parking lot. I got Heather's pack out of the truck and carried it in for her. It seemed like an extremely heavy pack and wondered how she could even lift it.

We went to the front desk and Heather asked what room her friend was staying in. We took the elevator up to the third floor and found the room. Heather knocked on the door.

"Heather.... it's been a long time," Susan said as they hugged each other. "Come on in." She turned toward me and asked, "Who's your friend?"

Heather introduced us and Susan gave me a hug. We sat down at the table and Susan lit up a joint. We passed it around as the girls caught up on old times. Heather got up from her chair and standing behind me put her arms around my shoulder from behind caressing my chest. She then kissed me passionately on the lips. Next thing I knew I could feel Susan tugging at my zipper and my pants. I offered little resistance as Heather continued to kiss me. The two girls moved me over to the bed with Heater still kissing me Susan took off her clothes and continued to undress me. Next thing I knew Susan was kissing me and Heather was getting undressed.

I ended up staying there for several hours, while the two of them had their way with me. Between the two of them, I was definitely overpowered... not that I would have resisted much anyway.

It was early in the afternoon before I left the room and got busy, doing my business in town.

"Come on back after you're done," Susan said. "We're going to stay here tonight and you're welcome to stay here with us if you want to. "I'll see how the day goes, but it sounds like an inviting offer!" I told them as I was leaving. It was early afternoon before I got out of there and got started on my list of things to do. I couldn't stop thinking about Heather and Susan waiting for me at the hotel. I didn't waste any time getting my business done, picking up groceries, gas and some things from Northern Hardware.

I went back and forth in my mind as to whether I should go home or go back to the room where the girls were waiting. It was a hard one to resist and I finally decided to give in and go back to the room.

It was about five o'clock in the afternoon when I knocked on the door at the hotel where Heather and Susan were staying.

"Come on in!" Heather said as she greeted me at the door. She and Sue were completely naked and smoking a joint. "Both of us took some acid about twenty minutes ago," Heather said. "Do you want some?"

"Sure!" I replied, having taken lots of acid in the past. I liked it a lot and thought it would be lots of fun with a couple of horny women.

257

Sue handed me a tablet; Take on of these," she said. I took the acid from her and popped it in my mouth and then took a hit off of the joint. The girls didn't waste any time pawing at me and getting my clothes off, pushing me down on the bed.

Heather climbed on top of me and started kissing me passionately. I was really turned on and kissed her back the same way. As we were making out, I felt something around my wrist, but was too involved with Heather to pay much attention.

Before I realized what was happening, my hands were tied with leather ties. The two girls wrestled with me until they had my hands tied behind my back. I was starting to feel the effects of the acid about this time and offered even less resistance. They tied my hands tightly behind my back so that I could not move them. I was powerless to do anything about it as they tied my feet together and tied them to my hands behind my back. I guess you would say I was completely hog tied and unable to move.

The acid was starting to come on pretty well by this time. The girls were getting off really well, too. With me tied up, they started fondling each other while I watched helplessly. I was really turned on watching them and feeling the effects from the acid.

They worked their way into a sixty-nine position next to me on the bed. I was trying to watch what they were doing, but the acid rushes kept on coming on and I had a hard time paying attention. I closed my eyes and the colors kept flashing in my mind. After a while, I started to forget where I was, as I got lost in the colors and hallucinations going on in my head.

I could hear the girls turning each other on as I lay there on the bed. I turned toward them and watched as Susan brought

Heather to a climax. They lay there for a minute and then it was Heathers turn on Susan.

Heather and Sue were still lying on the bed next to me, both tripping intensely. They were alternating between having sex with me and having sex with each other, with periods of time where we all just lay there in a state of bliss while we were all peaking on the acid.

After a while, Heather untied me. I sat up on the bed and experienced an intense acid rush that made me flop back down.

"It's my turn now, Louie!" Heather said to me and handed me a fistful of ties.

I was so stoned that I wasn't sure what she she was talking about. "Here, I'll help you," Sue said, as she took a tie from me and pushed Heather down on the bed. We both crawled on top of Heather and started tying her up. I was really stoned and it took a couple of tries before I could actually tie a knot.

She looked incredibly gorgeous, spread out on the bed, her smooth and completely hairless body. I was very turned on as I sat there looking at her.

Just then, Sue started kissing me on the lips. I got lost in her kisses, closing my eyes as the colors were flashing in my brain. I don't know how long she kissed me, it seemed like a long time. We were soon in a sixty-nine position on the bed, next to Heather. I reached my hand over and started touching Heather.

We both turned our attention towards Heather for a while and then decided that it was Susan's turn. It was a fantastic night of sex and drugs, ending up with the three of us falling asleep together and waking up the next morning.

In the morning I said goodbye and headed home to

Longstock. Heather asked me again before I left if I wanted to go with her. It was very tempting but I decided to go home. Heather and Sue checked out of the hotel that morning heading for the Queen Charlotte Islands.

On the way home, I was reflecting on my night of sex and drugs with Heather and Susan. Sex with Katy was nowhere near as fun or exciting. Sure, we had three kids, and I felt like I was committed to the family, which I was, but sex was like a reward that Katy dished out when she felt like it. Sometimes long periods would go by when she didn't feel like it. I was a young, horny guy and couldn't really help myself when beautiful women came on to me. If the opportunity arose, rarely did I pass up a chance to go to bed with a woman. It was a time of free love and lots of open relationships and not unusual for men or women to spread themselves around.

Katy could have been getting a bit on the side for all I knew. I kind of doubt it though, or at least since she got involved with the Elizabeth Lighthouse cult. Ever since then, oral sex was out, or anything other than the missionary position was too. Sex had rigid boundaries as far as she was concerned. In contrast to what I had just gone through with the girls it was a sparse and boring sex life that I had with Katy.

Chapter 11

Changes

I woke up one morning and looked out the window. It had frosted hard the night before and the ground was covered with a blanket of frost. A few light frosts during the week before had turned the leaves to reds, oranges and browns. They were like that for a week or so previous, but now the hard frost would make them start falling pretty fast. There was a cold wind blowing that morning and the air was thick with leaves fluttering to the ground. In a week or so, the trees would all be bare.

It had been a good year for gardening. We had the root cellar full of potatoes, carrots, beets, turnips and cabbage. Katy had made up dozens of jars of jams and jellies that stocked the shelves both in the root cellar and the cabin cabinets. Upstairs, a large crock was brewing a batch of sauerkraut. Another batch was already canned and packed away in the root cellar.

All in all, we had put up a sizable amount of food for the winter. We were not completely self-sufficient as far as food was concerned, but it was close. Between the vegetable garden, chickens, goats, hunting, and fishing, we were producing much of our own food. It was a good feeling to have nearly everything that made it to the table, day after day, produced on the land.

The boys were growing fast. Chico was already four years old, Zac was two and Chamuel was going on three months by the time the first snow started to fly.

I had a pretty good pot crop that fall. A cab driver from Prince George bought my whole crop. He would drive out to the landing every Sunday and I would meet him there with a couple pounds. It worked out pretty well, as he paid me cash every week and I was able to sell my whole crop to him over a couple of months.

Skid and Freddy took their crop to the States to sell. Skid went to Washington and Freddy took his crop to Alaska. They always returned with enough cash to make it through the year.

It was late November that year when the weather got cold enough for the ice to run on the river. The temperature dropped down to twenty below zero for a couple of nights in a row before the ice jammed up. Word spread around town that we would meet at the river to build the ice bridge the day after.

It was a cold morning, the sun was hanging low in the winter sky when Moose and I headed to the river to work on the ice bridge. The McCoby's brought their water pump and a bunch of fire hose. We were already there when they arrived.

I chopped a hole in the ice close to the shore and the McCoby's set the water pump up nearby. Soon more people arrived and a crew started cutting willows to mark the ice bridge. It was a town affair each year, a social event that everyone came to, even if it was only to watch.

The river was full of jagged pieces of ice, sticking up through about a foot of snow. It looked like the moon. We had to blow the snow off the ice with water pressure in order for the cold air to freeze the ice solid. We then chop holes in the ice and stuck willows in to mark the crossing.

Wayne McCoby got the pump set up and I worked the fire hose, blowing the snow off and exposing the ice. Many places, the ice was not frozen very much. The deep snow on top had actually insulated the ice from the cold. The ice was jammed all right and had lots of jagged pieces sticking up, but in between the ice jags it was not frozen...not enough to hold a person. I had to be really careful to avoid falling through the ice.

Ross brought me a thick piece of willow to carry with me, to stop me from going through if the ice broke. I shuffled across the ice with the willow in one hand and the fire hose in the other, blowing off snow about ten feet wide as I went. Moose was the only other person going out onto the ice. He was dragging a bunch of willow sticks with him and sticking them through the ice. He packed snow around the willows to keep them in place.

I slowly crept across the ice, careful to step on the thick pieces of ice as I fanned the fire hose back and forth. I was working along, not realizing how far out onto the ice I had gone. Over the sound of the water blasting out of the hose I thought I heard people yelling. I looked back across the ice. People were yelling and waving their hands at me. The fire hose snaked across the cleared-off ice and a few willows were sticking through the ice. Last time I looked, Moose had been working on the willows but he wasn't there now.

Wayne shut the pump off and the water stopped. I could just make out what people were saying.

"Moose fell through the ice!" I heard someone yelling.

"Holy shit!" I said to myself. I started shuffling back across the ice as fast as I could, being careful that I didn't go in too.

The top of the ice was covered with water, so that I couldn't tell where he fell through right away. My eyes searched the ice for Moose, all the while I was being careful about where I stepped.

Finally I saw him. He had managed to grab onto the fire hose. It was the only reason that he didn't get pulled under the ice by the current. The pump was shut off now, and the hose had gone limp and was starting to pull under the ice with him.

"I found him!" I yelled back towards shore. I had a hold of the fire hose as I shuffled around, trying to get some solid footing on one of the solid chunks of ice.

Moose was struggling to get his head above water as the current kept pulling him under. I grabbed the fire hose and pulled on it bringing Moose to the surface. When the ice broke, it opened a hole about five feet around. It was full of small pieces of ice that were floating on the surface.

"Come on Moose," I mumbled as I pulled on the hose. His head popped out of the icy water as he frantically tried to pull himself out. The ice kept breaking when he put weight on it. Every time the ice broke, Moose would slide back and go under again.

"Flatten yourself out!" I screamed, "don't try to climb out, let me pull you!"

Moose looked terrified as I pulled on the fire hose, trying to get him out. I could see that he was beginning to lose it. His grasp on the hose was starting to slip. I pulled hard on the hose and he came close enough to me for me to get a hand on him. I grabbed him by the coat and pulled, sliding him out of the hole and onto the ice. He tried to pull himself up, but the ice was too thin and broke again and in he went again.

"Lay flat, lay flat!" I yelled as I slid him back onto the ice again. He was just about to pass out as I got him back up on the ice. I grabbed his coat with two hands and pulled on him. This time I got him out and onto the ice. Water poured off of him and he was shaking profusely.

"Can you get up?" I said, looking him right in the eyes. He just moaned at me. His eyes didn't seem to focus.

I realized he was in pretty bad shape by this time. I wrapped the fire hose around him and yelled to the others waiting on shore, "pull the hose, I got him tied on."

Several people grabbed the hose and started to pull. I walked carefully along and helped him as they dragged him towards shore.

When we got to shore, Ross brought the team and sleigh down to the ice and was waiting for us. Moose was in pretty bad shape and couldn't move on his own at that point. We picked him up and put him into the sleigh, throwing a few coats over him. I jumped in the sleigh as Ross snapped the reins at the horses and they took off for his place.

Moose was starting to come around as we pulled up to Ross's house. We helped him out of the sleigh and into the house. Ross always kept his house very warm and today was no exception. He had stoked the fire before he left and it was hot inside. Moose peeled off all his wet clothes and sat next to the stove.

"Here, drink this!" Ross said, handing Moose a hot rum. "It'll help warm you up!"

It wasn't long afterwards, we were all sitting around having a game of crib. Aside from ending up with a righteous cold,

Moose was all right.

The McCoby's decided to leave the ice bridge overnight to freeze up and rolled up the hoses and took the pump home to thaw out. It was still twenty below and was going to get colder, so the ice would be in better shape the next morning, especially where the snow was blown off.

It was three or four hours later, when Moose was finally warmed up enough to go home.

Moose was living alone at the tee-pee now. Kathy had left in the fall, shortly after Heather did. She and Moose had been on the rocks for a couple months prior to her leaving.

"I just can't take the guy any more," she confided to Katy after she made the decision to leave. Moose had tried to talk her into staying, until one morning they had a terrible fight. In his rage, Moose told her to, "Get the hell out!" if she wanted to leave. That was it for them, as Kathy left on the next train.

He stayed at our place that night and went out to warm up the tee-pee the next morning.

The experience definitely traumatized Moose. Within a couple of days he took off for the States. Skid was down in Washington selling his pot and Moose went down to find him. There was a commune in Tonasket, Washington, that Skid was hanging out at while he did his business. The people there were into the Native American Religion practices including sweat lodge and peyote ceremonies. There were a few Indian people that lived there who directed the sweat and peyote meetings for the rest, who were mostly white hippies.

Moose met a beautiful, red-headed woman named Dolly there. He and Dolly really hit it off. She had been living on a commune in southern Oregon for the last few years and had just come to Tonasket to attend a peyote meeting. Moose told her all about Longstock and got her interested in coming back with him.

I got a letter from Moose just after New Year's, asking me if I could come to Washington to pick him and Dolly up and bring them back to Longstock. He wanted me to drive them to Oregon, where Dolly lived and pick up her stuff and then bring them north.

I was not terribly busy at that time and thought a break from Longstock would be fun.

It was around the middle of January when I left for Washington. It was pretty cold the day I left. I seemed to leave the winter behind as I drove south towards the coast. I had an old 1964 Ford pickup truck with a canopy on the back.

I followed the map Moose sent me, driving right to the commune a couple of days later. There were a group of makeshift buildings scattered around the eighty acres on the commune. The ceremonial sweat lodge was situated in the middle of the other buildings and seemed to have a lot of activity around it when I arrived.

Everyone I met there was very friendly. I walked around looking for Moose or Skid. I asked a couple of people if they knew where they were and was directed to the sweat lodge.

I walked up to the sweat lodge just as the group of people that were sweating were filing out, taking a break from the heat. Moose and Skid were among them.

"Hey, Louie!" Moose said as he offered his hand.

I shook hands with him and Skid came over and shook

my hand, too. It was always kind of weird talking to Skid, as one eye would look at you and the other glass eye seemed to be looking at something else behind you.

"I want you to meet Dolly," Moose said, as she stepped forward. "Glad to meet you," she said." I've heard a lot about you."

"I was afraid of that," I joked. She was a short woman with flaming, red hair and a friendly smile. She was standing in front of me, stark naked as everyone who was in the sweat lodge was. Wow! I thought to myself as I looked at her. She had a terrific figure and big firm boobs that were covered with freckles and a beautiful freckled face.

"Do you want to join the sweat?" Moose asked. "You can get in on the next round."

'What the hell!' I thought. "Sure, I'll give it a try," I answered.

Within a few minutes, people started piling back into the sweat lodge. I took off my clothes and piled them under a tree where other piles of clothes were and got in line to file in. It was dark inside. At first I couldn't see anything. After a while, my eyes started to adjust and the faint light coming from the door allowed me to see a little. The floor was covered with cedar boughs around the outside. There was a pit in the middle, where the hot lava rocks were placed.

After everyone was inside, one of the Indian men passed hot rocks in through the door, using a pitchfork to pass them to another man who received them with a couple of deer antlers. The rocks were glowing red. You could feel the heat from them as they went by.

After the rocks were inside a man closed the canvass door

making it pitch dark inside. A man named uncle Billy led the chants and prayers when the door was closed. He thanked 'Grandfather' for the air, water, the land, life and several other sacred things of this world. He repeated 'Grandfather' many times and each time the whole group would chant 'Grandfather.'

This prayer alternated with chanting and singing and then back to the prayer to Grandfather. The air was hot and heavy and my breathing became laborious as someone poured water on the hot rocks every few minutes. The steam seem to get hotter each time. I tried getting my head closer to the ground to avoid the heat on my nostrils.

This round in the sweat lasted about forty-five minutes. I was barely able to endure it to the end. I felt extremely hot everywhere, except my feet. Breathing the hot steam heated me up from the inside. I was sweating profusely from every pore, but I guess that was the point of the sweat.

The door finally opened, and people poured out of the sweat. The opened door let in a stream of cooler air as I waited in line to exit. When I got outside, people were pouring buckets of cool water over themselves or each other.

"Shall I?" Dolly asked me, as she stood there with a bucket of water.

"Oh yes, please do!" I answered, feeling about a thousand degrees fahrenheit after exiting the sweat. Dolly lifted the bucket and poured it on me. I gasped as the cool water hit me but boy did it feel good for a minute. I poured a bucket of cold water over Dolly as well. It was hard not to get turned on as I watched the water run down her body across her breasts. I seemed to heat up again right away. I got Dolly to pour another bucket over me. The second bucket seemed to cool me down considerably. People were all around me doing the same thing, as everyone mingled outside the sweat lodge.

There was a fire still going and two men were passing rocks from inside the sweat lodge where they were piled back onto the fire. There was about a ten-minute break between rounds, before people started going back inside. I didn't know if I should go back inside or not, given the struggle I had trying to breath with the extreme heat last time.

Moose, Skid and Dolly were filing back inside with the rest for another round as I watched.

"Hi, I'm Moonbeam!" a young woman said to me as I stood there. "What's your name?"

"I'm Louie," I smiled as I answered back.

"Are you going back in for another round?" she asked.

"Gee, I don't know if I should. It was pretty darn hot in there?" I said. "I don't know if I can handle another round or not."

"Sure you can!" she said to me, and grabbed my hand, leading me towards the door. She was a tall woman with long, dark hair and long legs. She looked very athletic, with average sized-breasts and a long, lean figure. Her muscles were well defined, especially on her stomach. She had dark, brown eyes and high cheekbones that were punctuated by a continuous smile on her face.

She held onto my hand and led me back in the sweat lodge. I probably wouldn't have gone back in if it hadn't been for her.

The second round was much the same as the first, with Uncle Billy saying prayers to The Grandfather, sometimes calling him the Great Spirit. Moonbeam sat with me, holding my hand and putting her arms around me at times all through the second round. It was actually the third round for everyone else, as I had started on the second round.

Each round of the sweat was supposed to hotter than the last and I could sure feel the difference. It was unbearably hot to me. Again I tried getting my head closer to the ground to try to breathe air that didn't burn my nostrils. It was all I could stand. I leaned on Moonbeam, as that was the only way I could move to get my head closer to the ground because of how crowded the sweat lodge was. I went into kind of a daze from the heat, but remained acutely aware of this naked woman pressing against me.

"Now that wasn't so bad, was it?" she asked as the door to the sweat lodge opened.

I could feel the cooler air coming from the door as the line of people moved slowly towards the door. Wow, does that feel good!" I said as I crouched through the door and out into the sunshine.

Moonbeam led me to the water buckets and poured one over my head. It was quite a rush, but felt good as the cool water poured over my incredibly hot body. I gave a shiver from the cold water and cool air for an instant, but heated up again right away after the water ran off.

"Would you like me to pour a bucket over you?" I asked her. "Oh yes, please do," she said.

I grabbed a bucket and lifted it up, pouring water over her head. She let out a gasp as the water ran down her body. I poured some of the water over myself, then the rest of the

271

bucket over her. It was not what you'd call a hot day outside, but it felt that way standing out in the sunshine.

There had been quite a crowd in the sweat and everyone was milling around outside by the water buckets. Soon, people started filing back in for the fourth round. Moonbeam grabbed my hand and led me back in.

I admit I was a little reluctant to go back in. The heat was excruciating on the last round and I didn't know if I could handle it again.

Moonbeam led me by the hand, offering encouragement by telling me "you'll be fine," and gently pulling me along. Before I had much chance to protest she was leading me through the door. We moved around the circle until we were situated towards the back of the sweat, the farthest from the door.

After everyone was in, the hot rocks were passed in, and the door shut. This was the hottest round, without a doubt. Our spot in the back of the sweat was nearly unbearable. I tried to get my head as close to the ground as I could, once the hot steam started burning my nostrils. Moonbeam seemed to handle the heat quite well compared to me.

I was so happy to see the canvas door open up at the end, even though we were two of the last people to get out. I felt like I had taken acid or something by the time we got out. We went straight for the buckets of water and took turns pouring them over each other. I was with it enough to appreciate how beautiful Moonbeam looked, both pouring the water over me and getting it poured on her. The water ran down her naked body, making her skin shimmer in the sunlight.

"How did you like the sweat?" Moose said, as he and

Dolly approached us.

"It was all right, though I thought I might not live through it at one point," I said.

"I see you've met Moonbeam," Dolly said to me.

"Oh yes, he has!" Moonbeam said, as she pressed her body up against me. "Let's go to the tee-pee and smoke a joint!"

The four of us grabbed our clothes and walked down a path through the trees. We came upon several tee-pees lined up in a row. Moonbeam led me into one of the tee-pees. The floor was mostly dirt, with a few beds on the outside wall, and some blankets and pieces of carpet circling a fire pit in the middle.

Moonbeam sat down cross legged on one of the beds and pulled out a leather stash bag and started rolling a joint. Moose and Dolly came in and sat down on the bed next to Moonbeam and I.

We passed the joint around as we talked and laughed, all the while sitting in the nude. After a while, Moose and Dolly got up to leave and I was going to leave with them until Moonbeam whispered in my ear, "stay here with me Louie, I want you to make love to me."

'Holy crap' I thought to myself. 'Am I in heaven or what.'

Moose and Dolly put their clothes on and left. They were not out the door ten seconds before Moonbeam was all over me. She was a really lively woman, swarming me with kisses. We made love passionately before she totally exhausted me. The heat from the sweat made me feel tired, as we both fell asleep, waking up a couple hours later. There were two other couples hanging out in the tee-pee when we awoke.

Aside from getting up to have something to eat, we stayed

in bed the rest of the day and through the night. She was lots of fun.

The next day Moose, Dolly, and I took off for Oregon to get Dolly's stuff. Skid was going to Oregon as well, but the truck was full with the three of us and Skid decided to hitch hike and meet us there. We drove out to I-5 and headed south. Skid got a ride out to the interstate with Uncle Billy and hitched from there.

It started to rain quite heavily before we got to Portland. As we crossed the bridge over the Columbia River, it was raining cats and dogs when we passed a hitch-hiker on the side of the highway. It was Skid. He had gotten to Portland ahead of us and was out there in the pouring rain. The traffic was too heavy to pull over right there, so I drove to the next exit and got off the freeway, turned around and went back over the bridge, got off again and turned around again, back over the bridge again and picked him up. It was a little crowded in the cab of the truck, but we squeezed him in.

It was another three hours drive to Roseburg and another half- hour to Dillard, where Dolly's cabin was. Dolly had built a small, frame cabin with a little help from friends, on government land. Unfortunately, the lands people found out about it and she had to move it or tear it down. The whole idea of moving the cabin seemed a little too much for her, so she had made arrangements for a friend to buy the cabin and move it. It was kind of hard to just walk away from it and was quite emotional for her to load up all her stuff and leave.

We stayed around a couple of days, filling the back of the pickup, then headed north to Longstock. Skid stayed in Oregon with his brother for a month or so and did not return with us.

We stopped in Tonasket on our way back and spent the night there. Moonbeam was there to greet me. I spent another night with her before leaving again in the morning. She pressed me to tell her all about Longstock and probably would have come with us, except that I told her about Katy and the kids. We both decided that it probably wasn't a very good idea and said goodbye.

When we got to the river at Longstock, there was a vehicle track across the ice. Old man Jamison had gotten a contract for plowing the roads in Longstock that winter. We were able to drive across the ice, almost to the house.

Moose and I got the sleigh hooked up, loaded Dolly's stuff and hauled it to the tee-pee. It was quite a shock to Dolly, having been used to the mild Oregon winters, to find herself in a cold northern climate, although she was really impressed by the sleigh ride.

Moose had the tee-pee fixed up to handle the weather and it was not too bad during a normal winter. The wood stove he had set up would keep the place warm in most weather, except for those days when the temperature dropped way below zero. It was pretty chilly on those mornings, even with the fire going full blast.

Moose banked the tee-pee up with snow about four feet deep when the cold temperatures hit. That made quite a difference making the tee-pee quite bearable.

Gypsy had a new girlfriend, too. She had moved in with Gypsy while we were in Oregon. Carol and Gypsy had met a couple of months earlier and had hit it off really well. She was a tree planter during the summer and usually took the winters off.

She was happy to have another woman living close by. Dolly and her became good friends.

Katy had made contact with a religious group while we were still in Colorado. The called themselves The Universal Lighthouse. They had been sending her literature for several years about their organization. They were headed by a husband and wife, Mark and Clara Summit, who believed that Gods spoke through them - not just Jesus or the Father, but angels and saints as well. I thought the whole scene was a bunch of malarkey, having gone to their church in Colorado Springs a couple of times.

Katy got more involved with them as time went on. As part of an everyday ritual, she would do a prayer chant at the kitchen sink while doing the dishes. It was the weirdest thing, because the chant had a drone to it, so that you couldn't tell what she was saying. It was all a blur of sound.

I usually left the house when she was doing her chanting. She was forever reading material that they sent to her and started feeling more and more like she needed them in her life. Frankly, it was very annoying, having to listen to her garbling up the house everyday with her incessant chanting. Somehow it made her feel like she was better than anyone else and she didn't hide it. The whole thing put a real strain on our relationship.

Mark Summit had passed away the year before and it was widely reported by The Universal Lighthouse that Mark had risen from the dead and ascended into heaven like Jesus and was now sitting on the left hand of God. Clara Summit had likened herself to the Virgin Mary. Clara had moved the Church to Pasadena, California, taking over the Pasadena City College

Campus. They were now teaching classes on their religion in hopes of increasing their membership. They sent Katy a lot of information about the classes they were offering. The classes were mostly concerned with what you should know to become a good Lighthouse Member.

She wanted to attend their university in Pasadena the following summer. She wanted to take the kids along because they had a preschool there they could attend. I had a pretty good year growing pot and had a bit of money saved and thought it would be a good excuse to get rid of her for a while. I agreed to pay her way.

The semester lasted for three months, starting the first week of April and ending at the end of June. She was going to leave the last week of March and stop in Fresno at her parents place. It would take her about a week on the train to get there.

The snow fell quite heavily that winter and by the middle of March it was very apparent that it was still along way from spring. I took Katy and the kids to the train station in Prince George on March 25th and put her on the train to California.

Shortly after she got there, I got a letter from her. It was a really weird letter. It sounded like it was from someone else. She said she was going to stay with the Lighthouse people and that I should sell the farm and give the money to them. She wrote about how the world would be coming to an end and that they were the only ones who would be saved. It was the same old holier than thou drivel that many cults and religions preach to shame people into joining them and giving everything they own to them.

I didn't buy it and I wasn't giving anyone the land.

I was worried about the kids. What the hell was going on with the kids if she was so far off the deep end?

Chapter 12

Trouble Brewing

Spring was a bit late in coming, due to the large amount of snow we had the winter before. The daytime temperatures were getting up in the 70s by the end of April, but there was just so much snow, the ground took a long time to show.

I was alone on the farm for the last month, since Katy and the boys went to Pasadena. I received another letter from her that sounded worse than the first one. It seemed like her mind had been taken over by The Universal Lighthouse people. She didn't seem to make any sense in her letters. She was still insisting that we should sell the farm and join up with them. It was the only way we could be saved when the world came to an end. I know it sounds crazy, but she actually believed it. According to her, we could not stay together if I couldn't see her way of thinking, which was actually The Universal Lighthouse way of thinking. If you ask me, I think she and they were completely off their rockers.

It would be another couple of months before her classes were over and I thought I'd go to Pasadena and try to talk some sense into her at that point. In the meantime, I could get the garden planted, a pot crop planted and all the goats and horses secured in the summer pasture, which would make it possible for me to leave for a while.

Moose and Dolly made it through the winter in the tee-pee, but were making plans to leave for the summer months and go to Tonasket. The Native American Church was becoming a bigger part of their life at this point. Skid was down in Washington until the beginning of May. He came back to get a pot crop planted. Freddy never came back that spring. Larry had taken over his pot gardens.

I had a few patches of pot in the bush. It was always the first thing I planted every year. I had put in a modest number of plants, hoping to pick up a few dollars off of it and have a supply for myself, enough to last the year.

It was early May, and I had been working on the garden when Larry showed up for a visit. I took a break and went in the house with him for a coffee.

"I got a couple hundred extra pot plants I'm looking for a place to plant," Larry said, taking a sip of coffee.

"Gee, Larry, I've got all my patches planted already. I don't know where I'd put them," I answered.

"Hey, what about Moose's garden? he said. "He's gone to Washington. He won't be planting anything there, will he?"

"No, I guess he won't," I said.

"I've already got plants all over the place. All the gardens are full and I got right around a hundred plants in buckets scattered around my place," he said.

Larry had been living alone on the land for a couple months. Faddus and Kathy had gone back to Alaska, Freddy was in Washington and Harry had taken a job in California. Lana still came by for a roll in the hay, but less frequently now, since she and Ross got married when she found out she was pregnant.

"How many plants do you have out now?" I asked.

"Somewhere around three hundred, I think," he said. "And how many plants do you have extra?"

"There's about a hundred and fifty or so," he said.

We took a walk out to the tee-pee area and had a look at Moose's garden. It had been planted the year before, and looked like it would be easy to work up.

"Man, this looks like a benevolent site to plant a garden!" Larry said. "You got a roto-tiller, don't you?"

I bought a small roto-tiller the year before at a second hand store. It was one of those front-mounted tillers - not a great piece of machinery, but it did the job.

"We could walk it out here this morning and get the ground ready today," Larry said.

I wasn't sure about just taking over Moose's garden like that, but Larry was really into it. "Aw, come on, Moose ain't gonna mind!" he said, trying to sound convincing.

We went back to the house and had another cup of coffee and a joint. After a while, I reluctantly agreed to go along with it. We walked the roto-tiller out to the tee-pee and roto-tilled the garden up. When we were done, Larry took off back to his place. He showed up an hour or so later with a wheelbarrow filled with plants. He wheeled the plants out to the garden. We found an old compost pile that Moose had piled up and we spread that on the garden. By early afternoon, the garden was planted with a hundred and fifty plants. The garden looked good with the little plants lined up in neat rows. We sat on a log and smoked a joint when it was all done, admiring our work. We agreed to split the crop when we harvested it in the fall.

I saw Larry pretty regularly during the summer as he stopped by to keep tabs on the plants.

I got another letter from Katy around the end of May. She sounded like she was even more messed up than before. She kept on giving me these ultimatums if we were to stay together. Now, I not only would have to give the property to the Lighthouse people, but I would have to quit growing and smoking pot, too. She considered it to be evil. It didn't seem to matter that it was pot money that had sent her to Pasadena to begin with. Maybe - the pot was evil, but the pot money wasn't! It was all too crazy for me to comprehend.

How did I manage to end up with someone like this, I thought to myself. I was ready to get rid of her at this point, but my main concern was for the boys. I couldn't just let them stay in the care of a woman that was obviously deranged without doing something about it.

I made up my mind that I had to go to Pasadena and see if I could somehow rescue them from this situation. Larry agreed to look after my place while I was gone. I took off hitch-hiking the last week of May, and got to Pasadena four days later. It was quite the culture shock, coming from the northern Canadian bush to the sprawling urban environment of southern California.

The last ride I got was with a woman hauling horses to the race track in Pasadena. She took me right to the Pasadena City College Campus where Katy lived. I asked a couple of people on the campus if they knew Katy and knew where she lived. I found her apartment pretty quickly. I knocked on the door. I don't know what I expected after the letters that she had written to me, but I was shocked when she opened the door.

It didn't even look like her. Her face was drawn in. She looked like a person who was malnourished or starving. She was so skinny that I hardly recognized her. She must have lost 30 pounds. She immediately started to back away from me, with this terrified look on her face.

"Don't come near me," she said. "I can see the entities crawling on you."

"What the hell are you talking about?" I said.

"Don't come near me," she said again. "The entities are all over you."

I rolled my eyes. "What the hell is wrong with you?" I said. "Are you insane? Where are the kids?"

"They're in school," she said, still backing away from me.

I couldn't get near her. There was no hugging or kissing or affectionate greeting, as she was sure the entities were gonna get her if she did. It was pathetic and disheartening.

We finally sat down across the table from each other. I tried to talk some sense into her, but it was no use, she was too far gone.

"I want to see the boys," I said.

"They're in school. They won't be out for a couple of hours, yet," she said.

"Where is the school?" I asked. "I want to see them and the school that they're in." After seeing her and how incredibly screwed up she was, I was concerned about what kind of a school they were in and what they were learning.

It was pointless to sit there, trying to talk to her anymore. I decided to find the school and go check out what was going on with the kids. I left her apartment, which was on the edge of the campus and walked towards what I thought was the center of the campus. After asking a couple of different people, I got directions to the school. As I approached the school, I noticed a group of children on the grounds outside the school building. There was a man and a woman leading the kids around the yard. The kids were chanting while they marched in a regimented fashion. I watched for several minutes and was able to pick Chico and Zad out of the crowd of kids. It looked like they were training them to be little Nazis. The adults that were directing the marching were yelling orders at the kids.

"Stay in line! Hey you, keep up with the group!" they were yelling.

What the hell kind of a school was this? I thought to myself. It looks like they're training soldiers. I couldn't believe what I was seeing. I was watching from the side of the grounds, when I was approached by a man and woman who seen me there. They asked who I was and what I was doing there.

"My sons are going to your school," I explained.

"Who are you and who are your sons?" they questioned me.

"I'm Louie Karmen. My sons are Chico, Zad and Chamuel. I just got here today from Canada," I said. "I would like to see them."

"Hello, I'm Joanne and this is Bill. You must be Katy's husband," she said to me.

"Yes, that's right," I answered. As we talked, the children filed back inside the school. An adult was yelling commands at them and they were saluting with a Nazi-type salute. The whole group of kids all saluted together, just like a group of soldiers. "I just came by to see the boys," I repeated.

"I'm sorry, but we can't let you see them," Joanne said to me. "You can't let me see my sons?" I said surprised.

"No, we can't," she said. "We got a call from Katy a few minutes ago, asking that we not let you see them."

"You've got to be kidding," I said. "These are my kids and you're telling me I can't see them?!" I was furious. "What kind of crap is this?"

"I'm sorry, Louie, but we have strict orders not to let you see them," she said.

While we were talking, Bill was making hand motions towards someone at the school and within minutes we were approached by five or six men. They were called over to keep the situation from getting out of hand. I hardly noticed them approaching, until I was surrounded. They gave the distinct impression that they were the enforcers, the goon squad.

I stood my ground. "I want to see my kids," I kept saying to them. "What gives you the right to tell me that I can't see my kids?"

"The children are in our care and we've been given instructions not to let you see them," one of the goon squad men said.

"They're my kids, and I'm not leaving here without seeing them," I said as the goons moved in closer around me. The situation looked like it could develop into a real bad one. I wasn't backing off and neither were they.

Someone in the school must have called Katy and told her that I was there. She already knew that I was going to the school. Maybe she thought she'd let the goon squad deal with me and I would just back off. It wasn't going that way and when it looked like there was going to be trouble, she was summoned to the school.

"What the hell is going on?" I said to Katy as she approached. "Is this how it's going to be? I have to go through these people to be able to see my own kids?" I was getting pretty mad by this time.

Joanne took Katy to the side to talk to her while the goons kept me there by surrounding me. They talked for a couple of minutes before coming back over to where I was.

"I'll go in and get the boys," Katy said to me. She went over to the school while the goons kept me there, returning a couple of minutes later with the boys.

As soon as they saw me, they started running towards me, yelling "Daddy!" I crouched down as all three boys hugged me at the same time.

"I missed you so much!" Zad said, hanging on to me tightly. We hugged for a couple minutes while the goon squad and Katy stood around us. We all started walking away. Katy followed behind us; as I looked back, I could see the goons watching intensely. I met eyes with one of the goons and gave him a dirty look as we walked away.

We walked to Katy's apartment from there. I was very uneasy being in the apartment with her, though it was nice to see the boys. It was obvious that they missed me terribly. They wouldn't let me out of their sight.

Katy was on what she called a spiritual diet. Diets like this were common among religious cults such as this. I read about these types of diets, that left people malnourished and made it easier to brainwash followers into believing just about anything that the cult wanted them to believe. Many of the religious cults of the day, such as the Moonies and the Church of Scientology, had used the same methods. There was no doubt in my mind that Katy was a victim of this method. She looked so unhealthy and her thinking was so unreasonable, that I think that she would have believed anything they wanted her to.

She even had the boys on her so-called spiritual diet, which consisted of mostly rice. No meat, eggs, bread, or milk products and very little fruits and vegetables. I didn't think it was a healthy diet for growing children. I tried to talk to her about it, but she wouldn't listen to anything unless Clara Summit said it was true.

I slept on the couch that night. It was the only piece of furniture in her apartment, besides the kitchen table and chairs. Katy and the boys were sleeping on a thin foamy on the floor. I guess she was calling it spiritual beds or something. The church teaching was that by depriving yourself of normal comforts such as a comfortable bed, it would make you more spiritual and holy. Of course, the leader of the church, Clara Summit lived in total luxury in her ashram in Los Angeles. It appeared that she didn't deprive herself of anything. Dressing in expensive clothes, traveling in a new Cadillac car with a driver that dressed in tails, like a Hollywood movie star would. Even the wallpaper in the ashram was made from silk, yet she required her disciples to deprive themselves of even the most basic comforts. This was supposed to make them more spiritual. It didn't seem to be working on Katy. There was a hierarchy that was taught by The Universal Lighthouse, that placed Clara Summit on a pedestal. She was looked at as the top of the hierarchy, ranking up there with Jesus and the Pope. There was nothing she had to deprive herself of. She was already the Holiest of the Holy in her own eyes and taught that to her disciples. There was nothing humble about her. She was the Queen and everyone was supposed to worship her. You could get in big trouble if you contradicted her teachings in any way, as I found out when I questioned her about some of the things she said and was met with a barrage of people defending her teachings to the point of threats of violence.

The next morning, I got Katy to agree to let me spend the day with the boys instead of sending them to the school for more Nazi training. She went to her classes and the boys and I hung around Katy's apartment. We took off to a park for a couple hours late in the morning and had lunch at a nearby restaurant where everyone got to eat what they wanted. All three of the boys opted for hamburgers and ice cream.

When I got back to the apartment, Katy was already there waiting for us. I didn't want to say much about what we had for lunch, as not to aggravate the situation, but the boys blurted it out anyway. Katy was not impressed.

She told me she had made an appointment with the church counselor for us to talk to about our marriage that afternoon. Even though I was reluctant to go to a counselor from this church, I thought what can it hurt? The way things were going, I couldn't see our marriage surviving much longer like this. I agreed to go, mostly because of the boys. Maybe, just maybe, it might help.

We brought the boys back to the school and met with

a counselor named Malcolm outside the auditorium on the campus. After introducing ourselves, we walked over and sat on the grass in the center of the campus.

Malcolm was very definitely on Katy's side, questioning me about why I wasn't willing to sell the land in Longstock and join the Universal Lighthouse Church. He supported Katy in her opinion that, if I wasn't willing to do it, then our marriage would not survive. I couldn't believe what I was hearing. This was a marriage counselor that couldn't, or wouldn't, do anything for our marriage. My frustration was evident. I wasn't getting anywhere with this guy.

Katy decided that she was going to have to divorce me after the meeting with the counselor. I wasn't going to join the church and that was necessary in her mind for us to stay together.

From my point of view, I couldn't see myself staying with a woman who was so screwed up on this cult. I really wanted to get the kids away from this situation. As far as I was concerned, Katy could stay there, but I couldn't abandon the kids to this fate.

I thought that I somehow had to get her trust in order to get the kids away from there. I took a long walk around Pasadena that evening after the boys went to bed and thought about how I could accomplish getting the boys away.

I decided that if I could get her away from Pasadena, maybe I could take off back to Longstock with the boys. Getting her confidence would be the first step. I made a conscious effort to convince her that I was coming over to her way of thinking. I attended several meetings in the auditorium where Clara Summit was supposed to have several different saints and even

Jesus himself, talking through her. Even though I viewed this as total bullshit, I pretended that I believed it. I could see Katy showing more and more confidence that I was coming around to her way of thinking, as time went on. It was working, even though I was rolling my eyeballs at what I was hearing.

It was a real struggle to keep my mouth shut when listening to the lectures that Clara Summit gave while she was supposed to be these different saints talking through her. While pretending to be Jesus talking through her in one session, Clara Summit said" If you're going to save someone in this lifetime, why not save yourself?" I found that completely contradictory to what Jesus said in the Bible. It is well known that the bible said, "He who seeks to save his own life shall perish." I believe that Jesus meant this in a spiritual sense, but Clara summit meant it in a material sense, convincing her followers to give money and property to her and buy into the church-sponsored bomb shelters that they were selling in order to save themselves. In one meeting in the auditorium, I sat there and witnessed the congregation give almost a million dollars in cash and property after a lecture by Clara Summit where she claimed to be John The Baptist speaking. I couldn't believe that these seemingly intelligent people could be so gullible as to believe that this was real and not a total con.

After being there for about a week, I suggested that we all take off for the weekend and visit my sister Cathy in Northern California. Katy agreed, but wanted to stop and see her brother in Big Bear Lake on the way. She borrowed a car from her friend Linda, who was also attending classes with Katy.

We drove out of Pasadena and up into the mountains to

her brother's place. Her brother was quite surprised when we pulled up and got out of the car. He was out in the yard, mowing the grass when we pulled up to the house. "What the hell happened to you?" he said as Katy got out of the car and walked towards him. Katy's whole appearance had changed drastically since the last time he'd seen her. She barely looked like the same person.

"Nice to see you, too!" Katy said, acting annoyed by his comment. Al was used to saying what was on his mind and told her straight out that she looked terrible compared to the last time he saw her. His straight forwardness had always been a problem with them, even when they were growing up. We all went in the house and sat around the living room, talking. Al's wife Judy had been out doing some errands. She showed up about a half-hour after we got there.

Katy and Judy were old friends from high school and had not seen each other for several years, since before we moved to Longstock. They were catching up on each others news when Al said to me "Louie, it looks like you could use a beer. Let's go!"

We drove down to the local bar and went inside. Al ordered a couple beers and we sat down at a corner table.

"What the hell is going on, Louie?" Al said to me. "Katy looks like hell."

I told myself I wasn't going to say too much to him, after all, he was her brother and it could really screw up my plan to get the kids back to Longstock and away from the cult.

"Why don't you ask her?" I said, reluctant to talk about the situation with him. Al kept pressing me for information. I was not saying too much, though he just kept up asking me and buying more beer.

I was starting to feel the beer and the pressure from Al was getting to me, when I blurted out, "She's joined a cult down in Pasadena and it's really fucked up everything with us. She and the kids have been there for months. She wants to sell the farm and give the money to the cult. If it wasn't for the kids, I'd be long gone."

"What the hell are you gonna do, Louie?" Al asked.

"I don't know!" I said, as my emotions swelled up inside me. I couldn't keep it together and started to get choked up. "I don't know what to do!" I said, not willing to reveal my plan to him.

"You gotta get the kids the hell out of there!" he said. "I know, but what the fuck am I gonna do?" I said.

"Take the kids and get out of here. Go back to Canada," he said. "And how do I do that?" I asked.

"I'll put you and the kids on a plane tomorrow if you want to," Al said.

I could see by this time that Al was on my side and feeling pretty drunk from the beer myself, I told him what I was going to do. I told him I was going to take the kids when we got to Northern California and go back to Canada. I had already arranged with a friend in Sacramento to go there and he would get us plane tickets north.

"If you need my help in any way, here's my number," he said, as he handed me a business card with his phone numbers.

We went back to his place shortly afterward. I felt that my secret was safe with him. We stayed one night with Al and the next morning left for my sister's place. Just as we were leaving, Al slipped me an envelope. I put it in my pocket. When I checked it out later in the bathroom in a gas station, I was surprised to find four fifty dollar bills in it.

It was an all day drive on the interstate north to Hayfork. We arrived late that evening. I decided to wait until morning to tell Katy I was taking the kids back to Longstock...but I did take Cathy and her husband Dennis aside and fill them in on what was going on.

They already knew something was up just by the way Katy was acting.

I waited until after breakfast the next morning and told Katy that I wanted to talk to her. We went into the living room and she sat down in a big easy chair.

"I'm gonna take the kids back to Longstock with me," I said. "I've pretty well had enough of these Lighthouse people and I think the boys have, too."

"You're not going anywhere with the kids!" she snarled back at me. "I'm going to take them back to Pasadena."

"No, you're not," I said.

"Oh yes, I am!" she yelled at me, getting up from the chair and lunging at me, fists flying.

I grabbed her by the arms and shoved her back into the chair. She attempted to get up again and by this time was screaming at me.

I pushed her back into the chair again. "Stay there," I said. She tried to get up again, but I kept pushing her back into the chair. She finally started to cry and remained there.

I had already arranged with Dennis and Cathy to take right off as soon as Katy left. We were afraid to take the interstate, just in case Katy went to the cops, which she did. Dennis knew the back roads pretty well around there. He took us on a gravel road for about 100 miles, connecting with the interstate way south of Hayfork. Katy would be telling the cops that we were headed north to Canada and all the while we were heading for Sacramento, about 300 miles to the south.

Cathy and Dennis left us at my friend Jed's place and headed back to Hayfork. We were there for about 5 days before we caught a plane back to Prince George.

I called David Parsons to let him know what was going on the day before we left Sacramento and to get him to meet me at the airport. He told me Katy was already back up there and was looking for me and the boys.

"Don't tell her you've heard from me Dave, OK?" I asked. "I'll see her when I get there."

I got off the plane with the boys in Prince George and Dave was waiting for us. He drove us to his place. Dave had given me a ride to the highway three weeks earlier. I parked the van at his place while I was gone.

Dave and Shirley weren't going to let me leave without filling them in on the details of my trip. They had already heard Katy's version of what went on and wanted to hear the story from me.

Katy had gone out to Longstock and was at the house when I arrived later that day. Her friend Linda that I met in Pasadena had driven her home and was still around. Linda had two kids with her as well.

The kids were glad to be home, and happy to see their Mom, though Katy was not thrilled to see me. She already set herself up to stay at Gypsy's cabin. Gypsy had been gone for a couple months, traveling with his new girlfriend and was not expected back until fall.

Katy's girlfriend Linda and her kids were staying in the house with me and the boys.

The situation was pretty tense, with all of us in the house during the day. Katy left for Gypsy's before dark each day and returned in the morning. I couldn't help thinking that she had some kind plan up her sleeve to grab the kids again. I kept a close eye on the situation so that she couldn't get out of there again without my knowing.

There was the added problem of the pot patch that Larry and I had planted at the tee pee. Katy had to walk right by it on her way to and from Gypsy's cabin each day.

Every morning, she would show up at the house and I would go out and work on the garden or whatever I could do outside. She and Linda would set up pictures at the kitchen sink of the Lighthouse deities and be chanting for a couple hours as they washed dishes and cleaned the house.

I wondered what had happened to the woman that left here six months before. Everything was so different with her now. I didn't know how I was going to live in this situation for long. The future looked pretty bleak. It looked like the end for us. What about the kids? Our whole life had been turned upside-down.

Chapter 13

Busted

$\mathbf{L}$arry was in the Inn of the North bar in Prince George, partying with some people from Dome Creek. He had harvested some of his pot crop and was trying to sell some.

People from the valley were not hard to notice when they were partying in the bars. It was easy to tell that they were hippies from the bush, in contrast to the city people. There was an undercover cop in the bar that night. Larry and the cop played a couple of games of pool together and got to talking.

He was dressed like a hippie with a beard and long hair

and hardly looked the part of a cop. He had Larry fooled as he became friendly and joined the group at their table, buying a round for everyone more than once.

The party was getting pretty loud and everybody was having a good time. Somebody suggested that they go outside the bar and smoke a joint. More than half the people at the table piled outside and around the corner, including the cop. A couple of joints went around and then everybody went back inside the bar.

The band was playing and much of their party was on the dance floor. Everyone was having a great time. It was common for people from the valley to party until 11 o'clock or so, then get over to the train station and catch the passenger train at 11:45. This night was no exception.

Larry had a room in town for the night. He wanted to stick around for a couple of days, or until he could sell the pot he had brought into town. Larry and a couple of other guys were left in the bar along with the undercover cop. It was the cop who suggested that they go smoke another joint outside.

"Okay," announced Larry, "I got one rolled," getting up from the table and leading the group outside and around the side of the bar. He lit up the joint and began passing it around.

"You know where I can buy some of this?" the cop asked Larry.

He was kinda drunk by this time and throwing caution to the wind, Larry answered, "I sure do!"

"What king of price are we looking at?" said the cop. "Depends how much you want," Larry responded. "How much you got?" said the cop.

"As much as you want," said Larry.

They finished the joint and the other two guys went back into the bar, leaving Larry and the cop to discuss their deal. After the other guys left, the cop announced to Larry that he was R.C.M.P.

"Oh shit!" said Larry, and tried walking away, back into the bar.

The cop grabbed him from behind and got him in a choke hold. "You're under arrest!" he said while wrestling with Larry.

Larry was struggling, trying to get loose from the cop but the cop had the advantage having Larry in the choke hold from behind. They stuggled for a few minutes and the cop wrestled Larry to the ground, stomping heavily onto his hand, breaking a couple of fingers on his right hand. The cop managed to get handcuffs on him, while shoving Larry's face into the concrete sidewalk.

They were only about two blocks from the Police Station. The cop got him up and walked him to the station, slapping and punching him numerous times on the way. He brought him in through the back entrance and up the elevator, stopping the elevator and beating Larry around the head and ribs.

He started the elevator and took him upstairs and booked him for possession. They found the key to Larry's hotel room in his pocket and went to searched the room, finding the pound of pot that Larry had brought to town to sell.

Larry was in big trouble now. He was not even a landed immigrant, but an American living in Canada illegally. They knew he lived in Longstock and figured there must be more out there. It took a couple of days for the cops to get it together to go there and search his house. Because there was no road, they had to arrange for a helicopter to get there.

I got up early that morning. Linda and all the kids were still sleeping and Katy was still out at Gypsy's cabin. I was expecting her to show up soon. I was having a cup of coffee before she got there; then I was going to leave the house. I couldn't really tolerate the chanting thing.

I turned on the radio to listen to the messages that came on every morning at 7:20, when I heard a report about a pot bust in Prince George. I turned up the radio, trying to hear more details, when I heard the names, "Larry Gaylord" and "Longstock."

"Oh shit!" I said to myself.

Within a couple minutes, I decided I'd better go to Steve's and make sure he knew and figure out what to do, because it was evident that the cops were going to come out here.

I quickly went out and saddled Daffodil, taking off for Steve's place. Steve had already heard the news when I got there and was getting ready to go over to Skid's and make sure he knew what was going on. He jumped on behind me on Daffodil and we took off for Skid's.

Steve slid off the horse ahead of me and ran up the path to Skid's while I tied up Daffodil. I could hear him pounding on the door and yelling for Skid. Skid was still in bed when we got there, but got up pretty fast, hearing all the commotion going on.

"The cops busted Larry!" Steve said to Skid when he opened the door.

"When did this happen?" Skid said nervously.

"Turn on your radio," Steve answered, "I heard it on the radio this morning."

Skid turned the radio on right away and set it on the table. We all sat around listening. Within a few minutes the report came on again. The reception was not that great. We had to strain our ears to make out what they were saying.

"The R.C.M.P. arrested a man in Prince George last night for possession and trafficking of a controlled substance. Larry Gaylord, a resident of Longstock, was taken into custody after trying to sell pot to an R.C.M.P undercover officer. Gaylord was also living in the country illegally. He will be appear in court this morning."

We were all at a loss for words, as the radio report moved on to other stories.

"You know, he's got pot all over his place and the cops are probably gonna come out here," I said, breaking the silence.

"We should clean the place out before the cops get out here," said Steve.

"You think they'll come out today?" I asked.

"I don't know. I suppose they might," Steve answered. "We could keep an eye on the place and if they don't make it today, we should get the place cleaned out tonight. It might be too dangerous to do it during the day."

Steve and I agreed that we would meet up at Larry's place just before sundown and get to work getting rid of all the pot plants.

Skid wasn't saying too much. His face was riddled with worry. "I think we should just get the hell out of here," he said. "We could end up in jail, too."

"And what are we supposed to do, just run off and let Larry go down without helping him?" Steve snapped at Skid.

"I don't want to get busted, too," said Skid.

"Let me explain something to you, Skid," said Steve. "Larry's in big trouble already. If they raid his place and find the weed he's got growing there, he's gonna be in really deep shit. It'll be way worse for him. If the cops come today, there's not much we can do, but if they don't, we can keep Larry from getting into deeper shit by getting rid of the pot he's got growing."

"How much has he got around his place?" I asked.

"I think it's about 300 plants. And they're all around six foot high," said Steve.

"Holy shit," I said. "Let's hope the cops don't make it out here today."

Skid still did not want to help get rid of the plants. All he wanted to do was get out of Longstock and head down to the States until everything cooled down.

"You chicken shit asshole, Skid!" I said. "You're gonna run off to save your own ass and leave your friend hung out to dry."

Steve and I ragged on Skid some more and he finally agreed to help, but made it clear that he was getting out of town as soon as we got the place cleaned out. We were both feeling pretty disgusted with Skid at this point. If he was ready to run out on Larry so quickly, it was a sure bet that he would do the same to either one of us, too.

I gave Steve a ride back to his place and headed home. Katy came out and met me when I got there. She had heard the report about Larry by this time and didn't know that I had already heard it.

She gave me the news as if she liked it. "They got your

friend Larry for pot, you know."

"I know all about it," I said, not wanting to talk to her about it.

I went in the house and rounded up all the pot I had there and put it into mason jars. When I was satisfied that I had it all, I went out to the barn and hollowed out a space in the hay and stashed it there. I was careful that Katy didn't see me. I didn't trust that she wouldn't tell the cops where it was if they came to the house. She already knew about the 150 plants growing out at the tee pee garden. I thought about harvesting those plants too but somehow figured that they would be safe, so I didn't. She didn't know, however, about the six other patches I had growing, scattered about the bush.

It was clear and sunny all that day. I kept my eye on the sky throughout the day, half expecting to see a helicopter appear in the sky, but nothing happened. It was evident that the cops were not going to show up by late afternoon. I was sure they would not attempt a raid late in the day. About 5 o'clock, I drove my tractor and wagon over to Steve's place and waited for Skid to show up.

Skid showed up at Steve's about a half hour later. I didn't want to leave the tractor parked in front of Larry's while we harvested the pot as it wasn't quite dark yet. We walked over to Larry's. Steve knew where some of Larry's patches were, so we followed him into the bush, coming upon a huge patch of at least a hundred plants, all over 6 foot tall, with some as tall as 9 feet.

I brought a machete from home. Taking it out of its sheath, I started chopping down plants and piling them up on

301

the ground. Skid and Steve were both chopping plants, too. It wasn't long before we had the first patch done. The pile on the ground was enormous.

We moved on to Larry's other patches, hacking the pot down and piling it up. It was amazing how many plants there were. I estimated it to be 500 plants. They were all over the place, even scattered across the land in buckets. The pile was humongous. Now what the hell do we do with so much pot?

"Got any ideas?" I asked after we were finished. "We can haul it out of here with the tractor, but where are we gonna take it?"

"What about taking it up the river?" Steve suggested.

"Do you think that this load is going to fit in my boat?" I asked.

"It'll be a full load."

"Hey, what about the old logging camp up at Driscol Creek? There's a couple of the old buildings still standing. Maybe we can hang them up there."

It was agreed that we would take the plants there.

It was starting to get dark as we carried the piles of plants closer to the road, where we could pick them up with the tractor and trailer. It was totally dark by the time we headed back to Steve's.

I gave the tractor a crank. It fired up on the first try and we headed back to Larry's. We had to tie the plants on the wagon with a rope to keep them from falling off. It looked like a big load of hay, but smelled a lot better. When the load was secured, we headed for the river.

I had been tying my boat upriver from the boat landing at

the end of the road near Ross's place. We managed to get to the river without anyone seeing us or our load. I carried the first load of plants down to the boat and then stayed in the boat as the other guys carried the plants down. It was dark, but there was just enough light to see what we were doing. The wagon load of pot filled the boat up from side to side and bow to stern, heaping up in the middle about five feet high.

It was 11 o'clock at night by this time and we thought it wouldn't be a good idea to go now, but wait in the morning for first light. After covering the pot with plastic and tarps and tying the boat up under some overhanging willows, we took the tractor and wagon back over to Steve's place and hung around there until about 4 a. m. It was still dark when we headed back down to the river. We waited until it was just light enough to see the water and shoved off and started upriver. We started with the tarps and plastic covering the plants, but it started to blow off when we headed upriver.

It was about a half-hour trip up the river to the old camp. Once it started to get light, it happened pretty fast. When we were about fifteen or twenty minutes into it, in a wide spot in the river, the first rays of the sun hit the boat. The big piles of green pot started to glow from the sunlight.

What a sight it was. A twenty-four foot boat filled to the brim with weed and glowing in the sunshine in the middle of the river. If the cops had been out early that morning and had gotten within five miles of us, we would've been caught. There's no way they would've missed us.

Steve was riding on top of the load. He turned and looked at me and said, "I hope those cops are sleeping in!" That said it all.

We weren't sure just where the old buildings were, so we let Skid out to go look for them before we docked the boat. Soon he was on the river bank a little downstream.

"Tie up down here!" he yelled to us.

I motored the boat down there and ran it up on the mud. We quickly unloaded the boat and piled the plants on top of the river bank. We each grabbed a pile and followed Skid to the building. I brought a bunch of baling twine from Steve's and started stringing it up to tie the plants to.

Skid and Steve carried plants up from the river while I hung them up. Within an hour or so, we were finished. It filled the entire building. It was so thick that you could hardly get through it.

Closing the doors as best we could, we got back to the boat and took off for Longstock. I gave Skid and Steve a ride back to Steve's place, then took off for home.

It was still early and no one was up when I got home. Even Katy hadn't shown up yet. I was feeling pretty tired, so I made some coffee. Katy showed up after my second cup and I figured it was a good time to split. I saddled Daffodil and rode down to Ross's.

It was a warm morning, Ross and I were sitting at his table, drinking a cup of coffee. Ross had a blazing fire going and had the door wide open.

"What's that I hear?" Ross said. I listened intently and I could hear the sound of a chopper. The cops were here. We both ran outside, trying to see where it was. There it was. It was one of those great, big choppers with two big propellers. It flew across Ross's field and headed up towards Larry's place.

I decided that I was going to stay where I was while the cops were around. It turned out that among the eight officers on the chopper were five R.C.M.P., two Immigration and one Fish and Wildlife Officer. They landed the chopper at Larry's place and piled out. They fanned out over the place and searched the buildings. Man, were they pissed off! They didn't even find one plant. All they got was a couple of roaches out of an ashtray in the house.

It was obvious that someone had beaten the cops to it, because of all the stumps. Even the pots had stumps in them. They proceeded to go to any house they could find, and search it. They fanned out all over Longstock, trying to find the missing pot. Unfortunately for Steve, he was home when the cops arrived. Steve was also in the country illegally. They searched his house and found an illegal pistol and about two pounds of dried pot. They also found about twenty plants that he had growing in the garden.

He was handcuffed and taken to the chopper and taken back to Prince George.

It didn't take long for the cops to make it to my place. While they were knocking on the door, some were already going through my buildings.

Maybe Katy thought it was a way to get rid of me for a while. I'm not sure, but she did tell the cops to look out by Gypsy's cabin and they would find some pot growing. The area was too small to land the chopper. Katy gave them directions and they walked out there.

Until Katy told the cops where the pot was growing, they hadn't spotted it from the air. The trees were too tall nearby.

305

They would have to fly directly over it to find it. Five of the officers walked the trail out to the patch and proceeded to pull the plants up by the roots. They dropped a couple of nets from the chopper and spread them out and piled the plants, roots and all, on them. A line and hook was lowered from the chopper and the plants were hauled up and flown across the river where a police vehicle waited.

I could hear the chopper flying around Longstock from where I was down at Ross's. It seemed to me they were flying on my end of town.

Some of the officers stayed around the house and went through the buildings, but they didn't find anything there. I guess they looked around the barn, but didn't want to disturb the goats.

I had Daffodil tied back in the trees with the saddle on, just in case I had to make a run for it. The chopper was still flying around my place when I heard a horse coming down the driveway. I got on Daffodil and was ready to take off into the bush. Peeking out from behind the trees, I could see it was Katy, riding Dondi.

I walked out from my hiding place. I could hear her saying to Ross, "Where's Louie? The cops are looking for him."

"Oh, yeah?" I said, walking up on them. "What for?"

"They found your pot patch and now they want to find you." Katy said, rather happily. "I just came down to warn you."

"Did they find anything else?"

"I don't think so. They just found the patch that was growing out at the tee pee."

Katy only stayed for a minute and didn't even get off the

horse before taking off back to the house.

I turned to Ross after she left and said, "I'll see you later, Ross. I'm heading off in the bush until the cops leave." I jumped on Daffodil and rode off into the bush along the river. When I felt I was far enough back that they wouldn't find me, I got off and tied her up and lit up a joint.

I surely didn't want to get caught out there. I figured I'd have a better chance getting off if I turned myself in later on my own terms. I stayed in the bush a couple of hours while the cops were still in Longstock. They showed up at Ross's place shortly before they left. By that time, they already had arrested Steve and confiscated a sizable amount of pot and didn't seem too interested in bothering Ross.

Skid had already high tailed it for Sinclair Mills on foot. His VW bug was parked there and he managed to get out of there before the cops could catch up to him.

I stayed in the bush until I heard the chopper leave back to Prince George. I took my time getting back to Ross's place, just in case they had left someone behind. It was almost dark before I got home again.

The next morning was another clear, sunny day. I knew the cops would come looking for me after a while if I didn't turn myself in. They hadn't found anything illegal around my house and I felt pretty sure I could beat the rap on the pot they did find. It was a long way from the house and they never saw me there. It was going to be hard for them to prove I knew anything about it.

I left the house that morning and went to Ross's place before heading into Prince George to turn myself in. Toad was there, having coffee with Ross when I got there.

"Did the cops come to your place yesterday?" I asked Toad.

"Yeah, they did," he answered. "They didn't stay long. They took a quick look around and left. I think they went down the tracks to Pierre's after they left my place."

I told him what happened at my place, about Katy telling them where to look.

"Shitty," was all he said.

I took my time going down the river and then stopping at the Purden Lake Restaurant. Toad's girlfriend Annie had an uncle (James) that had moved out to Longstock from Toronto a couple of months before with his girlfriend (Bonnie) and they were both working at the resort. They were living in a trailer just below the gas pumps. I stopped in on them and told them the story of the day before.

Bonnie cooked me up a steak for lunch. She said I should have a good meal now, in case I got locked up. James was no stranger to jail, having spent about fifteen of his thirty-five years in jail back in Ontario.

I used their phone to call a lawyer in Prince George. There was one lawyer in Prince George, Archie Dennis, who had been making a name for himself by defending a lot of drug cases.

I got Archie on the phone that afternoon and told him the story of the bust. He told me to stay right where I was until he had a chance to check things out.

I hung out at James and Bonnie's trailer until later that afternoon, when Archie called back.

"Okay, Louie, the cops are ready to let you give yourself up, but not today. I want you to meet me in the courthouse at

9 am tomorrow. Okay?"

"Okay, I'll see you there," I said.

"See you tomorrow," he said, and hung up.

I hung out with Bonnie and James the rest of the day and stayed at their place that night. I left to meet Archie just before eight the next morning.

I walked into the courthouse and stopped one of the lawyers in the hall. "I'm looking for Archie Dennis. Can you tell me if he's around the building?" I said; never having met Archie before, I didn't know what he looked like.

"Yeah, he's here," he said, looking down the hall. "There he is, down at the end of the hall with the gray suit," he said, pointing towards him. I thanked him and walked over to Archie. "Hi, Archie, I'm Louie Karmen. I talked to you on the phone yesterday."

"Oh yeah! Come on with me," he said, motioning for me to follow. I followed him down the hall and into one of the offices in the court house. It was one of the Crown Prosecutors offices, by the sign on the door. There were two lawyers in the office when we walked in.

"Could you fellows leave us alone for a bit?" Archie said, and the two lawyers left, Archie closed the door behind them.

"The cops want you upstairs," he said. "They want to book you, but they'll just have to wait. I got you on the docket and we could get called in any minute.

"So let me get this straight: They didn't catch you in the patch?"

"No they didn't."

"Was it on your land?"

"Well yeah, it was, but it wasn't by my house. As a matter of fact, it was close to a half a mile from my house."

"Did they find anything by your house?"

"No, nothing," I said.

"Anybody could have planted that pot out there, right?"

"That's right."

"It sounds to me that they don't have a case against you, Louie," Archie summarized. "Okay, let's go," he said, getting up and leading me out of the office and into the hall.

We were just hanging around, waiting for the clerk to call us, when I was approached by a plain clothes cop.

"Would you come with me," he said, grabbing me by the arm.

"No, he can't," said Archie, coming to my rescue rather quickly. "The judge could be calling us any minute. You'll have to wait."

The cop backed off.

Hours went by and the cop tried to get me upstairs a couple more times, but Archie wouldn't let him. Finally, after about the fifth time, Archie told him, "Okay, I'll give you five minutes with him. Can you do it in five minutes?"

"I guess so," the cop answered. "Come on," he said to me, leading me away.

We got in the elevator to go up to the station; "those were some pretty big plants you had there," he said. I didn't say a word. "Too bad about your buddy," he kept on. He kept on talking to me, trying to get me to respond, but I didn't say a word.

He took me to the fingerprinting room and got fingerprints. The camera was broken that day, so he didn't manage to get a mug shot. I was back downstairs pretty quickly. We probably waited another hour before they called my name. It was over in two minutes and I was out on a P.R. Bond. They would let me know when the trial was.

We went back to Archie's office and talked for a while. At one point, Archie walked over and opened a window and then pulled out a joint. We stood by the window and smoked it, blowing the smoke out the window.

He was sure that they couldn't make a case good enough to convict me and I would get off. I asked him about Larry's case. He told me that Larry had pleaded guilty the day before and had gotten three months on the hill.

Steve got a fine and was given 30 days to get out of the country.

Skid had already slipped out the day of the raid.

The cops had a picture on the front page of the paper that day of a huge pile of pot plants, claiming it to be three hundred pounds. Longstock had become infamous.

Chapter 14

Saving the Crop

I drove out and stayed another night with Bonnie and James at Purden Lake. They had a campground at the resort and James met a fellow from Idaho that was camping there. They hit it off pretty well. He brought him up to the trailer where they were drinking a few beers and having a good time when I got there.

Willy was a tall, lanky guy who wore cowboy boots and a leather jacket, the kind with two layers of fringe all around. He was one of those happy drunks, a real fun-loving guy who loves to drink. He was driving an old 1958 Ford station wagon.

Having just met Willy, I was a little reluctant to tell all the details of what had transpired over the last few days, but ended up talking about it a lot as we partied into the night.

Both Willy and I crashed out at the trailer after drinking and smoking until the wee hours. Bonnie and James had to get up and go to work in the morning. They were already gone when I woke up and Willy was sitting at the table with a cup of coffee that he got at the restaurant.

"There's a coffee here for you, Louie," he said as I stumbled into the kitchen. We sat around the kitchen table for as long as it took to drink my coffee and then went down to the restaurant for more.

"Coffee?" Bonnie asked as she flipped over a couple of cups and filled them up. "How are you guys feeling this morning?"

"I've felt worse," Willy answered. I just nodded. My head was pounding.

James was working the gas pumps. Every time he got a break, he would come to the restaurant and talk to us for a while until the next car pulled up to the pumps.

"So where are you going, Willy?" I asked as we worked on our second cup of coffee.

"Nowhere in particular," he answered. "Just traveling around. I've been on the road for about a month now. Spent some time in Calgary, a few days in Edmonton and points in between. I got an ex- wife in Idaho, been giving me a lot of grief, so I just took off for a while. I wouldn't mind checking out Longstock. It sounds like an interesting place."

"I'm going over there today. You're welcome to come over with me if you want to," I said.

"Well, I got no other plans for today, maybe I will come over for a couple of days," he said.

It was just past noon when we loaded up and headed for the landing at Longstock. Willy was surprised when he found out he couldn't drive his old station wagon across the river. He was afraid to leave all his stuff in the car. We ended up loading just about everything he had into the boat and taking it with us. Among his belongings were three old guns. One was an old-style, double- barreled, 410, side by side shotgun. Another was a lever action 30- 30 and the third was a bolt action twenty-two. All of the guns were made in the early 1900's. He wrapped them up in a sleeping bag and loaded them into the boat. He also had a couple of flats of beer and three or four bottles of hard liquor.

When Willy and I showed up at the house, Linda and her kids were the only ones there. Katy had gone to visit one of the neighbors with the boys.

Willy really took a shine to Linda and it seemed like she was interested in him, too. I went outside and dug the pot out of its hiding place in the barn and brought it back to the house. I rolled a couple of joints, gave one to Willy and went back outside. Linda and Willy were getting pretty friendly with each other by this time, so I left them alone and went for a walk in the bush. I walked out to the tee-pee. I wanted to check the patch out after the cops had raided it. They were sure sloppy about it, as I found three plants that had been pulled up and looked like they had fallen out of the sling. There were also six more that were still growing. They were off to the side of the main patch and had gotten so big that they were leaning over. I guess it made it hard to see them with the bush growing up around them.

I picked up the ones on the ground and carried them to the barn. I hung the plants up in the loft, where the goats couldn't get them and went back to the house. Linda's kids were sitting at the table, playing with coloring books and crayons. Willy and Linda were not in the house. The stove was going. I put a couple of pieces of wood in the stove and put on some water for coffee.

Willy and Linda walked in shortly afterwards. Linda's hair looked pretty messed up. I looked at Willy and he looked at me kinda funny, and then winked. It looked like Willy had scored with Linda already.

I went upstairs and crashed out.

I had been working on getting some of my own hay cut and put up prior to the cops raid. I didn't have a hay baler, so we were putting it up loose with pitchforks. The Allis Chalmers tractor that I had was equipped with a hay mower and I had an old dump-type hay rake. I was able to get the hay mowed and raked by myself, but needed some help to pick it up and load it into the barn.

The days had been really nice and sunny, with no rain: perfect haying weather. I checked the hay for moisture content that morning after the dew had burned off. It seemed ready to pick up. Loose hay could contain a bit of moisture and still be all right, as opposed to baled hay, which has got to be quite a bit drier so it would not mold when packed tightly.

Willy had agreed to give me a hand getting it picked up. The boys were out there with us as we worked. Chico was up on the wagon, walking around on the load, packing the hay as we loaded it off the field.

315

We then drove the tractor over to the barn and pitched the hay up into the hayloft. Willy was up in the loft and I worked the wagon, throwing the hay up to him while he pitched it to the back of the barn. We picked up about ten wagon loads from the field. There were a couple more left in the field.

I'm not sure how things happened, but Chico was down on the ground, playing alongside the hay wagon. We just finished loading a load of hay into the barn. Willy was getting ready to climb down the ladder and for some reason, he dropped his pitchfork down first. Normally, the pitchfork would just stick into the ground, but this time it ricocheted off the ladder. The pitchfork bounced into the air and hit Chico in the chest.

I was on the other side of the wagon and didn't realize what happened right away. Chico started screaming and I immediately ran over to him. The pitchfork had hit him and bounced off. Chico was holding his chest. I lifted up his shirt to see what was going on and I saw a little hole in his chest where the pitchfork had stuck him. The blood was squirting out in time with his heartbeats.

"Holy shit!" I said, and picked him up, running to the house with him. I was yelling to Katy as I got close to the house. She heard me from outside and met me at the door.

"What's wrong? What happened?" she said excitedly.

"Chico got stabbed with a pitchfork. It looks bad." "Oh, my God," she cried. "Let me see!"

I took him into the house and laid him down on the couch. He was starting to look like he was ready to pass out. Katy was a nurse and knew to put pressure on the wound to stop the bleeding right away.

"I'm going to a phone to get a chopper out here. You're okay?" "Yes! Yes!" Katy said. "Get going."

There was no time to saddle a horse or screw around with a tractor I took off running. The only phone in town was at McCoby's and even that was not a regular phone.

It was about a two-mile run to get to the phone I was in a panicked state by this time and ran out the driveway at a sprint. By the time I got to Greta and Dick's place, more than a mile away, I was starting to run out of gas. Dick was out front of his house as I was approaching.

I was gasping for air as I yelled out at him in between breaths: "Dick, Chico got stabbed with a pitchfork. We need a chopper, quick!"

As soon as he realized what I was saying, he took off running. "Go back home," he yelled back at me. "I'll make the call." He turned towards McCoby's and took off running.

I turned around and headed back home. I was totally out of breath and gasping for air. I pushed myself, making myself run all the way back home. I was praying and crying at the same time as I ran.

I finally got back, running into the house, gasping for air, I said to Katy, "How is he?"

"The bleeding has stopped. Is there a helicopter coming?"

"Yeah. I got as far as Dick's and he took off to McCoby's to call."

I went upstairs and got a white bed sheet. I went out in the hayfield in front of the house and spread it out on the ground, giving the chopper something to see so that they didn't have to look for us very hard.

317

There just happened to be a chopper about 30 miles away doing some forestry work. They got the call and immediately dropped everything and took off for Longstock. It was the longest 30 minutes

I've ever waited. Chico was looking bad. His face was losing color and he seemed to be starting to pass out.

I could finally hear the chopper coming and went out in the field to make sure they saw the sheet on the ground. They came in, circled and landed very quickly. The motor on the chopper was powered up during the landing so that they could take off quickly.

Katy carried Chico across the field to the chopper, with me close behind. We got into the chopper and took off. Even though Chico was in bad shape at the time, it was his first chopper ride and he was talking about it all the way into Prince George.

We landed on the landing pad in front of the hospital and were met with attendants that brought a wheel chair out to get Chico, wheeling him quickly into emergency.

The X-rays showed that the pitchfork had actually lodged between two ribs and bounced out. We thought that it had penetrated into his lungs or worse, his heart, especially the way the blood was pumping out. If it had gone straight in, it would have been much worse, but because of the angle of entry, it actually hit a rib, which stopped it from going any further.

After the doctor had treated him in the emergency room, they admitted him for the night. Katy and I decided that she would stay at the hospital and I would take the train back that night, retuning with the truck the next day.

I got home late that night. Willy and Linda were anxious

to hear the news about Chico. I assured them that it looked like he was going to be okay. Willy was feeling really bad and apologized profusely.

I took the boat across the river and drove into town the next day. I got to the hospital, parked the truck and went upstairs to Chico's room.

Much to my surprise, I found the room empty. "What the hell? Where are they?" I asked myself. Suddenly, I heard a voice. It was unmistakably Chico. I followed the voice into the next room and there was Chico, playing with trucks on the floor with another kid about his age.

"Hey, Chico. What are you doing?"

"I'm just playing, Dad!" he said, jumping up off the floor and running up to me, giving me a hug.

"You feeling all right?"

"Yeah!" he said. "Look!" He lifted up his shirt and there was a little bandage on the spot where the pitchfork had got him, with a smiley face on it.

Katy came into the room, "I think we're ready to go. It looks like he's all right."

The three of us went home. The ordeal seemed to bring us all closer together for a little while after that. Thank God it turned out okay.

Willy and I hung out together a lot over the next few weeks. I took him around Longstock to meet everybody that was still around. We drank Rum at Toad's, Berry cup at Ross's and partied pretty well non-stop for the next two weeks.

The pot was still hanging up in the logging camp up the river and had been there for almost three weeks. I kept quiet about the location. I still wasn't sure about revealing it to Willy. We even went for a trip up the river in my boat, going right by the camp. I went pretty close to shore when we passed the camp and thought I'd seen footprints on the river bank. Still I didn't say anything to Willy about the location of the weed.

We were talking one afternoon and I brought up the subject. "You know, Willy, there's a shack with three hundred plants hanging up in it that have got to be dealt with sometime soon.

"Is that a fact?" he said. "Your bullshitting me, aren't you?"

"No." I said.

"There really are three hundred plants hanging in a shack?"

"Yup." I said.

"Whose weed is it?"

"Let's just say it's just some that the cops didn't get."

"Where is it?"

"That's just it. The reason that I haven't gone to get it yet is that I'm not sure the cops ain't watching it. They knew they didn't get it all. What if they found it? They could watch it and see if someone comes looking for it. I'd want to be sure, if I got anywhere near it."

"Where is this building?"

"It's on the river. About halfway to Penney. We went by it the other day when we went up the river. I thought I could see footprints on the river bank. It makes me really leery of approaching it."

"I got it, man," Willy said. "You drop me off there with my shotgun and my sleeping bag. I'm going grouse hunting. I just hired you to take me up the river and pick me up later. We'll find out if there's any cops watching."

"That sounds like a really good idea. Then we can grab it if there's nobody there."

"So do I become a partner if I help recover the weed?" Willy said. "Yeah, I'd say you would."

The next morning, we left for the river on the tractor and pulled a wagon behind. It was a crisp, cool morning, even though the skies were clear. I tipped my hat down to cut the wind on my face. If I got it just right, the wind would push the hat tight on my head. After losing a few hats on the river, you tend to get the hang of it.

We were coming up to the camp by this time. I slowed the motor as I approached the river bank. Willy jumped out and I passed him his sleeping bag, a big sheet of plastic, his backpack, which contained mostly beer and his 410 shotgun. He piled everything on the riverbank and gave the boat a shove out into the current. We acted as if someone were watching, so if they were, our story would be believable.

"See you later!" I said, putting the motor in gear. I took the boat upriver a couple of miles and pulled it into a small creek on the opposite side of the river, tying it to an overhanging willow that was sticking out into the river. I shut the motor off and took out a bag of pot and rolled a joint.

I sat in the boat and smoked the joint. I figured I would give Willy about a half an hour and then go back down. If someone was watching the pot, I think that Willy would have flushed them out by that time. And if no one was watching it, Willy would have it packed down to the riverbank.

I had a fishing pole in the boat and a container full of worms, so I threw a line in and fished a bit while I was waiting. I managed to catch a two-pound Dolly Varden within a couple of minutes. It was the only bite I got during the twenty minutes or so I was killing time. When I figured enough time had gone by, I untied the boat and started the motor. Within a few minutes, I came around the corner, until the bank where I had dropped Willy off came into view. I could see something on the river bank, but I couldn't tell what it was at first. As I got closer, I could see Willy walking out of the bush dragging a big pile of pot plants wrapped up in plastic. He threw it down on the river bank right next to his sleeping bag, which was already filled with pot. Willy sat down on the bank, cracking open a beer waiting for me to pull in.

I swung the boat around to face upriver and steered it into the bank, throwing the motor into neutral just before landing. I then shifted it back into forward gear so that the motor would hold the boat against the bank.

Willy and I loaded the two piles of pot into the boat and backed out into the river, turning the boat down river and taking off. The pot took up way less room now that it was dry. Willy went to the rear of the boat so he could talk to me as we went.

"Well, there was nobody watching. There was no sign of anybody even being there. I cased out the area first before I approached the shack," he said. "When I realized I was alone, I started cutting it down and rolling it up."

The plants were bulging out of the plastic and the sleeping bag. Even dry, it was quite an impressive pile. It was about eleven o'clock in the morning by this time and the sky was still clear. I couldn't help feeling nervous as we motored downriver with the weed. I kept my eye on the sky, just in case any choppers or planes were flying that morning.

We managed to make it all the way back without anyone seeing us. It was too risky to transport the crop anywhere in the daylight. We stashed the bundles under some brush along the river and decided to wait until nightfall.

We drove the tractor back to the farm and hung around there for the day, careful not to arouse any suspicion. I spent some time catching up on the garden work and later went to sleep for a couple hours in the afternoon.

Willy and Linda spent the day hanging out together. At first Katy was really bothered by their relationship, Willy not being a fellow who lived up to the Lighthouse ideals, but as time went on, she softened up.

I think she was following Linda's lead and began to act friendlier towards me, too.

She actually came to the bedroom and got in bed with me that afternoon. I awoke to find Katy laying next to me and wanting to seduce me. It was the first time I had been intimate with Katy since before she left for California, almost eight months before.

I think she was just horny, though. Nothing else had really changed. Maybe she just felt bad about turning me in to the cops.

Willy and I stayed around for dinner, seeing as how things improved that day. Katy left for the Gypsy cabin just before it got dark and Willy and I left shortly afterwards.

We took the tractor and wagon to the river, picking up the two bundles of pot.

We managed to make it all the way to Larry's place without anyone seeing us. I drove the tractor around back of the house so it couldn't be seen from the road. We took one of the bundles inside. Before lighting any lights, we covered all the windows in the house so that anyone driving by couldn't see any lights coming from the house.

Three hundred plants take a really long time to clean and bag up. It took Willy and I five nights straight, working all night, right through to eight in the morning, to get all the plants handled. We would go to the farm during the day and try to get a few hours sleep, while not letting on what was going on.

After the fifth night of cleaning, we finally finished. The following night, I brought my scale to Larry's and we bagged it all up in one- pound bags. It came out to thirty- three pounds. Those were the days when the whole plant was smoked, except for the large and discolored leaves. Nobody had heard of buds. The pot seemed to be very good. Willy and I had been smoking it right through the whole ordeal. It was kind of risky to leave the thirty-three pounds there while we were trying to sell it, so we put it in old feed bags and hid it in a big hole that I had been dumping trash in for three or four years. We threw it in the hole and covered it up with some old trash so it looked like it was part of the trash. That's where the crop lived for about the three weeks it took to find a buyer.

I ran into George one day, a guitar player friend of mine. He asked me if I knew where he could buy any weed. I had known George for a few years and thought he was trustworthy enough to let him in on it. I also wanted to sell the weed.

I made a deal with George to sell the crop to him. He drove a taxi and every Sunday morning at 11 o'clock, George drove his taxi to the river at Longstock. I met him there with the boat and five pounds. The price was $200 a pound. George paid me $1000 every week when he picked up the pot. He bought thirty pounds. We kept the other three pounds, of which Willy, Larry and I each got a pound. We stashed the pound for Larry in the root cellar under his house.

We split the money up on the thirty pounds, with each of us getting $2000. It was late November when Larry got out of jail and was deported. They sent him to Seattle first and then he took the Alaska Ferry back up north to Ketchikan. I put the money away until I got a letter from him saying he was back in Alaska.

I wrote back, saying that I would come up to Ketchikan and bring him his share of the money. It was already early December when I finally heard from Larry. Willy was still around and he thought it would be a good idea to go with me. Willy and I stopped at James and Bonnie's trailer on the way back from Prince George one night. We were talking about going to Alaska. James decided he wanted to go with us.

The three of us headed off a couple days later. We drove the five hundred miles out to Prince Rupert and took the Alaska Ferry north to Ketchikan. It was a six-hour ride up the coast to Alaska. The scenery was breathtaking. At one point on the trip, there was a school of dolphins chasing the ferry. I went out on the deck and watched them. They shot through the water like rockets as they followed the ferry for quite a long way.

The three of us were hanging out at the bar when we heard the ferry's engines slow down. We were approaching Ketchikan. We left the truck in Prince Rupert and were traveling as foot passengers. After we got off the ferry I phoned Larry's place to let them know that we were on our way. We then grabbed a cab.

Larry came outside the house and met us. Willy and Larry didn't know each other until now. Larry was really happy to see us. We went in the house and Larry rolled a couple joints and passed each of us a beer.

I took Larry over to the side and gave him his share of the money.

He was really surprised.

We sat around for hours, drinking, smoking joints and swapping stories. After a while, Kathy came over and joined us. Shortly afterwards, a girl named Connie and her boyfriend Roy showed up. And then a couple more girls, Barbara and Judy.

We partied at Larry's until about 7, then took a cab to the Arctic Bar. It was a cool little bar on the waterfront. The outside deck was built out over the water and had its own dock for people who came by boat. Larry was in a real party mode, once we got to the Arctic he was buying drinks left and right.

"I'm gonna show you every bar in this town," Larry boasted. "We'll start at the bottom and go up from there. Let's go." Larry led our group of nine out of the Arctic, down the street to a bar called the Shamrock.

"This is the bottom, my friends," Larry announced to us all before we went inside. Larry led us in and to a table in the back. We had been drinking tequila with beer chasers over at the Arctic, so it seemed reasonable to order the same here. I guess you might say we were quite loud and were feeling no pain by this time. Larry, James, Willy, and Roy were sitting at one end of the table and Connie, Kathy, Barbara, Judy and I were at the other end. I had my eye on Judy. She told me she

326

was single and it looked like the interest was mutual. There were a couple of other groups of people sitting at some of the other tables. The bar was not full. There were probably about thirty people in the bar, besides us. We were getting pretty loud, laughing and carrying on. We were also spending Canadian money. It wasn't long before the whole place knew there were Canadians at our table.

I wasn't sure how things got started, but there seemed to be some friction going on between our table and another table close to us. I was feeling pretty loaded by this time and my thoughts were directed towards Judy.

At one point, I noticed that there was a heated exchange of words between our table and another. Someone yelled something about "The Fucking Canadians." At that point things became even more heated. James and Willy were both tough customers. James had been hardened from his time spent in jail and was no stranger to fighting. As a matter of fact, he liked to fight. He had a couple of scars on his face from past fights and a scar on his side from a jailhouse fight where he was stabbed with a home made knife. Willy was a tall, lanky cowboy who could fight. He had won every fight he had ever been in. His long reach and a powerful punch had laid many a man out. Though he tried walking away from fights most of the time he was someone to be reckoned with if you pushed him into it.

I really didn't realize that things were getting out of hand until I got up to go to the can. The urinal in the can was halfway ripped off the wall. I pissed in it anyway. I guess I thought that it was supposed to be like that; after all, we were in the sleaziest bar in town. I came back out and sat down next to Judy again.

Things were going pretty well between us.

A fellow came over to our table, clutching a big pipe wrench. Standing next to the table, he said, "Okay, which one of you guys ripped the urinal off the wall in the can?"

James and Larry started laughing; "What the fuck are you talking about?" James snarled at the guy.

"One of you guys ripped the urinal of the wall," he said again.

"Fuck off, buddy. Who the fuck are you anyway?" James said.

"I'm the maintenance man here."

"Well then, you better go fix it!" James said, laughing about it.

Nobody took the guy seriously. We were all laughing.

"Hey man, it was already ripped down when I saw it," I said to the guy.

"Yeah, well, it was up when you people showed up here," he said. The guys at the other table were paying close attention to what was going on. Yelling out remarks like," fucking Canadians, go back to Canada, fucking assholes!"

James was starting to get mad and the exchanges were getting pretty hot. The maintenance man was standing in front of us, slapping the pipe wrench against his hand in a threatening kind of way.

James pushed his chair back and stood up face to face with the maintenance man. "How would you like that wrench stuck up your ass, buddy?" he said. The guy started to shake and didn't say a word as James stared him down. "That's what I thought," James said, crowding him. "Now get the fuck away from our table, right now!"

The maintenance man slowly backed across the room and disappeared. James sat back down and the happy mood returned at our table again. My attention shifted back to Judy.

Before we ordered the next round, Kathy said, "Hey, let's blow this place! It ain't very friendly here and we got about forty more bars to hit yet." We slugged down our remaining drinks and all got up to leave. Judy and I had our arms around each other as we started to walk out of the bar.

As we were leaving, the maintenance man appeared again with a length of pipe in his hands. He was standing near the door when Judy and I walked out. He followed us out of the bar and the entire bar piled out onto the street. We probably could have gotten out of there if we had just taken off quickly, but somebody yelled some obscenities at us and James started yelling back.

"Come on man, let's just get out of here," Kathy said, trying to keep us all moving.

"Fuck them guys!" James was yelling as we slowly walked away from the bar.

"Fuck you, too!" one of the other guys yelled from behind us. James stopped and started walking back towards him. We all kind of followed James. He was walking back into this crowd of maybe thirty people. I was pretty drunk at that point and went after James, grabbing him by the arm. "Come on, man, let's get the fuck out of here!" I said. James looked over at me and I don't even remember what he said, when all of a sudden, out of nowhere, a piece of pipe hit him right in the teeth. All I remember about it was that there was a big crack and teeth were flying. Next thing I knew, Willy dropped the guy with the pipe, hitting him square in the mouth. He went down like a ton of bricks. We all circled James, trying to protect him. Reaching down, I grabbed his arm and pulled him up. His teeth were gone, or at least the ones in the front of his mouth that I could see. His mouth was full of blood.

"Give me your knife!" he said knowing that I had an old-timer, folding knife in a sheath on my belt. By this time, Willy was engaged with a couple of guys. The first guy took a solid punch, his eyes rolled and down he went. Larry and Roy both got jumped by several people and were swinging it out. I unsnapped my sheath and took off my coat, handing it to one of the girls. James grabbed the knife out of my sheath and went to work.

I turned around just in time to see a fist flying at me. Dodging the punch, I let one fly, landing on the nose of the guy throwing the punch. It knocked him back, blood flowing out of his nose. At this point, it was thirty against the five, Kathy was the only girl who got into it. Each of us had three to five guys on us. I remember just getting ready to throw a punch and the lights went out. Someone hit me from behind with a hammer. I think it was a hammer, by the shape of the bruise I had on my back the next day. It hit me right in the shoulder blade and apparently knocked me out.

James stabbed four people before the crowd overwhelmed him, knocking him to the ground. Both Larry and Roy fought hard, managing to hold their own pretty well, but were eventually overwhelmed, too. Willy was knocking guys down left and right. He had a wrecking-ball punch that would leave few men standing after he hit them. The crowd of guys got around James

330

and were kicking him all over, in the head, in the ribs in the back.

I don't remember a thing, but James told me later that he could see me from the ground, where he was getting kicked. "You kept getting up, and they kept knocking you down again!" It must have been true, because my knees were really hurting the next day. As a matter of fact, it took more than two years before my knees felt right again after that.

When I came to, there was a guy shaking me. Not hard, but he was trying to determine whether I was seriously hurt or not. I heard him saying "Hey, buddy, are you all right?" He was the first thing I heard and saw when I came to. He was looking me right in the eyes. "You okay?" He repeated himself several times before I was coherent enough to answer. "Yeah, yeah, man, I'm okay." I totally remembered what was going on when I had been knocked out. I looked around, the Shamrock was across the street and I was on the sidewalk at the sea wall. There was a pipe fence and the waves were crashing below.

'How did I get over here?' I thought. 'Right next to the water and I was totally unconscious. I could have fallen in the water in the dark.' I looked the other direction. There were lights flashing. There were cop cars and a couple of ambulances there. I started to walk over there, when Barbara and Judy caught up to me and stopped me.

"You okay, Louie?" Judy asked.

"I don't know. My arm or shoulder might be broken."

"How about we stay over here away from the cops," Judy said as she took me by the arm and led me back across the street. She checked out my arm and shoulder, and deduced that it wasn't broken.

"Who went in the ambulance?" I asked Judy. Kathy and Connie walked over to us just then and filled us in.

"James and Larry went to the hospital. James got severely beaten up after he stabbed those guys. He got four of them, cut them up before they got the knife away from him. All four of those guys went in the ambulance. Larry got a shot in the head. I don't know if it was a punch or not, but he was talking crazy afterwards. Roy and Willy are still talking to the cops. Don't know if they're going to be arrested or not."

We hung around a little while longer. The cops let Willy and Roy go. We grabbed a cab back to Larry's. His house was open. Everybody came in and I made a few phone calls, trying to track down information on James and Larry.

My shoulder was really hurting. Judy helped me get my shirt off and we had a look at it. I had to look at it with a mirror. It was a perfectly round bruise in the shape of a hammer head. It was right in the middle of the shoulder blade. The rest of my back was streaked with broken blood vessels on the surface. It looked terrible. About an hour and a half later, Larry walked in. He had a bandage around his head, under which they shaved some hair and gave him six stitches. He seemed all right at that point.

I asked about James.

"They ain't letting James go. Besides being really beat up, the cops have charged him with assault. He's in pretty bad shape. He got a couple of ribs broken and there is damage to the fluid that surrounds the lungs. Not only that, but the guys that got stabbed were the Guildermores, from the family of Guildermores that own the sawmill and pulp mill here. The family is among the founding fathers of Ketchikan. None of those guys are gonna get charged."

"They were hitting people with pipes and hammers!" I said, turning and showing Larry my back.

"Holy cafesus," said Larry.

I spent the night at Judy's place. She just lived a few doors away from Larry's. It was a really uncomfortable night. I could only lie on my uninjured side. Any other position hurt like hell. I couldn't stop thinking about James getting charged and the other guys not.

The next morning I took some painkillers and went down to see the cops. I tried to plead my case to them, but was told that it's in the hands of the prosecutor now. It was him I should talk to.

I found the prosecutors office and after a long wait, I finally got in to see him.

"I'm inquiring about the case of James Dayton. I'm wanting to know where things stand."

"Mr. Dayton is charged with assault with a deadly weapon. He has a hearing in court tomorrow morning," he said.

"Is anyone else being charged?"

"No, nobody else, just Mr. Dayton," he said.

"Why not? James wasn't the only one with a deadly weapon. There were guys swinging pieces of pipe and hammers around."

"Hammers?"

"Yes, hammers! Look at this!" I took off my coat and shirt, exposing my back. By this time it looked real ugly. My entire back was black and blue. The perfectly round mark from the hammer head stuck right out.

"That looks pretty bad! Did you see who did it?"

"No, but I saw who knocked James's teeth out with a piece of pipe.

That's what started the fight."

"It was the maintenance man at the bar. I saw him, hell, we all saw him with the piece of pipe, he was holding it before we even left. They came outside after us. It was a sucker shot. I saw him hit James with the pipe."

He was taking notes by this time. "You didn't see who hit you, huh?"

"No, man, they got me from behind!"

We talked a while more about the case and he said he would look into it. It was the first he had heard about the other guys having weapons, too. The cops hadn't said any thing about it.

"Talk to me tomorrow. I'll see you at the court house." I left feeling optimistic.

I went over to Judy's after I left the prosecutors office. Shortly after I got there, we got a call from Kathy. She said that Larry was in the hospital again. I guess he passed out just walking down the street and somebody passing by hailed a cab and took him to the hospital. Kathy was going down there to check it out. She said she would call later.

A couple hours later, Kathy showed up at the house with Larry. They had checked him out in the hospital and confirmed that he had a concussion. He was supposed to take it easy for the next week and not do anything strenuous.

I filled Larry in on what happened at the prosecutor's office. It seemed that James might be able to claim self-defense. He was going to court in the morning and we all planned on being there. We got word that Bonnie would be coming in on the next ferry. The ferry was getting in the following afternoon, after James court appearance.

All eight of us showed up in court the next morning. Bob Faddus came with us as well. It was a short appearance, taking less than ten minutes. James was in the prisoners box, looking really bad. He had a hard time walking and the look on his face revealed he was in a lot of pain. They set his bail at $20,000. A bondsman would take 10% to put up the money. Nobody else was going to get charged.

I talked briefly with the prosecutor. He told me that James was going to be the only one charged. Self-defense might be an issue, but that was going to be decided at the trial. He asked me if I would come to his office later that afternoon. He seemed in a big hurry and rushed off.

As we were leaving the courthouse, Bob took me aside. "I can put up the money to get James out," he said. "I don't really know the guy though, he's your friend. If I give you the money, it's going to be a loan to you. You gotta make sure I get it back."

"As long as James comes back to go to court, the bail gets returned, or most of it anyway. I think the bondsman charges 10 or 15%," I said. "Let me think about it for a bit."

Bonnie would be in on the ferry later that day. I would talk it over with her before I made a decision. We all went back to Larry's place and hung out there until afternoon when the ferry came in. Willy and I went to the ferry dock to meet Bonnie and to my surprise, Willy got on the ferry. He didn't really tell me that he was going to leave. Bonnie got off and we hung around until they started to load the ferry.

"I'll see you in Longstock," Willy said as he was leaving. Bonnie and I grabbed a cab back to Larry's. She wanted to come with me when I went to see the prosecutor.

We walked into the prosecutor's office late in the afternoon. He asked us to sit down, and closed the door behind us.

I introduced Bonnie to him and we both shook hands with him. He sat back in his chair and started to talk: "I know you're concerned about your friend, but the situation is not good. Three of the men that he stabbed were Guildermores. Not being from around here, you may not know who they are. The Guildermores are one of the most influential families in Ketchikan. No charges are going to be brought against them. As a matter of fact, there is a lot of pressure to make an example out of Mr. Dayton. What I'm telling you is strictly off the record, you understand. I really can't talk to you about the case. I'm going to give you some advice, though. If you get Mr. Dayton out on bail, I suggest you get out of Alaska and don't come back. Your friend has quite an extensive criminal record," he said, handing me a paper with a print out of James's record. "Things are not going to go well for him if he goes to trial here."

I started to read the print out. I counted thirty-five convictions, for everything from assault and robbery to drunkenness and impaired driving. He had spent fifteen of his thirty-five years in jail in Ontario.

He let me keep a copy of the print out and opened the door for us to leave.

"I guess you knew about this," I said to Bonnie. "I think that was a pretty clear warning."

Bonnie was pretty upset and didn't talk much on the way

back to Larry's. We got out of the cab and before we went into the house, I stopped her.

"Bonnie, we've got to decide what we're going to do here. My friend Bob said he would lend me the bail money. Understand that it's a personal loan. If James doesn't come back, I'll end up owing Bob $2000. That's not something I can afford. I have got my own problems. The only way I'll borrow the money is if you guarantee me the money is getting paid back or that James will come back to court."

She looked at me with tears in her eyes, "I have to call my Dad."

We stood outside for a few minutes while Bonnie got herself together and went in.

She called her Dad in Ontario and talked to him for over an hour. It turns out that her Dad was a bondsman in Toronto. She got her Dad to call the bondsman in Ketchikan, and see what he could work out.

Her Dad called back about an hour later. It seems as if the bondsman was expecting James to run when he got out. The odds were not good in getting a fair shake, considering that he had stabbed the Guildermore boys. The Alaskan bondsman was reluctant to take the customary 10% as bond, with the risk of James not appearing being so great.

He was going to call the bondsman back in a little while and try again. He said he'd call Bonnie back.

James finally got out of the hospital. Bonnie, Larry, and I went to visit him in jail. He looked really bad. He moved like an old man. We told him about what was going on with his bail.

I looked him in the eyes and asked him point blank, "James,

if I stick my neck out for the $2000, I want you to promise me that I'm not going to lose the money, that you either come back and go to court, or if you do take off you will make sure I don't get stuck with it. You've got to pay it back. Deal?"

He looked up at me. His face was full of pain...maybe because he knew I was going to get screwed and he was going to screw me. Maybe James had done too much jail time in his life to take the chance. Maybe Bonnie just wouldn't let him do it.

"I promise either way. You won't get screwed." He looked me right in the eyes when he said it. I wanted to believe him, so I did.

Bonnie's Dad finally convinced the Alaskan bondsman to take the $2000 as bond and get James out. I got the money from Bob. We got James out and the three of us got the ferry the next day back to Prince Rupert. We drove from there to Longstock. I left Bonnie and James at their trailer at the resort, crossed the river, and went home. The next day they both took a bus back to Toronto and I never saw them again.

Chapter 15

Changing seasons

When I got home, Katy and the boys were the only ones there. Linda, Willy and her kids split back to the U.S. a couple days before I got there. According to Katy, they were getting pretty friendly by the time they left.

There was a ton of work to do. The snow was already deep and the woodpile was getting kind of low. I spent quite a few days cutting and hauling wood with the horses. Chico was old enough to help out with loading and unloading though some of the blocks were too big to lift. Of course, the sleigh rides in between were fun. Katy had seemed to be less intense about the Lighthouse cult and we actually had a nice Christmas.

We had the New Years Eve party at our place again. It was another cold night. The temperature got down to 40 below zero. It was a mixture of sleighs and ski-doos coming out for the party this time. Ross had his bobsleigh going and had Bob and Paula Hooty with him. Harry was using Freddy's cutter. Toad and Annie came out in the new sleigh that he built during the summer. The McCoby's came out on their ski-doos.

Lana rode a horse out and she was so cold when she got to the house that she rode her horse right up on the porch. I heard someone yelling outside and went out to find Lana so cold that she couldn't even get off the horse. I helped her off and she stumbled inside. I tied her horse up for her. It was cold.

The party was a little subdued this year, with only Harry from the Alaskan group there. We missed Bob's drunken version of 'What I say,' but the party was quite lively anyway.

Ross was on the arm-wrestling kick and ended up arm-wrestling everyone including the girls before the night was over. He really wasn't that strong, though. He only beat Bob McCoby and a couple of the girls. He couldn't beat Paula, even though he tried three or four times, she put him down every time. He seemed to get weaker every time she beat him...but the drunker he got, the stronger he thought he was.

It was another cold, clear night, with a bright moon lighting up everything as if it were daylight. The party was kind of uneventful, except for Lana nearly freezing her feet and Harry taking off with the horse not hooked to the sleigh and too drunk to correct the situation. I ran after the horse and got him hooked up again.

The next morning, there was a trail of stuff that used to be in the sleigh lining the road. I guess Harry took the corner too sharply and flipped the sleigh over. Sinbad didn't have any trouble pulling the sleigh for a couple of miles upside down. It was the last trip that that sleigh ever took. I was in the Purden Lake restaurant one day and I heard a bunch of loggers talking a couple of tables over. I heard one of them say that they were looking for fallers. I had no experience at that time as a faller, except for the day I spent in bush with Bud. I walked over to the table and said," I heard you say you were looking for a faller."

"That's right," said one of the guys at the table. "You a faller?"

"Yup!" I answered.

"When can you start?" he asked.

"When do you want me to start?"

"How about Monday?"

"I'll be there," I said. "Where are you working?"

"You know where the Walker Creek road is?" I nodded. "Turn left just before the bridge. You can't miss it." I knew exactly where he was talking about. A couple of friends of ours, Benny and Marie, lived down that road. We had been to their place quite a few times.

"Okay!" I said. As I was walking out of the restaurant, I was thinking 'It's a good thing he didn't ask me who I worked for or how much experience I had!

I had a couple of days to get ready. I went back to Prince George the next day and bought a Ski-doo. I was going to have to cross the river every day on the ice in order to get to work. I also bought supplies that I would need for the job: wedges and tool pouch, an extra chain, files, etc.

On my first day on the job, they sent me into an area to start falling trees. The foreman told me to go to the back of the skid trails and work towards the front. I guess I went a little too far back and down the hill into the creek bed. After I fell about forty trees or so, I stopped to gas up the saw, I could hear someone yelling at me from the top of the hill. I grabbed my gear and walked up the hill. There was a cat at the top that came to skid the wood I was falling. As I approached, the operator climbed out on the track of the cat and said, "How in the hell am I supposed to get that wood out of there?"

I turned around and looked down the hill at the down timber. "I don't know," I said. I was told to go to the back and start."

"Yeah, but you can't fall trees down below the hill, cause I can't get them out. Start at the top and then work your way out. Don't go down the hill."

"Okay," I said, feeling kind of stupid.

"You're new at this, ain't you?" he said to me.

"How did you know?" I said. He just laughed.

"I'll give you a half an hour or so to get some trees down and I'll be back," he said, getting back into the cat and driving away. He was back in a half hour, like he said and started skidding my wood. I managed to stay ahead of him for the rest of the day.

Things seemed to go better after the first day. My falling lesson with Bud a few years before proved to be really valuable. Within a few days, I was falling a couple hundred trees a day, which was a reasonable count for a new guy.

I took to it really well and was making around $200 per

day after the first couple weeks. The pace was grueling though, getting up at five in the morning and getting home after six at night. I did a lot of tough jobs over the years, but I think falling was probably the hardest, over-all. I gained about 15 pounds in the first month, wading through a lot of pain on the way. Slugging through the snow with a chainsaw and all of my gear day after day put me in the best shape of my life.

Katy and the boys were still living at the house, but she was talking about wanting to move into Prince George. Chico was old enough to start kindergarten and Katy was not really happy living on the farm anymore. Even though things weren't all that bad at the moment, Katy and I both knew that our marriage was pretty well over and we were probably going our separate ways.

We were communicating pretty well at the time. We decided that we would get her a house in Prince George. We got a hold of David Parsons to see what was available. He sent us out to look at a place on Old Summit Lake Road. It wasn't a bad looking place. There was a little over an acre of land and it had a board fence around the whole property. The house wasn't that great, but it was certainly livable. There were at least four other out buildings on the property: a little cabin, a shop and two utility sheds. They were asking $18,000 for the property.

I took the deed to the farm into the bank and used it for collateral for $6000 for the down payment. The farm in Longstock was always in my name only. I forget why that happened, but at this point I was glad about it.

It took a month or so to get the deal straight and completed. I was still working in the bush when Katy moved into town.

This meant that I was having to get up even earlier to feed the animals, now that she wasn't there to do it.

Every two weeks, on the Friday of the second week, I would go into Prince George to see her and the kids. I had done it for the first few months she was living in Prince George. When I went into Prince George two weeks after she left, I found the house that we had bought empty.

I ended up calling Dave Parsons place to find out if he knew where she was. Dave told me she had moved into an apartment. He gave me the address. I went over there right away. I knocked on the door.

"Oh, hi! she said, opening the door.

"What's going on, how come you're in here and not at the house?" I said.

"Oh, I just decided I didn't like it."

"That would have been a good thing to decide before we bought it," I said.

"Well, when I got into town, I went to the transition house. Then my dad came down here from Alaska to help me move. He took one look at the house and said he didn't want me living in such a dump. He convinced me that if I went to welfare, that they would get me and the kids a place. I did and they did and here we are."

"What are we supposed to do with the house we bought?" I said. "I don't know and I don't care."

"What do you mean you don't care? I still have to pay for it! I put up the farm to get that place!" I was really upset.

It seemed that Katy couldn't care less. I realized that I wasn't going to get anywhere with her, and decided to let it be for now. I hadn't seen the boys for a couple of weeks, so I turned my attention to them. We had a good visit. I even went to bed with Katy before I headed back home to Longstock for another grueling two weeks.

That was pretty much the drill for the rest of the winter. I came into Prince George to see Katy and the kids every two weeks, had a good visit with the boys, had sex with Katy and left.

I worked falling until the end of March and then went up in the mountains, slashing. That's when you cut down all that is still standing after the logging is done. Most of the time it's the less desirable species, like cedar, birch, poplar, or alders. Those trees were cut down and left in the block. The forest service burned the blocks by dripping burning liquid down onto the ground from helicopters. The standing trees impeded this process, making it dangerous for the helicopters. I stayed up in the logging camp in the mountains while I worked this job. I had arranged for Ross to throw out hay for the animals while I was gone.

It took two weeks to finish the job. Break-up had set in by the time we were done. The roads were falling apart. There were about 15 people in our crew. We all left together the next morning in a caravan of eight vehicles. The roads were thawing out, but still had frost in most of the road, though it was about a foot below the mud in many places. Every now and then, we would come across a spot where the frost was completely out of the road and the mud had no bottom.

It took us four hours to go the first 12 miles. The last five miles of the road was good, and only took ten minutes.

It was Friday, so I thought I would go into Prince George

and see the kids before going home to Longstock. I got into Prince George about 4 o'clock in the afternoon that day. I drove over to Katy's place and parked in the front of the house. I got out of the car and walked up to the house, something was not right. There was a big window right by the steps. I looked in, the house was empty. There was no furniture, nothing.

I went to the house next door and knocked on the door to ask if they knew what happened. She told me they moved out a couple weeks ago.

I went to David Parsons office. I walked right by the secretary, right back to David's cubicle. "Dave, Katy is gone from her apartment. Where did she go?"

"I know," he said. "Her dad was here, and took her and the kids back to Alaska. I would have let you know, but I couldn't get in touch with you."

"Oh, fuck!" I was devastated. I left with Dave and we went to his place. We talked for a while, but I knew I had to go home. I hadn't been there for two weeks and Ross was looking after the animals. I left back to Longstock.

By this time break-up was in full swing. The roads were a mess and the river ice was pretty well impassable. I was stuck on the farm by myself.

The population of Longstock had thinned out considerably. It seemed strange to be the only one living on my place. There had almost always been somebody else there. Gypsy was gone back east, Moose and Dolly were in Washington, none of the Alaskans were there.

Greta and her boyfrind Dick were still there. The McCobys and Ross were there, and that was it. It was the lowest population since I moved there.

It was quiet and lonely around the farm. I was slipping into a deep depression. It wasn't so much that Katy was gone, it was mostly the kids. Things had been on the rocks with Katy and me for over a year and I was resigned to the fact that we would most likely split up. There was a definite difference this time. Not knowing where the boys were or when I would see them again, was really upsetting.

The snow was melting and the ground around the house and the garden started to show through. I had been feeding three cows, twelve goats and two horses all winter. I couldn't see the point in keeping them all now.

I decided to sell all of them except the two horses. I put an ad in the feed store in Prince George. I put my mailing address on the ad, seeing as I had no phone. Within a week I had a couple of letters from people interested in buying the cows. A couple days later, I walked the cows out to Sinclair Mills and loaded them into a trailer. Within a week I had sold all the goats, too.

Having only the horses left made the situation much easier. Once they were out to pasture, they more or less took care of themselves.

Harry showed up at the Alaskans place by himself around the end of May. If it wasn't for Harry coming around and egging me on, I probably wouldn't have even planted the garden. Harry and I hung out together a lot. We ended up going into Prince George about once a week to party at the Canada Hotel bar.

There was an acoustic coffee house that went on Sunday nights at the old cop shop that we started to frequent. It was on one of these nights at the coffee house that I met a woman named Sara. I played a set with my guitar and sang a song called 'Poncho and Lefty' that I had learned off a Emmy Lou Harris album. Apparently, I had some of the words wrong.

I was approached by this woman. She was stunningly beautiful, with long dark hair and dark eyes. "Hi," she said. "I'm Sara, I've seen you around, and I wanted to meet you."

I was quite taken with her and a little speechless at first.

"Well hello, ah... it's nice to meet you, too, I'm Louie," I said, reaching out to shake her hand. She held onto my hand for what seemed like a long time.

"I'll have to teach you the right words to the 'Poncho and Lefty' song," she said, still holding on to my hand.

"Did I get them wrong?" "Yeah, you did," she said.

We hit it off right away. She had kinda of a gypsy look to her. A couple inches shorter than me, she had dark skin and fiery eyes. Her hair flowed and curled around her face, hiding part of it. She seemed to be always peeking out at me. Mysterious, beautiful, charming, and sexy, she was simply irresistible.

She invited me to her house after the coffee house. Harry figured out what was going on and told me not to worry about him, that he would get home okay. There was a train first thing in the morning. Sara had come there with her sister Marie and her boyfriend Mark. We all went back to Sara's place. Mark was a guitar player, too, and we ended up playing and singing for hours afterward.

It was pretty late when Marie and Mark went home. Sara and I stayed up and talked for what seemed like a long time. I thought that she might ask me to stay, but I wasn't sure. After all, we'd just met that night.

Suddenly Sara got up and went into the bedroom. I thought

she was coming right back when I heard her calling me.

"Louie, come here," she said. I went into the bedroom and Sara was already under the covers. "Want to stay with me?"

"Yeah, I do!"

"Come to bed, then," she said.

I got undressed and crawled under the covers. She pulled me towards her and wrapped herself around me.

That was the start of my relationship with Sara, though she was really not the marrying kind. We both pretty much knew that from the beginning and never really felt committed to each other in that way. We were just having fun and enjoying each other, with no strings attached. It was a good relationship for me to be in at this stage in my life. I was lucky to know Sara. She was one of those beautiful people that comes into and touches, your life forever.

She came out to Longstock with me for a couple of days. It sure changed my outlook on life. All of a sudden, I was full of energy. With Sara's help, I got about fifty pot plants planted in the bush.

We took the horses for a ride every chance we got. She loved to ride. She rode a lot as a kid. When she was ten years old, her parents got her a horse of her own.

Sara and I spent a lot of time together after that. She would come out to the farm sometimes and I would stay at her place in Prince George. I felt really good when I was out with her. Her magnetic personality and stunning beauty made me the envy of all the guys, no matter where we went. She loved music and dancing and we did quite a bit of both. The Sunday night coffeehouses were a regular event for us.

349

About the beginning of June, Moose and Dolly showed up at the farm. A couple of days later, Gypsy and his new girlfriend Jennifer got off the train. All of a sudden, there were people around again. Sara was a hit with everyone. Gypsy especially liked her. Her gypsy look and exciting personality were really attractive to him. He flirted with her all the time, even in front of Jennifer and me.

The house was a bustle of activities compared to the last year. Katy's chanting had not only kept me out of the house, but it also affected how much company we got. Sara was spending more time there, too. We split our time between Longstock and Prince George.

I still had the two horses and was feeling ambitious one day. I plowed up about three acres, and planted it in oats for the horses.

It was about the middle of June when I got a message that a company called Beavertail Steel wanted to talk to me about doing a concrete foundation contract. They had gotten my name from another company that I worked for previously.

I called them from Sara's place and got an interview the same day. It was a big industrial job. Beavertail steel sold large industrial steel buildings that were made in Ontario, shipped to B.C. This building was 150 feet by 100 feet.

I got the contract and had to get a crew together. I hired Moose and Skid, who just showed up a couple of days before. I worked with Moose back in Colorado. Sara worked on the job, too. She might have been the best worker I had. Moose and Skid stayed in Sara's mom's basement for the two weeks it took us to do the job.

Sara and I were at her mom's place one night after work

and her mom was looking for someone to go to the wrestling matches with her. There was a big-time wrestling show going on in Prince George. The wrestling only came to town once a year, so she didn't want to miss it. I was really not into that sort of thing, but Sara took me aside and asked me. "Would you take my mom to the wrestling, Louie? She really wants to go."

I reluctantly agreed. Joyce was a older woman. She was in her sixties, just a year or so from retirement. Why she liked the wrestling so much was beyond me. I had never been to a wrestling show before, though I 'd seen it on TV. It always looked fake.

It was a sold-out crowd and the fans seemed to be in a frenzy. The first couple of matches were not all that exciting, but then they had the cage match. All the fans were yelling when the matches started and Joyce was no exception. They put these guys in a cage and it's supposed to be fight to the finish. When this match started, Joyce leaped out of her seat. She starts screaming at the wrestlers, "Kill him, kill him, rip his eyes out!" I wasn't even sure who she was rooting for.

The match went on and on and Joyce went on and on. I couldn't believe that this frail, old woman could, or would, carry on like this. I was pretending that I didn't know her while she kept screaming at the wrestlers all through the rest of the program.

"Well, did you have fun, mom?" Sara asked as we came back.

"Oh yes, I did. I had lots of fun," she said as Sara looked at me. I just shrugged my shoulders and rolled my eyes. "Later," I said.

On the drive to her place, I told her all about the wrestling. We got a good laugh.

Chapter 16

Louie and the Cops

It had been about ten months since the Longstock raid.

I got a message from Archie that the trial was coming up in a few

days. About a week before the court date, Shirley Parsons and my friends Benny Perkins, Harry, Sara, and I went to the drive-in to see the new movie 'Star Wars' that had just been released. We all couldn't fit in my pickup truck, so I borrowed a van from a friend. I made arrangements with my friend Vincent to meet him at the Canada Hotel Bar after the movie. It was early in the year and we were a little short on pot. I think we only had a couple of joints between us, so we stopped by the liquor store and picked up a bottle of tequila to take to the movie.

We smoked one of the joints soon after we got there, and saved the other one for about the halfway mark, while passing the bottle of tequila around steadily until it was gone. I don't really remember much about the movie. I may have been too loaded. After the movie, I was still feeling kind of buzzed from the tequila and drove the van down to the Canada Hotel Bar to return it to Vincent.

We pulled up in front of the bar and I shut the van off. When I pulled the van over, I hadn't noticed, but an unmarked detective car had pulled over right beside us. I was just opening the door to get out and there was a cop at my window. As I was starting to get out, he asked me to stay in the van. I closed the door and rolled down the window. He asked for my license and registration. I dug through my wallet and showed him my license. Looking through the glovebox, I searched for the registration, but couldn't find it.

"Is this your vehicle?" the cop asked.

"No, it's not," I answered, trying not to get too close to the cop, in case my breath smelled like tequila. "It 's a friend of mine's van. I borrowed it to go to the drive-in and I'm returning it to him here. He's in the hotel bar waiting for me," I said, pointing across the street at the hotel.

The second cop had gone to the other side of the van, where Harry and Benny had already gotten out. Sara and Shirley were still in the van. Harry nonchalantly walked beside a building that we were parked next to and proceeded to have a piss. The cop was busy with Benny and the girls, getting everyone to show him ID. Harry came out from beside the building and walked across the street and into the bar, unnoticed.

It was a few minutes later that one of the cops says, "Hey, what happened to that other guy?" Benny and I looked at each other and talked at the same time: "What other guy?"

The cop seemed sure that there was another guy, but we all denied that there was anybody else.

One of the cops went back to his car to call in and check us out, when Vincent came out of the bar and walked up to the van. He was feeling no pain, having been in the bar the whole time we were at the movies.

Harry had slipped away and on into the bar, telling Vincent,

"The cops have got Louie pulled over with your van right outside the bar!" Vincent went outside to investigate.

"What's the problem, guys?" he asked, walking across the street to the van.

"This is the guy who owns the van," I said to the cop.

"Is this your van?" said the cop.

"It sure is!" said Vincent, in kind of a smart-ass tone.

"Got a registration?" he asked. I guess Vincent kept the registration on the sun visor, one place that I didn't think to look. While he was dealing with the other cop, the one who went to the car to check us out came back to my window and gave me everyones ID.

"You're the guy that grows three hundred pounds huh?" he said to me.

"Yeah, right!" I replied.

Walking around the car to the other side where his partner was, he said, "Hey Bill, let's get out of here!" He quickly gave Vincent back his registration and both cops got in the car and took off.

We were talking and laughing about the cops taking off so quickly and walked across the street and into the bar. There was Harry on the crowded dance floor, dancing with a 300-pound Native woman.

While we were in Prince George, working, strange things were occurring in Longstock and Penney. The cops launched a boat at Penney and brought two drug squad cops downriver to Longstock. They had a couple of dirt bikes they unloaded and used to get around on. Two cops took off from the river on their motor bikes and headed up towards the center of town.

354

Their first stop was at Chad's place. There was nobody home. Chad had been living in Prince George, working as a counselor for Corrections at the halfway house. He only came home every other weekend and then sometimes only for the day. The house was locked up and so was the building that they had moved from across the river several years before. The cops ripped the lock off the doors of both buildings and got in. They searched through his house, looking for pot, I guess. They found nothing in the house and proceeded to break into the other building.

They didn't find any pot, but they did find a case of beer that Chad had locked up in the shed. They cracked the case of beer and each had a couple while they were looking around his place.

They went from there to the Alaskan's place. There was nobody home at the time, as Harry was in Prince George that day. They went in the house and searched the place, sitting down at the table and making themselves at home while having another beer.

They left there on their motor bikes and went up to McCobys. Bob and Wayne were outside working on their woodpile when the cops drove up. They didn't identify themselves as police, but acted like they were old friends that just stopped to make small talk. Both Bob and Wayne thought it a little weird when these complete strangers offered them a beer. They both refused, thinking, this a bit strange, but the cops cracked a couple of beers, anyway.

They drove across the tracks to Toad's place. Toad, hearing the motor bikes coming up his driveway, came outside and met the cops before they had a chance to knock on the door. "Can I help you fellows?" Toad asked.

"Yeah," answered one of the cops. "We're looking for Louie Karmen's place. Can you tell us how to get there?"

Toad gave them directions to my place, telling them that I wasn't there. He talked to them for a while, trying to find out more about them and what they wanted. They told him they were old friends of mine and were just stopping by for a visit.

As they drove off, Toad stood outside watching them leave. He had a feeling that something was strange about these two guys. They didn't exactly look like people that I would be friends with and they didn't seem to care that I wasn't home at the time.

They rode their motor bikes out to my place, leaving the gates open as they drove up to the house. They walked around the house and looking in the window, saw a tray on the table that had a little bit of pot on it.

The house was unlocked. I didn't have a lock on the door. I never felt that I needed one, but in this case, they probably would have broken in if I had. They went into the house and searched it, looking through all the cupboards and emptied everything out on the floor. They went through the dressers in the bedroom and all the bookshelves. They made a real mess of the house as they did not put anything back.

I had some 410 shotgun shells in a bowl on the counter in the kitchen. There were probably five or six of them. I don't know if they thought it would be a good joke or what, but they put them in the firebox in the cookstove. If undiscovered, they would undoubtedly go off as soon as the fire was lit. After they finished

356

making a mess of the house, they drove their motor bikes around in my field of oats and shot all my chickens. That's right, shot my damn chickens! I only had about 7 chickens and a rooster, but there was nothing but feathers left by the time I got home. They made a point of leaving all the gates open. They must have gone out of their way to open the gate to the horse pasture, because it's not one they needed to open to get to the house.

I guess there were a couple more cops motor-biking around Penney at the same time. The boat that had brought them down the river came back and picked them up, taking them back to the Penney landing later that afternoon.

Coincidentally, I had gone to court on the pot charges on Wednesday, the day before the cops were ransacking my place. The prosecutor said that he had a surveyor at the court house and he was going to testify that the pot was on my land. Even so, I don't know how they would ever prove that I knew anything about it anyway, being as it was a half a mile from my house.

The prosecutor came over to where Archie and I were talking and asked to talk to him. They walked out of my hearing range and exchanged a few words. Within a minute, Archie came back. "The prosecutor offered a deal. I told him I didn't think you would take it, but I'm obligated to tell you anyway."

"Okay, what's the deal?" I said.

"He said he's got a surveyor to testify that the pot was on your land, but if you pleaded guilty to possession that he would drop the cultivation charge."

"What's the difference?"

"There is no difference. They carry the same maximum sentence."

"Well, what's the point?

"He has no case. That's the point."

"Well, Archie," I said, "I think you should go over there and tell him that he should stick his deal up his ass. Let's see him prove cultivation."

Archie jumped up from his seat enthusiastically and walked back over to the prosecutor. I couldn't hear what they were saying, but I could see that the prosecutor was pretty upset by the time Archie left.

"What did you say to him?" I asked Archie.

"Just what you told me to," he answered. I had to chuckle.

It wasn't long after that we got called. Archie and I went into the courtroom and sat down. Then we had to stand up while the judge came in and then sit down again.

The bailiff stood up and read the charges. Archie and I stood up again while they read the charges and he acknowledged that he was representing me. Then the prosecutor stood up and announced that the Crown wanted to stay the charges.

Archie got up and walked out of the courtroom. I was sitting there in the chair and I wasn't sure what happened. I looked towards the door and through the little window I could see Archie waving at me to come out. I got up and walked out.

"What the hell happened?" I asked. "It's over. You got off."

"Well, shit, that was easy!"

"They can reopen the case if they get some proof within a year, but they won't. You beat it, it's over!" Archie explained.

We went back to his office and smoked another joint, blowing smoke out the window again.

I finished work early on Friday and decided to go out to

Longstock for the weekend. We still had a few days work to finish the contract, but word had it that Beavertail Steel had some more jobs for me.

I drove out to the landing and took my boat upriver to the landing on the Longstock side. I drove the power wagon home. On the way, I saw Greta and Dick on the road out in front of their place. They lived in the house that Katy and I used to live in while I was building my house.

"Hi Louie, how ya doing," said Dick as I stopped to talk. "Did you hear about the cops coming out here yesterday?"

"No! What were they doing here?" I answered, not thinking too much about it.

"They were on motor bikes, driving all around town. They passed here about noon and they were heading out to your place."

My place was the only place past Greta's, so if they were going in that direction, they had to be going there. "Not long after they passed here, we heard a bunch of gunshots." Greta said.

"Gun shots!" I exclaimed. Seemed pretty strange that they would hear shots coming from my place. I didn't know what to expect, so I invited them to come with me down to my place and check it out.

They got in the power wagon with me and we drove to the farm. The first thing we noticed is that the gates were open. I drove through the gate and up to the house. Both of my horses were grazing in my field of oats.

"Oh shit, the horses are in the oats!" I said. "We'd better catch them and put them back in the pasture!" The three of us walked out and got the horses. It looked like they had been tramping through the oats for a while, having tramped down much of the field. There were lots of motor bike tracks as well. While we were leading the horses back to the pasture, passing the chicken yard, we noticed feathers blowing around in the wind. I went up to the fence to have a closer look. There were no chickens, but lots of feathers and chicken parts scattered around.

"What the fuck!" I said, not believing that they had actually shot my chickens. "Well, that explains the shots you heard."

The gate was open in the horse pasture. We put the horses in and went to the house. The door was open. We went inside. I was shocked. It was obvious that they had been in my house. There was stuff scattered all over the place.

"Look at this shit!" I said in disbelief. We started cleaning up the kitchen, putting stuff back into the cupboards. When we had most of the stuff on the floor put away, I grabbed a handful of kindling wood and opened up the stove. I ripped a hunk of birch bark off the wood in the wood box and stuffed it into the firebox and lit it. As soon as it started to catch, I stuffed the kindling in on top of it. I was waiting for the kindling to start crackling before I put the bigger pieces of birch in.

We were talking among ourselves about the 'fucking cops' when there was a loud bang. It came from the firebox. "What the hell!" I exclaimed, when I heard a second bang.

I noticed that the shotgun shells were missing from the bowl on the counter. They had been there in the bowl for months prior.

"Let's get out of here, you guys," I said. We quickly got out of the house. While we were outside, we heard several more shots go off. We stayed outside for awhile while the kindling burned itself out and the shots stopped. After going back in, I open the stove and went digging through the firebox. I found the burnt out casings of six 410 shotgun shells in the stove. I was so pissed off.

"Those #@%#*## cops!" I ranted and raved about the cops for what seemed like a long time.

Greta and Dick headed home after a while and I cleaned up the mess the cops had left. I was just boiling about it the rest of the day and the next. I left early in the afternoon on Sunday and went back into Prince George. I went over to Sara's first and told her about what happened. David Parsons showed up at her house, looking for me and I told him what happened. I had to do something about it. I couldn't just let it go.

"I'm going down to see the cops. I gotta do something," I said. You guys want to come with me?"

Sara wasn't going to let me go by myself and David figured he'd better come too, for moral support.

We walked into the cop shop and up to the desk. There was a cop at the desk.

"What can I do for you?" he said.

"I want to file charges. My place has been ransacked, and my house as well."

"And who are you filing these charges against?" he said, getting ready with a pen and paper to write down names.

"Well, you tell me what the names of the cops who ransacked my place last week in Longstock."

He seemed to know that the cops had been out there. He put down his pen and looked at me and said, "That was the drug squad. They had a writ. You can't file charges against them."

I instantly flew into a rage, yelling at the cop, "What the hell do you think this is, communist Russia? You fucking cops think you can ransack my place and I can't do anything about it? You're out of your fucking mind!"

"You better get out of here! Because if you keep yelling at me that way, I'm going to arrest you!" he said.

Sara and David were literally dragging me out of the place while I screamed at the cop. "Communist bastards," I yelled as they were dragging me out the door. I was pissed.

We went back to Sara's place. I was so agitated! It took me a while to cool down. I just couldn't believe the cops telling me that I couldn't do anything about it. I hardly slept at all that night.

We were still working on the Beavertail Steel job the next morning. I got away from the job for a few minutes and phoned Archie's office, but wasn't able to talk to him. He was out of town. Archie's wife, Jill Dennis, was a lawyer as well and I ended up talking to her about it.

After listening to my story, she said, "You know, Louie, I think your best bet is to go public. There's a reporter at the newspaper that would just love to hear your story. He's not a fan of the cops and this story is pretty juicy. His name is Udo Wenzel. Give him a call."

I took her advice and phoned the newspaper. I got Udo on the phone and briefly described the situation to him.

"When can I meet you and talk to you about this?" he asked.

"I start work at eight. Any chance of meeting me before that?" I said.

We agreed to meet in the Simon Fraser Inn Restaurant at 6:30 the next morning. When I got there, Udo was already waiting for me. He had a copy of Mondays newspaper with him, which had a short article about the case that he had written, based on my phone call. Udo had no love for the cops and was eager to make them look bad, as he had on several other occasions.

He listened intently, taking notes in shorthand and stopping me every once in a while to ask me questions. I told him about the chickens being shot, the shotgun shells in the stove and about the deal that I was offered by the prosecutor the day prior to all this happening.

"This is quite the story, Louie! I'm going to enjoy writing this one. I think you have a legitimate complaint here. I'll get the story in the paper, but I think you'll have to file a official complaint with the R.C.M.P." he said. "I'll be calling them to get their response, but the guy you want to talk to is Superintendent Banes. He's the top dog for the R.C.M.P. for all of northern B.C."

"How do I find him?"

"I think he's going to want to talk to you after I speak to him and after the article comes out in the paper. I'll give you a call this afternoon and let you know what he says when I talk to him."

I gave him Sara's phone number and left to go to work. On the way home from work that afternoon, I stopped and picked up a newspaper, hoping to see an article about the case in there. Sure enough, there was an article on page three. The headline said, 'Man Claims Harassment. It took up six columns, and spelled out the whole story in detail.

Udo called me at Sara's that evening. He told me that he had spoken to Superintendent Banes and that he did want to see me. "Can you make it in to see him tomorrow afternoon?"

Udo asked.

"Sure, I can do that," I answered.

"If you go to the front desk and tell them you have an appointment with the superintendent, they'll be expecting you." he said. "Do you want me to go with you?"

"Yeah, that sounds like a good idea." I called Udo the next afternoon and we went to to see the superintendent together.

The cop at the front desk was the same one who had told me that I couldn't do anything about it a couple of days before. I snickered and made a comment: "Maybe I can do something about this, eh?" Looking at Udo, I said, "This is the guy who told me that I couldn't do anything about it because they were the drug squad and they had a writ." I said this right in front of the cop and then looked at him. He didn't say anything. Udo took out a pad and pencil and scribbled some notes in shorthand.

We were let in through the security door and led upstairs into the superintendent's office. Udo sat there quietly, all the while taking notes as I told my story to Banes.

"If even half of what you've told me is true, it worries me!" he said. "What are you going to do about it?" I asked.

"First we'll have to investigate it and then decide what to do."

"And how long is that going to take?"

"Give me a couple of weeks," he said, giving me his card. "Give me a call in a few weeks."

I went into the Canada Hotel Bar after leaving the cop shop to meet Sara. She was already in the bar when I got there. The waitress came over to the table and I ordered a beer. When she came back, she had a whole tray full of beer and proceeded to

364

unload the entire tray on our table and wouldn't take any money.

The word went around the bar that I was the guy who was taking on the cops and everybody wanted to buy me a beer. The waitress came by with several more trays of beer, filling the table until it wouldn't hold anymore. For the next month, every time I went in the Canada bar, I had a table full of beer,

I even got pulled over by the cops on two occasions, and as soon as they knew who I was, they let me go immediately. I guess they were being careful not to harass me any further. I felt untouchable.

I got a call at Sara's from the cops a couple of days later. It was from a Sergeant Blair. He wanted to know if I would take him across the river to Longstock. He was assigned to the investigation and wanted to spend some time in Longstock to dig into things.

I arranged to meet him at the river the next morning. Sara and I left Prince George and drove out to the landing. I had my riverboat tied up a little ways upriver. I walked up through the bush, untied the boat and brought it down to the landing. Sara had been waiting at the truck while I was getting the boat. Sergeant Blair showed up, driving a marked police 4x4. He parked the truck and got out. Sara noticed right away that it was the same cop that was behind the desk at the cop shop the day I went in to report the incident - the one who had told me that there was nothing I could do.

As I pulled the boat into the riverbank, Sara and the cop were waiting for me. I had to look twice. I couldn't believe that they sent this guy out to investigate the complaint.

They both got in the boat and I turned out into the current

and headed off. The cop was up towards the bow of the boat, on one of the seats. The noise of the motor made it hard to talk to anyone who wasn't sitting right next to you. Neither Sara nor I said anything to the cop.

We landed the boat and got into the power wagon for the drive to the house. Sara and I rode in the cab and the cop rode in the back. When we got to the house, the Sergeant wanted to see the chicken yard, which was still littered with feathers. Taking notes all the time, he checked out the motor bike tracks through the oat field. He wanted to see which gates had been left open.

I took him into the house and showed him the cupboards that had been gone through and the burnt 410 shells that I had fished out of the fire box. "How did you manage to get assigned to this case?" I asked the cop.

"It's just an assignment," he answered, volunteering little information.

After spending about an hour around the house, looking over things, he said he wanted to talk to some of the neighbors. I gave him directions to the McCoby's and Greta's, agreeing to pick him up at the crossroads in a couple of hours. As I didn't offer him a ride, he headed off, walking to the neighbors.

"I don't like the looks of this situation," I remarked to Sara after the cop left.

He stopped at Greta and Dick's place and questioned them about the incident. They told him about the cops riding by on the motor bikes and then shortly afterwards, about their having heard gun shots coming from my place. They recounted the morning I came home and about their going to my place with me and finding my house upside down, the doors and the gates open and the shotgun shells going off when I lit the fire.

From there he went to McCoby's house and questioned them. They went over their story about the two cops showing up at their place on the motor bikes with a case of beer and offering them some.

"They said Chad had given them the beer, but we knew Chad wasn't even here in Longstock. He had a job in Prince George that he worked during the week," Wayne told the cop. "He was out here last weekend, though and came by and told us that somebody had broken the lock into his shed. Chad had apparently had a case of beer in the shed that was missing."

After leaving McCoby's place, he walked to the crossroads and turned west towards the Hooty's. They were both startled when the sergeant walked up on them. Paula was working in front of the house on some flower beds and Bob was sitting on the front porch, reading a book. They both stopped what they were doing.

"Hi! What can I do for you?" asked Paula.

The cop introduced himself and said that he was investigating a complaint that I had filed. He was asking them if they had any knowledge of the goings on here involving the cops. Had they seen anything that day?

"Only what we've heard," answered Paula.

They were both taken by surprise when he cop said, "We know that Karmen is a pot grower. We know what he's doing, and we think that he made the whole story up." He asked a lot of questions about me while not many about the cops. The Hooty's were real friendly towards the sergeant, even offering

367

him a cup of coffee while he was waiting to meet me for a ride back across the river.

Their place wasn't very far from the crossroads where I was meeting the cop. The sergeant left and walked to the crossroads to meet me.

He was already there when Sara and I drove up in the power wagon. We drove to the river and took him back across. We dropped the sergeant off across the river and headed back to the farm. Sara and I were spending the night in Longstock.

Shortly after we got there, Bob and Paula showed up at the door. "We had a visit from the R.C.M.P. today" Paula said.

"Yeah, I know. He was out here investigating the cops that ransacked my place," I answered.

"Yeah, well, that's maybe what he told you, but he was asking a lot of questions about you, Louie," Paula said.

"What!" I said, surprised. "What kind of questions?"

"He told us that they know that you grow and sell pot and he thought that you made the whole thing up," said Bob.

"Why, that asshole! He came out here to investigate those fucking cops and now, instead, he's investigating me!" I said.

The next morning we got an unexpected visit from Dave McCoby. "I just got a call from the cops this morning. They asked me to pick one of them up across the river at 12 o'clock. I thought you should know, so you don't get surprised."

"Did they say what they wanted?" I asked.

"I guess they're still investigating the two cops who came out on the motorbikes," he said. "Didn't say very much. Only that he needed a ride across."

"You know the asshole was asking Bob and Paula questions

about me as if I were the one under investigation."

"Maybe you are," said Dave. "It sounded like that from what he was saying to Wayne, too, though he didn't come right out and say it."

"Well, he said it to Bob and Paula. This guy is starting to piss me off!"

Dave left for the river and I could not help feeling very agitated. I was pacing back and forth in the kitchen, talking out loud, trying to decide what to do.

"Maybe he's trying to prove a point. Didn't he tell me that they were the drug squad and I couldn't do anything? It sounds like he can take the focus off of the cops if he shifts it onto me. You know, I'm going to meet this guy at the crossroads, before he ever gets here and tell him that I know what he's saying to my neighbors. That's it, I'll tell him I want him to take himself off the case. As far as I'm concerned, he's investigating me instead of the cops."

I went out and saddled up Daffodil and rode her up to the crossroads. I waited around for twenty minutes or so, when I heard a truck coming up the road from the river. Dave's truck pulled up to the crossroads. I could see from a distance that the cop was his passenger. I was still on the horse when they stopped and the cop got out of the truck.

"I want to talk to you," I said, riding up closer as he got out of the truck. "What are you saying to my neighbors about me, my friend?"

"What do you mean?" he answered.

I rode Daffodil up real close to him. She was almost stepping on his toes. "Don't give me that shit! You know exactly what I mean! You're supposed to be investigating your buddies, not me!"

"Well, ah, I'm looking into it," he said, nervously.

"Horse shit!" I said. "Aren't you the same guy who told me that there was nothing I could do?" Not waiting for an answer, I said, "Here's the way I see it. Your mind is already made up. That makes you the wrong guy to be on this case. I want you to take yourself off the case. In other words, you're fired. You can't do this job properly because I'm putting you on notice that you are not allowed on my land." Looking over at Dave, who couldn't believe what I was saying to the cop, I said, "If you step foot on my land, I'm going to file charges against you for trespassing. Dave will be my witness that I've told you. If you think I'm bluffing, just try me!"

The cop was speechless. He just stood there with a stupid look on his face like, 'what do I do now?!' It was the first time in twenty years on the force that he'd been fired by a citizen.

I reined Daffodil around, facing her towards home and yelled at the cop, "Go back to town, my friend, you got no business here!" I kicked Daffodil and off she went into a gallop, heading for home.

I rode my horse right up to the house. Sara came outside, asking how it had gone. I sat on the horse and told her what I had said to the cop. I finally calmed down enough and got off the horse and Sara and I walked her over to the barn to get her unsaddled. I could see the driveway from where we were at the barn. I saw somebody walking down the driveway. It looked like the cop!

"What the fuck!" I said. "We'll see about this."

I hurried across the field to meet him, thinking that he was coming on the land in spite of what I had told him. Sara stayed at the barn and watched from there. He walked right up to the gate and stopped there.

"I thought I told you to keep off of my land!" I said angrily.

"I'm not on your land!" he said. He was right. He had only come to the gate.

"I've got something to check out." He took off walking down fence line on the eastern boundary of my property.

"What the fuck is he doing?" I said to myself. He disappeared into the bush as I stood at the gate, watching him, when it occurred to me that I had a pot patch growing in the bush in the direction he went. "Oh well, if he finds it, it's not on my property, so it won't stick either, just like the last one."

I think that he was acting on some information that they had gotten out of Katy the year before. She knew that I had a patch in the bush down that way, but had only been out there once and wasn't really sure how to get there. It was really well hidden.

Sara walked over to the gate from the barn where she had been waiting. "What's going on?"

"I think he's looking for one of my patches," I answered. "Maybe Katy told them about it. We'll see if he finds it. They won't make it stick anyway. Too far from my house."

At first, I could hear the cop crashing through the bush, but after a while I couldn't hear him. Sara and I went back to the house and rolled a joint. We walked out to the barn and hung out and smoked it.

Suddenly, I could hear some crashing through the bush again and the cop appeared by the gate. Sara and I kept out of sight while watching him. He got out onto the driveway and turned towards the crossroads, walking.

"That's a sure sign of who's being investigated," Sara said to me as we walked back to the house.

A couple hours later, I went down to check my patch to see if he had found it. Everything looked fine. He hadn't been able to find it.

I didn't hear anything from the cops for the next couple weeks and then one day I had a message from Udo at the newspaper. He wanted me to call him.

"The cops have been trying to get a hold of you," he told me on the phone. "They want you to come to the station. They have apparently finished their investigation, and they want to talk to you about it."

"Did you hear about my telling the cop they sent out to investigate to take himself off the case?" This was new information to Udo. I filled him in on all that had happened.

"Do you want to go to the station with me?" I asked. "If you want me to, yes, I would!" he answered.

I called and talked to Superintendent Banes. He asked me if I could come in that afternoon. I got hold of Udo and we went together.

When we walked into Banes' office, there were five other high- ranking cops in there. It was intimidating. I was glad I had Udo with me. He evened the score quickly by pulling out his note pad and pen and getting poised to take notes.

Banes started by saying that disciplinary action had been taken in regard to the two officers.

"What kind of action?" I asked.

"We're not at liberty to tell you that," he said.

"What? Why have you called me here if there's nothing you can tell me?"

"I am telling you that our investigation resulted in disciplinary action."

"This is pretty good, you know! The day after the charges get thrown out of court, my place gets ransacked and you can't tell me anything about the action you've taken? What kind of shit is this?" I was feeling quite brazen with Udo sitting beside me taking notes.

"That was just a coincidence."

"Do you expect me to believe that?"

"Whether you believe it or not, the raid on Longstock and Penney was planned two months before. It was just a coincidence that it happened the day after you went to court. Isn't that right?" he asked, turning to one of the other officers in the room.

"That's right!" said the officer. "I don't believe you!" I said.

Things started to get a bit heated when Banes said, "You know, you really didn't help things by throwing the officer off your land."

"I fired him, too! Did he tell you that? And I did it because he was focusing on me and not on your boys. They were the ones who were supposed to be investigated! What was he doing, asking questions about me? He was supposed to be asking questions about your cops!"

The argument went back and forth a few times. I was developing a nasty tone towards the cops, but every time one of them started to get nasty back, Banes cut them off. There was a reporter in the room and he wasn't going to let things get out of hand.

We spent nearly an hour talking and arguing with the cops before we left. I pressed Banes for an apology before I would leave. He looked at me, and then at Udo, who was busy taking notes, and then reluctantly apologized.

We left right after that. Walking out on the street, I turned to Udo, "Thanks for coming with me, man!"

"No problem!" he said. "I wouldn't have missed it for the world!" The next day, there was another article in the paper about the meeting with the cops. That made the fourth article on the incident that came out in the paper.

I was still drinking for free at the Canada Hotel Bar.

Chapter 17

Hippies Gone Bad

It was the end of July by the time the whole fiasco with the cops was over. Gypsy and his new girlfriend Jennifer had been staying with friends at Fraser Mills for the last month. Gypsy got a job at the mill. It was the first real job he had since he had come to Canada.

His last girlfriend, Heather, was independently wealthy and had no problem supporting him...she even gave him an allowance each week. Gypsy was quite comfortable having women taking care of him. To him it was part of the Gypsy lifestyle.

Jennifer, however, was not a wealthy woman. She came from a Jewish family and had grown up with a stringent work ethic. She wasn't going to let Gypsy get away with living off of her money. They stayed a couple of weeks in his cabin on the farm, though Jennifer kept pressing him to get a job, but Gypsy wasn't the kind of guy that just anyone would hire. His appearance was quite outlandish and his personality even more so.

Jennifer got him to go to the sawmill at Fraser Mills and apply for a job. He was just as surprised as anyone when they hired him. It was actually some friends of Jennifer that lived and worked at Fraser Mills that had agreed to let them stay there, as it wasn't a foregone conclusion that Gypsy would be able to hold on to the job without quitting or getting fired. This was kind of a wait and see situation.

Gypsy's appearance at the mill was startlingly noticeable. The first time he walked into the noisy, crowded cook house, he brought the crowd of two hundred or so to a standstill. The entire room quickly turned silent as Gypsy stood by the door, glaring across the room. His dark, penetrating eyes seemed to freeze the entire room into silence. His cold glare was disarming, and once the room went silent, nobody wanted to be the first one to talk. Gypsy stood there for a very long minute, and when he felt he had established control of the situation, he walked across the room and got in the cafeteria line. People relaxed and started to talk again.

Moose and Dolly had taken off to McBride to stay with friends while the cop fiasco was going on. Both Moose and Dolly were Americans living in Canada illegally and did not want to talk to any cops.

They were both in Longstock the day that the cops had been riding around on their motor bikes. Moose had been helping Ross out, repairing and servicing his haying equipment now that haying season was not far off. When they had heard about cops in Longstock, they got out of town fast. Ross took them across the river in his boat the same day. They took off to McBride.

They showed up back in Longstock around the end of July, after everything had cooled down.

Just about the same time, Skid surfaced again, too, and he had a new girlfriend with him when he returned. Krista had a five year-old daughter named Dedra. Skid picked them up hitch-hiking down in the States, where he had been while waiting for the heat to cool down in Longstock. It turns out that they had some mutual friends in Washington and ended up getting together. Skid told Krista about Longstock and she was interested in checking the place out.

Lana had been living at Ross's for the last few months and had become pregnant. She and Ross were talking about getting married before the baby was born.

Sara and I were down at Ross's having a three-way game of crib one day, when Skid appeared with Krista and Dedra. Krista was a tall, good-looking woman with long brown hair and blue eyes. I couldn't understand how a homely guy like Skid could get such a beautiful woman.

Moose and Dolly showed up that day, as well. It ended up being a party with everybody there. Ross broke out a gallon of Berry Cup to celebrate a reunion of sorts. Ross was drinking at lot more these days, ever since Lana moved in. Lana loved to drink. Both she and Ross ended up getting pretty hammered that afternoon.

I got word from Beavertail Steel that they had a couple more jobs for me to do if I wanted them. Both Moose and Skid were interested in getting some work. Neither of them were legally entitled to work in Canada, but could get away with it if they worked for me. I wasn't really interested at the time, but thought I would run it past those guys and see what they thought. They were really interested and encouraged me to go after the contracts. Sara wanted to work, too.

I went to the Beavertail Steel office to check out the jobs. One was a commercial building for the new Atlas Aluminum Plant in Prince George, the other job was up north, in Fort

Nelson, about 500 miles from Prince George.

I took a copy of the plans back home with me and spent a couple of days figuring out a bid on the jobs. The guys at Beavertail Steel liked me and accepted my bids.

All of us went to Prince George and stayed at Sara's while we worked on the Atlas Aluminum plant. Skid had a van to sleep in that he parked in her driveway.

The first job went really well, taking us a week and a half to complete. After getting paid for the job and paying everyone else, we took a couple of days off and went to Longstock. Ross had just started on the haying when we got back. We all went down and helped out for a few days before we were to start the Fort Nelson job.

The job in Fort Nelson was much more complicated. We had to haul steel, forms and virtually all the materials except the concrete, from Prince George. It was a long days drive north to get up there. The roads were not the greatest, riddled with potholes and frost heaves. I rented a 5-ton truck to haul everything up there. It was a big job. The building was 200 feet by 150 feet and sat right on the property line. The property was the same size as the building, which left no room for error.

We traveled together in a three-vehicle caravan on the way up. Moose and Dolly drove his pickup, Skid, Krista and Dedra went in Skids van and Sara and I were in the five-ton. I took the concrete forms and pipes up on the first load.

It was a twelve-hour drive to get there, first over the pass to Dawson Creek and then the first leg of the Alaskan Highway from Dawson Creek to Fort Nelson. We got into Fort Nelson late, though it was still light, being so far up north. We set up

378

camp at a local campground that night.

The next morning, Moose, Skid, Sara, and I went over to the site to unload the five-ton. At this point, it was just a vacant lot, but the survey lines were in. Sara and I laid out the building, driving pegs in the ground to mark where it was going to be.

It was going to be built on concrete caissons. Caissons are drilled holes varying in diameter and drilled down to a hard surface like bedrock. A retaining wall of concrete generally connects the caissons with a paper material called void under the retaining wall. It's called void because it rots out quickly and creates a void space under the wall, leaving room for the ground to expand and contract. This is very important in cold climates where the ground freezes hard

Moose and Skid got the truck unloaded and went back to the campground while Sara and I finished laying out the sixty caissons that were required. I called a drilling company to try to get a rig to drill the caissons that afternoon, but there were no rigs available. It turned out that I couldn't get a rig for a couple of days.

Sara and I went back to the campground and told the others we were going to have to wait around for a few days. The five-ton truck I was driving was a rental and I still had the rest of the steel reinforcement bar to bring up from Prince George. We brought enough for the caissons on the first load, though we still had to get all the steel for the walls.

"I'm thinking of going to Prince George and trying to get back before the rig comes. I wonder if I can make it?" I said.

"You got all the caissons laid out?" Moose asked.

"Yeah, they're all laid out and ready to drill," I answered.

"I've got strings up on the two property lines. You know that we've got no room to spare. It's a two hundred foot lot and a two hundred foot building. We're going to make it 199 feet, 11 and a half inches. A quarter inch on each side. That's what we've got to play with."

"Don't sweat it, man! If the rig gets here before you get back, Skid and I will get them poured," he said.

"There's almost 60 caissons, you think you can do it, man?"

"Yeah, no sweat!"

"You know that you can't get over the property lines? You've got to make sure of that."

"Yeah, yeah, don't worry," said Moose, appearing to be annoyed.

Moose worked with me in Colorado and on quite a few jobs since then. I had no reason to think that he couldn't get the caissons drilled and poured properly.

Sara and I left early the next morning for Prince George. It was late when we got in. We went right to Sara's place, parking the five- ton in front of her house. The next morning, we went to Beavertail Steel to pick up the steel. It turned out they didn't have enough at their yard and were waiting for a truck to come in. It was supposed to be there by early afternoon.

The truck came in on time, but the steel that we needed was on the bottom of the load. They had to unload three quarters of the load before they got to it. By the time we got loaded, it was four o'clock in the afternoon.

We decided to leave first thing in the morning, driving the truck back over to Sara's. I got a call that night from Moose, saying that they hadn't poured the caissons yet. I told him that we would be there by the following night.

We took off early the next morning, arriving about six o'clock that evening. I was totally beat from the drive, and went straight to the campground where Sara and I had a tent set up.

Moose, Skid and the girls were in camp when we pulled up.

"Hey man, I got them caissons poured today," was the first thing he said.

"All right! We can start tomorrow," I said.

The next morning, we all went to the job site. Now that the caissons were poured, we could start building. I backed the truck into the middle of the lot, thinking that the steel could stay on it for the time being. Sara helped me check the layout pegs while the guys started spreading out 2x4's and forms.

It was then that I realized there was a problem. The caissons were over the property line. Not by much, but they were over. There were only about two inches of each caisson on two sides that were over. That made half of the sixty over the line. 'This couldn't have happened' I said to myself. I checked over the surveyors pins that I had taken the line from. It appeared that it really was happening.

I was walking around the job checking things out, oblivious to anything people were saying to me. When I finally realized that there was no doubt, I yelled to Moose to come over. Sara came over, too.

"You fucked up, man!" I said.

"What do you mean?" said Moose.

"Those caissons are over the line," I said, turning and looking at him.

"No, they can't be!" he said, walking over to the line. It

wasn't hard to see, when you looked down the string I had stretched out. "We drilled them right where the pegs were. I don't get it."

"It was the property line that was important. I thought I told you that. The edge of the caisson was supposed to be on the line. If it isn't, it's over."

"What are we going to do about it?"

"I'll tell you what we're going to do, nothing. We can't do anything until we get this worked out. We might have to take them out." I walked over to the truck, feeling disgusted. Sara followed me.

"They're over the line?" she asked. "Yeah! They sure are."

"What are you going to do?" she said.

"I'll have to get hold of the guys at Beavertail and let them know. Maybe they can work out a deal with the neighbors, or maybe we'll have to pull them out. Either way, it's going to cost."

I got in the truck, motioning Sara to come along and drove to a nearby restaurant where there was a phone. I phoned Beavertail and told them about the situation. They really didn't seem to be too excited about it right away. They asked me to go to each neighbor and give them their phone number and they would negotiate it with them.

I went back to the job, where Moose and Skid were still checking things to see if we weren't making a mistake.

Moose came over to me, saying "looks like I made a big mistake, man. I'll take full responsibility for it, whatever it costs to fix."

"Okay man, I hear you. But for now, we've got to get these neighbors in touch with Beavertail and see what they can work out."

I went and talked to each of the neighbors. On one side was a man named Wilbur Smith, who lived in a single-family house. After I told him what was going on, we both took a walk out to the line and had a look. He wasn't happy at all but agreed to give Beavertail Steel a call.

On the other side there was an empty lot owned by the Methodist Church. The church was on the next lot over. I went and knocked on the door of the rectory and talked to the priest. He seemed like a good-natured person and walked out to the line with me and looked the situation over.

"It shouldn't be a problem," he said to me before going back home.

I got in touch with Beavertail Steel and let them know that I had talked to both neighbors. Wilbur Smith had already been in touch with them. They had tentatively agreed on a cash settlement of

$5000 for the easement on the two inches that had been encroached upon. It was going to be a few more days before the legal papers were drawn up and signed, before we could begin work again.

At that point, they had not heard from the church yet. In the meantime, we were stuck in Fort Nelson, unable to do anything on the job.

Sara and I were sitting in a restaurant one afternoon, when a fellow recognized me and came over to our table.

"Hi Louie, what are you doing up here?" he asked.

"Hey, Johnny!" I answered, recognizing him right away. "Have a seat."

It was Johnny Stafford, a contractor from Prince George who was working in town.

"I'm doing a job for Beavertail Steel," I said. "We got held up on our job and are waiting it out for a couple days." Johnny Stafford was in the foundation business, too, and I had met him on several occasions in Prince George. "So, what are you doing up here?" I asked.

"I got contract for a foundation for West Coast Gas. They're building a new office a little south of town," he said. "I am, however, looking for a crew. Do you have a crew here?"

"Yeah, I do. How big is the job?"

"Oh, it's a pretty good-size job. Probably about ten days work. I was going to try to pick up a crew here. How long are you going to be delayed?"

"I'm not sure, I'm hoping it's not too long."

"Maybe you should come out and look at my job. I could get you and your guys working right away. We could start on the footings tomorrow."

"Okay man, let's go check it out!" I said.

I left my truck at the restaurant and Sara and I rode out to the job with Johnny. The excavation was dug and Johnny had all the forms and steel already on the site. He spread the blueprints out across the hood of his pickup and we went over them. I agreed to bring my crew to this job if we could negotiate a price.

"What are you going to charge me for your crew?"

I took a few seconds to mull it over, and then said, "I'll charge you by the man-hour. Fifteen bucks a man-hour, plus twenty bucks a day for expenses." I was paying Moose $10 an hour, and Sara and Skid $8 each per hour, leaving a profit that would offset the loss that we were going to take on the other job.

He put out his hand to shake hands on it. "It's a deal! We can start tomorrow."

"Deal!" I said, shaking hands.

Johnny drove Sara and me back to the truck. We went back to the campground and let Moose and Skid know that we had a job to work on while we waited.

The next morning, we all went to Johnny's job and got things started. We had all been getting bored, sitting around waiting for something to happen. Everybody was in good spirits that morning as we started on Johnny's job.

We had the footings poured within a couple of days and started setting up the forms for the walls. We were close to being done setting up the forms, when I got in touch with Beavertail Steel to see how progress was coming along with the easement on the church side.

Negotiations with the church were not working out so well. They refused to accept any kind of an easement. It looked as if we had to dig out the caissons.

I called several places before finding a backhoe that was capable of pulling them out. Leaving the rest of the crew on Johnny's job, I went back to the Beavertail job to supervise the caisson removal. This was no easy task. The caissons were 16 feet down in the ground. The backhoe had to dig each caisson as deep as possible in order to be able to get them out. It was a long day before we had all the caissons out of the ground, the ground leveled off and all the concrete hauled away.

I wanted to give the ground a few days to settle down

before drilling them again. I would have to make another trip to Prince George to pick up another load of steel in order to put them back in. I left Sara and the guys on Johnny's job while I took off to Prince George.

It was a three-day trip to get to Prince George and back. I rolled in late on the third night with the truckload of steel. They poured concrete on Johnny's job the day before I got there and had just a couple of days clean-up left to complete the job.

Sara came with me to the Beavertail job. I got a drilling rig to redrill the caissons the next morning. We were done drilling by early afternoon and managed to get them poured.

They finished up on Johnny's job and Skid and Moose came back over to the Beavertail job to work on the walls. We were another week, and some, completing it.

I got word from Beavertail that the cost of fixing our mistake was $17,000. $5,000 was for the easement, and $12,000 was the cost of removing the caissons and putting them back in. The labor price for the entire job was $22,000, which left only $5,000 to pay everybody. Johnny's job would give us another $5,000.

Beavertail Steel provided all the materials, steel and concrete, etc., but I had to pay the truck rental, the campground and food for the Beavertail portion of our stay in Fort Nelson, which was close to

$1600. If I pooled the money from the two jobs, I could at least pay everyone their agreed-on wage, but there would be no bonus this time.

Dolly, Krista and Dedra had been at the camp the whole month we were there and were anxious to go back to Longstock.

We had just about finished the job, with clean-up being all that was left, when Skid and Moose asked if they could leave a day early with the girls. We would be leaving the next day anyway, so I didn't see it as any problem.

It was a long drive back the next day in the 5-ton, carrying the load of forms. The sense of hurry up was not there as it had been on every other trip north over the last month. We pulled into Sara's place late that night.

It felt so good to sleep in a real bed after a month of sleeping in a tent. We slept in until almost noon, after which Sara followed me in my pickup while I returned the forms and the truck. Afterwards, we went to Beavertail Steel and picked up the money for their job. Johnny Stafford was back in town, too. I called him from the Beavertail office.

"Hey Johnny, how's it going?" I said, getting him on the phone. "I want to come over and pick up a check. When is a good time for you?"

"Didn't your guys tell you?"

"Tell me what?"

"They came up here yesterday and I paid them."

"What! What the hell are you doing, paying them? Your deal was with me!"

"Well, they came here looking for money. I paid them. You've got to take it up with them."

"You're goddam right I'm taking it up with them! If I don't get that money, I'll be taking it up with you! You had no right paying them.

I've got expenses to pay. You should know that." I said as I hung up the phone.

"Problem?" Sara asked.

"The fucking cheese-head paid those guys!"

"What guys?"

"Moose and Skid!"

"So that's why they wanted to leave early!"

"Well, let's go find them." We left for Longstock.

We got to Longstock that afternoon and immediately went looking for Moose and Skid. There was nobody at the tee-pee, so we went over to Skid's place and found both of them there.

"Moose, Skid, I want to talk to you guys!" I yelled in through the open door. They both came outside.

"Moose, what are you guys doing picking up money from Johnny?" I said.

"Well, we did the work there, why shouldn't we?"

"Why shouldn't you? Did you forget that you were the ones who fucked up the other job?"

"That was your job."

"Exactly! And so is Johnny's job! Neither of them are yours!" I looked at Skid, who was trying to avoid looking at me. But I couldn't look Skid straight in the eye. The glass eye was screwing things up. I can't figure out which one to look at when they face different directions.

"So where is the money?" I asked with a snarl in my voice. "We split it up."

"Are you going to give it to me and have it dealt with fairly, or what?"

"No! I don't think so."

"You realize that you're fired for life. You'll never work for me again. And I'm going after my money in court. People like you make me lose faith in people! You're hippies gone bad. There's been a lot of crazy people that have come through here, but you could always count on them being honest. But you two, you're a couple of dishonest pricks."

"What about you making all that money from Larry's weed. I should have got a cut of that." Skid barks out.

"Gee man, you should have got my cut. That's after I paid back the

$2000 for bailing James out of jail. Fuck you, Skid!" I added.

I could see I was getting nowhere with these guys. Sara and I left.

We had been friends for a long time, especially with Moose. We had known each other for a couple of years before we moved to Longstock. It was disheartening to have a friend screw you over in such a way. Moose knew the drill from having worked for me a lot over the years. Sara and I talked it over and thought that I might be able to recover the money from Johnny, seeing as the contract was between me and him. The money he paid to them shouldn't count.

We went back to Prince George and I filed a small claims suit against Johnny. I got a phone call from him that evening at Sara's. He was irate. He was too intense to listen to and I hung up the phone on him.

It was a couple of weeks before we got into court and as it turned out, the judge agreed with me. He did, however, deduct the amount of Moose and Skid's pay and awarded the rest to me, a total of

$3,560.

I was feeling pretty cocky that I had won the case. I even

had a lawyer approach me, saying, "good job, my friend, you're a natural, you should have been a lawyer."

I went out in the hallway and waited for Johnny to come out. I wanted to ask him when I could pick up the money.

Johnny was a big man: probably about 6'3" and 230 lbs. He looked even bigger when he stormed out of the courthouse and was walking right towards me. I don't know if he saw me or not at first. He swerved around me as he went by.

"So when can I get paid?" I said as he hurried by. I didn't want to get in his way.

"Never! I'm going to appeal it!" he said on his way by, without missing a stride.

'Well, that sounds like a refusal to me,' I thought. I went downstairs, directly to the Sheriff's Office. My next step was to show them my order and commence garnishee proceedings.

Johnny was served that afternoon with the garnishee notice. In the case that you got the right bank and the money is in the account, the court takes the money and holds it for three months. During that time, the person who is garnished can try to recover the money through the court if they wish. If they are unsuccessful, or if they don't try, then the money is paid.

I thought that I knew the bank that Johnny dealt with, but it turned out that I got the wrong one. The Sheriff had served the notice and nobody noticed that it was a bank where Johnny had no account.

I called his house that evening to see if he had changed his mind about paying me. His wife answered the phone.

"Hello, this is Louie Karmen. Is Johnny there?"

"Yes, he's here, but he doesn't want to talk to you." "I just

390

want to know if he's ready to pay me yet?"

"Well, you garnished our bank account!" "Can I come over and pick up a check?"

I could hear that she covered the phone with her hand while she talked to Johnny.

"If you come right over, you can pick up a check."

"Okay, I'll be there in ten minutes," I said, hanging up the phone.

Sara drove with me over to Johnny's place. I left the truck running while I walked up to the door. I knocked. All of a sudden, the door flew open and there was a teenage boy on the other side. His arm jutted out at me and he gave me an envelope and quickly shut the door.

"Oh, man!" I remarked to myself. I decided that I was going to have a look at the check to make sure everything was right before I left the house. I ripped open the envelope and pulled the check out. It read $3,560, just as it was supposed to. I was just turning to leave when the door flew open again. It was the teenage boy.

"You are Louie Karmen, aren't you?"

"Yeah, I am he," I said, snickering. I guess he could have given my check to the milkman or someone else.

That incident pretty well ruined the friendship between Skid and Moose and me. I never did another job for Johnny, and those guys didn't either, though Beavertail Steel did give me several more contracts over the years.

Chapter 18

Sexy Women

It was getting to be the end of August. I went out to Longstock to help Ross finish the rest of the haying. The baler was working really well this year and he managed to get most of his field hayed off, with just a couple of days left to go. Ross, Lana, and I were picking the last load off the field when it started pouring rain on us. Ross pulled the wagon under the barn roof and unhooked it to unload later and then took off for the house with Lana and me hanging onto the tractor. We were soaking wet by the time we got to the house. Ross quickly built a fire and Lana went into the back room, coming out with a gallon of Berry Cup. She poured each of us a glass and sat down at the table.

Ross had a pot of mulligan stew on the stove that he started that morning. He stoked up the fire in the morning, leaving it cooking until the fire went out while we were out picking up the hay. He pushed the mulligan onto the heat after getting the fire going.

The first few gulps of Berry cup sent a warm glow through me, chasing the chill out.

Lana and Ross had been living together for more than a year and had recently found out that Lana was pregnant.

"Hey Louie!" Lana leaned over the table and said softly, like it was a secret, "Ross and I are getting married."

"Hey, congratulations, you old fart," I said jokingly to Ross. "When are you going to do this?"

"Pretty soon. We've already got the license and blood tests."

So it was a double celebration, having the haying done and getting married. Ross served us all up a bowl of mulligan and tumblers full of Berry Cup. A couple more glasses of wine and we were all getting pretty drunk.

It wasn't long before Ross got up, staggered to the bedroom and passed out. He was no sooner out of the room than Lana started coming on to me. She actually came over and sat right beside me and unbuttoned her blouse.

"Lana what the fuck are you doing? Put them fucking things away." I said to her as she took off her blouse and started fondling her tits.

"You like them?"

"Yea, yea, they're nice now put them away." I said and started to laugh.

She started to laugh too. "No, I want you to touch them." "Come on Lana cut it out. Ross is right in the next room."

"Don't worry about Ross, come on touch them," she said laughing as she talked. "Come on Louie." Lana sat on my lap facing me and grabbed my head and pulled me into her chest. I was trying to get away from her and the chair tipped over and we went crashing to the floor.

I thought for sure Ross was going to wake up. She wouldn't let go of me. I was trying to get up off the floor with her hanging on to me. We made a lot of noise and couldn't stop laughing. Ross snored right through it all.

I finally got up off the floor and got away from Lana. She crashed around on the floor for a minute trying to get her feet. She finally got up and wasted no time coming after me again.

"I've got to go!" I got up and went for the door. She wasn't going to let me get away that easily, grabbing and fighting with me as I managed to make my way out to the power wagon and drive away.

"Holy shit! That woman is crazy!" I said to myself as I drove away. About a week later, I was staying at Sara's place in Prince George.

Sara was out at the coast picking mushrooms. She'd been out there for a couple of weeks.

Ross talked to me a few days earlier about picking him and Lana up at the river and take them to town to get married.

They had an appointment with the Justice of the Peace at 9am. That means I had to leave town by 6am to pick them up at the river by 7:30.

I stopped at the 7-11 and picked up a cup of coffee when I was leaving Prince George. I arrived at the river a few minutes before them. I could hear the boat coming down the river. I walked down to the riverbank and soon Ross's boat came around the corner. A couple minutes later, he pulled into the riverbank. Lana jumped out while Ross brought the boat a couple hundred feet upriver to tie up. That was something that people frequently did so that the boats were somewhat hidden from view.

Ross gave me a few things to carry up to the truck. Lana and I walked up the bank and put everything in the truck and waited for Ross.

Lana wouldn't leave me alone once her hands were free.

"You're a crazy woman! You're getting married today!" I said, trying to keep her away from me as she was grabbing at me.

Ross finally showed up and Lana stopped pestering me. We got in the truck for the drive to town. They were getting married by a Justice of the Peace at the court house at 9:00. Lana's parents came down from Alaska for the occasion. It was just the five of us, the Justice, and his wife. The ceremony lasted under five minutes and we were all out of there. They were married.

We then went to the Simon Fraser Restaurant and had brunch to celebrate. I drove them around town to pick up groceries, feed and a few hardware items and then gave them a ride back to Longstock. We loaded the boat and I gave the boat a shove and watched them take off up river.

"Good fucking luck, Ross! Good luck with that one!" I said under my breath, watching them go. I walked up to the truck and drove back to town.

I got to back to Sara's about 5 o'clock, and the door was open. Sara's sister Lynn had shown up from Vancouver a couple hours earlier. Sara had told us that she might show up. She also had a friend with her.

Lynn met me at the door, giving me a hug. "Hi, Louie! How are you?" she said. "This is my friend Julia. She's celebrating her 19th birthday today."

"Nice to meet you, Julia," I said, extending my hand.

"Nice to meet you, too. Lynn has told me about you," she said while shaking hands with me.

I went into the living room, rolled a joint and crashed out on the couch in front of the TV. I got up early that morning to pick up Ross and Lana and was feeling kind of tired. Julia and Lynn both came in and sat down and smoked the joint with me. We ordered a pizza for dinner and the girls started getting ready for their night out.

We smoked another joint when they were all dressed up and ready to go. The girls looked great. Julia was a tall and slender girl, with long legs and big boobs. She was dressed to kill, with plenty of cleavage showing. Her hair was pulled up in a pony tail, making her facial features stand out. I had a really hard time keeping my eyes off of her.

After we smoked the joint, they got a taxi downtown and I remained in my perch in front of the TV.

I hadn't heard from Sara for a couple of weeks. Out where

she was there were no telephones, so there was no way to get in touch. She would probably just show up one day with no warning.

I finally shut off the TV and went to bed around midnight. I was sound asleep at 2:30 when Lynn and Julia got back and I didn't even hear them come in. Lynn had bumped into and old friend and had brought him along, too. There was some pot on the coffee table in the living room. Lynn rolled a joint while they talked and laughed, making a lot of noise, even though, I didn't hear a thing. After smoking the joint, Lynn and her friend Brian went to her room, leaving Julia alone.

Julia was feeling no pain and looked around until she found where I was sleeping. She got undressed and slipped in under the covers with me. I thought I was having a wet dream at first, waking up, I realized what was happening. My first thought was, Sara is home and she was really glad to see me. My first reaction was, again, more or less instinctively, to go with the flow.

Something definitely seemed different, but under the circumstances, that's not where my attention was focused. It was actually some time before I realized that there was another woman in my bed. I finally realized, when she said something that it wasn't Sara's voice and even then I didn't know who it was. Yet this did not deter me! I figured that I would just find out later.

Sara had finally finished picking mushrooms and was on the way back to Prince George in a van with a bunch of other mushroom pickers. They had been driving for 14 hours when they rolled into Prince George. They dropped Sara off in front of the house at about three in the morning.

She noticed both my truck and Lynn's car parked in front of the house. "Oh, Lynn's here." she said to herself, walking up to the door. She opened the door with her key and walked in. She went to Lynn's room first, lightly knocking on the door.

"Come in!" Lynn said. Sara opened the door a crack.

"So you made it!" she said.

"Yeah," she said, leaning over so that Sara could see Brian.

"Oh! I'll see you in the morning," Sara said. "Did Julia come with you?"

"Yeah! I think she's in your bed with Louie."

"Hmm," said Sara, closing the door, as she went to take a shower.

Meanwhile, back in the bedroom, things were getting hot and heavy with Julia and me. At one point, she whispered in my ear, "I'm a virgin!"

I was thinking, 'What are the chances of this? Being woke up in the middle of the night by a nineteen-year old virgin in bed with me. Isn't that every man's dream?'

I heard the shower running, but didn't think anything of it. I thought it was probably Lynn, having no idea that it was Sara. She came out of the shower and quietly opened the door and slipped in.

It was just minutes later that I felt another body get in bed with us. 'Okay, who is this now?" I was thinking. To my surprise, she joined right in the fun. I realized that it was Sara after a few minutes. I had never known Sara to like women before, but she obviously did and knew what to do to.

Things continued hot and heavy with the three of us. It

398

was the first time in my life that I had had sex with a virgin.

Afterwards, we were all laying together, feeling worn out. I turned to Sara, saying, "I didn't know you liked women."

"Sometimes. I guess this is one of those times," she answered. But I like you, too," she said, leaning over and kissing me.

"I like you, too!" Julia said, punctuating it with a kiss.

Julia slept with Sara and me a couple more nights before she and Lynn went back to Vancouver.

Every once in a while, Sara and I would bring home a girl and have a threesome. It came as a surprise to me how much easier it was for a guy and a girl to pick up another girl than just a guy trying to pick up a girl. They were surprisingly interested and, of course, we would make them the center of our attention for the evening.

There were times in my life when I couldn't seem to attract girls, even if my life depended on it. Then there were times that I attracted anything with boobs. I don't know what causes these times to be so radically different, but they were. Right then I appeared to be a magnet for women.

I was driving back to town from Longstock one day and I saw two girls on the road, hitch-hiking. I pulled over and picked them up.

They were from Montreal and had been traveling across the country. They both had large backpacks, complete with camping gear and a tent. Just before we got to town, it started raining cats and dogs.

"Gee, I hate to leave you girls out in this downpour," I said. "My girlfriend has a place here in town. You're welcome to come over and wait it out."

They talked it over between themselves and agreed.

I drove over to Sara's with the girls. I went in the house first and told Sara what was going on. It was still raining heavily when we got there.

They left their backpacks in the truck and came in with me.

"I picked these girls up hitch-hiking in the pouring rain. I thought they could wait it out here," I said to Sara. We introduced ourselves to each other, and went in and sat around the table.

One of the girls was named Danielle and the other was Sonya. Danielle was really out-going and friendly, though Sonya was kind of reserved. Danielle seemed to like me and was acting a bit forward, seeing as how we just met.

"We have an extra room, if you girls would like to stay the night," Sara offered.

They had been mostly camping on their trip. It had been a couple of weeks since they had stayed in a house and they seemed to like the idea. The girls talked it over for a minute and accepted the invitation.

Sara and I had a short conference while they went out to the truck to get their backpacks.

"That Danielle is pretty cute and sexy," I said to Sara.

"It looks like she likes you, too," she answered.

We agreed to feel things out with the girls and see what would happen.

They came back in with their heavy pack sacks and put them in the spare room. Sara cooked some spaghetti for dinner and we had dinner together.

After dinner, Sara went over to her Mom's for a couple of

hours, leaving me with the two girls.

"You're welcome to take a bath or shower if you like," Sara said before she left. "Help yourself"

Danielle went first in the shower, while Sonya and I watched TV. She seemed a little nervous about the situation.

"Your turn," Danielle said as she came out of the bathroom. Sonya got up and went to take a shower.

Danielle sat down with me on the couch. She was very talkative and outgoing, unlike her friend and even though the TV was on, neither of us paid much attention to it. She shifted position on the couch, crossing her legs in front of her and turning towards me.

She was telling me about their trip across the country, yet, as I was listening to her, I couldn't help thinking about how cute she was. She was a very tactile person, grabbing my arm while punctuating her words. It was as if we had known each other for a long time. In the course of the conversation we got a little closer to each other and she grabbed my hand.

I thought I might as well go for it and asked her straight out if she would like to go into the bedroom and smoke a joint.

"What about Sara?" she asked.

"Sara's not going to object," I assured her. "She might even join us if she comes back."

She looked at me curiously, as if she wasn't sure how to take it. I rolled a joint and we went into the bedroom to smoke it. We had hardly finished smoking the joint before we were all over each other. I heard Sonya come out of the shower and the other bedroom door close as Danielle and I made out on the bed.

We were just laying in bed afterwards, when I heard Sara

401

returning. We got our clothes on and went back into the living room. Sara and Sonya were sitting on the couch, watching TV, when we appeared. It was pretty obvious what had been going on. Sara smiled, winking at me as I sat down.

Later that night I retired to the bedroom again with Danielle. Sara was trying to put the make on Sonya, but it wasn't working. She finally gave up and joined Danielle and me. Even Danielle was reluctant to have sex with Sara there. We moved slowly with her. Her resistance crumbled more and more as she got more turned on.

The room was dark and I don't think she could actually tell which one of us was kissing her.

The girls left in the morning. I drove them to the highway and said goodbye.

I had some friends in Dome Creek whom I had met at David Parsons place. They were Americans who immigrated to Canada and had become very good friends. I seemed to always be bumping into Marie, either at the bar or in the bar car on the passenger train and we became drinking buddies. She knew Katy and had been to our place many times. Katy and I had been to their place in Dome Creek too.

Marie and I became the best of friends and had many nights out at the bar where we ended up together. We never had a serious romance going, though we had talked about taking off to Mexico together. She was the kind of friend that I could tell all my troubles to.

Marie was short and very curvaceous. I remember leaning across the table many times, thinking of how much I'd like to sleep with her. We definitely had something going between us, but amazingly, it stayed under control, never getting beyond making out with each other every once in a while. It's probably true, that if we were not both married we probably would have ended up together for a while, anyway.

It was a running joke between us that anytime we went drinking, we would always go to the Burger King and get some french fries first. Then we could go to the bar and drink enough to get the french fries floating.

"Hey, Marie! You want to go float some fries?" That was our own personal code for, 'Let's go to the bar'.

Our relationship was living proof that beautiful, sexy women could be great friends.

Then there was Deserea. She moved into Pierre and Betty's to care take their place for the winter. Pierre had been working at the mill at Upper Fraser for more than a year, just coming home on weekends.

Betty was holding down the fort at the homestead. She was not looking forward to spending another winter in that situation.

Pierre moved Betty and their two kids to a house in Upper Fraser for the winter. Deserea moved in to take care of their place. She traveled overseas to Thailand and the Far East the year before and was looking for a place to hold up during the winter. They met each other through mutual friends, finding out that Deserea was looking for a place to stay, they offered their place. They only had one cow and a calf to feed for the winter and were happy to have someone to stay there and take care of the place.

Deserea was definitely a hippie chick. She wore long, flowing, patchwork dresses and had very long brown hair, reaching almost to her knees. She was very much into the occult, especially astrology and the Tarot.

Sara and I had been seeing less of each other at about that time. She got a job in Prince George, working at one of the local bookstores. I was cutting firewood and getting ready to go falling for the winter. It was a pretty good job being a faller; nobody bothered me much and I could make my own hours. The only requirement was that I had to have trees on the ground for the skidders. As long as I was ahead of them, I could come in and leave when I wanted to.

I was out in the woodshed, stacking wood one day, when I heard an unfamiliar voice.

"Hello, Hello."

I came out from the woodshed, walking towards the house where I could hear her calling. "Hi, and who might you be?" I asked, as I came around the corner.

"I'm Deserea. You must be Louie!" she said, smiling back at me.

"That's right. What can I do for you?"

"I'm care-taking Pierre and Betty's place. I was out for a walk, just checking out the town and thought I'd drop in. Betty told me about you. I thought I would drop by and introduce myself."

"Well, come on in!" I said, leading the way into the house. "Would you like a cup of tea?"

"Yes, that sounds good," she said, following me into the house.

It was a chilly, fall day, with a cool wind blowing that made it even cooler. The fire was going in the house. The warm, dry, wood heat felt good. I put a pot of water on the stove for tea and we sat down across from each other at the table.

Deserea was really talkative. I don't know if she was nervous in my presence, or what. I had found that sometimes when people were nervous, they tended to talk a lot. Then again, it could just be her nature.

I wasn't sure if I should offer to smoke a joint with her, but before I could, she got one out of a leather bag she was carrying.

"Do you mind?" she asked, lighting the joint before I had a chance to answer.

She told me about her travels in Thailand and the Far East. She was going back there in the spring. It felt like she was an old friend that had come to visit. I took her for a tour around the farm. We casually walked around, visiting the garden and the horses.

Daffodil was pregnant and about to drop a foal. It was fall and not a great time for her to be foaling. The spring was always better, so that the foal would have a summer to grow before winter set in.

Deserea stayed around for a couple hours and invited me to go home with her.

"There is a trail through the bush that we can walk in less than half the time. I'll go with you and show you," she said. It was a good three-mile walk to her place on the road, yet if we went through the bush, she was my closest neighbor. I took a machete and a roll of surveyor's tape with me, for clearing out the trail and marking it so it would be easy to find.

Another good thing about using the trail, besides being a lot shorter, is that nobody could see us traveling back and forth.

One of the drawbacks to living in a small place like this is that every time you went anywhere, somebody was sure to see you and then everyone knew what you were doing.

I wasn't the only one interested in Deserea. A single girl living alone in Longstock was rare and several of the single guys were interested and paying her visits. I was at her place on more than one occasion, when somebody knocked on the door. Bob McCoby was there several times. He looked a bit disheartened when he saw me there.

Deserea and I went back and forth on the back trail often. I told her about Sara and she didn't seem to mind a bit that I was seeing her once in a while.

We had been spending a lot of time together. We helped each other cut firewood, split it and put it up in the woodshed.

I had been keeping a close eye on Daffodil, hoping that I would be able to see the foal being born. I could tell it was going to happen soon, when one day as I was checking her, I noticed a fine stream of milk squirting out of her teats. I think that having a foal is kind of a private affair when the horse is not confined to a barn stall. Daffodil disappeared for a couple of days in the pasture. I walked all over that pasture looking for her for the two days prior, but couldn't find her. Granted, the pasture was about 40 acres and mostly in bush, but it was rare that I looked for her and couldn't find her.

She finally appeared on the second day with a little painted filly. I had a hard time getting near the filly to catch her. She always kept Daffodil between us, circling back and forth as I pursued her. I finally got a lariat and tried throwing it over Daffodils back. After about the fourth try, I got her and the fight was on. Having never had a rope on her before, she freaked right out, dragging me along as I held onto the rope.

I slowly pulled her towards me and got my hands on her, rubbing her neck and back. She was all tensed-up at first, but gradually relaxed and seemed to enjoy my rubbing her. After that, I roped her every day for the next two weeks or so and spent about an hour a day rubbing her. Finally she got to the point where she was looking forward to it and I was able to catch her without the rope.

I looked forward to catching her and petting her every day, too. A close bond was created between me and the filly which would last for her whole life. Many times, nobody was able to catch her, even old Ross, who had handled horses all of his life, couldn't get a hold of her. He would drive to my place and get me. "Your horse is in my field. I got all the others but I can't get her! I've been trying for two days! You want to come over and catch her?"

It would really piss him off when I'd get her in the first ten minutes. Yet that's the way she was. I give credit to those first two weeks, when I handled her everyday.

Even though I was close to the filly, I couldn't decide on a name for her. It was going on three weeks and I still hadn't named her.

Deserea had stayed at my place that night and we stayed up late. It was 2 or 3 o'clock in the morning. I suddenly was awakened by a loud noise I had heard in a dream. It was a whistling, eerie roar. I woke up, startled by the sound and not knowing what it was. Deserea was still asleep next to me. I got up and went downstairs. I couldn't get the sound out of my head and I didn't know what it was. I stayed up for an hour or so before going back to bed.

We were sitting downstairs by the fire in the morning. I was drinking a cup of coffee and Deserea was having a cup of tea. I had forgotten about the dream that had awaken me when Deserea remarked, "I had an awesome dream last night!"

"Tell me about it."

"The wind was blowing and I went out to meet it. The wind spoke to me; I told it my name and it told me its name. It was loud and clear."

"What was its name?" I said, suddenly remembering my own dream and the sound of the wind that woke me up.

"It said, 'my name is Nika.'

"Holy shit! I had a dream, too! And it was the wind that was in my dream. It woke me up."

"Did it tell you its name?"

"No, but I think it's trying to tell me something."

"Tell you what?"

"It's telling me the name of my filly!"

"Nika?"

"Yeah, that's it, Nika."

"Wait a minute. That's the name of the wind that I heard. You can't use that name"

"What do you mean? Why can't I?"

"No, you can't! That's the name of the wind, not the name of a horse."

"What are you talking about? I've been waiting for a name to show up and attach itself to my filly for weeks. Now, there it is. Nika, I'm going to name her, Nika."

Deserea got really mad. "You name her something else, you can't use my name. That's my name. It's already the name of the wind."

"Are you nuts or something?"

She got up and left. She was really pissed-off. I couldn't believe it. Why the hell should she have so much trouble with my using the name Nika for the filly?

For reasons that she only could understand, she stayed pissed-off at me and didn't want to see me anymore. That was it for us, all because of the name Nika.

I didn't change it. The filly was named Nika and kept the name throughout her whole life...

The sound of the wind
Came to me in sleep
Frightening footsteps
Naming words that I keep.
And the sound of nothing
That I would call by a name,
I won't give it up
Even pressured by shame
The sound runs and shivers
Not owned by the heart
And Nika, Oh, Nika,
You're not really that smart!

Chapter 19

A Fall to Remember

It was early October and Fall had definitely set in. The entire previous week had poured rain. Flocks of Canada geese flying at high altitude, crossed the sky over Longstock every day. It had become quite windy and cool, the trees were quickly losing their leaves. I had been harvesting the garden for the last couple of weeks. The pot was looking pretty good, too. I liked there to be a day of frost or two before I cut it down.

It was the week before Canadian Thanksgiving and I had been out at Longstock for a couple of weeks by myself. Sara had a message on the morning messages to pick her up across the river at 2 o'clock. The only thing I had that was running was the tractor, so I drove it to the river just before 2 o'clock and took the boat down the river to get Sara.

She was waiting on the river bank when I got there. We loaded a box of groceries and a pack sack she brought with her and turned out into the river, heading home.

We were just about halfway back when I thought that I saw something in the river.

"Is there something in the river up there?" I asked Sara.

"Where?" she said, squinting her eyes, looking upriver. "Yeah, there is something in the river! What the hell is it?"

"Is that a moose?" I asked, straining my eyes to trying to make it out. I had the motor wide open and the distance was beginning to close. As we got closer, it started to look more like a bear. The river was high and wide from the recent rains and the bear was only about halfway across the river when we finally got close.

"Holy shit! That looks like a grizzly!" I could see only his head and the hump sticking up out of the water. The grizzly was distinguishable from black bears by the huge hump on his back and this one was definitely a grizzly.

I didn't want to get too close. I heard stories of grizzlies turning around and going right for the boat. A bear this big would almost certainly swamp a boat and sink it. I kept a safe distance from him while powering the motor down about 40 feet away from the bear. We stayed in the current, moving across the river with the bear as he swam.

The river bank on the opposite side was almost straight up and down, where the bear was heading. Having us cruising right beside him seemed to give him a sense of panic.

Well, let me tell you, we couldn't really see just how big this grizzly was while he was in the water, but when he got to the shore and came out of the water, it was apparent that this bear was huge. It was without a doubt the biggest bear I'd ever seen.

When he came out of the water, the water poured off him like a waterfall. He started up the steep bank with a bound. Because the bank was so steep, every movement up was a bound.

"Holy shit!" both Sara and I exclaimed from our viewpoint in the boat, as he bounded up the bank. He had to be at least nine or ten feet tall, weighing near a thousand pounds. There were three huge rolls of fat across his back, which jiggled and bounced as he went up the bank. I especially noticed his legs. His thighs were as big as tree trunks.

Sara and I were staring at this beast in awe. It was without a doubt the most spectacular sight that I'd ever seen in the wild - especially to see it so close to us.

The power of this bear was clearly evident as he went up the bank. The bank was sliding down as he went up, yet he continued to make ground, tearing down small trees and brush. He finally disappeared into the bush. This was definitely something that we would both never forget.

We think it was the same bear that was sighted several other times that fall by the McCobys. Everyone was talking about it because it was so big.

It was a couple of weeks later Dave McCoby was out hunting moose. He took a boat down river from Longstock and was hunting in the bush across the river from where Sara and I had seen the grizzly. Dave spotted a big moose in the

412

bush close to the river. He got it in his sights and shot, but the moose didn't go down right away. It took off running towards the river, finally collapsing just on top of the riverbank. Dave pursued the moose, coming upon the fallen animal and finished him off with a shot in the head.

It was a pretty big moose and Dave didn't have a boat big enough to transport it home. He cut the moose's throat to bleed it out and gutted it before leaving to get some help to get it home.

It was a couple of hours later before he returned with brother Bob and his riverboat. They landed the riverboat where Dave had shot the moose. He had hung a piece of red tape from a tree on the bank so that he could find the spot. They tied up the boat and climbed the bank, expecting to see the moose on top of the bank, but it was gone.

Something had dragged it away. It was obvious that it had been moved, by the marks on the forest floor. Bob hadn't brought a gun, thinking that they were just going to pick it up and go home.

"I'll go first," Dave said to Bob, seeing as he was the one with the gun. The trail was clear, they followed it back to where the moose was. They came upon the moose between a couple of Cedar trees. It was partly covered up with duff from the forest floor.

"Looks like a grizzly dragged it off!" Dave said, turning to Bob. "I wonder where he is now?" he said, looking around. "Well, we can't just get this sucker in the boat now. It's too far from the river. We're going to have to cut it up."

They both went back to the boat and got a meat saw that they brought with them. Usually, a bear would take off when it heard the noise of the boat motor and people talking. Even though they figured that the bear was gone, they were quite aware that he could still be around.

Dave was in front as they walked back to where the moose was. He had his rifle in hand, carrying it at hip level. It happened so fast that there was no time to think: the grizzly was still there and wanting to defend his kill. Even though he didn't kill the moose, he considered it his.

The grizzly jumped out in front of Dave with a roar, a few mere feet in front of him while he walked. There was not even time to take aim. Dave was only able to get the rifle up to his hip and shot while the bear was closing on him. The first shot hit the grizzly in the chest, stopping his forward progress and knocking him back, but not down.

Dave cocked his rifle and shot again. The grizzly hesitated and then lunged forward towards him again. Dave had ten bullets in the 30-06, firing in rapid succession and emptying his gun. The bear collapsed on the eighth or ninth shot, though Dave kept shooting after it fell.

Bob was watching the whole incident from behind Dave. Everything had happened so fast that he didn't have time to react.

Dave and Bob had managed to get both the grizzly and the moose back to their place with the help of a come-a-long and a few extra people. The grizzly was out on the grass beside the house. It was quite impressive. I don't know if it was the same grizzly that Sara and I saw swimming the river, but it could have been. It was certainly big enough.

It was a frosty morning, with the sun shining on the nearby

mountain. It was also a mail day. Toad had been working at the mill at Upper Fraser and Annie, her brother Dale, and his girlfriend Kate, were at his place. Toad still had his horse Flicka.

Kate saddled up Flicka that morning and rode down to Deserea's. It was about an hour later that she was riding Flicka back to Toad's. The road followed along the railroad tracks about 200 feet away, with bush on both sides and descended into a gully and up the other side.

Up on the tracks, the section crew was working. They traveled the tracks on a motorized cube called a speeder. It enabled the section crew to access the tracks in their section for maintenance and repairs. One of the crew, Vince Bono, had a gun in the speeder just in case he saw a moose.

Kate was just descending into the gully when Vince grabbed his rifle, thinking that he had heard a moose running. He aimed down into the gully, watching through his sites. As Kate got to the bottom of the gully, she came into Vince's view. In his eagerness to shoot, Vince pulled the trigger, with the rest of the section crew looking on.

Kate heard the boom and Flicka went down, throwing Kate over her head.

Kate didn't know what had happened at first and then realized that someone had shot Flicka.

Kate got up off the ground, and could see that Flicka had been shot. "You fucking asshole! You shot my horse!" she yelled at the top of her lungs.

Flicka thrashed around on the ground for a few seconds and managed to get up. When she stood up, it was apparent that she had been hit in the rear, right leg. The bullet had shattered the bone, leaving her leg twisted and dangling.

Kate was furious and screaming at the top of her lungs: "You shot my horse, you fucking asshole!" she repeated several times.

Vince and a couple of the section guys ran down from the tracks through the bush to where Kate and Flicka were.

"Are you all right?" one of the section guys asked.

"No, I'm not all right! You just shot my horse!" Kate screamed at them. She was crying and screaming at Vince and the section guys as she was checking out Flicka. The section foreman was there when Vince had pulled the trigger. He made his way through the bush to where Kate and Flicka were. He tried to talk to Kate, but she was too irate.

Kate screamed at the section foreman and the crew to fuck off. There was little that anyone could do for Flicka at this point, her leg was so badly mangled that the only thing holding it together was the skin. Flicka held the leg up off the ground and it was swinging around as she moved.

The section crew went back up to the tracks. Kate managed to get Flicka to walk up the hill and back to Toad's on three legs. Dale and Annie came running out of the house when they saw Kate and Flicka coming.

"What the hell happened?" Dale asked frantically. Flicka was walk hopping on three legs.

"One of those fucking section guys just shot Flicka." she answered.

She led the horse around to the barn as the three of them looked on, trying to figure out what to do.

"I think we'd better call Toad and tell him about this," Annie said. "Dale, you want to go down to Ross's and get him up here to take a look at Flicka."

Dale took off, walking to Ross's and Kate and Annie went back into the house. Within a few minutes, Vince and the section foreman knocked on the door.

Annie answered the door, but refused to talk to them. "I think you'd better fuck off, assholes!" she said before slamming the door in their faces.

Dale got back with Ross and they all went out to take another look at Flicka.

Ross took one look at the horse and turned to Annie, saying, "This horse is finished! There's no way you can fix her leg! It's shattered right to the bone. You'll have to shoot her."

Kate and Annie both started to cry. Ross went into the house with them and got Toad's 30-06 rifle. The girls stayed in the house while Ross and Dale went back out to the barn. Dale led Flicka out of the barn to the edge of the field. It was easier to lead her to a spot now than to try to move her after she was dead.

Boom! Ross shot her in the head, putting her out of her misery.

The girls heard the shot from inside the house. Flicka was dead.

Dale went to McCoby's and used the phone. He was not able to get Toad on the phone, but left a message for him to call right away, there's been a catastrophe.

It was a couple hours later that Toad phoned; Wayne McCoby answered the phone and told him what had happened.

Toad was able to get off work right away and drove out to the landing and came home.

I was at the landing when he arrived. I went to Prince George the day before and was just returning home. I just finished loading some supplies into the boat when Toad pulled up.

"Hey Toad, how's it going?" I said as he was getting out of his truck.

"Not so good. It seems that somebody just shot my horse this morning."

"What!"

"Yeah, one of the section guys shot her while Kate was riding her."

"Holy shit!"

"Yeah, they called me at work. I'm going to check it out."

I took Toad across the river and gave him a ride to his place. We walked out to where Flicka laid. He was really upset and vowed to 'make somebody pay for this.

He went to McCoby's and phoned the cops. He then phoned the C.N. police.

Dave McCoby showed up at my house in the morning a couple of days later.

"The cops want you to pick them up across the river this morning.

They want to investigate the horse shooting." "What time are they going to be there?"

"Eleven o'clock."

"Okay. I'll go over and get them." That still gave me about an hour. I went to the river where my boat was tied up, but it was gone. I had completely forgotten that I had loaned the boat to Ross. He had gone up the river, moose hunting, about halfway to Penney.

His little plywood speedboat was tied downriver a couple hundred feet from where I had tied mine. His speedboat was only about 14 feet long and had a three-person capacity. He had an older 20 horsepower motor on it. I borrowed his boat several times before, when he was using mine.

I didn't think too much of it as I pushed off and started down to get the cops. It was a cold day. The temperature was well below freezing and the ice was starting to form on the edge of the river as I headed downriver.

I pulled into the river bank on the other side and there were two cops waiting on the river bank.

I drifted the boat into the bank, running the bow of the boat up on the sandy bank. "Get in, fellows!" I said to the cops. The two of them climbed in the boat. I reversed the motor and pulled out into the current.

We made a little small talk, but it was not easy to talk over the roar of the motor. As we traveled upriver, we were going right into a cold wind. The cops were wearing winter jackets and hats. It was about a five-mile ride from the landing to the Longstock side and we were about halfway there when I heard a clunk come from the motor.

It startled me, and thinking, 'I wonder what that was?' I took the cover off the motor to investigate. When I lifted the cover off, there was a steady stream of water spraying out of the motor. It looked like a head bolt had popped out and the water was spraying out of the hole. As I was looking things over on the motor, I didn't notice that the spray was directed towards the front of the boat and was spraying on one of the cops. Because of the temperature, it was pretty well freezing when it landed on him.

My assessment of the situation was that it really wasn't hurting anything, as far as the motor running well enough to get us up the river was concerned. That was until I turned around and noticed that the water was spraying on the one cop. He was moving around, trying to get out of the spray, to no avail. The boat was too small and there was no place to go.

We were traveling against the current, so that while I was working on the motor, we drifted downriver a little, losing a little ground each time I stopped. After a while, I noticed the cop was getting quite covered with ice from the spray.

I decided to put the cover back on the motor and interrupt the spray of water. With the cover back on, it stopped the water from spraying on the cop, but was spraying water all over the motor now, shorting out the spark plugs. The motor started running very badly, missing and sputtering.

"Sorry, guys, but I'm going to have to take the cover off again or we ain't going to make it!" I said to the cops as I removed the cover. The water resumed spraying all over the one cop.

By this time, the plugs were already wet and the motor was still running terribly. The one cop had a layer of ice on his hat and jacket about an inch thick. Things were not looking too good. We drifted back down quite a ways while I was working on the motor. It was pretty cold. One of the cops was getting really wet and I thought that maybe we should forget it for today and try again tomorrow.

The motor finally died and we were drifting down the river. I didn't want to get stuck on the wrong side of the river, so I paddled the boat over to the bank on the Longstock side.

I jumped out of the boat and pulled it into the bank. Both of the cops were looking at me as if to say, 'what the hell are we supposed to do now?'

"Hey, look, fellows, we're not going to make it today. I'm getting out here so I can walk up the riverbank and get home. You guys are going to just have to drift back down to the landing. Use the paddle to get yourselves across and tie up the boat. If you come back tomorrow at the same time, I'll pick you up with a different boat."

I gave them a shove off into the current and away they went. As I started up the bank to walk back, I glanced out at the cops. The layer of ice was glistening off the jacket and hat of one of them.

It took me a couple of hours to get back to Longstock through the bush. It was really thick along the river and not very easy walking. My tractor was up at Ross's place, so I took the long walk to his place to get it and noticed smoke coming from the chimney of his house.

"Hey Ross, did you get a moose?" I asked as I walked in the open door. The fire was blazing and the house was like an oven.

"No, but lots of sign up there." "See any?"

"One cow, that's all."

Ross's whipped up a couple of hot toddies and we sat down. Lana wasn't feeling good and was in the bedroom sleeping. She was quite pregnant these days. It was only a month before the baby was due.

I told him the story about the two cops and the bolt flying out of the head on the motor.

"Where's the boat now?" Ross asked. "Down at the landing."

"Let's go get it now. We can just tow it up. The river could be froze in a couple days, the ice is starting to run."

We took Ross's tractor to the river and took my boat down to get his, towing it upriver and pulling it out of the water with his tractor.

The next day I took my boat down to pick up the cops again. It had been cold that night and the river ice was getting thicker and the pieces bigger around. At this point, the river was about half full of ice. It was impossible to travel without the ice scraping the side of the boat. When it did this, it made a really loud noise. Every once in a while, I would come to a spot where the ice chunks were closer together and I had to power the boat through it, breaking the ice. It was really noisy.

When I got down to the landing, there was only one cop waiting this time. I noticed that it was a different cop today.

I pulled into the bank and jumped out with the rope. "It's just you today?" I asked.

"Yeah, just me."

"What happened to those other guys that were out yesterday?" "Oh, they won't be coming out again."

I chuckled as I got back in the boat. "Let's go." "It's okay with all that ice coming down?"

"Yeah, yeah, come on!" I said, waving him to get in. He finally got in the boat. I reversed us out into the current. It seemed like the ice was getting thicker by the minute. There was definitely more ice in the river than when I came down. I could still get through, though it was even noisier than before.

The loud noise the boat made going through the ice was making the cop nervous. He was crouched down in the middle of the boat, with one hand on each side, seemed like he was hanging on for dear life. I swear that there were gouges in the wood from his fingernails.

We finally made it up to the landing, pulling the boat as far out of the water as possible, to keep it away from the flowing ice. I gave the cop a ride up to Toad's place, and arranged to pick him up in about an hour. I went home.

The cop questioned Kate about what had happened, and pretty well assured her that there was going to be an arrest. They already knew that Vince Bono was the one doing the shooting and now that they had a statement from her, they could arrest him.

I showed up at Toad's an hour later and picked up the cop and took him back across the river. The ice got even thicker in the last hour and a half. At no point in the trip down were we not crashing through ice. The cop had resumed his position of holding on for dear life in the center of the boat.

"I'm glad that's over," he muttered when we finally landed. He gave the boat a push off as he got out.

The trip upriver was the slowest yet. The ice had got even thicker and in the narrow spots in the river, I pretty well had to break ice all the way through. The usual ten-minute trip took over an hour. I finally got up to the landing. I hooked the tractor up to the boat and pulled it out of the water. It looked as if this would be the last trip this year.

Lana went to bed that night, not feeling well at all. She got up a couple of times, having a hard time sleeping. It was about two o'clock in the morning that the pain started to get really bad and that she realized that something was terribly wrong.

There was a pounding on my door at about 2:30 am. I was sound asleep and hadn't heard Ross's tractor pulling up to the house.

I opened the door and Ross was standing there. "What's up?"

"I got to get Lana into town. I think she's having an appendix attack."

"What about the river? The ice was heavy this afternoon." "It's still moving!"

"You think you can get through?"

"I can try. Will you drive her to town?"

"Yeah, okay," I said. I got dressed quickly and we took off for his place.

Lana was in pretty bad shape when we got there. She was in a lot of pain. We hooked up the wagon and threw a bunch of hay in it for her to lay on, then took off for the river. I had pulled the boat out of the river about twenty feet from the waters edge.

We unhooked the wagon and put Lana in the boat before backing the tractor up to it and pushing it back in. There was ice on the rivers edge about twenty foot wide. Once the boat was on this ice, I got in and Ross gave it a push and then jumped in. The boat slid across the ice and right into the current. Most of the river was ice at this point. I got the motor down and got it started. Our way was blocked by many huge, slow-moving chunks of ice, pretty well all the way down to the landing. Lucky for us that the ice was still moving downriver, the direction that we were going, so as long as it kept moving, we would get there eventually.

Lana was still really uncomfortable. The ice was crashing on the sides of the boat.

Once we started going, I turned the controls over to Ross. It was pitch dark, and I thought that he might be better at getting us there than I would be. After all, he had run this river for over fifty years in all kinds of conditions.

It took us over an hour before we pulled into the landing on the other side. The shore ice was quite far from the landing. We had to break it to get to shore. I jumped out with the rope and tied up. Ross helped Lana out of the boat and up the riverbank, while I got the truck started, and warming up.

Lana waited in the truck for a couple of minutes while I went down to the boat, untying it and giving Ross a shove back into the ice laden river. The ice was moving really slowly by this time, and seemed to cover the whole river.

"Good luck, Ross! I hope you make it back!" I said. Ross gave me a wave and started upriver. The boat made lots of noise as it inched up through the ice. I was hoping he would make it back up to the landing. If he didn't that would mean my boat would be stuck in the ice for the winter.

I watched him as I walked up the riverbank to the truck. It was going to be a long haul on the way back. Hopefully, the ice would keep moving long enough for him to get back.

Lana was still in a lot of pain as I got back in the truck and headed to Prince George. I drove as fast as I could on the way in, making it there in record time. I pulled up to the front door of the hospital, getting out and running inside.

"I've got a woman outside, I think she's having an appendix attack!" I said to the nurse at the front desk.

She got on the phone, and within a minute or so, a couple of guys showed up with a wheelchair and went outside and got

Lana out of the truck and brought her in.

I parked the truck while they were taking care of her. She went immediately into surgery. Her appendix was apparently close to bursting and they wasted no time in getting her in.

The river ice had almost come to a stop as Ross plowed through, trying to make it back. There were several times when the ice was so slow that it took more than one attempt to get through it. It was especially thick where the river curved around the bar where Hungary Creek dumped into the river. Ross ran the boat back and forth a couple of times before the ice chunks broke and allowed him to get through. After almost two hours of trying, he managed to get up to the landing, when he ran the boat up onto the shore ice. By this time, the ice was thick enough to hold the boat up. Ross got out, walked across the ice, got the tractor and pulled the boat out of the river.

"I didn't think I was going to make it!" he told me the next day. It had been only a matter of a couple hours afterwards that the ice jammed up and stopped moving. That was it for the winter. We would not see the river flowing again for the next five months.

Lana was doing fine the next day when I saw her, but they wanted to keep her in the hospital for a couple more days just to be sure, on account of her pregnancy.

I stayed at Sara's for a couple of days and then took the train back to Longstock with Lana.

When the train pulled up to the station at Longstock, I could see Ross and Toad waiting there for us. Lana was pretty slow getting off the train, still feeling sore from the operation. Ross had the wagon half full of hay. We got Lana loaded in the wagon for the ride home. She and Ross took off and I went over to Toad's with him for a while.

On the way to his place, Toad told me that he had heard back from the cops about the shooting. They had charged Vince Bono with dangerous use of a firearm, destruction of property and unlawfully carrying a weapon on the speeder. The cops also went to his house and confiscated all of his guns. Vince was out on bail until he went to court. The railroad had also suspended him from working until the matter was settled.

The cops told Toad that these were criminal charges, but in order to get compensated for his horse, he would have to bring a civil suit against Vince for damages. Toad talked to a lawyer and was told that he could sue Vince for whatever amount he wanted, and could expect to get it. He filed a lawsuit for $2,500.00 for compensation for Flicka.

Vince had heard that I was somehow involved in turning him in to the cops and bringing them up the river to investigate the shooting.

Word had spread around that Vince was going to beat the crap out of me for my part in turning him in to the cops.

I was on my way to Prince George on the train one day, and Vince happened to be on the train. I could hear him talking from where I was sitting. I don't think that he knew what I looked like or that I was on the train that day.

"When I catcha up with that guy, I'm-a going to kicka his ass," Vince was telling his friend that he was sitting with. He had a reputation as a scrapper and got into fights frequently. It was not unusual to see him with a battered face or black eyes. Though he liked to fight, he was not really that tough and got his ass kicked a fair amount of the time. He was also very loud and could be heard throughout the rail car. I was not the only one who heard him boasting about how he was going to teach me a lesson.

The word spread throughout the train about what Vince was saying. Johnny was working the baggage car that day and had heard all about the incident prior to this. One of the train crew had gone to the baggage car and had told Johnny about what was going on back in the coach. Johnny knew Vince because they both worked for the railroad and he didn't like him very much. As a matter of fact, Johnny and Vince had tangled one time in the bar in McBride, a year or so ago. Johnny had proceeded to kick the crap out of him, breaking his nose and finally, knocking him out.

Suddenly I heard Johnny's voice from behind me. "Hey Vince, what's this about you going kick the shit out of Louie for turning you in?"

Vince didn't say a word.

"You shot the fucking horse with a girl riding it, didn't you?" Still not a word from Vince.

"Listen to me, asshole!" said Johnny. "You're not kicking anybody's ass. 'Cause if anybody gets their ass kicked, it's going to be you. You shot the fucking horse, now you're gonna take your lumps, whatever they be."

Still not a word from Vince.

"I know the girl who was riding the horse and I know Louie, too. And I like them people way more than I like you. If I hear of you even talking about going after anybody, then I'm coming after you and I'm going to fuck you up really good."

I turned around and looked up the aisle towards them. Johnny had his face in Vince's and was raising his voice, making it clear that he meant what he said.

"Do we understand each other?"

I assume that Vince must have shook his head, yes.

"Okay." Johnny walked away, and went back to the baggage car.

Though I knew who Vince was, I don't think he knew me. When I got off the train, I walked right by him. I never heard another threatening word again.

Vince got a fine of $1,000 and lost his right to own guns, and could not get a hunting license for five years. Toad's lawsuit was successful as well, and he was awarded the full $2,500.

Chapter 20

Chilling Out

It was early December, and the ground was covered with snow, and the temperature was dipping down to -20 the last couple of nights. I went to the Post Office to get the mail and to my surprise, I had a letter from Chico. I had not heard a word from Katy or the kids since the previous spring, when they had disappeared from the apartment.

The postmark on the letter was from Alaska; I opened the letter quickly and read;

Dear Dad,

How are you? I am fine. We are living in Wasilla, Alaska. I am going to school and having fun. My brothers are doing good. I miss you a lot and want to see you. Please write back.

I Love You Chico

I was moved. It had been a long time since I had had any contact. I walked home, wanting to answer Chico's letter. It was hard to keep from crying as I hurried to get home.

I sat down and got out some paper and started a letter to Chico. It was a difficult letter to write. I was so moved by his letter that I was taken over by emotion every minute or so. I ended up crying all over the letter and had to rewrite it. I missed the boys very, very much. Although I had missed them terribly since they disappeared, I had not really let myself grieve like this.

I wrote back, telling Chico how I missed them and that I would try to come to see them as soon as I could. Christmas was coming up soon and now that I had an address, I would get off some Christmas gifts right away.

It was a relief of sorts, going shopping and getting the packages ready to send. It gave me a sense that I was doing something important for the kids. I bought them each a toy and a piece of clothing, wrapped it up in Christmas wrapping and sent it off.

It was going to be a quiet Christmas this year: Sara was going to Vancouver Island and I would probably just stay home. There were always a few things happening in Longstock at the neighbors and they were extra friendly, especially to a person who was alone.

I was totally planning on staying in Longstock until I ran into Benny and Marie on the train coming back from Prince George. We were sitting in the bar car on the passenger train, when Marie asked what I was doing for Christmas.

"You should come and spend Christmas with us!" Marie said to me. "A whole bunch of friends are coming up here from California. Jed and Betty are coming up, too!" Jed and Betty helped me escape with the kids a couple of years back. "It'll be fun!" I could see that Marie was not going to let up until I agreed to come.

"Okay! I'm in!"

"Just bring a present that's worth about ten bucks, we're going to draw names," she said. I agreed.

I took my snowmobile across the river and drove my pickup out to their place on Christmas Eve day, arriving at their place in the early afternoon. The people from California started arriving three days before. The house was bustling with people. Benny and Marie's house was quite large and built in the shape of an octagon, with the downstairs being one big, open room. They had just done the floors with hardwood, which looked so good that it looked like it belonged in a bowling alley.

Benny's brother Jed was there, and his wife Betty. Benny's parents and sister Joyce showed up, too. There were a few other friends that I met for the first time: Jose', Roberto and Maria, who had all come up from California. There were also a couple other girls, Karen and Nancy, that lived in a cabin nearby.

Food was all over the place. The counters were full of every kind of snack you could imagine. I guess that I was supposed to bring something, too. Oops! I did bring the present. There was a Christmas tree in the living room area and decorations all around the house.

There was a designated smoking area for all the pot smoking that went on while Benny's parents were around. There were several easy chairs and an old antique couch in front of the big picture window that was the smoking area. The kitchen was off limits. There on the coffee table was a wooden container full of pot, cigarette papers and roach clips, ashtrays and such. The wood stove was blasting out the heat, creating a warm and friendly atmosphere.

I took turns introducing myself to everyone that I didn't know. I was really taken with Benny's sister, Joyce. She was a tall woman, with dark hair and dark eyes. She was a school teacher in California and was on her Christmas break.

Benny's parents were a retired couple. The chance to spend some time in the bush was something they never passed up. His Dad had spent time here when Benny was building the house. They lived in a tent for two months while they were building. His Dad, Rich, didn't look his age at all and was full of energy. He and his wife Dotty were in the kitchen, pumping out the food and drinks. There was enough food there to feed us all for a week. I remember thinking that most people tend to slow down when they get older. That was not the case with them.

I had a few drinks, so I wasn't sure how much time went by, but soon the music got cranked up and the dancing began. Rich and Dotty started it off, and one by one, we all took to the dance floor. The furniture got pushed out of the way, making a really nice area for dancing.

I kind of got partnered up with Joyce and we danced every

dance for a long time. It was more fun than I had had for quite a long time. We hit it off pretty well and the relationship might have come to something, except for the distance between us and the fact that neither one of us was going to move.

Benny had an area outside, where he had set up a couple of home made log benches. It was cold, and the sky was clear as a bell. The Northern Lights were beginning to streak across the sky. The moisture crystals in the air sparkled from the cold temperature as we sat outside. Joyce snuggled up close to me to stay warm as we took in the beauty of the winter night. The sound of music was spilling out from the house and we could see bodies dancing away inside. The cold temperature eventually got to us and after about twenty minutes, we headed back inside.

It seemed as though the music had turned up while we were outside and the dancing had gotten more vigorous. Marie and I both knew how to jitterbug and it wasn't long before she was pulling me on to the dance floor.

The party and the dancing went on until the wee hours of the morning. It seemed like Rich and Dotty were never going to get tired. They just kept on.

The party finally started to wind down. Sleeping bags and foamy's were laid around the floor and people started to crash out. Joyce and I made a bed on the floor and crashed out together. The floor was covered with bodies the next morning when I woke up.

It was Christmas morning, Rich and Dotty were making coffee and breakfast for everyone as soon as they woke up. It was a Christmas to remember and they were loving the experience. We exchanged presents and talked about the night before, having some good laughs. Everyone pitched in and we had a fantastic Christmas dinner. There was a turkey with all the trimmings and a very big salmon, cakes, pies, cookies, sweet potatoes, several different salads and just hoards of food. We went through gallons of rum and eggnog, and feasted until we could hardly move.

Christmas day was pretty slow, as people laid around, recovering from Christmas Eve. Late in the afternoon, Rich and Dotty got a group together to go for a hike in the snow. Joyce and I joined the group for a while, but returned to the house early. She was not used to such cold temperatures and was beginning to get pretty cold by the time we started back.

It was kind of a lazy night, with a lot of worn-out people around the house. The next day, the crowd started to thin out. I left for Longstock, saying goodbye to Joyce; she would be leaving for California early the next morning.

Even though it was lots of fun, I was acutely aware of how much I missed the kids, especially after I got home.

I was only home a couple of days, when I got a visitor: Dennis was a fellow who lived in a little cabin near where the Torpy river dumped into the larger Fraser River. Dennis and I had met on the train many different times. We had something in common, in that his ex-wife had taken off with his kids, too. It was nice to have him around for a couple of weeks. It distracted me from the issue, even though we talked about it.

Right after Dennis arrived, the weather took a turn for the worse. The nighttime temperature had dropped to -50 degrees. It was the beginning of the longest cold snap I had seen yet, lasting right into the end of January. For the next five weeks, the thermometer never came above -10 in the daytime, and stayed -20 to -50 at night. It was too cold to do much outside, except to cut a little wood in the daytime and keep shoving it into the stoves.

Dennis and I were out getting some wood one day and noticed a bunch of grouse really high up in a big poplar tree. There must have been forty of them. I went to the house and got the old 410 shotgun I had gotten from Willie years ago. I loaded two shells and got right under the tree. Aiming straight up, I fired and three grouse fell. None of the others moved, except to keep pecking at the buds high in the tree. I fired again, and three more fell.

I looked over at Dennis, and said, "That should probably do us, eh?"

"Yeah! Looks good!" he said. We walked back to the house. The other grouse in the tree just kept pecking away at the buds, just as if nothing had happened.

I picked up a newspaper just before leaving Prince George. The headline on the paper read: 'Mountie Killed by Mad Trapper.' There was a picture on the front page as well. I recognized the picture and the name: Michael Buddai was one of the two cops I had filed a complaint against a year before. The story took place up north, in the Yukon, at a place called Teslin Lake. The trapper apparently shot a moose and broke into a cabin along the lake, dragging the moose inside and butchering it. He then took out for his cabin way back in the bush. The cops in Whitehorse got the complaint and went out to to bring him in. There were a dozen cops in the posse that went out to get him, and the man in the lead was Michael

436

Buddai. The trapper was aware that the cops were coming for him and he hid behind a tree close to his cabin. When the cops got close, the trapper fired the first shot and shot and killed Buddai. After the first shot, his gun jammed and the remaining eleven cops filled him full of lead.

After the harassment investigation, the cops would only tell me that disciplinary action had been taken, but they wouldn't tell me what it was. The mounties had a history of shipping cops who got into trouble up north for duty. And now it seems that this is what happened to Buddai. I admit that I was very pissed-off at those cops after the ordeal, but Buddai being killed was not something that I wanted to see happen. I said a silent prayer for the man after reading about his demise.

The cold snap broke at the end of January and I felt that I should go out and try to find some work. Trying to get to work and back when the weather was so cold was no easy task from Longstock. Aside from being terribly cold to travel and work in, it was a big ordeal trying to get my pickup started every morning. I worked in that kind of weather before, but it did not usually stay around for so long. Many times, the job would shut down for a couple of days until there was a break in the weather. It always required getting to my pickup with a little kindling wood and building a fire under the oilpan without burning the truck up. It would take about 20 to 30 minutes to warm the oil up enough to start the engine. By the time I got it started, I was usually frozen to the bone.

There were a couple of logging outfits working in the area. Now that the weather had warmed up, they were trying to make up for lost time. I managed to get a job, falling trees for a company called Silvertip Logging. They were working close by, on the Longstock access road that had been built recently from the river to the highway. Because there were only about six weeks left to log before break up, we worked a lot of six-day weeks. I can't remember anything about that time, except work. I got up at 5am, left the house at 6:30am, got to work at 7:30am, worked until 5:00pm, got home at 6:00pm, made dinner, fed the horses and went to bed at 9:00pm and then started all over again. By the sixth day, I was totally beat, doing as little as possible on my day off.

By the middle of March, I was ready for a break. Sara and I talked about taking a trip down to San Francisco, traveling down the Oregon coast on the way there and back. I asked Ross if he would mind throwing hay out for my horses while we were gone and he said that he wouldn't mind at all.

We decided to go to Vancouver first and visit Sara's sister Fran. It was the first of April when we left Prince George. We were planning on taking a month to make the trip, so our pace was very leisurely. I bought a canopy for my pickup the year before, so we were able to pull over and camp any time we felt like it. I guess you would say we were taking our time: it took us two days to get to Vancouver. We hit the city limits During rush hour and bumper-to-bumper traffic. We had a map to Fran's house that Sara drew from directions that Fran gave her over the phone. We smoked a joint just before we got into the heavy traffic and ended up getting lost trying to find her place. We missed one turn and then, thinking we could get off at the next exit and turn around and come back to it, I realized that it was a mistake. Every time we got off, there was no entrance to get

438

back on going the other way. We ended up going farther and farther in the wrong direction, away from Vancouver, almost to the U.S. border.

We did find Fran's place, finally, and spent three days with her before taking off for the U.S. It was a sunny spring day when we left. I knew that it was a little risky to take any pot across the border but it might be hard to find down there, so we decided to stash a bag in the truck. There was a panel in the inside corner of the cab on each side, a kind of triangle shape about twelve inches high. A mouse had recently gotten stuck in one of these panels and died, it created quite a stink. I tried washing out the cab with water, trying to get rid of the smell and that's when I found out that the panels were sealed and filled up with water. I managed to fish the dead mouse out of the panel with a coat hanger, but it was impossible to get the water out. A hot day with the windows rolled down created quite a smell. After the first time, I always left the windows cracked, yet the smell persisted, though it was not as bad.

I sealed up a baggie of pot and put it inside of another one, compacting it as much as I could, and shoved it down in the water in one of the panels. I didn't think they would look there because of the smell. I rolled one joint out of the bag before I stashed it, for us to smoke on the way to the border.

It was a beautiful spring day when we left Vancouver. Sara lit up the joint even before we were out of town. It was only about a half hour drive to the border. We were really stoned when we got there. Miraculously, the customs guys, after only a few questions about citizenship, let us through. We waited until we were quite a way from the border before getting the pot out. Sara opened the bags, and found that it was still dry. She rolled a couple of joints and we stashed the bags back in the panel again.

We were about halfway from the border to Seattle when Sara noticing two hitchhikers, and said, "Hey Louie, stop for these guys."

I pulled the truck over to the side of the road, passing the hitch hikers and stopped in front of them.

"Hi! Where are you going?" Sara asked.

"San Francisco."

"You're in luck!" Sara said as they put their packs in the pickup box. Sara slid over next to me on the seat and the two of them squeezed in.

"I'm Richard, and this is Liz."

"I'm Sara and this is Louie," she said, reaching out to shake hands. "We're not traveling very fast, but we are going to San Francisco."

"This is faster than we were going," Liz said. "We're in no hurry."

Our pace was pretty slow. We got off the freeway shortly after picking up Richard and Liz and took the road out to the coast. We stayed at a campground on the Olympic Peninsula in Washington the first night out. Richard and Liz were traveling with a tent and camping gear, and Sara and I were sleeping in the truck canopy. Richard went right to work getting a fire burning and collected a pile of firewood to last into the evening.

It was a warm, spring night and the sky was clear, as we sat around the fire. I got my guitar out of the truck, and started playing some instrumental blues. Richard rummaged through his backpack, looking for a harmonica.

"Hey, look at this! I've got an A and a C," he said, waving the harps, one in each hand. We jammed on harp and guitar for a while, until Richard started making up words:

I went to a party
Had too much to drink
Next thing I knew
I'm over the bathroom sink
I'm puking in the bowl
When I get some bad news
Looks like I'm getting attacked
By the diarrhea blues
I found out what happens
When you mix tequila and wine
My head started spinning
Now that's a bad sign
I went for the couch
I just wanted to snooze
It was keeping me awake
Those diarrhea blues

We played for hours, until my fingers were sore. Most of it was just jamming along on guitar and harmonica, but I did play just about every song I knew, as well. The one song that was the highlight of the night was Bob Dylan's, 'Down In the Easy Chair,' because everyone knew the words. Sara liked to sing and she was pretty good, although a little shy. Liz was not shy at all, but tended to drift a little off key once in a while.

Sara and I had planned on taking this trip very slowly,

covering an average of about 100 miles a day, taking lots of time to stop and explore along the way. It was about 1,000 miles to San Francisco. Richard and Liz were in no hurry, either, so off we went the next morning, heading south and out to the coast.

About noon the next day when we were driving next to the Hood Canal. It is a large body of inland tidal water on the Olympic Peninsula. As we passed, we could see, by the shoreline, it was low tide and that there were a lot of people out on the tidal flats.

'I wonder what they're doing?' I thought.

"Oysters!" said Richard, reading my mind. "They're getting oysters off the rocks; peeling them off with knives."

"Really! Why don't we get some too?" I pulled over on the side of the road and parked the truck. We grabbed a few knives and a bucket and took out across the tidal flats. Oysters live at a level such that it's only on very low tides that they are exposed. Even then, it is only a few hours from the time the tide exposes them until the water covers them again. We wandered around in the tidal flats for a couple of hours, managing to collect about a half-bucket of oysters. We drove on a little farther that day before finding a place to camp and feasted on them.

It was the next day that we crossed the Columbia River into Oregon and got to the coast. From that point on, we were camping on the beach. We seemed to find a deserted beach every day, where we would set up camp for the night. The beaches weren't very crowded at this time of the year, and even though it wasn't what you would call, summer weather, the wind blowing in off the water wasn't cold. Each night, we would gather enough firewood to last the night and sit around

442

playing and singing. Several times, we were joined by people who were camping nearby and heard the music.

It was a fun and laid-back trip down the coast to San Francisco, with us camping at a different beach each night. Every night, around dusk, Sara and I took a walk along the beach, just out of reach of the waves crashing on the sand. Sometimes we walked for an hour or more before returning to our camp. It was a very romantic time for us and it drew us even closer together. On the way back to our camp, in the darkness, we could hear the waves crashing in the surf as we walked, holding hands. We could see only a dim outline of the foaming waves and lights coming from ships that were far out to sea. Richard always seemed to have a fire going on the beach by the time we returned. It helped us find our camp in the darkness.

It was a Friday, the seventh day after leaving Vancouver that we finally got to the Bay Area. Richard and Liz lived in Berkeley, and they invited Sara and I to stay at their place. They lived in an upstairs apartment in a residential neighborhood. We had been on the road for a week and were excited about getting there, wanting to take in as much of the city as possible. We picked up a copy of the previous Sunday paper that had an entertainment section that

listed all the music and shows that were taking place in a fifty-mile radius of the city. The following night was Saturday, and Chicago bluesman Charlie Musselwhite was playing at a bar in Berkeley called "The Basement." It was a small place located in a basement room near the center of town.

After relaxing at Richard and Liz's place the first night

in town, we made plans to go out to The Basement the following night.

Both girls were dressed to kill. Sara had on a sexy, red dress that she had brought along with her. She looked fabulous in the tight, low cut dress, with her long, dark hair flowing down her back. Not to be outdone, Liz was dressed in a short, black dress that had a slit up the side that exposed her thigh. She looked fabulous, too.

We piled into my pickup and drove to downtown Berkley. The Basement was actually in a basement, with a long, narrow flight of stairs going down to it. It wasn't a very big bar and was pretty well full when we got there. The band was already playing and the dance floor was crowded when we walked in. We managed to get one of the last empty tables, just in time, as people were still coming in.

The house band that was playing when we came in. Shortly after we got there, Charlie Musselwhite joined them. Charlie was a blues harmonica player that sang, as well. The music definitely rose to another level once he joined the band.

Sara and I didn't spend much time sitting at the table. We danced to nearly every tune. We only stopped to have a quick drink and then we were back on the dance floor. There was no stage to speak of. The band was at the same level as the dance floor and it was so crowded that the people were pushed right up to the band. There was almost no room to move on the dance floor. We were bumping into people constantly. The band took a break about once an hour, for about ten minutes. As the night went on we were all getting loaded and the group at our table grew. Because there was a shortage of tables, we were joined

444

by several other couples.

One of the couples that joined us was Rod and Tamara. At one point, when the music started up again, Rod asked Sara to dance. I took a cue from that and asked Tamara. It was a wild night. Charlie Musselwhite and the band had the place really rockin'.

It was two o'clock in the morning before the band stopped playing and we were all pretty loaded by that time. Rod and Tamara invited all of us along with a bunch of other people over to their place for a party after the bar closed. They lived within walking distance from the bar. We followed them to their place. Sara and I were not really paying a lot of attention to where we were going from the bar, but rather, we just followed the crowd.

They lived in an upstairs apartment somewhere in downtown Berkeley. There were at least a dozen other people that showed up there after the bar closed. I remember a large living room with a few sofas, easy chairs and a lot of people. Sara and I both passed out on the couch, when we woke up, it was getting light outside, people were still partying. Richard and Liz were gone when we woke up, having taken a cab home.

Sara and I hung around for a little while and then decided to leave. We weren't exactly sure how to get to Richard's place, but had the address and figured that we would find our way. We left the apartment and went down to the street, realizing at that point, that we had to find the truck. Not knowing where we were, we didn't know which way to go to the truck. We walked around the streets of Berkeley for at least an hour before we came across the bar we had been at the night before. After circling the blocks nearby The Basement, we finally found the truck and got back to Richards place at about eight o'clock in the morning. Sara and I slept most of the day on Sunday, getting up around five pm. Richard picked up the Sunday paper during the day, and scanned it for entertainment for the following week, circling shows that we might be interested in seeing.

We hung around the apartment that evening, recovering from the night before. The next day, we set off to explore the city, starting with "Fisherman's Wharf." It was a sunny and warm day, as we took a bus into the city. A couple of transfers later, we got off at Fisherman's Wharf. We left the bus right by the cable car stop. Having heard a lot about the San Francisco cable cars, we decided to start out the day with a ride on the cable car. The street was already packed with people and there was quite a crowd waiting for the cable car. There was a big hand-painted box with a man inside at the cable car stop. There was a sign painted on the front of it that read, 'The Human Juke Box'.

"Hey, let's see what this is all about!" Sarah said to me, grabbing me by the hand and leading me over to it. It was a large box, similar to what a refrigerator might come in. There was a list of songs on the outside, and a slot to put money in. Deposit .25, it read just below the slot.

"We'd better try this out!" Sarah said as she put a quarter in the slot. A few seconds later, a flap raised up, and there was a man inside with a trumpet. A penny whistle sounded as the flap opened and then the man started playing, 'When the Saints Come Marching In' on the trumpet. Sarah got out her camera and raised it up to take a picture. The man inside, even while he was playing, raised up and started waving, a sign that said

446

'Photo Tax: .25, Sarah deposited another .25 while the man played. He put his sign away when she put the quarter in the slot. It was a short version of the song, the flap closed and he was quiet.

"I've got to do that again!" said Sarah. She put another quarter in. Up came the flap, and this time it was 'Zippity doo da.' It was quite entertaining.

Just then, the cable car pulled up and we got on. It took off squealing and clanking, heading up the steep streets, leveling out at each intersection to stop and load passengers off and on. It was powered by cables under the street. I couldn't help thinking what would happen if the cable ever broke, but luckily it didn't. Sarah and I both hung on to the side like the people in the Rice-a-Roni commercials. It went up and then came down again, leaving us off at the stop with the Human Juke Box. There was a group gathered around him while he played 'When the Saints Come Marching In.'

We headed off down the street towards Fisherman's Wharf. The street was really crowded, with street performers all over the place. There was a man dressed in a tuxedo, with tails and white gloves, who was playing an upright piano that was in the back of a little Datsun pickup truck. There was a basket hanging off the side of the pickup box with a sign that said, 'Please help put this boy through music school'. The basket was more than half full of money. We stopped on the street to listen. He was playing a whole array of pop songs, not stopping at all as he went from one song to another.

While we were stopped there, listening, a policeman walked up. He looked at the parking meter and noticed that it was expired. He then tapped the man on the shoulder, to get his attention. The piano player stopped playing and turned around. The cop didn't say a word, but just pointed to the parking meter. The man jumped out of the pickup onto the sidewalk, fishing through his basket of money, he came up with a quarter and turned to the parking meter and deposited it. The cop gave him a wave of approval and walked on down the street. The piano player climbed back into the pickup and sat down and started playing again.

The next street performer that we saw was the one-man band: an old hippie-looking guy with a number of instruments strapped onto him that he played all at once.

Then there was the mime: a very tall man, with his face painted white, wearing a black suit with tails as well. Gathered in a big circle, there was a huge crowd of people around him on the sidewalk. While was doing his mime thing, he would walk briskly to the edge of the circle and stop suddenly, just inches from someone's face and be perfectly still. He seemed to pick the biggest guy in the crowd and walk right up to him and stop, staring him in the face without moving a muscle. The target person could not keep a straight face, moving around laughing. The mime would not move or crack an expression in any way, and then, without warning, he would slowly move across the circle to the next big guy he saw in the crowd. He had a basket on the sidewalk that people put money in, and it too, was more than half-full with bills and change. After a while, we moved on to see what other street entertainers down the street.

There was a courtyard with a podium in a little mini-mall, where a comedian/juggler was performing. He seemed very professional, like someone you would see on television. He talked and told jokes as he juggled various items. At one point in his act, he was juggling pins similar to bowling pins, having as many as five going around at once. Just when I thought that juggling five pins was quite a feat, he kicked off a shoe, getting it into the rotation going around with the pins. He never stopped talking through his entire act. He proceeded to catch the pins one by one, and then, catching his shoe, he put all of the pins down and picked up five machetes. He started to juggle the machetes one by one, until he had all five going. He then quickly reached in his back pocket and next thing I knew, he had a carrot going around with the machetes. Then he added a shoe as well. Now there were five machetes, a carrot and a shoe, all going around at once. He talked constantly as he was juggling. I thought it was quite amazing.

The courtyard was crowded with people as the juggler/comedian brought his act to a close, catching all the items he was juggling one by one, except the last machete, which fell on the floor next to him. "Aren't you glad you weren't sitting there?" he said jokingly as he picked it up. There was loud applause from the crowd as he took a bow to wind up his act.

Sara and I wandered around for a couple more hours and then took the bus back to Berkley. We recounted our adventure at Fisherman's Wharf to Richard and Liz, with Sara and I taking turns telling them about it.

Richard had picked up the Sunday paper and we looked through it. There were a couple of shows that interested us. On Monday night, Dan Hicks and his Hot Licks were playing in Mendicino, and John Lee Hooker was playing in Santa Cruz on Wednesday.

Sara and I drove to Mendicino for the Dan Hicks show on Monday night. It was a concert setting for the show, in contrast to the bar where Charlie Musselwhite had played. The room was packed with people, though it was a totally different kind of crowd there. Dan Hicks and his band played a high energy set, yet there was nobody dancing. There wasn't really a dance floor area in the room, but it was hard to just sit there and not want to dance. Sara and I found a place in the back of the room to dance. There was one other couple that joined us dancing, but everyone else at the show just sat there and listened.

On Wednesday, we drove to Santa Cruz to see John Lee Hooker. John Lee was a well known bluesman, but hadn't yet attained the star status that would come later in his career. It was a five-dollar admission. The bar was not crowded at all, with perhaps twenty-five or thirty people there. We sat at a table right on the edge of the dance floor. The dance floor was bordered by a wooden railing that encircled it. John Lee sat on a chair while he played the blues, backed by a bassist and drummer. A few other people danced besides Sara and I but most of the time we were the only ones.

There were a couple of girls that were sitting at a table close to the stage. When John Lee and the band took a break, they went and sat at the table with the girls.

"Let's go say hi to John Lee!" Sara said to me." I chatted with the blond in the ladies room." She got up and grabbed me by the hand; "Come on Louie, come with me!" she said, coaxing me to come with her.

We approached their table and Sara introduced us. "Hi, I'm Sara, and this is Louie," she said looking directly at John Lee. Sara was looking very beautiful, which prompted a response from him.

"Hi, Sara," John Lee said as he stood up and extended his hand and shook hands with her. He then turned to me, "Hi Louie," shaking hands with me, he invited us to sit down with them. Everyone introduced themselves as we sat down at their table.

John Lee had a very polite manner about him. He had been an entertainer for many years and was very gracious with us, as he always was with his fans.

I had first heard about him in the late 60's, when the blues revival had hit the U.S. The blues had actually almost died out in North America and had come alive again in Britain and had been exported back to the U.S., with groups like John Mayall and the Blues Breakers, The Yardbirds, Eric Burdon and the Animals, and Cream. When this happened, many of the black bluesmen in North America gained notoriety as a spin-off. John Lee was one of those bluesmen that benefited from this trend.

After a while, the band went back to play another set. As soon as they started, Sara and I took to the dance floor again and sat at their table every time they took a break.

We stayed until closing, dancing to almost every tune. It was a rare opportunity to see the John Lee in an intimate setting. He would become very famous, years later.

We had been in the Bay Area for about a week by now, and had been having a really good time. Both Sara and I were starting to get a little antsy to get back on the road by this time. We said goodbye to Richard and Liz on Friday morning and headed north over the Golden Gate Bridge and out to Coast Route 1. The fog was lying over the wind-blown trees along the road when we got to the ocean north of San Francisco.

451

By early afternoon, the fog had burned off and Sara and I stopped at a beach. There was a cool wind blowing off the ocean as we walked along the beach. We took off our shoes and walked in the sand close to the water. The waves would chase us up the beach, every now and then one would catch up to us. After spending a couple of hours there, we got in the truck and drove for an hour or so, stopping again at another beach. We camped on the beach, as we would for the next few days, traveling only a couple hours a day on the way back north. We had a campfire on the beach every night, and I played my guitar in front of the fire.

Ooh wee, ride me high
Tomorrow's the day
My bride's gonna come
Ohh ohh, we gonna fly
Down in the easy chair (Bob Dylan)

It took us almost two weeks to make it back to Vancouver, after having a ton of fun and leaving us with memories we could not forget.

I wrote a song about it:

Sara, do you remember when
We traveled down the coast
Walked in the salty wind
And Sara, do you remember when
We sang that same Bob Dylan song
A thousand times again

Chapter 21

Whole Earth Summer Solstice

$\mathbf{A}$ lot of people had come and gone in Longstock over the last few years. Harry was the only one of the Alaskans who was still there. Toad and Annie were still there too, living in the old house that had been there when they bought the place. The house was in very bad condition. It was basically sitting on the ground and listing to one side. Annie had been getting on Toad's case to build a new house for a few months. He finally decided to give it a try. Toad wasn't really handy as far as building things were concerned. He had attempted building a shed the year before and he would still be building it if Pierre hadn't come over and helped him finish it.

Toad got a bunch of logs together to build a log house, piling them by a site close to the old house. He had a tractor with a front-end loader that he used to lift the logs, managing to get three rounds up on the building.

I went over to Toad's place one day, he invited me out to take a look at the construction.

"What do you think?" said Toad rather proudly.

"Looks great!" I said, trying to be encouraging. Looking closer, I noticed that the logs had cuts in them. They were cut three-quarter of the way through. "What are those cuts there?" I said, pointing at them.

"Oh, I had to cut them to make them lay flat."

"But... it looks like they're cut almost all the way through."

"That's the Baloney Principle."

"The Baloney Principle?"

"Yeah! Haven't you ever heard of the Baloney Principle?"

"No, I can't say that I have. You want to tell me about it?"

"Haven't you ever noticed that if you fry a piece of baloney, it bubbles up in the pan. If you want to get it to lay flat, you have to cut it. When you do, it lays flat in the pan."

"And somehow you think that the Baloney Principle applies to log houses, too?"

"Why, of course! There were big spaces in between the logs, and when I cut them, they laid right flat on the one below."

"Yeah, but you cut right through them in some places. Don't you think that that would weaken the log walls?"

"Hey, sometimes you got to put a big cut in the baloney, too."

It was clear to me that I wasn't going to deter Toad from

454

using the Baloney Principle. He had it all figured out in his own mind. I rolled my eyes and changed the subject. The house never got finished, anyway.

The population in Longstock had been decreasing steadily over the last few years. People seemed to be moving out all the time, with nobody moving in until one day a family had bought a piece of land on the river, about halfway to Penney. Gunther, his wife Karen and two kids were planning on moving out there as soon as Gunther could get a house built on the property. Gunther had a big team of workhorses that he planned to use to build a house with. He also had a 28-foot, aluminum riverboat with a 454 cubic inch V8 in it that he used to haul supplies the seven miles upriver to his property.

Gunther hauled the majority of his building supplies downriver from the Penney landing, as it was easier going down with the current with the heavy stuff. Because of that, nobody in Longstock knew that he was moving in until he started to use the Longstock landing with his boat. His property was closer to Longstock than it was to Penney, making the river trip closer, but upriver.

Gunther walked his horses in through the bush from the highway, about three miles away. He didn't waste any time getting started on his house as soon as he got them to the property. There were a lot of trees on the property that would make good building logs. He started cutting and skidding logs for his house right away.

After getting a pile of logs up to the building site, Gunther rigged up blocks and cables in the trees around the house. He used the team of horses to lift these big logs up in the air and right into place. It was amazing how fast he got the place built, taking less than a month to finish the log work on the walls and roof.

I met Gunther at the landing one day as we were both loading our boats after going to Prince George. He just about had his house built before I even knew that he was living up there. We talked for a while on the riverbank, and he invited me to drop by for a visit.

I waited for a couple of days, until Sara came out and the two of us took a boat ride upriver to Gunther's. It was hard to see his house from the river, even though I knew approximately where his place was. As we approached I could see a faint outline of the house well back in the trees. There was a little back eddy that was hidden behind a big cottonwood tree that was leaned out over the river where Gunther's boat was tied. I noticed his boat tied behind the cottonwood and tied up next to it.

There was a trail from the boats up to the house where Gunther was working with the horses. He had a big log pulled up in the air and was positioning it over the house. It was quite impressive watching Gunther get the log in place. He was on the ground, getting the horses to stand still, he was pulling on ropes that were tied onto the ends of the logs in order to position it just right. When he got it in the right position, he backed the horses up slowly, lowering the log in place.

Sara and I stood back and watched as Gunther worked. Afterwards, he gave the horses some grain, taking a break to visit with Sara and I. I was amazed at the size of the house and the logs he was using. The site had piles of plywood, lumber, roofing paper and all kinds of building supplies.

Gunther came from Germany and talked with an accent, having escaped over the Berlin Wall several years before. His wife Karen and their two boys, were going to be showing up in a couple of weeks and he wanted to have the house finished enough to live in by then.

We didn't stay too long, as it was obvious that Gunther wanted to get back to work. Sara and I went fishing at Driscoll Creek after leaving there, getting a couple of nice Dolly Varden and headed home.

A couple of days later Sara and I were lying in bed in the morning, when we heard a knock on the door. I got up and went downstairs. There was a person that I didn't recognize at the door.

"Hi, I'm Dan Hamel! I've been walking the railroad tracks from Jasper. I stopped in Dome Creek and a guy I met there told me that I should stop and pay you a visit."

Sara got up, and came downstairs, "who's that, Louie?"

"Come on in," I said, turning to Sara. "Sara, this is Dan."

I looked back to Dan: "Who did you say sent you?"

"Benny and Marie. They told me that they were friends of yours and that I should stop and pay you a visit."

"Oh, yeah! Benny and Marie! How are they doing?"

"Yeah! They're doing good! I stayed at their place about a week."

"You're walking the tracks? Where are you coming from? Where are you going?" I asked in rapid succession.

"Well, I used to be a stock trader in Calgary. I did that for over ten years, then one morning I got up and decided that I didn't want to do it anymore. It was really high stress and long

457

hours. I thought that there had to be more to life than doing that job every day. So I quit. I walked out of my office in the middle of the day. I couldn't take it any more. Never went back."

"Okay, so what made you start walking the tracks?" Sara asked.

"Let's put it this way: I knew that I wanted out of Calgary, but I didn't know where to go. So I figured that if I started walking the tracks, I would figure it out eventually."

"And how long have you been walking?"

"Oh, about a month."

"How long will you be sticking around here?" Sara asked.

"Don't know."

Dan did stick around for a couple of weeks with us. He could not stand being idle and was continually finding things to do in the garden, or working on the woodpile, or cleaning the house, etc., etc., etc.

After a couple of weeks, he packed up and started walking down the tracks again, heading west, towards the coast. We had become very good friends in the time he spent with us and always wondered what became of him.

Harry and I were taking the train to Longstock from Prince George one night. We were riding in the bar car, along with several other people from the valley. The table next to us had several people from the McBride area. As always while riding the bar car, everyone there talked to each other across the tables. It was one big, happy party.

There was a big fellow sitting at the next table, whose name was Harold. Harry was a big guy, too, and they got to talking back and forth. It wasn't long before we were sitting with the

McBride bunch and the two big guys, Harry and Harold, were joking back and forth. It seems that they had a few things in common. They were both originally from California. Harry was 6'2 1/2", and wore a size 14 shoe, and Harold was 6' 4", and wore a size 12 1/2 shoe.

"I got it now!" Harold announced to Harry in his half loaded state, "We came out of the same mold and they turned a little more under for feet on you." The arithmetic added up, the shorter guy had the biggest feet.

"You should come out to my party! "Harold told us. "Every year on the summer solstice, I have a party. We roast a couple of sheep on hot rocks."

"Hot rocks?" I asked.

"Yeah! We build a fire and let it burn for a few hours in rocky ground. After the fire has burned for a while, we shovel all the fire out of the hole and wrap the sheep in wet burlap, burying it in the ground with the hot rocks. It cooks in there for about four or five hours, then we dig it up. The meat is so good and tender cooked this way. You've got to try it."

"Where is the party?" I asked.

Harold gave us directions to his farm. The party was always held on the summer solstice weekend, which was only a couple weeks away.

"We'll be there!" Harry yelled back at Harold as we got off the train that night.

I told Sara about meeting Harold and about the party. She was really interested in going. There were a few others from Longstock that decided to go to the party, too. Besides Sara and I, there were Lana and her friend Sandra, and Harry.

We left Longstock at 10 o'clock on Saturday morning, with all five of us crammed into the cab of my pickup. It took about three hours by the time we got across the river and drove the 75 miles to the turn-off. There was a hand-painted sign by the highway, about 12 miles from McBride, with a large, red arrow that read, 'Whole Earth Summer Solstice.' We left our vehicle at the top of a very steep hill and walked down to the farm. The parking area at the top of the hill had several vehicles parked and a few more arriving right behind us. Everyone grabbed sleeping bags and I grabbed my guitar. We all started down the road towards the farm. The road was spotted with a line of people walking down the hill to the party. The road twisted and turned down the long hill, crossing the railroad tracks at the bottom. After crossing the tracks, we could see some buildings and cleared fields ahead of us. As we got closer, we could see a bonfire burning and a lot of people around.

We followed the road towards the crowd of people gathered around the bonfire, when someone yelled out, "The Longstockians are here." Harold spotted us as we approached the bonfire.

"I'm glad to see you guys made it." Harold said, leaving the crowd around the fire to greet us. He was a very friendly person, making us feel welcome right away, shaking hands with everyone in our group and introducing himself to the girls whom he had not met before.

"We're just getting the lambs ready to bury, Harry. Do you want to give us a hand?"

"Sure, man, I'll give you a hand!" Harry answered. "Where should we put our gear?"

"You guys can camp out in the hay shed over there," Harold said, pointing towards the shed. Just pick a spot under the roof and put your sleeping bags and stuff there." I took Harry's sleeping bag and pack from him. Me, Sara, Lana and Sandra all took our things to the hay shed. There was a layer of hay about three feet thick spread out across the floor. The floor had a couple dozen sleeping bags already scattered across the hay. We picked a spot in the corner that hadn't been taken yet and spread our bags out.

It was early in the afternoon, there were people all over the place already and a steady steam of people still coming in. Most of the people were from the McBride area, though I saw a few faces that I recognized from traveling on the train, and there were many people I didn't know.

After setting ourselves in the hay shed, we migrated over to the fire where they were burying the lambs in the hot, rocky ground. The fire had burned down to a pile of hot coals that had been dug out of the pit by the time we got there. There were several people around the fire pit helping to get the lambs in the hole and burying them in the hot rocks. The pit was about two feet deep, with the lambs wrapped in burlap in the bottom, covered with hot rocks and gravel that had been dug out of the hole. The rocks were heaped up about a foot high over the pit when they were done.

"Let's see, it's 1:30 now, we can dig them up at 5:30," Harold said, looking at his watch. "We got to leave 'em in the ground for four hours."

We hung around the pit for a while after that, talking. The crowd of people was growing all the time, as more people arrived by the minute. I saw a few people coming in with guitars, hand drums, and several other instruments. I recognized my friend George, the cab driver from Prince George, carrying a guitar. George played in a band called, 'The Rocky Mountain Express' that I had seen at the Canada Hotel in Prince George several times before. He came with the other band members and their acoustic instruments, including acoustic guitars, fiddle, conga drums and a stand-up, or doghouse, bass. All the music was acoustic, as there was no power for electric instruments there.

The hay shed had a roof off to one side that Harold used as a pen for the lambs. It too, had a layer of hay on the floor. It looked like a good place for George and his band to set their instruments. It wasn't long after they had gotten set up that the music started up. The music played pretty well constantly from that point on, until the sun was shining brightly the next morning.

While the music was playing at the lamb pen over by the house, there was a volleyball game going on. Sara and I both got into the game for a while, on opposite teams. There was an incredibly tall guy on Sara's team. He was really skinny and when I asked him how tall he was, he told me that he was 6' 11". In a volleyball game, every time the serve changes, all the players must rotate around. Each player gets to play all the positions and to serve each time around. During the course of the game, I was rotating around the court and so was he. At one point, he was playing close to the net and I was playing across from him. The top of the net was at his chin level and he was waving his hands back and forth.

As the afternoon went on, more and more people showed up. After a couple of games of volleyball, Sara and I decided to sit out and let some others play. We met back up with Lana and Sandra, who were mingling and wandering around the farm, checking the place out. In the farmhouse, people were preparing lots of food. A table made with a couple of sheets of plywood was set up for the food by the hay shed. At 5:30, Harold dug up the sheep, unwrapping them from the burlap, laying them on the table and slicing them up, one by one. As he was cutting the meat, the table started filling up with huge amounts of food including salads, rice, perogies and pasta dishes, etc. By this time there were probably around 250 people there.

Sara, Lana, Sandra, and I were lined up, waiting for them to start serving the food, when I noticed that Skid was there.

"Hey, Skid!" I yelled.

He looked over at me and waved. That's when I noticed that Krista and Dedra were with him. "I heard there was a party," Skid said to me, slurring his words a little. "Decided to come check it out!" It was obvious that he was already drunk.

We all got a plate of food, walking back over to the hay shed to eat. The band was playing in the lamb pen right beside us, never stopping for more than a minute between songs.

A fire was restarted in the pit where the lambs were cooked. There was still a line of people arriving coming down the road. I had about half an ounce of mushrooms. We split them up between us after we ate. I even gave some to Skid, who was pretty hammered already, but I thought it might mellow him out. He seemed to be looking off in all directions at once, with the glass eye staring at who knows what. Every time anyone looked or talked to him, he just burst out laughing. He had his pockets full of Milkbones, pulling them out one at a time and sticking them in his mouth, holding them in his teeth like a cigar and chewing on them.

After Harry showed up, the whole group of us started to migrate over to the lamb pen where the music was coming from. George and the boys sure had it going on over there. There were about 15 or 20 people in the lamb pen with instruments, creating quite a big wall of sound. There were a bunch of guitars, fiddles, banjos, the doghouse bass, washboards, shakers, tambourines, a guy with a sitar, a trumpet and a guy playing the spoons. I took my guitar out of the case and joined in the music. George must have known thousands of songs, as he led the musicians through hours of songs. There was always a guitar player close at hand that I could pick up the chords from and 90% of the songs used the same three chords anyway, C, F and G. The musicians were crammed into the lamb pen, and pretty well filled it up. There were lots of dancers dancing out in front of it and farther away, a ring of people standing around, watching.

There were so many instruments playing at once that I could not hear my guitar when I was playing it. The sound just got absorbed into the wall of music. I was starting to feel the effects of the mushrooms and really got into playing those three chords. I was getting down and loving it, for a while, anyway, until the mushrooms started to get more intense. There came a point where I thought I'd better stop and I put my guitar in a safe place.

I stumbled out of the lamb pen and put my guitar back in the case. I had just got the case snapped up and was going to take it over to the hay shed where our sleeping bags were, when I heard some one call my name.

"Hi, Louie!" said Lana from behind me. She was looking like the mushrooms had kicked in on her as well. "What 'ya doing?"

"I'm gonna take my guitar to the hayshed." "I'll come with ya," she said.

She grabbed onto my shirt as we wove through the crowd of dancers on our way. We got to the hayshed, both of us were so stoned on the mushrooms that we weren't sure which of the sleeping bags were ours. It wasn't really dark, but not exactly light, either, we searched around for the right ones. I knew our bags were against a wall. When I thought we had found the right place, I put my guitar down and laid down on the sleeping bag. Lana quickly lay down beside me, and immediately started kissing me. There was nobody else in the hay shed at the time, although just on the other side of the wall there were lots of people.

I was pretty stoned and reacted by kissing her back. A couple of minutes later, I forgot who it was I was kissing. Lana is tearing at my clothes, trying to get them off, undressing herself at the same time and I can't remember who the hell she is! It was just dark enough that I couldn't see her face.

'If she talks, then maybe I can tell,' I thought to myself. She didn't talk or make any sounds that I could distinguish. I made love to her there in the hayshed, though I had no idea who it was I was making love to, until we got dressed and went back outside the hay shed. 'Oh, it's Lana.' I thought to myself. I took a pinch of mushrooms and gave her some.

The area outside the lamb Pen was even more crowded when we got back there. Lana was hanging on to me with both hands as we weaved back through the crowd.

Just then, Sara came out of the crowd and grabbed me by the arm. "Louie, over here!" she said pulling me towards her. Lana was still hanging on.

Skid, Harry, Krista, Dedra and Sandra were all dancing, though Skid didn't look so hot. He looked like he was about to fall down. Sara, Lana, and I all started in dancing, too. There were people dancing all around us, it was pretty crowded.

It was then that the music stopped and Harold got everyone to quiet down, and made an announcement.

"Friends and neighbors! I want to thank you for coming to this years Whole Earth Summer Solstice Party. It has been great to put these parties on over the last five years but I want to tell you this years party is going to be the last one, so enjoy yourselves!" The response was a mixture of sighs and cheers as the music started up again.

"That's too bad," I thought, "this was my first one."

I started dancing again and was really getting into it, only looking up long enough to grab a joint or pass one. We were all dancing in a mass of people and not really with each other, when I noticed that I kept bumping into Sandra. She started dancing really close to me, grabbing my hands, pulling me towards her. Between the mushrooms and the joints, I was pretty stoned and went right along with her, offering no resistance. She led me a little away from the others and started to dance with me very seductively. She ended up leading me to the hay shed and back to the sleeping bags. We were kissing and again I forgot who she was, and then I couldn't even remember where I was. The only thing I did remember is how to make love to her.

Again I had to get outside the hay shed, where there was light, before I could see her and still I wasn't sure who she was, having just met her.

We got back to our friends who were still dancing away in the crowd. I was in one of those states of mind where I see and I hear, but when I try to think, nothing happens. It seemed like no time at all before I was getting led away by Krista and we were getting it on in the hay shed and then twenty minutes later, pushing through the crowd, we went back to dancing.

I took some and passed around the last of the mushrooms about that time. The party was starting to peak and so were me and my friends. It was starting to get light and I don't remember much after that, but woke up with Sara in my sleeping bag with me, with Lana and Sandra beside me.

Could it be? I didn't want to ask.

Chapter 22

The Summer After The Morning After

I was awake for at least an hour before I could get my eyes open. I could hear things going on around me, people were stirring around, talking and laughing. I had women snuggled up to me on both sides, but I just could not get my eyes open to see who they were. It was as if my eyes were stuck closed and my brain was in a thick fog. I wanted to wake up, but my head would not cooperate. I don't remember getting undressed the night before, but I could feel bare skin on both sides of me under the sleeping bag. I could tell I had at least one naked woman on each side of me as I lay there with my eyes closed.

The hay shed was full of people, some moving around and some not. As I opened my eyes, I was looking at Sara, who was still sound asleep, lying on one side of me. I rolled my head to the other side to see who was there. I looked right into Sandra's eyes, looking back at me. She immediately gave me a kiss and pushed her body right up to me. Lana was also fast asleep and snuggled up to Sandra. I could hear music coming from the lamb pen as a guitar and fiddle jammed in the distance.

We all lay there in different levels of consciousness for some time before anyone made a move towards getting up. Sandra and I were the first ones to move, getting up and dressed, while the other two girls still slept.

"There's coffee over at the house!" I heard someone say from across the hay shed.

"Let's go get some coffee!" I said to Sandra. The two of us headed for the house with Sandra holding onto my arm. I wasn't sure why she was being so affectionate towards me, but as I woke up a little more, I started to remember little by little, the roll in the hay we had had the night before.

The house was crowded with people as we walked in. "Which way's the coffee?" I asked. A couple of people just pointed, We went in the direction they were pointing. I poured a couple of cups and wandered back outside towards a picnic table that was in the yard and sat down. In a matter of minutes, I had the first cup downed and went back in for a second. By the time I finished the second cup, I was starting to come alive again.

Sandra and I both went in for another cup, then went back over to the hayshed to see how the rest of the gang was doing. She was still being quite affectionate towards me on the walk back. When we got to the hay shed, Lana and Sara were still lying in the sleeping bag. Sara was still asleep, but Lana was awake, though still lying there. Sandra was still holding onto my arm and she made a point of staying close to me as we went in and sat down in the hay. It was as if she were staking her claim on me.

The three of us sat around, talking about the night before. In a few minutes, Sara started to wake up. She lay there in the sleeping bag, eventually joining in the conversation. Both Lana and Sandra knew that Sara and I had been seeing each other for quite a while, but both of them were flirting and touching me affectionately right in front of her.

Skid, Krista and Dedra were sleeping nearby, and were waking up by then. Skid looked like the walking dead when he finally got up. It looked like a bird had hit a bulls eye from the rafters of the hay shed, as Skid had bird shit on his forehead and in his hair. He came over to where we were, without realizing it, he kept wiping his head, smearing the bird shit all around. It was getting hard to keep from laughing before Lana finally blurted it out, "Skid, for Gods sake, go wash your face, you got bird shit all over your head."

"Huh?" Skid answered, as if he didn't get it. "A bird shit on your head, man!" she said.

Skid wiped his hand across his face, smearing the bird shit all over his forehead. "Oh shit!" he said, finally realizing it. We were all cracking up, laughing as he got up and went off, trying to find some water to wash it off.

I don't know where Harry was, but while we were all sitting there, I realized that I'd slept with all four of these girls the night before, while we were all doing mushrooms. I wasn't sure if I should be elated or embarrassed. We all sat there, talking and laughing. It was almost noon by the time we all got up and got moving. Sara was the last one to get up and dressed, throwing aside the sleeping bag and standing up stark naked in the midst of us while getting dressed. She got everyones attention for the moment as she slipped on a pair of tight jeans and a tee shirt.

Skid found the creek that ran through the property and washed the bird shit off his head and face. We were ready to pack up and leave by the time he showed up back at the hay shed.

We all packed up our things and got ready to make the long walk up the hill to the truck. We finally found Harry over by the house. He and Harold were still hanging out talking, when we told him we were going to take off. Saying goodbye to Harold and whomever we ran into on the way out, we started the slow plod up the hill.

Harold stayed true to his word, making this the last Whole Earth Summer Solstice Party.

The parking lot was packed with vehicles when we got there. There were vehicles parked along the road all the way to the highway, as well as both sides of the highway around the turn off. Skid and Krista followed us in his VW bug back to the landing. It was about 4:00 in the afternoon before we crossed the river and got back to Longstock. Everyone was feeling pretty tired and worn-out by that time. We all piled into the power wagon. I made the rounds, dropping Lana and Sandra off at Ross's place, Harry at his place and Skid, Krista, and Dedra off at the railroad tracks, where they took off walking the tracks back to Skid's.

Sara and I went home, being dead-tired by the time we got there and crashed out, sleeping straight through, until 9:00 the next morning.

The sun was shining in the window when I opened my eyes. Sara was still sleeping as I slipped out of bed and went downstairs to make the coffee. I was sitting there in a bit of a fog, having a first cup, when she came downstairs. We sat in the kitchen, drinking coffee and talking about the party. It had been a really fun time and we were both glad we had gone.

"I'm going to be leaving soon," Sara said to me. I thought she was talking about going back to Prince George.

"When do you want to go?" I asked.

"I'm not just going back to town," she said. "I'm going to be moving, Louie. I've enrolled to go back to school to get my nursing degree."

"Oh, yeah! That sounds like a good idea. Where are you going to go to school?"

"That's just it, Louie. I'm going back east."

"Back east? Where back east?"

"Nova Scotia. I got accepted into a school in Nova Scotia."

"Holy crap! That's like four thousand miles away."

"I know."

"Soo......... when are you doing this? I mean when are you leaving?"

"In about a week."

"Oh shit..... Sara..... you're going to leave." I said, half to her and half to myself. "I'm going to lose you."

"Ah, come on, Louie, you got women hanging around you

472

in droves. You could have any woman you wanted."

"Ah man, come on."

"Come on, come on yourself. How many women did you sleep with at the party?"

"I don't know. I was pretty stoned."

"And they all got the hots for you. You won't miss me for long."

I was shocked at the thought of her leaving. It made me think of times over the last few years when Sara and I hung out together. Meeting her at the coffee house when I sang the wrong words to 'Poncho and Lefty' and her correcting me. Dancing at the Canada Hotel. The trip to down the California coast and back. We did a lot of things and it seemed like whatever we did turned out to be fun. I can't remember any bad times.

I put my arms around Sara, holding her in a long embrace. It had been a couple of years since we met and even though she was still with me for a few more days, I started to miss her right away.

She stayed with me until the next day, when I took her back to Prince George. I decided that if we only had a few days left, I would try to spend that time with her.

I helped her pack up her apartment and move her things over to her Mom's place. She was taking the train back east, so the amount of stuff she could take was limited.

The night before she left, there was a farewell dinner at her Mom's place.

I took Sara to the train station the next morning to see her off. After checking her bags, we went across the street to the Iron Horse Restaurant and had breakfast while we were

473

waiting for the train.

"I'm going to miss you, Sara."

"I'll miss you too, Louie, but I don't want you to get hung up on me. You know we were not destined to be partners for life. Our time was a good time, a lot of fun, but now is the time to get on with our lives. I've been planning on doing this for a long time. I have relatives back in Nova Scotia that I can stay with while I'm going to school."

"I got family back east, too. I guess I'll have to come out and see you the next time I go to visit my family."

"Listen Louie, I think it's better for the both of us if we just say goodbye right now. My life is going to change drastically and I'd feel better if I knew that you were getting on with yours."

"But Sara, I have feelings for you."

"Yeah, I have feelings for you, too, but this is something I've got to do. I'm going to be gone a long time and I don't want you to be waiting for me."

I held onto her hand as we sat and talked, until it was time to go. I hugged her and gave her a kiss and watched her climb aboard the train. I stood on the platform and watched as the train pulled out and disappeared down the tracks.

Sara was gone.

I picked up a few groceries before heading back to Longstock later that day. I couldn't get Sara off my mind. I must have felt more strongly about her than I realized. After getting to the river, I didn't cross right away. Sara's leaving was weighing heavy on my mind. I got the groceries loaded in the boat and then sat on the riverbank and watched the water go by. There was something soothing about watching the river flow. It gave off a kind off energy that I couldn't explain, but just sitting there watching and feeling the power and ambiance seemed to help fill the emptiness I was feeling. I decided that I needed to be close to the river for now. I got in the boat and cruised upriver for no other reason than that it felt good. It seemed to soothe the feeling in my heart.

I traveled up the river on the opposite side from Longstock passing the Longstock landing, Ross's farm and the river bar where Patty's Creek dumped into the Fraser. It was a warm, sunny day and the trees along the riverbanks were glistening in the sun. I continued around the bend and towards the rocks. Up river from the rocks Driscoll Creek poured clear water into the muddy Fraser. I passed the spot where the old cook shack was, where we had hung the 300 pot plants in some years back. I continued turning the corners where the horse shoe shape created a large peninsula that the water had cut out over many years of traveling this route to the faraway ocean. Up ahead of me, the river turned east again, following the railroad tracks and widening out to accommodate the large sand bars that occupied the middle. It was one of these sand bars that Ross, Steve, and I had got the boat stuck on with a big load at 2:00 am on the return trip from Prince George years ago.

I had no other reason for going so far, except for the voice inside me that told me to keep going. Soon I could see the familiar bee- hive burner from the old abandoned sawmill at Penney. There were a few people on the river bank as I cruised by the Penney landing and disappeared around the bend in the river. I kept going for another 30 or 40 minutes, and was just coming to the bridge at Dome Creek. As I went by the big house by the bridge that Ben lived in, I could see some people hanging out along the river bank. I steered the boat closer to the bank and recognized Ben among them. I had been traveling for about an hour and a half by this time, and decided to stop and pay Ben a visit.

It looked like they were having a barbecue by the water as I got closer and eased the boat towards shore.

"It looks like Louie from Longstock!" I heard Ben say as I pulled in to shore. There was an old engine block on shore that I tied the boat up to, then walked the trail up the bank.

There were about half a dozen people sitting around in lawn chairs and Ben cooking burgers over a fire. I had been outrunning the bugs on the river, but they caught up to me as soon as I stopped and were quite lively here.

"Hey Louie, what brings you up here?" Ben said to me as I approached.

"Nothing in particular, just out for a boat ride today. I probably would have turned around by now, except I noticed you guys, so I decided to pull in and visit before I head back."

"Well, you're just in time," Ben said, handing me a paper plate with a burger." The fixings are over there," he said, pointing to a picnic table nearby.

It was late in the afternoon and I had not even thought about being hungry. The situation with Sara was all I could think about up to then and it was handy that I came upon food without even trying, though I did have groceries in the boat.

We smoked a joint after eating and Ben coaxed me to come with him to do something, I wasn't sure what. We walked along the riverbank, away from the fire.

"You look like you got something on your mind, Louie," he said to me out of the blue.

"You can tell?

"I can tell."

"You remember Sara?"

"Yeah, the gorgeous chick with the long hair. Yeah, I do."

"Well,....she got on the train for Nova Scotia this morning."

"What's going on there?"

"Nursing school."

"She's going to nursing school?"

"Yeah.... but that's not all. It's probably over. It's rather sudden." I looked at Ben, and he put one arm around my shoulder and gave me a one arm hug. "I'm just blowing off some steam. The river felt good, so I just kept going." He didn't say anything. We walked around a bit and then went back to the fire.

Ben invited me to stay there for the night. I almost did, but thought I needed some time alone and that would only postpone my time for solitude.

It was getting late in the afternoon, the mosquitos were getting quite ferocious by the time I left. The sun was still out when I headed downriver, bringing the boat up to speed and leaving the bugs behind. One thing about going home, is that the current pushes you an extra four miles per hour, so it takes less time going back. I was back in Longstock in a little over an hour, pulling the boat into the landing.

I'd been at home for a couple of days before Sandra showed up at my house. I had been trying to keep a low profile and take some time with the loss of Sara. It was true, however, that as soon as I had Sandra coming around, I missed Sara less.

She had been right for the near term, but as time went on, I found myself thinking of her at the most inopportune times: like when I was making love to Sandra, poof! There was Sara in my head. It started to happen more and more often. Finally I couldn't take it any more I had to see Sara.

Needless to say, Sandra wasn't very happy with me after I told her that I was going back east to see Sara. It was the end of August and Sara had been gone about two months when I took off from Longstock and drove east. It was early in the evening when I got to Edmonton. Sara had given me a phone number and address where she was going to be staying in Nova Scotia. I decided to call and let her know I was coming.

I was surprised when she answered the phone.

"Hello, Sara, is that you?" I said, recognizing her voice.

"Louie! Oh, what a surprise!"

"I've been thinking a lot about you lately."

"Oh yeah."

"Yeah, matter of fact, I'm on my way. I'm coming to see you."

"Where are you?"

"I'm in Edmonton."

"Louie, don't come out here! Turn around and go back."

"Sara, what are you saying? I want to see you."

"Don't you see Louie, it's only going to make it harder if you come out here."

"Ah... man. Sara, come on. I want to see you."

"Don't come, Louie. Don't come."

I stood there, speechless, holding the phone for a minute. I didn't know what to say. I wanted to see her so badly that it

478

never occurred to me that maybe she wouldn't want to see me.

"Are you sure, Sara, this is the way you want it?"

"Yes, Louie," I could her her sobbing on the other end. "Yes."

"Okay, that's the way you want it. Goodbye, Sara." I could only hear her sobbing as I hung up the phone. "What a bummer," I said to myself. I went back to my truck and sat there for awhile. "Fuck it! I'm going to Denver. I'm not going back right away." I got back on the highway and took the turn south towards Calgary and the U.S. border. Shortly after making the turn south, I came across a long stretch of highway that was lined with hitch hikers. There were at least ten people hitching there and one by one I stopped and picked all of them up. Three were sitting in the front with me and the rest were riding in the pickup box. It was warm and sunny, a perfect day for riding in the back.

I dropped people off in intervals on the way to the border. There was a sliding back window in the cab. When someone's stop was coming up, they would knock on the window and tell me where they were getting off. There was only one guy that I picked up that came across the border with me. He had come from the north slope of the Mckenzie River in northern Alaska. He had lived up there for two years straight, way back in the bush. He was going to Vermont. His clothes were made from Caribou hide and greased up with bear grease. If you never have smelled bear grease, let's just say that it pretty well stinks and anyone wearing it stinks, too. He had a dog with him and the dog was wearing a pack made of Caribou hide and greased with bear grease. He rode all the way to Denver with me and let's just say that the guys at the border weren't too thrilled about keeping us there any longer than it was necessary.

I let him out on the highway that skirts the city when I got to Denver. Then I went to look up my friend Bobby Mach. It had been years since I saw him. The last time was when he came up to Longstock and helped me on the house. I went to the Barton Brothers office and talked to Joe Barton. He told me where to find Bobby, drawing me a map, of sorts, I headed off to his place.

I was driving down the street, trying to read house numbers, when Bobby drove past me and into his driveway. I recognized him right away and pulled in behind him.

"Hey, Bobby!" I yelled to him as he got out of his car.

"Holy shit! It's Louie!"

I got out of the car and greeted him with a hug. "Man, it's been a long time. What, it's got to be five or six years."

"All of that," I said.

We went inside and Bobby rolled a joint and broke out a couple of beers. We sat down at the table, reminiscing about the times in Longstock when Bobby was there. Since Bobby had come back from Longstock, he had gotten married to Peggy. She was still at work and showed up about an hour later.

"I've heard all about you! Bobby talks about you a lot," she said when we were introduced. I stayed the weekend with them and then headed off east again. Bobby told me about George and Louise. They left Denver and bought some land in Ava, Missouri. He didn't know their address, but was pretty sure it was a small place and it wouldn't be that hard to find them. It seemed like a good place to stop on the way, so I headed for Missouri.

It was about 8:00 pm when I drove into Ava. It was a really small town, with just one main street. Most of the stores were closed, with only a couple of bars and a pool hall open. It was kind of late to be trying to track someone down, but I remember having a photo album with me, with a picture of George and Louise in it. I hunted around in my things until I found the picture and took it into the pool hall.

There was a guy at the desk in the front. I showed him the picture and asked if he knew these people. Looking at it, he said he wasn't sure and then yelled out across the pool hall, "Hey, anybody know these people?" There was about a dozen guys playing pool. They all stopped what they were doing and came up to the front to look at the picture.

"Yeah, I know them!" one fellow said to me. "In fact, I'm driving right by their driveway on my way home."

"Well, that's cool, when are you leaving?"

"Just getting ready to now. Just follow me and I'll point it out when we go by."

"Okay, man."

We left the pool hall and I followed him for about five miles, until he slowed down and stopped, pointing at the road from the truck. I gave a couple of beeps on the horn, he drove off as I turned down the driveway. It was a long, twisty drive to the house. I came around the corner and my headlights shined on the house. I could see people moving inside, then the door opened and George came out on the porch. I shut off the truck and got out.

"Hey, George, you old fart! You sure made yourself hard

to find."

"Louie? Louie is that you? Holy crap, Louise, it's Louie." he yelled towards the house before coming down off the porch and grabbing me in a bear hug.

"Man, how did you find us?" he said as Louise came running out of the house.

"Oh, my God!" she exclaimed throwing her arms around me. "Oh, my God!" she kept saying.

Once the initial excitement died down a little, we all went into the house. There were two little boys, twins that were peeking out from their room where they were supposed to be sleeping. Come on out, kids!" George called to them.

"This is Eli and Matthew," George said, introducing the two boys. "And this is my friend Louie," he said to the boys. They both reached out their hand to me to shake hands. "Okay, kids, you'll get to see Louie again tomorrow, so off to bed."

The two boys scampered off to bed and we moved into the living room, where George rolled a big one.

I told the story of showing their picture around in the pool hall and one of the guys showing me their driveway.

They discovered that Louise was carrying twins shortly after they left Longstock. After spending the first year in the city with the kids, they decided to get out of town. The place in Missouri was on a multiple listing and they found out about it while still in Denver, bought it and moved. They had been there for almost five years.

Louise worked the next day and the boys went to school, leaving George and me alone at the place. We went out hunting pheasants in the morning and cut some firewood in the afternoon.

I filled him in on what had happened with Katy and also, most recently, with Sara. It was really nice making contact with old friends. It was excellent therapy, with the Sara thing still weighing heavily on me.

I spent about a week with George and Louise before taking to the highway again, towards Massachusetts.

I didn't make any more stops, except to sleep, before rolling into Springfield a couple of days later. It had been years since I had seen my Mom and sisters and their families. It seemed like every night I was staying up late talking with one or the other of my sisters or mom. I had years of catching up on news, both mine and theirs. I built a bar for my mom while staying there for about a month. I had to go visit my grandmother while I was there, taking her to the dog races that she loved so much. Her vision wasn't that good by this time. I discovered that she couldn't really see the dogs, she couldn't see the results board, but she could see the program. I would go buy the tickets on the dogs she wanted for her, but she rarely won anything. She just loved going. It didn't matter at all if she won or lost. It was a wonderful day out to the races, and she insisted on taking us all out for ice cream on the way home, getting bent right out of shape if anyone tried to pay for anything.

I still could not stop thinking about Sara. I wanted to see her so much, but I was afraid to call her because I thought she would say no again.

I tried to keep it under my hat, but the feelings kept creeping in. I wasn't very far from where she was living, and if I was going to see her, now would be the time.

Just before leaving, I talked to my sister Pat about it. I told

483

her what Sara had said to me on the phone. Her advice, "Let her go. If she doesn't want to see you, just let her go." It was not what I wanted to hear.

It was a crisp, fall day as I loaded the truck up with my things and got ready to depart. I spent about a month with my family, but it was time to get back on the road. I left early in the morning and drove north through the Berkshires, crossing the line into Vermont with its hills of exceedingly beautiful foliage. I crossed the border back into Canada in the late afternoon, stopping at a motel about a half hour from the border. I got a burger from the Burger King and went back to my room at the motel. It took a while to get the nerve up to try to call Sara again. I ate the burger and picked up the phone. I held the phone for a couple of minutes, looking at the phone number before I started to dial.

"Hello," a voice said from the other end.

"Hello, is Sara there?"

"Yes, just a minute." I waited.

"Hello."

"Sara."

"Oh, hi, Louie."

"I've been thinking about you a lot, Sara."

"I'm thinking about you, too. Ever since your last call .....a month and a half ago."

"In one way I really want to see you, but in another, I don't."

"You know, Louie, it's exactly the same for me."

"I don't know what to do..."

"It's a tough choice. I'm choosing a career right now, but I gotta say I didn't know it was really love until I was losing it. I thought it was sex, drugs, and rock and roll."

"So.. what do we do now? Part of me really wants to see you."

"Where are you?"

"Just east of Montreal."

"Oh, shit."

"I was visiting my mom in Springfield."

"Well, here's what it comes down to. If you come here, then you've got to stay here until I finish school. If you're not going to do that, don't come."

"How long is that?"

"About four years. Think about it."

I didn't sleep much that night. Got up early and went over to the motel restaurant. The desire to see Sara was huge. She was only about a day's drive from where I was now. I wanted to get an early start. It was about an hour and a half drive to the trans-Canada highway going east to Nova Scotia and west to B.C.

The thoughts were going through my mind all about the great times I had had with Sara. The way she looked, her long black, gypsy hair and beautiful eyes. The thought of seeing her was overwhelming.

But then I thought of my boys. They were already far away from me, in Alaska. I hadn't seen them in a long time. A move to the east coast would complicate that problem further. I could feel the emotions well up inside when I thought of my sons. I could not abandon them. I had to keep trying to see them, even if I did move. The signs appeared as I neared the turn-off to the trans-Canada.

485

There was a rest stop a couple of miles before the turn. I stopped there. I was going back and forth. My mind was racing. I was trying to make a decision, but it seemed that I was only hanging on by my fingernails. I had to act decisively. I got in the truck and pulled out onto the highway. The turn was coming up.